Agricultural Economics

Agricultural Economics

John W. Goodwin

Regents Professor
Oklahoma State University

Reston Publishing Company
A Prentice-Hall Company
Reston, Virginia

Library of Congress Cataloging in Publication Data

Goodwin, John W
  Agricultural economics.

  Includes Bibliographical references and index.
  1. Agriculture—Economic aspects—United States.
I. Title.
HD1761.G66   338.1'0973   76-30724
ISBN 0-87909-020-0

©1977 by John W. Goodwin

10 9 8 7 6 5 4 3 2 1

Printed in the United States of America

To

James S. Plaxico

without whose support,
encouragement, and occasional prodding
this book would not have been written.

Contents

Illustrations

Tables

A Word to the Reader

This text is designed for a one-semester or two-quarter sequence introduction to agricultural economics. It is designed to provide the reader with information concerning the role of agriculture in today's American economic system and with a knowledge of the relationships that regulate the entire economic environment. These two objectives are reached through a study of the basic economic principles upon which rational managerial decisions must be made. An acquaintance with some of the broad problem areas facing American agriculture and an indication of the vast array of opportunities available to those trained in agricultural economics can be gained from the examples used to illustrate these basic principles.

Agricultural economics is the social science that is concerned with human behavior during the process of producing, processing, distributing, and consuming the products of farms and ranches. Many of the students who will take the introductory course in agricultural economics may be defined as a basic raw material of agricultural origin. When these people leave the farm or ranch to enter college, they are engaged in "processing" themselves from a raw material into some sort of finished product. The supply of and the demand for the products that they will ultimately become will determine the "market prices" (or salaries) that they will receive when they finally go into the job market. Premiums and discounts from this price will reflect any differences in product quality.

It is important that the college student recognize his or her educational endeavor as an exercise in economics. A college education is nothing more or less than an investment. As with any investment, the only way to evaluate the advisability of investing is through an analysis of costs and returns. All too often, college students haven't the foggiest idea of how much they are paying for a college degree. Even worse, they have even less idea of how good a living a particular major will enable them to earn. It is to be hoped that each and every college student will analyze the alternatives economically when selecting a major field of study, and will use economic standards for evaluating his or her progress in the pursuit of the chosen major field.

Each year of a college education involves two elements of costs. First, there is the *out-of-pocket* cost covering room, board, tuition, books, etc. Second, there is the *opportunity* cost of income foregone—that is, the income which an individual would receive if he were working rather than going to school. These costs—accumulated over the course of a baccalaureate degree—comprise an individual's investment in the future. The difference in what he might have earned without the college education and what he actually does earn *with* that education is the return—or the interest—on his educational investment.

If you were to go to work directly out of high school, you might earn about $95 per week, or $4,900 per year. At the end of four years, you might be making about $115 per week or $6,000 per year. The average annual earnings over this period would be in the neighborhood of $5,500. Thus, your *opportunity cost*—the cost of income foregone—might be about $5,500 per year, less the amount earned during the summer. If your summer earnings as a college student amount to $1,500 then your opportunity cost for going to college would be about $4,000 per year.

Most students will be surprised at their out-of-pocket costs. These are estimated on the basis of living in a dormitory while attending Oklahoma State University as an in-state resident student.

Room and board @ $125 per month for 9 months	$1,125
Tuition @ $14 per semester-hour (16 hours per semester)	448
Books and supplies @ $100 per semester	200
Clothing (probably underestimated)	400
Dating @ $10 per week (underestimated)	360
Hamburgers, beer, coffee, Cokes, etc.	300
Total	$2,833

It will be noted that transportation, laundry, etc., have been omitted. If a student has a car, and if he drives that car an average of 10,000 miles per year, we can add $1,500 to our cost estimate to cover gasoline, oil, tires, depreciation, insurance, etc. From the looks of the parking lots on most university campuses, every student has at least one car. Without question, more than half the undergraduate students in most universities do drive automobiles, so perhaps we should add the $1,500 annually for the car, bringing our out-of-pocket costs to $4,333 annually.

Of course, the $4,333 out-of-pocket costs can be reduced by the amount one earns during the year and by the amount that it would cost the student to live either at home or in an apartment while working for wages. If we allow $135 per month in living expenses that would have to be paid whether or not the student were in college, our out-of-pocket costs amount to about $3,100 per year.

The investment that the average student makes in education each year, then, includes about $4,000 in opportunity costs and about $3,100 in out-of-pocket expense. This totals about $7,100 annually. If he belongs to a fraternity, or she to a sorority, a minimum of $200 per year can be added to this figure. Thus, the total investment for a four-year education is about $28,500! In addition, each state invests upwards of $1,500 per year per student in terms of university operating expenses and depreciation upon the facilities used. Over a four-year period, a state will normally invest about $6,000 in each baccalaureate degree.

The total investment for a college degree will run from $35,000 to $40,000! If a student is enrolled in a five-year course or takes five years to complete a four-year course, the cost is even greater. The question that I as an economist am forced to ask of students is, "ARE YOU GETTING YOUR MONEY'S WORTH?" If we break the investment down to a per classroom hour figure, it amounts to $15 to $17 per hour spent in the classroom or the laboratory. Students who cut classes are robbing themselves of $15 to $17 each time they do so. (It should also be pointed out that professors who come to class poorly prepared rob each student enrolled by a similar amount.)

We have defined the cost of a college education. How good is the investment? The only way this question can be answered is in terms of the return to investment that an education will earn. Some fields of study will earn more than others. College advisors and counselors should be able to provide information as to the relative earning power of the various degrees that the institution offers, but it has been estimated that a college degree increases one's earning power by about $175,000 over his working life. If we average this out over a forty-three-year period (i.e., from age 22 to 65), it amounts to $4,700 per year. In terms of our $35,000 investment, this translates to a 12 percent annual return on investment! This is better than stocks and bonds, better than land, and there are no capital gains taxes to pay!

What does this pep talk you've just read have to do with the onerous chore you face as you study this book and subject yourselves to the tender mercies of the professor who is to guide your study of agricultural economics? First of all, economic principles are a *personal* thing. The concepts and ideas to which you will be introduced in this book may be used by you in your everyday personal business decisions. Second, economic principles to a degree regulate the world within which you must live. Any violation of those principles will create inefficiency and waste. This is fine, so long as we can afford it. But the time comes when it becomes necessary to trim back on waste in order to accomplish other goals and objectives. Third, since graduation from college is probably among your most immediate goals, the principles may be used to guide your use of ability, money, and time in order that you may gain the greatest value from your educational investment.

If you should encounter a passage of this book that seems to you to be a little suggestive, rest assured that such was the intent. Economics is not necessarily a dry and colorless study. Even the most ribald side of human existence (and some phases of college are unquestionably ribald) is subject to economic forces.

John W. Goodwin

Agricultural Economics

1

Agricultural Economics Defined

The recorded birth of organized society in almost any civilization has invariably coincided with the time that man began to regulate his environment through the cultivation of crops and the husbandry of animals. Thus, agriculture provides the basis for civilization itself. Unless man can find some means for harnessing the natural forces in his environment, it is impossible for him to progress far beyond the savage state in which he found himself at the beginning of time.

As man has progressed from the cave man era into the enormously complex and sophisticated circumstances found in today's economic environment, certain behavior patterns have emerged that regulate the manner in which he goes about attending to his daily affairs. These behavior patterns are concerned with the interactions between and among groups of individuals, and between individuals and groups as these people go about the economic activities of production, consumption, and exchange.

The relationships that may be observed are not of the physical "test tube" variety that can be duplicated (or "replicated") repeatedly in a laboratory. Rather than being physical relationships that may be physically sensed—i.e., that may be touched, tasted, smelled, or heard—these relationships are of the more elusive variety contained in the psyches and souls of men. Such relationships are *social* in nature, and a study of these relationships is a *social* study.

As knowledge concerning social relationships is accumulated, it may be systematically classified into a body of general truths that will provide for a formulation of general laws that must be tested and verified. When the classification and systematization of any body of knowledge is accomplished, the end result is known as *science*.

3

Thus, when the body of knowledge is concerned with social phenomena, a *social science* is the result. If the social phenomena in question are concerned with relationships of production, consumption, and exchange—all of which are economic variables—then the social science that has been developed is *economics*.

For purposes of this book, economics is defined as a *social science that deals with the allocation of scarce resources among the unlimited and competing alternative uses to which those resources may be put.* This definition embraces the general laws that govern the production, consumption, and exchange of goods, and the interactions—individual and/or group—that are generated in these processes. Resources (including the human resource) provide the basis for production. The needs of people—that is, the end uses to which products may be put—provide the basis for consumption and exchange in society.

Agriculture may be defined as the production, processing, marketing, and distribution of crops and livestock. These four activities were all farm-centered at one time. However, with improvements in technology, division and specialization of labor have moved some of these activities away from the farm into certain strategic central points.

In view of the definitions of economics and agriculture, we can define agricultural economics as the *social science concerned with the allocation of scarce resources among those uses associated with producing, processing, and consuming the products of farms and ranches.* Within this definition, the objectives of this book may be specified:

1. To define the role of agriculture within today's American economic system.

2. To define the general economic laws that regulate not only agriculture, but also the entire environment within which agriculture exists.

3. To examine some of the broad problem areas that face the managers of individual agricultural businesses, and other problems that face agriculture as a whole.

4. To describe the basic principles upon which rational economic decisions may be made, not only for the management of farms and ranches, but also for the management of other agriculturally related businesses.

The first two objectives will be examined in the early chapters in this book, and the third will be given attention throughout. The fourth objective of describing the basic managerial principles will receive the most detailed attention.

2

Our National Economy— Some Basic Choices

Economists like to think that the science of economics is an independent science and that economic forces are immutable and will eventually prevail, regardless of the political and economical institutions that help form the environment within which these forces operate. This could not be further from the truth. The facts are, we live in a *political* economy. (Indeed, the earliest economists recognized this fact. Economics was originally termed "political economy"!) Economics are shaped by politics, and economic forces in turn change the face of political activity.

Types of Politico-Economic Systems • Since mankind does exist in a political economy, and since modern American politics are filled with references to politico-economic systems, it seems appropriate to define the sort of political economy with which we will be dealing in our study. There are four basic types of politico-economic systems.

COMMUNISM: All economic goods are owned by the population at large. In theory, individuals contribute to the production process according to ability and consume the goods produced according to need. In practice, the term communism is used to describe totalitarian states, such as the Soviet Union, in which the means for production (i.e., capital and land resources) are owned and managed by the state. The individual's right to hold and control property is recognized only in the case of consumer goods.

SOCIALISM: All or a large part of the productive resources in the society are owned and operated collectively. Income tends to be more evenly distributed than in capitalist societies, but socialist societies—unlike communist societies—typically allow free elections. Thus, the politico-economic system may become more or less "socialistic" as a result of the expressed will of the citizenry. Example of societies that tend toward socialism include Sweden, Norway, Denmark, and the United Kingdom.

CAPITALISM: In theory, productive resources are owned, controlled, and managed by private citizens with a minimum of direct economic intervention by government either in resource or commodity markets. In practice, those socities that combine private resource ownership with a substantial degree of public supervision by a government freely elected are said to be capitalistic. The United States, Canada, and Japan are examples of nations that might normally be classified among the capitalist societies.

FASCISM: While resources tend to be privately owned, extensive and far-reaching governmental economic direction is present. Government is characteristically totalitarian. Extreme nationalism and patriotism, racism, glorification of the chief of state, and suppression of civil liberties are all frequently associated with fascist states. Hitler's Germany, Franco's Spain, Mussolini's Italy, and many of the Arab and emerging African states are examples of fascist societies.

Obviously, no society can be classified as fitting purely into one or another of these general classifications. Almost any society may possess elements of each of the general types. One might view these various sorts of politico-economic systems as being on a "circular continuum" (Figure 2.1). While communist and fascist societies have historically denounced one another in the vilest of terms, the two are similar, both being totalitarian states that practice extreme suppression of civil liberties and exert an enormous degree of control on the private lives of their citizens. It should be pointed out that they have said some pretty unkind things about capitalists and socialists as well. Fascists and communists don't like anyone—least of all each other. Because of the political freedoms and the minimization of government economic control, capitalism could be viewed as the direct opposite of *both* communism and fascism, with socialism fitting somewhere between communism and capitalism.

Since the United States does tend toward capitalism most of our discussion will assume the capitalistic politico-economic system. While the author admits to being a capitalist of the rankest sort, capitalism—as well as other forms of politico-economic organization—may come in for some lumps. Angus Black, in *A Radical's Guide to Economic Reality,* has described capitalism as "Big Business—or Screw the Consumer and Full Speed Ahead."[1] While there is some justification for Mr. Black's description of capitalism,

___

[1] Angus Black, *A Radical's Guide to Economic Reality* (New York: Holt, Rinehart, and Winston, Inc., 1970), Chapter 1, p. 1.

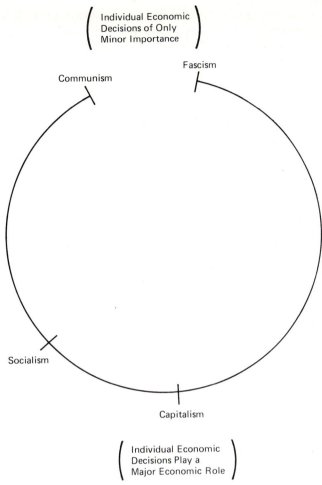

Figure 2.1 The politico-economic systems on a "circular continuum" measuring the degree of influence of economic decisions made by individuals.

communism might be described as "Screw *Both* the Producer and Consumer— Full Speed Ahead." These descriptions suggest that the only decision that can be made by the individual citizen is whether he wants it in one ear or both. But this is not the full story. It must be pointed out that Mr. Black could publish his views—and sell them *capitalistically—only* in the capitalistic society he so roundly damns.

    There *are* some problems in this capitalistic society of ours, and we will be examining these problems and the efforts that have been made to solve them. These problems include not only those faced by society in general, but also those faced by particular individuals within that society. Most of us are interested in society's problems primarily in terms of how they and any of their proposed solutions will affect the socio-political and politico-economic environment within which each of us must find ways of doing our thing. Therefore, the focus of our discussion will be primarily on individual problems.

The Basic Economic Problems of Society • Any economic system, whether that system be an individual, a household, a business, a community, a state, or a nation, faces a set of basic economic problems. Traditionally, most economic texts have listed three of these problems:

1. What to produce,

2. How to produce it, and

3. For whom to produce.

In deciding *what* is to be produced, an economic system must determine not only which commodities are to be made available, but also the quantities in which those products are to be created. That is, the *composition* of the total produce must be determined. For example, any major university must determine what portion of its annual effort will be devoted to securing quality classroom instruction; how much will go for enrichment programs; and how much will be devoted to improving, enlarging, and maintaining the dormitory, classroom, and laboratory facilities utilized in the educational process. In this fashion, a university *economizes.* The decisions as to *how many* courses to offer, *what* (if any) outside speakers shall be permitted to come on the campus, and the quality of campus facilities all go together to determine just what sort of educational opportunity is to be available at that institution. The student, on the other hand, economizes by selecting a blend of formal education and extracurricular activities.

In decisions as to *how* goods are to be produced, the method of production is determined. Where will production occur? What resources will be used? What level of technology will be employed? Continuing our educational example, should a university limit class size to 40 (or 30 or 25) students? This would involve a large number of decisions:

1. Should we limit enrollment to the numbers of students that can be handled by existing faculty and classrooms and still conform to the class size limitation?

2. Should we increase the size of our faculty by hiring larger numbers of less well qualified faculty in order to handle the teaching load, which would increase as a result of limited class size?

3. Should we have only small classrooms and laboratories?

4. Should we offer certain courses only every other semester or every other year? Or should we eliminate certain courses of study entirely?

The question of *for whom* goods are to be produced deals with the question of who is to get the goodies. In other words, how do we distribute the available goods among our total population? Is the bulk of our productivity to be used by the very rich? Or should it be distributed more or less evenly so that most of our people enjoy about the same level of living? If our decision is in favor of giving all or the bulk of our population an even break to share in the goodies, how are we to prevent a small group of the very wealthy from hogging the available goods? An old adage suggests that the rich get richer and that the poor get children. How are we to break such a cycle in a capitalist society? Even more important, *should* we attempt to alter such a pattern?

There are two additional general economic problems that have emerged in economic literature in recent years. These problems are concerned with economic progress:

4. How intensively are resources to be employed, and

5. How rapidly shall the total size of the economy expand?

The degree of intensity of resource use is concerned with decisions about the size of the total economy; the degree of fluctuation of such items as prices, income, and employment; and the acceptable levels of such factors as employee safety and environmental pollution. These questions focus on the conflicts among and between political and economic objectives. Reducing the rate of environmental pollution, for example, can be accomplished through a reduction in the intensity of resource use, but only at the cost of a reduction in economic efficiency. Thus, society must choose how much economic efficiency (as measured by the cost of production) it is willing to sacrifice in order to improve the environment. Much of the inflation in food prices during the early 1970s can be traced to bans on the use of certain agricultural chemicals having high residual properties. The long-lived residual nature of pesticides such as DDT, Dieldren and Aldrin is precisely the characteristic that made these substances desirable for the control of pests such as the gypsy moth and corn root worm. The short-lived residual nature of alternative chemicals preferred for limiting the environmental impact causes increased frequency of application and hence increased production costs. As a result, consumer food prices have been forced to increase—due to decisions regarding the intensity of resource use.

The question of the rate of economic expansion is closely related not only to the questions of what and how to produce, but also to the intensity of resource use. It involves deciding on the blend of investment (capital) goods versus consumer goods; that is, deciding on the provision of *new* economic activities. This immediately involves the question of for whom to produce, since a decision to distribute more income to lower income families is a decision in favor of increased consumer goods.

All of these functions must be performed in some fashion in every society. The role of the individual citizen is the basic source of difference in the various politico-economic systems. In the capitalist system, individual economic decisions are of enormous importance, especially in achieving answers to the what, how, and for whom questions. These individual decisions are of relatively minor importance in the communist and fascist societies.

In solving the five basic economic problems, economic systems perform their major functions. Whether or not they are performed well is dependent on one's own set of values and objectives. But the facts are these functions must be performed in some fashion *regardless* of the economic, political, or social system, and regardless of the state of economic development. All of these economic problems have arisen as a result of a single unpleasant fact of life—*scarcity*. If we had access to unlimited resources, every conceivable human want could be satisfied. Therefore, it would not matter if resources were combined unwisely. If every person could have as much as he pleased of everything, it wouldn't matter how income was distributed. If there were no problems of resource scarcity, there would be no need for "economizing" or for studying economics. If resources were unlimited, no good would command a price. Everything would be as free as the air we breathe (which is no longer all that free—witness the increased cost of automobiles resulting from the addition of emission control devices that are intended to reduce air pollution).

The idea (or law) of *scarcity* is basic to the entire field of economics. As small children, each of us encountered the law of scarcity. We knew that one dime would not purchase both chewing gum and a Coke, since both were priced at ten cents (and weren't those the good old days!). We had only one dime, and were therefore forced to choose between the two—dimes were *scarce.*

A child's wants are simple. As he matures and as the means by which he is able to acquire goods increase, his aspirations increase. As an individual attains college age, he can generally afford to buy both Cokes and chewing gum. But the range of his wants is much broader than it was twelve to fifteen years earlier. Rather than the Cokes and chewing gum of grade school days, now he aspires to cigarettes, whiskey, beautiful women, and fast cars. (Or we can turn that around. He also likes beautiful cars and fast women.) However, these commodities are expensive and the college man's coins are still scarce. So he works out some combination of these items that he feels will permit him to achieve the highest level of satisfaction possible with the scarce resources that he has at his disposal.

Economic Definitions   •   In Chapter 1, we defined economics as the *social science that deals with the allocation of scarce resources among the unlimited alternative uses for those resources.* This definition embraces the five problems of any economic system. It deals with the questions of what, how, for whom, how big, and how fast that we face as individuals. You personally decide whether you will study tonight or go to a wrestling match at some secluded campus trysting place. In so doing, you are deciding:

1. *What* kind of education you get (formal, physical, or sex),

2. *How* you are to achieve that education (participant or observer),

3. *Toward Whom* that education will be directed (you or?),

4. *How Intensively* your resources will be employed (several hours or ???), and

5. *How Rapidly* you will grow (so far as educational skills are concerned. No further comment is necessary).

In the more general sense, the definition of economics may still be somewhat confusing. What does this definition mean when we translate it into English? Let's break it down into parts and perhaps we can get a better idea of what this business of economics is all about.

First of all, what are *resources?* Resources provide the basis for production. Generally speaking, almost any productive resource will fall into one of four broad categories—land, labor, capital, or management. Some authorities contend that land is a special type of capital and that management is a special type of labor. But for our purposes, we will treat the four as separate types of resources. Land, of course, includes the soil and other natural resources. Labor is obviously the resource provided by the rank and file of wage earners. Capital is normally defined to have been created when the "original factors of production" (that is, land and labor) are stored in the form of goods. Thus, a tractor would be capital. Livestock could be capital. Money—the means for acquiring goods in an exchange economy—and other financial assets such as stocks and bonds are not capital as such, but can *command* capital goods. Management is the resource that must be used to organize (or allocate) the other resources for the purpose of production.

Next, let's examine the term "unlimited alternative uses" for resources. Why do we use resources at all? Resources are the basis for producing the goods and services that are used for the satisfaction of human wants. The wants of humanity are unlimited. No person ever has everything he could possibly want. Because of the insatiable nature of human wants, the uses for the resources that provide the means for satisfying those wants are unlimited. There are at least four places to spend every dollar an individual can lay hands on. Thus, there are an *unlimited number of alternative uses for that dollar.*

Our definition of economics, then, embraces the five problems of any economic system. But let's consider our national economy and the economic environment within which we live. The individual decides whether he wants chewing gum or Coke. A farmer must decide whether to plant an acreage in barley or bermuda grass. Nations must make the decision between public and private goods—the classic "guns or butter" decision.

The Production Possibilities Frontier • We have already recognized the basic economic fact of life that scarcity of resources forces us to choose among commodities that, because of resource limitation, must likewise be scarce. These choices must be faced at the national as well as the individual level. Consider our economy, which at any moment in time has only so many people, only so much technical know-how, only so much land, water, power, and other natural resources. In making the decisions of what and how to produce, the society must really decide just how these resources are to be allocated among the thousands of possible uses. How much land should go into cotton production, and how much into pasture? How many factories should produce hair dryers and how many should manufacture motor bikes? How much skilled labor should go into machine shops and how much into beauty salons?

These problems are fiendishly complex even to define, let alone to face the complexity of achieving solutions. Therefore, let's simplify the problem by assuming that there are only two economic goods—goods for private consumption, as represented by beef; and public goods, as represented by usable "green space" (that is, open areas unused for agricultural purposes). This represents the problem faced by all governments—namely that of choosing some blend of public and private goods. There can be no public goods that have not first been wrested from or denied to private individuals.

The problem is illustrated in Figure 2.2. If we use all our resources to produce beef, there will be some maximum quantity of beef that we can produce in a year. Let's say that 50 million head of cattle a year is all we can expect to slaughter if we apply the best technology and use all of our resources in that effort. If, on the other hand, we use all resources to produce usable "green space," perhaps a maximum of 100 million square miles can be available if we are really willing to forego beef.

All green space or all meat are the limits of the alternatives we face. If we are willing to give up ten million head of cattle a year, we can have about

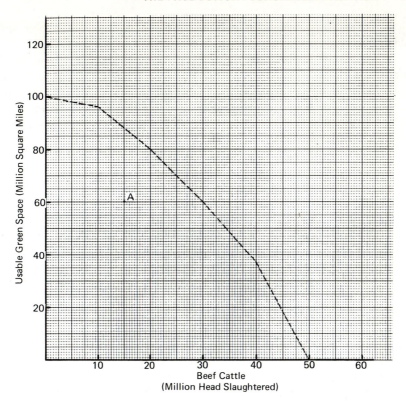

Figure 2.2 Possibilities for transforming usable green space into beef.

37 million square miles of green space. If we are willing to give up still more meat, we can have still more green space. Some resources are better suited for producing one good than another—heavily forested areas are not especially suited to beef production and the buffalo grass areas of the Great Plains are not particularly useful as green space since major cities are few and far between. (Further, those who come from the Great Plains will recognize that the areas are only too rarely green!)

As we move away from producing *only* beef or *only* green space, it doesn't "cost" a great deal initially to substitute one good for the other. In Figure 2.2, we see that we can produce ten million head of slaughter cattle without giving up much green space. But the next ten million head cost a good many square miles of green space, and the next ten million head cost still more in terms of open area.

This relationship is known as a *production possibilities curve*. It represents the fundamental fact that an economy in which all resources are employed must always give up something of one good in order to increase the availability of another. The production possibilities curve defines the array of choices that can be made. Any point on or below the curve is available, but points outside the curve are unavailable because of resource limitations.

When some resources are not fully employed, the economy is operating somewhere under the production possibilities curve (point A in Figure 2.2). If resources are idle, we can have more beef *and* more usable public areas by putting these resources to work. That is, more lands could be rendered "usable" for public purposes by the addition of some items such as camping facilities and picnic tables.

There are several reasons a society might leave some resources idle, electing to operate below the production possibilities curve. For example, during the 1960s, large acreages of land were placed in the so-called Conservation Reserve, reducing agricultural production in an effort to maintain higher prices for farm commodities. We have from time to time removed land from agricultural production in order to provide wildlife habitat. In the early 1970s, we saw great efforts made by environmental interests to prevent the construction of nuclear power facilities. These same groups worked diligently to prevent the development of oil and gas deposits off the New England coast, giving rise to bumper stickers in Texas and Louisiana advising that we should "Let the Bastards Freeze in the Dark!"

As we learn more and more about the world in which we live, technology shifts the production possibilities curve outward—that is, the resources we have become more and more productive. This is the situation we have had in American agriculture since World War II. We have discovered ways of making each acre more productive, and as a result we can either produce the same amount of food and fiber with fewer acres or we can produce a great deal more with the same acreage. In the case of the example shown in Figure 2.2, the practice of sprigging (setting bermuda roots—or "sprigs"—in an improved pasture) native grass pastures to bermuda grass greatly increased the beef production capacity, particularly on acreages in the southern United States (Figure 2.3). The maximum level of usable green space would not have been affected by this particular sort of technological improvement; hence, the change in the curve would rotate around the point at which the production possibilities curve intercepts the "Usable Green Space" axis. Thus, in the case of the example in Figure 2.3, after the technological development, an annual beef slaughter of 50 million head could be achieved while leaving 45 million square miles of usable green space. Prior to the technological development, this level of slaughter could have been achieved if and only if all usable green space had been sacrificed to beef production.

It should be pointed out that a production possibilities curve in no way suggests what decision a society *should* make. It merely shows the array of choices available. Once a decision has been made to operate at some point on or below the curve, then the choice of that point may reveal society's solutions to some of the basic economic problems. Suppose that Point B in

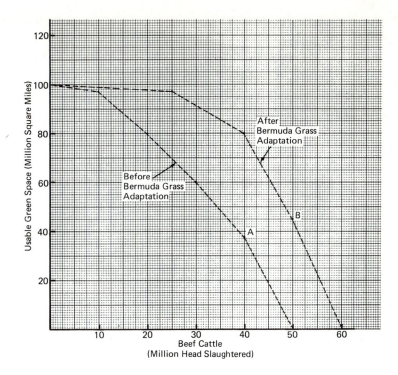

Figure 2.3 Example of technological growth's shifting the production possibilities curve.

Figure 2.3 has been selected. This point reveals the society's "what to produce" decision. Since Point *B* has been selected rather than Point *A,* we also have an indication of the "how to produce" decision. That is, society has opted to allow the bermuda grass technology, even though numerous citizens may manifest allergic reactions to this plant.

"For whom" goods are to be produced cannot be determined from the production possibilities curve alone. However, from the product mix that may be shown, we can get some glimmer of who is to enjoy the benefits of productivity. If there are a great many luxury cars in relation to the numbers of subcompacts in the product mix, it is a pretty safe bet that it has been determined that the wealth and income within the society is distributed such that we have a few very wealthy people, a very small middle class, and a great many very poor people. This is the case, for example, in many of the oil-rich Arab nations. The oil wealth has been confined to a very small portion of the total population.

The position a society selects on a production possibilities curve between basic necessities of life and luxuries can characteristically show the state of economic development in a nation. A very poor (or underdeveloped) nation will be forced to devote almost all its resources to the production of food. As the nation develops and adapts new technology, or as it invests in capital goods, the production possibilities curve can shift upward. If productivity is increasing faster than population, while the production of basic necessities may be increased somewhat, the real increase will come in the luxuries such as washing machines and automobiles. Thus, a relatively larger share of the available resources will be devoted to the production of the non-necessity items.

So far as the questions of economic growth and the intensity of resource use are concerned, the production possibilities can only suggest the decisions that have been made. If the allocation between consumer goods and capital goods is weighted toward the creation of capital, a decision has been made in favor of growth. The degree of weighting will suggest the relative growth rate chosen. As already suggested, the decision to leave resources idle might be reflected by having selected a point below rather than on the production possibilities frontier.

The Question of Economic Growth • In recent years, economists have become vitally interested in the processes of economic growth. W. W. Rostow, one of the nation's leading theorists in economic development, has defined the stages of economic growth to be:[2]

1. The Traditional Society. This is a period of economic stagnation such as has historically been found in primitive cultures. Most of the labor force is involved in food production. Tribal or clan organizations are a major force in maintaining social order.

2. The Preconditioning for Take-Off. "Social overhead" capital items such as roads, schools, a marketing system, etc., are created. Agricultural production becomes efficient enough to begin to release some labor to non-food production. The monetary system increases in importance. An effective, centralized national state is created.

3. The Take-Off Period. Total productivity increases so rapidly that economic growth is perceived as the normal condition. A major portion of the benefits from the increased productivity is reinvested in capital goods for still further increases in productivity. Population begins to congregate to establish large cities.

4. The Drive to Maturity. Economic growth has become steady and dependable, if occasionally erratic. Increases in productivity regu-

---

[2] W. W. Rostow, *The Stages of Economic Growth, a Non-Communist Manifesto* (Cambridge: Cambridge University Press, 1962), Chapter 2, pp. 4–10.

larly exceed increases in population, allowing steadily increasing standards of living. Population becomes primarily urban rather than rural.

5. The Age of High Mass Consumption. The leading economic sectors focus upon consumer durable goods (automobiles, refrigerators, etc.) and upon services.

In the earliest stages of economic development, man is basically a parasite of nature. He simply takes what he finds and lives from it. During this period, he accidentally discovers some of the secrets of nature and a rudimentary agriculture develops. This sort of production technology is perpetuated through tradition until some factor allows the society to move into the pre-conditioning for growth phase. Rostow points out that except for the case of England, this pre-conditioning phase occurred as the result of some intrusion from outside.

Obviously, a society that is forced to devote almost all its resources to the production of food is "locked" into the traditional period at what may become a threshold of starvation. If the production possibilities curve is to be shifted upward, either through investment or technology, some savings must occur. That is, some consumption must be delayed. It's a little tough to delay consumption when all resources are devoted to producing the basic necessities of life.

When a society is at the threshold of starvation, almost all of the production must go into current consumption for purposes of merely maintaining the present population. In this situation, it is virtually impossible to provide internally for both economic growth and increasing standards of living, *regardless* of how many natural resources that country has. The development of natural resources requires that some current production be set aside for purposes of capital formation. For example, the machinery for drilling and pumping an oil well is expensive. The equipment for digging and smelting copper ore is not free. It costs a lot of money to develop improved varieties of wheat seed that will increase per-acre yields of wheat. It costs a great deal to drill an irrigation well that will make desert land productive.

Unless funds can be set aside for acquiring such capital equipment, the natural resources cannot be developed, and the production possibilities curve for that society is locked into position at the starvation threshold. An example of this is the current situation we see in many of the new Asian and African nations and to some extent in Latin America. The idea behind foreign aid as practiced by the United States since World War II has been to provide nations that are locked into the starvation threshold with the wherewithal to shift their production possibilities curves outward.

The adoption of new technology and investment in capital goods both cost money. The primitive or traditional societies cannot delay consumption in order to make these investments. Hence the reason for Rostow's observation that the basis for growth has most commonly come from outside sources.

But like anything else, economic growth had to start somewhere. The earliest major instance of rapid economic growth that we read about came with the Industrial Revolution. The Industrial Revolution began in England and spread from England into Western Europe. From these areas, it spread into the rest of the world.

How did growth begin in England? Knowing Mama Nature's inclination to insure the preservation of every species, and recognizing man's disinclination to deny himself the joys of an active sex life, how were the influences of this partnership between man and nature overcome to a degree large enough to permit any degree of economic growth ever to occur?

Horrible as it is to visualize, England suffered a couple of very fortunate disasters. The epidemic of bubonic plague and the Great Fire of London during the seventeenth century reduced the numbers of people that had to be fed. As a result, England escaped from the "starvation threshold" that had bound so many resources into the production of food. It was then possible to rapidly increase the creation of capital goods, which in turn permitted the production of not only more goods for current consumption, but also the production of still *more* capital items. In this fashion, England ceased to be an insignificant agricultural island and became a nation of merchants. These merchants exported capital items from Europe into the New World and into Africa and Asia in the form of colonialism. From these seeds grew the highly productive societies of the Western Hemisphere and from these same seeds came substantial development of certain Asian and African economies.

As economic growth progresses, economic units become specialized, producing more of their specialty product than they can possibly use at home. They then sell this product and exchange the proceeds of the sale for purposes of buying the other products needed for home use. Government expands more and more into a regulatory role since there is necessarily more interaction between and among economic units. Money becomes increasingly important as a medium of exchange since there are so many more exchanges occurring. As the large cities of the Take-off and Drive to Maturity periods develop, there is no choice but to devote more and more resources to the government sector to provide the public services of fire protection, police protection, urban planning, parking meters, parks and playground.

Economic Growth in a Developed Economy • Rostow is vague regarding his expectations of what happens in a society once the Age of Mass Consumption has been achieved. But this is a crucial question to Americans, who have reached this stage of economic development. Continued economic growth can come from further capital investment, from investment in research or from some combination of the two. In general, investment in research has proved to be even more productive than investment in capital equipment (witness the "spinoff" developments associated with the space program).

Through technical progress, two types of growth can be accomplished. First, improved ways of utilizing present resources, and second, development of new forms of resources (for example, atomic power and solar energy). In agriculture, this has been illustrated by mechanization and development of new seed varieties. Through mechanization and the new methods of cultivation associated with mechanization and fertilization, the productivity of a given piece of land has increased. Planting hybrid corn or grain sorghum under the new methods increases productivity to an even greater degree.

Selected References

Black, Angus, *A Radical's Guide to Economic Reality*. New York: Holt, Rinehart, and Winston, Inc., 1970.

Heady, Earl O., *Economics of Agricultural Production and Resource Use*, Chapter 8. Englewood Cliffs, N.J.: Prentice-Hall, Inc., 1952.

Heilbroner, Robert L., *Understanding Macroeconomics*. Englewood Cliffs, N.J.: Prentice-Hall, Inc., 1965.

Lipsey, Richard G. and Peter O. Steiner, *Economics*, Chapter 1. New York: Harper and Row, 1966.

McConnell, Campbell, R., *Economics, Principles, Problems and Policies*, 2nd ed., Chapter 2. New York: McGraw-Hill, 1963.

Rostow, W. W., *The Stages of Economic Growth, A Non-Communist Manifesto*. Cambridge: Cambridge University Press, 1962.

Samuelson, Paul A., *Economics, An Introductory Analysis*, 6th ed., Chapter 2. New York: McGraw-Hill, 1964.

3

Our National Economy— Wealth, Productivity, and Income

We saw in Chapter 2 how the various production possibilities curves define the limits within which our economy must operate and the limits within which economic growth can occur. We saw that the questions of economic progress and decisions of what, how, and for whom to produce must be determined by any economic system because of the scarcity of resources. In the case of the American economy, these decisions are made largely by way of the price system.

We have all heard that the forces of supply and demand provide for the regulation of the economy. The mechanism by which regulation is achieved is price. Households provide the major part of the demand for consumer goods, and business firms supply those consumer goods. But the questions concerning basic economic problems are not transmitted directly from households to business firms. If consumers need and want more peanut brittle and fewer automobile tires, they make their wishes known in the market place by "balloting" in favor of peanut brittle. The polls for this very democratic process of casting ballots are located in the market place (Figure 3.1). The "ballots" are the dollars bid for the available peanut brittle. As the votes in favor of peanut brittle are increased and as peanut brittle prices begin to rise relative to tire prices, business firms get the message that the peanut brittle racket is more profitable than the tire business. Consequently, more resources will be devoted to the production of peanut brittle.

In a capitalistic economy, individuals in the general public (i.e., households) control the supply of resources. Each household has a certain amount of labor at its disposal, and perhaps some land, capital, or management as well. As the business firms get the message that peanut brittle has won the election, they go into the resource market to buy the ingredients for peanut brittle. This effort, in turn, spawns a second "election." They discover that

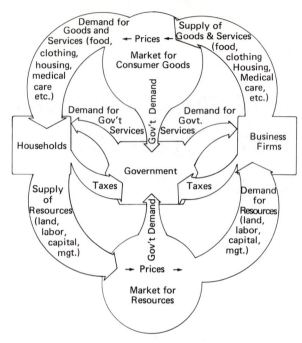

Figure 3.1   Flow chart of the capitalist economic system.

competing firms have also gotten the message that peanut brittle is a highly desirable item and that these competing firms are trying to cut themselves in for a piece of the peanut brittle action. Because of the expanded demand for peanut brittle-producing resources, the prices for the ingredients of peanut brittle begin to rise relative to the prices for the ingredients of automobile tires.

The results of this second "election" ultimately get to the owners of resources by way of the prices bid for the ingredients of peanut brittle, relative to those for the ingredients of tires. Rather than planting more rubber trees, these resource owners will devote more land, labor, capital and management to the production of peanuts, sugar beets, and sugar cane. In a capitalist society, then, price is the means of communication that makes the system work.

Central to this whole procedure in a capitalist economy in the Age of Mass Consumption is the role of government. Government takes claims to resources from both businesses and households in the form of taxation. The funds derived from taxation are then used to purchase the necessary materials and to hire the necessary labor for providing the government services that are essential to the orderly performance of that society. These services are demanded by both industry and individuals. Both these groups require roads, police and fire protection, research and educational facilities.

Government policy can also influence the rate of growth. Through manipulation of taxation, spending, or the money supply, government can either accelerate or retard the rate of economic activity. If the growth rate is such that the demand for goods and services is outrunning the ability of the economy to produce such goods, prices begin a rapid upward spiral. Through increased taxation (or through reduced government spending, or a reduction in the supply of money), government can reduce the demand for goods and services to a point where the current rate of production can meet this demand. Conversely, when the rate of production begins to outrun the demand, government can help ameliorate the effects of such a development by reducing taxes, by increasing government spending, or by increasing the availability of money. In either case, the level of consumption will be increased.

The Place of Government • It should be noted that the markets provide the connecting link between the general public and business. In some cases, the markets are also the connecting link between government and business and between government and the general public. However, government has a much more direct and intimate connection with these two sectors. The pocketbook of every business and every individual has a special corner that belongs exclusively to the tax collector. Through the tax collector and through government spending, government exercises a strong voice in all five of the basic economic decisions that must be solved within any society. Within the limits imposed by government action, the price system determines the questions. But government action (a price freeze, for example) can negate and/or disrupt the price messages that are necessary for the decisions to be made.

We are all acquainted to some degree with the direct role of government in the agricultural sector of our economy. But as has just been suggested, the impact of government is felt throughout the economy. The effect of government action upon other sectors filters indirectly into agriculture. Let's consider, for example, the growth of government expenditures.

Before World War I, federal, state and local government expenditures amounted to a bit more than eight percent of our Gross National Product (Figure 3.2). During World War II, our national production expanded tremendously due to the war effort, and government expenditures took about half this total output.

Gross National Product (that is, the *total value of all goods and services produced either for consumption or investment*) has risen steadily in the United States for more than a century. The only real exception to this trend was during the early years of the Great Depression from 1929 to 1933. We can see from Figure 3.2 that there have also been short periods during which Gross National Product (usually abbreviated GNP) moved sideways or perhaps even declined slightly, but overall, the tendency has been for a steady

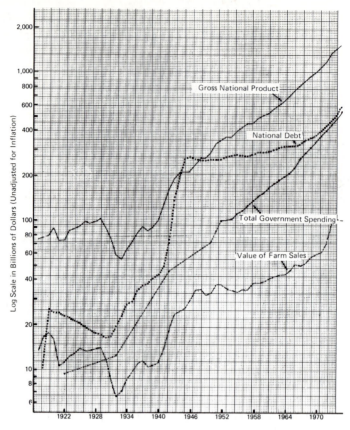

Figure 3.2   U.S. Gross National Product, national debt, gross value of farm sales, and all government expenditures, selected years, 1916–76.

increase. (The periods in which GNP failed to grow for short periods are called recessions. The official definition of a recession is that GNP declines for two successive three-month quarters.)

Over this same period, we see upward trends in several measures of general economic conditions. Gross Farm Income (that is, the total value of all farm production as it leaves the farm gate) has risen steadily over this period. At the beginning of World War II, Gross Farm Income accounted for about 11 percent of Gross National Product. By 1964, Gross Farm Income made up less than 7 percent of GNP. By 1970, Gross Farm Income had declined to a bit under 6 percent of GNP, but with the dramatic increase in agricultural exports and the relatively rapid increases in farm commodity prices during the early 1970s, Gross Farm Income rebounded to about 6.5 percent of GNP. Thus, it is evident that over time, farm production has become less important as a share of GNP. But the early 1970s suggest that there may be some reversal of this direction.

Gross National Product has increased from an annual rate of about $100 billion in 1940 to almost $1,500 billion in 1975—an increase of about 1,400 percent. Gross Farm Income over this same period increased by less than 800 percent. When we consider that the total volume of farm production has almost doubled over this period, it is apparent that while the efficiency of the American farmer has increased very rapidly, much of this improved efficiency has been given away in the market place through relative reductions in farm prices (when compared with other prices). The American public today spends a smaller proportion of income on food than has *any* population in *any* country at *any* period in the history of mankind. Less than 20 cents of the American Consumer's dollar has gone for food since the early 1960s, and the farm producer has received only 40–42 percent of this relatively small food expenditure.

Two other factors with which we may concern ourselves are the levels of national debt and government expenditures. These two factors are related, since any time a government spends more than it takes in, a debt is incurred. If government spending outruns tax collections over a long period of time, the accumulation of deficits progressively enlarges the national debt.

There are two striking observations that can be made about the national debt and government spending. First, these both increased relatively more rapidly in the 1970s than did the Gross National Product. In 1940, federal, state and local governments spent something less than 20 billion dollars, and the national debt was just over 60 billion dollars. By 1970, federal spending alone had increased to $197 billion, and the national debt was more than $370 billion. In 1975, federal spending was $374 billion and the national debt had increased to $570 billion. Thus, in the five years between 1970 and 1975, GNP increased by a bit less than half while federal spending increased by 90 percent and the national debt by 54 percent. This suggests that as our economy has become more and more productive, moving further into the Age of Mass Consumption, the function of government has grown even faster. As our population has grown, and as a larger and larger share of this population has moved into the close quarters of major metropolitan areas, it has become necessary to increase government spending in order to provide the roads, schools, and other public facilities necessary to accommodate this urban population. Because of the shift in population, many of these same facilities in rural areas have been under-utilized and in many cases abandoned. In terms of a production possibilities curve between public and private goods, we have moved around the curve toward public goods such that we are spending a larger share of our production on public functions, and a smaller share on private functions.

A second observation that we can make concerning government spending and the national debt is that the greatest rates of increase have come during times of war or other national emergency. The periods during which the national debt and spending increased the fastest were during World Wars I and II, during the Great Depression of the 1930s, and during the very serious economic recession of the 1974–75 period. For a short period during and following World War II, the national debt actually exceeded Gross National Product. Since the 1950s the national debt has moved upward, but at a rate generally more comparable with the increase in GNP.

Gross National Product   •   Gross National Product (GNP) is the term that is used to describe the dollar value of the total annual output of all "finished" consumption and investment goods produced in a nation. Gross National Product has several characteristics that should be kept in mind. First of all, only the *finished* goods are included in GNP. We are concerned with the total *value* of all the goods and services that are ultimately available to the individuals and businesses within the economy. Thus, we do not count the value of goods in the various level of production (i.e., the intermediate goods). When we compute the value of GNP, we do not, for example, add up the values of beef cattle, carcass beef, retail cuts of beef, raw hides, tanned hides, and shoes. When we buy shoes, the value of the shoes includes the cost of the tanned leather, and when the shoemaker buys the tanned leather, the price he pays includes the cost of the green hide. Likewise, the price of steak in the meat market is inclusive of the cost of carcass beef to the retailer, and the price the retailer pays for carcass beef includes the price the packer paid for the live animal. Embodied in the cost of finished goods are the costs of all the ingredients that are included in the finished item. So we add only the values of finished items when we compute GNP.

A second point that should be clarified concerning GNP is that there are several sorts of finished goods. The two basic types are consumption goods and investment goods. However, the difference between the value of goods that leave the United States and those that come in from outside during any given year must also be accounted for.

If total exports exceed total imports, then the difference is a *net export* (that is, there is a positive trade balance). If the reverse condition prevails, we have a *net import* (a negative net export, or a negative trade balance). Net exports may be either in the form of goods for consumption or goods for investment.

The excess of imports over exports was the reason for the much-publicized "gold drain" of the 1960s. What happened was that foreign businesses sold more products in the United States then were shipped out of the United States. The dollars which paid for these products were converted by the foreign businessman into the local currency (say francs in the case of France). The foreign government then presented the dollars to the U.S. Treasury and said, "All right boys, your paper dollars may be good here, but they don't spend for sour apples in France. How about cashing each 35 of these greenbacks in for an ounce of the pretty yellow stuff buried at Fort

Knox?" So we bought our paper money back with gold and the end result was that we had more goods and more paper money, but some of our gold had gone overseas to pay for Belgian barbed wire, Scotch whiskey, and French wine.

In the very early 1970s, the United States ceased redeeming dollars for gold at $35 per ounce. We allowed the value of the dollar to "float" in terms of other currencies, and hence in terms of gold. Thus, gold became a substance to use for filling teeth rather than the basis for settling international accounts. With the advent of the energy crisis in 1973−74, there was great concern that the dramatic increases in Arab oil prices would create an enormous balance of payments deficit in the United States and consequent erosion of the value of the dollar. However, the increased volume and value of farm exports almost perfectly offset the increased cost of the imported oil, thus limiting the impact of the energy crisis on the U.S. economy. The relationships regarding the net export component of Gross National Product will be examined in some detail in Chapter 5 when we discuss the question of economic policy decisions.

The key to a third characteristic of Gross National Product that should be kept in mind is the government sector. Government purchases and production of goods and services may be for either consumption or investment purposes. For example, purchases of agricultural commodities for a school lunch program would represent public consumption items, while the purchase of equipment used in the pursuit of governmentally-sponsored agricultural research activities represents public investment. Likewise, the services of a municipally-paid fireman represents public consumption, while roads and schools are public investment. In the calculation of GNP, *all* public expenditures, whether for consumption or investment, are commonly included in the single category of government purchases.

A fourth point that should be made concerning GNP is that it is at best an approximation. The inexact nature of GNP is inescapable since the values of some items are much more difficult to measure than are those of some others. For example, it is a fairly simple matter to add up the value of all the bubble gum manufactured in the United States, but an accurate computation of the value of the services of residential rental units is almost impossible. Rents on certain public housing units, for example, are adjusted to the income of the tenant. Yet, who is to say that the value of a given unit occupied by a family with an annual income of perhaps $6,000 is worth less than if that unit were occupied by a family with an income of $12,000? Or physicians may adjust fees to levels they feel a patient is able to pay. Yet who can say an appendectomy is worth less for one person than for another? These situations complicate the calculation of the value of Gross National Product, but medical services and rental housing are a part of GNP just as surely as are the receipts of all the bubble gum vending machines.

A second weakness in the calculation of GNP is that services which are bought in the market place are included, whereas those same services—such as charity medical care or rent-free housing provided by one's parents—are not included when they are obtained free. The salary of a housekeeper, for example, is counted as a part of GNP. But suppose the master of the house marries the housekeeper; he buys the cow in order to get free milk. Gross National Product has declined in the amount of the wages that are no longer paid, even though the housekeeper's original duties are included in her responsibility as a housewife.

The number of men who marry the women who are *paid* to keep house for them is unquestionably small. But the number who "buy the cow" is *not* small. For example, a great many people own their own homes rather than paying rent. Net rental income would be a part of GNP, but the same value of an owner-occupied home is not. Many people eat the vegetables grown in their own gardens. These are not included in GNP, although the same value of vegetables purchased at the food store would be so included. The problems of assigning a reasonable value to the goods and services that are produced and used but not paid for is a source of fiendish complexity in the calculation of GNP.

Even with all its limitations and weaknesses, GNP is the best (indeed the *only*) measure we have of overall economic performance. The computation is normally seen in equation form as:

$$GNP = C + I + G + NE$$

It is calculated by adding up the values of all finished goods purchased for consumption, of all the goods purchased for investment, and of all government purchases, and then adjusting the total for net exports or net imports. The equation (GNP = C + I + G + NE) is one that you will see frequently. You will often read about the various components of GNP in the financial and business sections of your newspaper.

National Wealth: The Basis for Production • We now have some fuzzy notions about what GNP *is* and about what GNP *is not*. We also have some idea about which items are and are not included as a part of GNP. We have recognized that Americans spend less of their income for food than any other people, suggesting that the United States must be the world's wealthiest nation. How does our national production relate to our national wealth? Or more specifically, precisely what is *wealth*?

When the first astronauts viewed the earth from space in the 1960s, what do you suppose was the most tangible evidence they saw of human existence? The most striking thing must have been the stock of wealth from which any society's gross national production must flow. By *wealth,* we mean

TABLE 3.1

STOCK OF TANGIBLE NATIONAL WEALTH, UNITED
STATES, 1968

ITEM	VALUE (BILLIONS OF DOLLARS)
Domestic non-farm wealth	
Residential housing	682.7
Private non-residential structures (business buildings)	288.7
Institutional structures	55.7
Government structures	459.8
Producer durables (machines and equipment)	377.0
Consumer durables	233.8
Business inventories	172.7
Government inventories	14.0
Privately owned non-farm land	418.6
Total non-farm property	2,703.0
Domestic farm wealth	
Farm buildings	50.0
Farm machinery	29.5
Farm inventories (crops and livestock)	29.5
Privately owned farm land	152.6
Public lands	144.2
Total farm property	405.8
Net foreign assets	67.6
Total material wealth	3,176.4
Human wealth (1970)	
Urban population—149.3 million	?
Rural non-farm population—44.2 million	?
Farm population—9.7 million	?

Source: *Statistical Abstract of the United States,* Social and Economic Administration, Bureau of the Census, USDC, 1973.

the tangible goods such as land, forests, farms, and factories which we can observe. Table 3.1 partially inventories the wealth that might be observed in the United States. This estimate is incomplete since we cannot possibly estimate the value of people. The income of an engineer is greater than that of a day laborer. But how can we estimate the value of a group of engineers, physicians, or day laborers? Worse yet, how does one value a stock of highly paid hard-rock musicians whose primary product is hearing loss among young people and ulcers for their parents? The presence of technology (and the people trained to implement that technology) unquestionably enhances the value of other resources, but how can we assign a value to it? What we are really talking about in our estimate of wealth is in a very general sense the national stock of resources.

We can classify the properties listed in our inventory of wealth into the four factors of production we discussed earlier. The resources provided by nature—the soil, water, and all the mineral riches—are normally classified as *land*. The human population would normally be classified as *labor* and *management*. The third category of *capital* would include the man-made items that are of crucial importance in almost every contemporary economic activity.

Capital is of crucial importance as a portion of national wealth. Capital is man-made and can therefore be reproduced. Man-made *capital* in 1968 consisted of all our buildings, our machinery, our producer and consumer durables, inventories, and net foreign assets—almost $2.5 *trillion*! The stock of capital at any time may be considered to represent the sum of everything that has ever been produced in the United States from the beginning of time until the present but that has not yet been consumed. Capital formation occurs when consumption is delayed and some of the product of current human activity is set aside to be used in further production. Capital represents that portion of the total national wealth that is reproducible, and therefore over which man can exert immediate control. Natural and human resources are extremely important, but in a freely elected government associated with a capitalist economy, these items cannot (and probably should not in any society) be manipulated with the speed and unconcern that we observe in the case of capital.

Our discussion of national wealth has ignored some items that each of us would individually consider in calculating our personal wealth. If we apply for a loan at the local bank, the first thing the banker asks for is a financial statement. In that statement, we would be asked to enumerate such items as accounts receivable, accounts payable, cash on hand, funds in savings accounts, and all financial assets such as stocks, bonds, deeds, and mortgages, as well as real assets such as automobiles, land, and art objects. If financial assets are a part of our consideration when we estimate personal wealth, why are they not included in national wealth?

Are stocks and bonds wealth? Or are they merely *claims* to wealth? The factories, machines, and land that make up the real assets represented by stocks and bonds have been included in the estimate of national wealth. Stock certificates merely specify who *owns* these assets; they are not the assets themselves. Bank accounts likewise are merely *claims* against physical wealth. The value of a dollar bill as an object is almost zero. It wouldn't even be good toilet paper. But that dollar bill *does* give the holder an official and legal claim to the objects for which it is exchanged.

The physical wealth over which stocks, bonds, and money give us a claim have already been included in our estimate of national wealth. If we counted these financial assets as a part of national wealth, we would be counting both the physical asset and the claim to that asset, hence greatly overestimating total wealth. The title that Americans hold to overseas investments *are* included as a part of the national wealth since these represent a claim that the U.S. economy holds against physical assets in other nations.

The Relationship Between National Wealth and Gross National Product • We've made a big deal of the ideas of Gross National Product and of national wealth. What is the relationship between the inventory of wealth a nation holds and the level of living enjoyed by the citizenry? Many nations hold enormous resources, but unless those resources are utilized in productivity, living standards remain low. Brazil, for example, has always had an enormous reservoir of resources, but only since World War II has it begun to develop and utilize these resources, increasing productivity. India has more cattle than any nation. But because Brahma cattle are considered to be sacred among the Hindus, these cattle do not raise the Indian standard of living. In all probability, these cattle actually reduce the Indian standard of living because they consume feeds grown on acreages that might otherwise produce food for the satisfaction of human needs.

The presence of wealth provides a *basis* for an elevated level of production. But unless that wealth is *utilized,* output remains low or declines. If population is increasing under such circumstances, living standards may decline substantially. Local attitudes, customs, and institutions can reduce or even eliminate the potential benefits embodied in a large inventory of wealth.

In late 1973, the stock of national wealth in the United States was not greatly different from that stock in late 1974. If anything, the 1973 inventory of wealth was most probably a bit below that of 1974. Yet consider what happened to productivity. Figure 3.3 compares the actual Gross National Product with the level of production that our economy could reasonably have been expected to achieve, based upon the available wealth and labor force. Why did our rate of productivity decline by about ten percent over this twelve-month period? Or even more important, why did our national economy perform at or above full potential during the latter half of the 1960s, and consistently at much less than full capacity during the 1950s and 1970s?

The relationship between national wealth and gross national product involves the decisions made by *people.* Since human decision is by no means a completely predictable variable, the relationship between wealth and production is a *social* rather than a mechanical relationship: Thus, the reason for economics being termed a *social* science.

In our modern interdependent society, we have a tremendous stock of

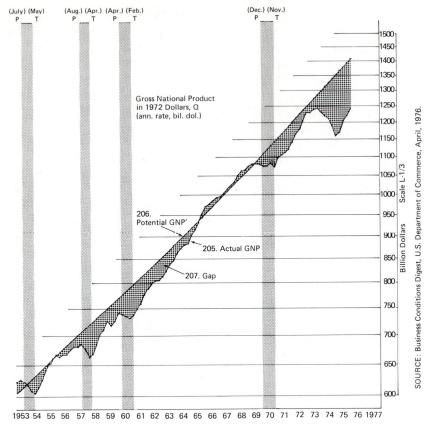

Figure 3.3 U.S. actual and potential Gross National Product, 1953–75, by quarters.

national wealth that creates an equally tremendous potential for production. Yet there are times when we make full use of our wealth and other times when we use it at less than full capacity. These are the periods of "boom" such as we saw during the 1960s, and the periods of "bust" such as we saw in 1974.

Stocks and Flows • Why do we have the ups and downs in our economy? To explain this, we must first understand the difference between *stocks* and *flows*. To illustrate this difference, consider a windmill, a storage tank, and a water tap (Figure 3.4). A *flow* of "production" is created as man combines labor and management with the natural and capital resources at his disposal. That is, a *flow* of water results when the natural force of wind interacts with the capital *stock* of the windmill that has been set in place with labor and other capital. This *flow* of water becomes a *stock* when it is held in the storage tank, and again becomes a *flow* when the tap is opened.

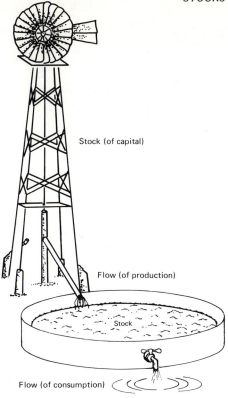

Figure 3.4   Relationship between stocks and flows.

A *flow* of production is created when the *stock* of national wealth interacts with a *flow* of labor that comes from the *stock* of population. When this *flow* of production reaches a finished stage, the flow of production becomes a part of the *stock* of national wealth. The *flow* of consumption is drawn from this stock of national wealth. If the *flow* of consumption exceeds the flow of production, the *stock* of wealth is reduced. If production exceeds consumption, then of course, the reverse is true.

In the case of the United States, the factors of production are privately owned. When we study Gross National Product, we are analyzing the total activity of all people and resources involved in the production process. The services of the factors of production are offered in the market and the users of those factors bid for resources in that same market. The products created by the people who combine these factors for purposes of production (we call these people entrepreneurs) are also offered for sale in the market and are in turn purchased by the general public.

We have suggested that the flow of production turns into a flow of consumption at the point where a finished good is created. The benefit or utility embodied in a product *flows* throughout the period that the product

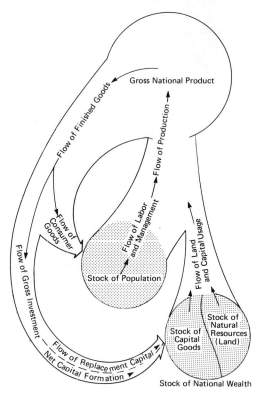

Figure 3.5   Stocks and flows in Gross National Product.

lasts after it reaches its ultimate destination. The length of time that this *flow* of consumer utility lasts depends upon the nature of the particular product. In the case of food, the flow lasts but a few hours or days at most. In the case of products such as refrigerators, however, utility will flow over a period of several years. These items will be recognized as the *consumer durable goods* listed as a part of our inventory of national wealth precisely because of their long life.

Associated with the production and consumption flows is still a third type of flow. A major portion of the final goods and services goes into consumption but there is another portion that goes into a flow of *investment.* Thus, some of the current production is withheld from consumption to be used for further production; that is, some of the current production is used as *capital.*

Capital goods are not simply used up as they give off their flow of *utility.* They are producing other items and are carefully repaired and replaced. These items *flow* into the *stock* of national wealth, where they will be preserved, maintained, and renewed.

The *flow* of GNP which is used to maintain and increase the stock of capital is referred to as *gross investment* (Figure 3.5). The portion of the gross investment flow that goes to replace the capital consumed in the process of production is referred to as *replacement capital*. If the flow of capital consumed during production exceeds the flow of gross investment, then we have a situation of *net disinvestment*. When gross investment exceeds replacement, we can say that *net capital formation* has occurred. When we have net capital formation, there has been an increase in the stock of national wealth.

We have discussed stocks and flows as they apply to Gross National Product. The *stock* of national wealth is made up of a *stock* of natural resources (or land) and a *stock* of capital. The stock of capital is that portion of the stock of national wealth which is the result of human effort—that is, capital is that part of national wealth resulting from man's organization of the factors of production and creation of goods that are to be used for still further production. We likewise have a *stock* of people at any given time, These three stocks are the sources of *flow* of production services that make up the *flow* of production. When production reaches the stage of *finished* goods, the *flow* divides into a *consumption flow* and an *investment flow*. The consumption *flow* returns to the *stock* of population to provide for maintenance and growth, and the investment flow returns to the *stock* of national wealth for purposes of maintaining and/or increasing the capital *stock* portion of national wealth.

The Flows of Production, Consumption, and Income   •   Production in an advanced capitalistic economy does not occur as a result of changeless tradition as it does in some of the pastoral or village economies of the frontier stage. Nor is it the result of forcibly combined labor and material resources as in the centrally-planned communist economies of Eastern Europe and Asia. Rather, production in an advanced capitalistic society results from the infinite numbers of economic decisions that are made in the market places where men buy and sell resources with a minimum of government intervention.

The function of the market place in combining the factors of production under the supervision of a manager (or an entrepreneur) is not mysterious. Any businessman—farmer, grocery store owner, or industrialist—has an intimate knowledge of this process. The crucial factor that enables these people to run their businesses is *demand* for the products or services they produce. If there are no buyers who wish to purchase the seed of ragweeds, farmers are not likely to incur the cost of cultivating ragweeds. In order for *demand* to exist, buyers must have the money necessary to meet the prices at which goods are offered. Demand, then, is made up of two components:

1. The *desire* of consumers for a product, and

2. The *ability to pay* the price for that product.

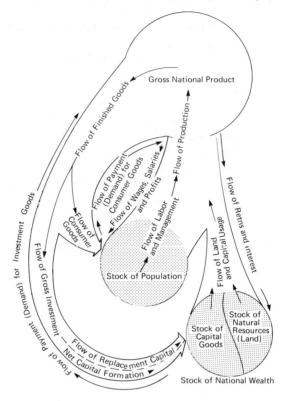

Figure 3.6 Flows of physical goods and payments for those goods in Gross National Product.

Consumers simply by existing create a desire for goods and services. This desire is based upon the *need* for and the *utility derived* from these items. But the *ability to pay* is not so automatic. India, for example, desperately *needs* American wheat. But unless some means can be devised outside the normal market channels to pay the American farmer for producing wheat, the inability of the Indian consumer to pay will prevent the shipment of American wheat to India. As it happens, these "extra-market" channels *have* been created, and American wheat goes to India in the form of foreign aid under Public Law 480, which created the Food for Peace program. The burden of payment has been assumed by the American taxpayer.

How has the American taxpayer acquired the ability to pay? In other words, how does demand come into existence? How has the American taxpayer gotten control of the dollars that represent a claim to that portion of Gross National Product made up by the Indian wheat shipments? Obviously, these dollars are a part of the taxpayer's *income*. But how is this income generated?

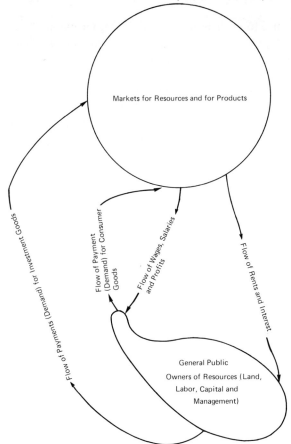

Figure 3.7   Circular flow of funds (payments) in Gross National Product.

Consumers acquire their incomes because in some fashion they have contributed to the process of production. They have provided some of the resources that have gone into producing the items now being sold. Thus in Figure 3.6, showing the flows that connect resources and production, we can add four new flows that move in directions opposite to the directions of the flows of production, consumption, and investment. These are the flows of income to land, labor, capital, and management, and the flows of expenditures for consumption and investment. In other words, any time there is a physical flow of *resources, products,* or *services,* there is a flow of monetary *income* that moves in the opposite direction to pay for these items.

If we look at the income flow alone (Figure 3.7) we see that the flow forms a sort of rough circle with the market place forming one side of the circle and the general public of resource owners the other. Income leaves the market place in the form of *wages and salaries* that provide money income to labor. Income in the form of profits goes to management, and in the form of *rents* and *interest* provides the return to land and capital. These incomes return to the market place in the form of demand for consumer goods, demand for replacement capital, and demand for net capital formation.

In this fashion, we see that output results from *demand,* which results in *payments* to firms and factors of production. Payments to firms resulting from the market demand for their products create the basis for the demand for resources. Payment to these resources (*wages* in the case of labor) provides the basis for the demand for consumer goods, which again results in payment to firms and factors. Thus, income flows in a circular pattern. A given dollar is likely to be split in the market place with a part going to pay various resources that produce any item. The prices of most consumer and capital items will include payments to all four factors of production.

The Circular Flow Model

This chain of payments and incomes contains the key to the operation of our capitalistic economic system. Obviously, it would be humanly impossible to keep track of all the market transactions that actually occur daily. Therefore, we are forced to reduce the problem to manageable dimensions in order to reduce confusion. We do this by pulling from the real world those economic events that history has shown us are of primary concern. From these primary links, we create a *model* of the economy that shows the important characteristics of its real-life counterpart. An *economic model* is in no way intended to *report* the real world but it does describe the chain of events that will help up to *understand* the real world.

Initially, we will ignore certain important factors in our effort to sort out this economic bucket of worms. For example, we will ignore changes in people's *tastes,* and assume that everyone can be depended on to demand the same sorts of products. We will assume that population does not grow—an heroic assumption since it ignores Mother Nature's tendency to sabotage even the best laid of family plans. We will further assume that there is no change in the way of doing things—i.e., there is no new technology and therefore there are no new products. We will ignore net capital formation in order to eliminate growth in the base of resources. In this manner, we can *stabilize* the economy into a *static,* imaginary world. This is much like stopping a movie film in order to examine one frame of the film very carefully without the fiendish confusion of having everything changing at once. Once we understand what we see in a single frame of the film, then we can begin to add frames and understand what happens as each of these changes is introduced.

Let's start with an imaginary gross national product that we shall imagine as having become available all at one point in time. This product comes from the farms, factories and offices where it was produced during the past year. The product is now lurking in the market place, prepared to pounce upon us unwary buyers. What we must now determine is whether enough income was generated in the process of production to provide the basis for us to sell all the finished goods at full costs of production.

Those with farm experience are only too well acquainted with an occasional inability to sell production at prices that will cover full costs. No farm operator is really very concerned about anyone's income except his own. What concerns him is his *cost*. But those costs he incurs represent *income* to someone else. Let's look at a farm cost summary for some mammoth farm operation that covers, say, several counties in an agricultural state (Table 3.2).

TABLE 3.2

HO AND RAIKE FARMS, INC.
Farm Cost Summary

ITEM	AMOUNT
Wages, salary and employee fringe benefits	$ 10,000,000
Rents	50,000,000
Interest	5,000,000
Outside purchases	40,000,000
Taxes (other than income tax)	15,000,000
Depreciation	15,000,000
Profits payments (dividends)	5,000,000
Total	$140,000,000

We can immediately recognize many of these cost items to be payments to factors of production. Wages obviously is the payment to labor, and Rents represents the payment to land. Interest is the payment to capital— that is, the payment to the banker who has lent the farmer money in order to help him carry out his productive operation. The Outside Purchases category represents payments for such items as fertilizer and fuel. Many of these expenditures will eventually find their way into the cost summaries of oil and chemical companies and eventually will be allocated back to original factors in their cost summaries. Taxes represents income to various governmental units and Depreciation is the cost of maintaining and/or replacing capital equipment.

The inclusion of Profits as a cost may seem a bit peculiar. However, there must be some payment to investors if they are to risk their resources in this business rather than burying them in a coffee can. This payment represents a special kind of payment to "entrepreneurial managers" for their assumption of risk. We'll discuss profits in some detail in later chapters, but for the moment let's consider them as a part of the cost of doing business.

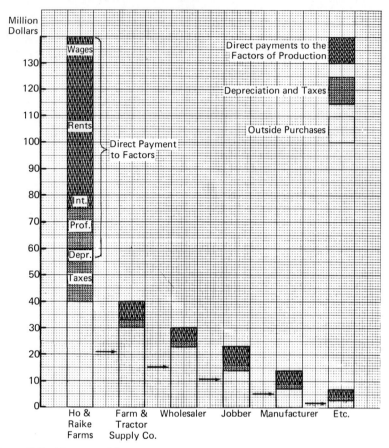

Figure 3.8 How outside purchases made by one firm appear as factor payments, taxes, and depreciation for other firms.

Now let's look at our cost summary. The payment to outside purchases will appear in the cost summary for some other firm and will be allocated to the factors of production from that point. What actually happens is illustrated in Figure 3.8. Suppose that Ho and Raike Farms make all outside purchases at the local Farm and Tractor Supply Company. In F & TS Co.'s cost summary, there will be some direct payment to factors and some cost for outside purchases from the wholesaler. The wholesaler makes some direct payment to the factors of production and buys some items from the jobber. The process is repeated until all payments for materials and supplies have been allocated either directly to the factors of production, to government in the form of indirect business taxes, or to depreciation. Taxes will be allocated to the original factors in the form of government expenditures. Depreciation represents the cost of maintaining and replacing capital equipment and thus does not represent new production.

The illustration of our cost summary in Figure 3.8 shows several important relationships. The "other costs" of depreciation and indirect taxes cover the costs of maintaining the productive plant and the indirect costs of doing business. The costs for outside purchases represent the payment made to some other firm for the firm's contribution to Ho and Raike Farms' productivity. The payments made to the original factors of production are shown by the Wages, Rents, Interest, and Profits categories in our cost summary. The value of these items represents the net contribution made by Ho and Raike Farms to the total value of the products produced in the operation. Thus, *the total of the payments made directly to the factors of production represents the total value that Ho and Raike Farms has added to Gross National Product.*

When we begin to aggregate the annual cost summaries for Ho and Raike Farms and for all the other firms in the economy, we derive an estimate of the total contribution made to the Gross National Product "pie" by *all* the productive efforts during the year (Figure 3.9). When we set aside funds to pay the depreciation on capital equipment, the amount left over represents *net national product,* (that is, total product or GNP less the capital used up in the productive effort). This leaves a smaller pie. When we set aside still more funds to cover the costs of indirect taxes, the resulting estimate is one of *national income*–a pie that is smaller yet. *National income is the sum of all payments made directly to the original factors of production.*

National income, then, is exactly what the name implies; the total amount of earnings paid to all the factors of production in the nation. If we consider the factors to be capitalistically owned by individual households, then we can see that factor payments result directly in household incomes. Thus, if factor costs were the only costs involved in production, the problems of selling GNP at full cost of production would be very simple. But since payments to the original factors were only a part of the cost summary, it is apparent that household incomes alone cannot possibly buy all of GNP. We

Figure 3.9   Relationship between Gross National Product, net national product, and national income.

still have government activity and depreciation to consider, and until these items are accounted for, there is a shortage in our Gross National Product that is shown by the two outer circles in Figure 3.9.

We've already shown how much of the cost of outside purchases made by Ho and Raike Farms would appear as payments to original factors in some other firm's cost summary. As we looked down the chain of payments made for materials and supplies, we saw how at each succeeding step these payments are distributed among payments to the original factors, to outside purchases, and to the other costs of depreciation and taxes.

These "other costs" of taxes and depreciation that are paid by the farm supply and intermediate firms with whom Ho and Raike does business are carried along in the guise of costs of materials used by Ho and Raike Farms. The sum of these costs for *all* firms in the economy will make up the difference between national income and GNP. The tax portion of this obviously goes to governmental activity. Taxes go to pay for goods and services that are provided by government—items such as roads, schools and national defense. The government expenditures for these items will eventually be used to pay for the original factors of production that are used in the *government sector* of our economy. Thus, a part of the difference between national income and GNP is accounted for. Government spending will pay for much of the GNP that will not be covered by national income and will create a demand for goods and services in the market place.

Depreciation is the only portion of GNP for which we still have to account. Why isn't depreciation a part of someone's income? Let's go back to our definition of the stock of national capital. National capital represents the sum total of all the production that has ever occurred in the nation and has not yet been consumed. The income for producing this capital has been paid to the original factors of production in some previous period. While a firm does not have to submit payment to anyone for depreciation, some allowance must be made for maintaining and replacing buildings and equipment, and this allowance included in the price of products sold. If this allowance were not made, not all the resources used in the process of production would be accounted for, and profits would be overstated. Further, if depreciation is *not* covered, the firm will reduce the productive resources and ultimately be forced out of business.

The essential need for covering depreciation can be illustrated in the case of a beef cow herd. About a third of the heifer calves are typically retained each year to be grown into replacements for the mother cows that depreciate. A rancher who reserves no replacement heifers—that is, if he makes no allowance for depreciation of cows—is going to find himself with a much less productive breeding herd in four to six years. Some cows will fail to breed because of advancing age, and others will die from various causes, including old age. Within ten years, if he does not provide for cow depreciation, he will probably be out of business entirely. By selling the heifers that should have been saved to cover depreciation, he has consumed the substance that provided the original base for his productivity.

The Stationary Circular Flow Model for the National Economy • Our analysis of GNP is just about complete. We have traced the elements of cost into the corresponding income payments. In this fashion, we have determined that there is enough income paid out to allow the entire Gross National Product to be sold at prices that cover full costs of production. We have shown how three different streams of expenditure flow from households, businesses, and government. Each of these streams of *expenditure* represents a stream of *income* to some other sector. For example, household expenditures for consumption items represent income to business and government.

Figure 3.10 should give us some indication of how the complete circuit is made in the national economy. The cost of producing the Gross National Product pie is divided into payments to each of the three sectors:

1. Households are paid for the use of factors of production,

2. Governments are paid taxes, and

3. Business receives payment for depreciation on capital equipment.

Each of these *incomes* is then paid out in the pie of *expenditures* used to satisfy *demand*.

1. Households pay for consumer goods and service,

2. Governments pay for government goods and service, and

3. Businesses pay for replacing capital equipment.

Each of these payments represents *receipts* to factors, taxes, and depreciation and when these receipts are collected, we find ourselves again with the pie showing the costs of producing Gross National Product.

This analysis again brings us to the relationship between GNP, *net national product,* and national income as illustrated in Figure 3.9. Gross National Product can be defined as either the total *costs* that are incurred in the process of producing the Gross National Product, or as the total *expenditures* made in purchasing this same Gross National Product. Since *depreciation* represents the production of some previous period, it is deducted from Gross National Product, leaving an estimate of *net national product.* Indirect taxes (real estate taxes, cigarette taxes, sales taxes, and the like, that must be paid for the privilege of merely doing business) represent an expense that is paid over and above factor costs. When these are removed, we have an estimate of *national income.*

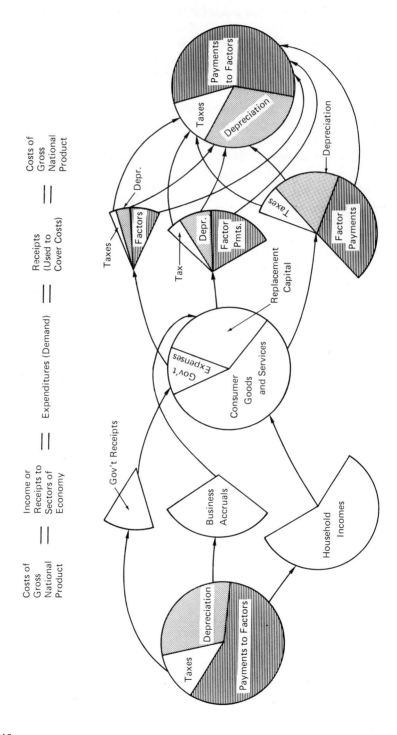

Costs of Gross National Product = Income or Receipts to Sectors of Economy = Expenditures (Demand) = Receipts (Used to Cover Costs) = Costs of Gross National Product

Figure 3.10 Flow of costs and receipts in Gross National Product.

What we have constructed in Figure 3.10 is a model of the national economy showing the circular nature of the flow of payments and receipts. This model economy regularly and dependably buys back everything it produces. There is no question that this model is unrealistic. However, it does provide a very useful standard for comparison and a framework within which we can examine other questions. The model economy we have constructed is said to be in *stationary equilibrium*. The changeless flow of costs into receipts and receipts back into costs is called a circular flow. A circular flow economy in stationary equilibrium cannot experience recession or boom since everything that is produced is consumed. This static situation will be the norm that we can use as a basis for comparison as our analysis progresses.

The Impact of Savings and Investment   •   So far in our analysis of our national economy, we have examined the relationships between wealth and output, and between output and incomes in the strictly *static* sense. We have constructed a "bench-mark," circular flow, model of the nation's economy in *stationary equilibrium*. Now, let's relax some of the static assumptions and consider the more realistic question of the impact of savings and the investment upon our static model.

Let's briefly review our study of the economic flows. You will recall that the flow of national production resulted from an interaction between national wealth and labor under the guidance of the managerial resource. The payments made to these original factors provided the purchasing power that created an effective *demand* for the finished goods which flowed into one of three channels: consumption, government, or investment. In our circular flow model, each round of expenditures found its way into a stream of purchasing power just large enough to cover the cost of again producing exactly that given scale of output. We recognize that the static circular flow model is highly artificial, since economies rarely continue simply to reproduce themselves. More often they either grow or decline. The key to economic growth or decline may be found in the investment sector.

In the circular flow model, the flow of investment was assumed to be exactly equal to depreciation. This assumption omits the most dynamic factor in economics—the continuing creation of new capital and the resulting enlargement of the resource basis for production. It is through the formation of new capital that society has progressed beyond the cave-man era. That is, if man had *always* consumed everything he produced, the only means of securing food today would be through hunting, fishing and reaping of wild crops. Man would thus still be a parasite of nature.

How does a nation increase its stock of national capital, and what is the impact of this capital accumulation upon the static model we have created? We have already defined capital to be the sum total of all production that has not been consumed. Anything we have failed to consume has been *saved*. In terms of the buying and selling, paying and receiving discussed in our construction of the circular flow model, *savings* is simply *refraining from consuming all or part of current income (or production)*.

In our discussion of the circular flow, it was apparent that the three flows of expenditures were critical links in the operation of the economy. If saving is *non-consumption*, and hence *non-spending*, then it would appear that savings could cause us to be unable to buy back all of our national production and would thus force us into the downward spiral of recession and eventual depression.

But simply non-consuming is not the total story of savings. We know that investment (i.e., spending money to direct factors into the creation of capital goods) pre-requires an act of saving in some previous period. The funds used for investment *cannot* be used for consumption. Hence, savings is prerequisite to the process of investment and growth.

Let's reexamine our diagram of the circular flow model and see what savings does to that model. In Figure 3.11, a portion of the payment to the original factors—household income in our model—has been set aside rather than being spent on consumer goods. The result is entirely predictable. The cost of GNP is still equal to the income of the sectors, but these are no longer equal to the total expenditures for goods and services (i.e., the aggregate demand). Consumer demand is *not* equal to factor costs, and hence households are not going to buy back as many consumer goods as their incomes suggest they should. A piece of the aggregate demand pie is missing. The producers of consumer goods will be unable to sell all of their product at full cost as a result. Thus, it begins to look like we are finding the reason for the hard times that we have experienced from time to time.

The gap in demand introduced by a deficiency in consumer spending might very well be the cause for unemployment. You may either believe or refuse to believe this: In either case you would be partially correct. The first answer to any question in economics is "that depends." Whether or not savings causes economic recession and unemployment depends on whether the household "ratholes" the funds that are being saved or whether these funds are *being put to work* in some other sector. In other words, we have introduced savings, but we have ignored the fact that the coin of savings has another side—*investment*.

We can draw two conclusions from our analysis thus far. First, the act of saving creates a deficiency in aggregate demand. Unless we can devise some means for closing this gap, the economic system will begin to deteriorate because employers will not be able to cover all costs. Second, since a gap in demand results from saving, a nation is forced to choose between a static (or stagnant) economy and a growth economy. If our society chooses to have a dynamic, expanding economy, we must be prepared to face the problems that are created by saving, since saving is prerequisite to the investment in the

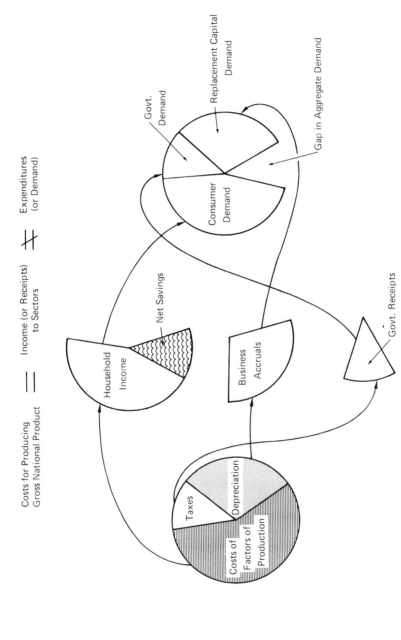

Costs for Producing
Gross National Product

Income (or Receipts)
to Sectors

Expenditures
(or Demand)

Figure 3.11 Impact of household savings upon aggregate demand.

49

capital goods essential for generating economic growth. If we wish to avoid these problems, we can close the gap by urging consumers not to save. This can be done by manipulating interest rates, and by legislatively providing for all the financial contingencies of modern living.

If we wish to avoid the problems of saving completely, we must be prepared to accept an absence of economic growth. Obviously, this is not an either-or choice. We can choose "pieces" of growth by the number and magnitude of "stagnating" forces that we introduce into the economy. In many instances we may be able to maintain growth by countering a "stagnating" move such as increased social security benefits with some offsetting growth-stimulating move such as a corporate investment tax credit.

How do we close a gap in demand? If the gap is the result of household savings, the gap must be closed by increasing the expenditures (or demand) in either the government or the business sector. In this fashion we can offset savings in one sector by increasing activity in the other. This may be done in several ways. Among these are:

1. Household savings can be borrowed through the sale of corporate bonds. The borrowed funds can then be used for business investment, thus increasing business activity. This gives the households that buy these corporate bonds a claim on the future receipts of the borrowing corporation.

2. Household savings can be borrowed through the sale of government bonds. The funds may then be reinjected into the income stream through increased government expenditures. Again, this gives the household lenders a *claim* on future government *receipts.*

3. Business can float new stock issues, thus incorporating the savings of the public into the ownership of the business sector (i.e., the households would then enjoy a claim on the assets of the business sector). The funds derived from these stock issues can then be used to expand business activity.

4. Business and/or government can both borrow from financial institutions such as commercial banks, using the funds to increase demand in the government and/or business sectors. This gives the financial institutions a *claim* on the future receipts of the borrower. Since the financial institutions acquire their loanable funds from the public at large, the households would have an indirect claim against the future receipts of the borrowers by way of the financial institutions.

In our discussion of national wealth, we pointed out that while bank accounts and stock ownership said much about our personal wealth, they merely represented *claims* to national wealth. The four methods we have outlined for closing the demand gap (that gap that results from savings) are all concerned with *claims* on wealth. These *claims* show that funds have been obtained by either business or government from some other sector of the economy, that those sectors have a *claim* on a part of the wealth or assets of the government and/or business sectors.

Figure 3.12 shows how savings in the household sector can be siphoned into the business sector through the sale of corporate bonds or through new stock issues. These stocks and bonds give households a claim on the future receipts or the physical assets of the businesses selling the stocks and bonds, and the proceeds of the sales provide funds for increasing the demand of the business sector for new capital formation. In this fashion, the gap in aggregate demand resulting from household savings may be closed through an expansion in investment demand.

The beauty of the full circuit in savings translated into business investment funds and ultimately into new capital formation is illustrated in the cost for producing GNP in the subsequent period. The new capital, which has enlarged the national wealth and hence the resource base, has enabled us to have a larger pie! This illustrates that savings and investment are the very foundation of economic growth.

A result similar to that of the transfer of savings from the household to the business sector would be observed had the transfer been from households to government. Rather than through an expansion in business activity, the gap in aggregate demand would have been closed through enlarged government activity. Whether the growth in GNP would have been similar would depend on which government activities were enlarged. If the increase had come in the payment of unemployment benefits or other welfare, the immediate impact would be an increase in demand for consumer goods. But the ultimate impact on economic growth would most likely be less than if the increase had been on items such as developing new sources of energy or increased research effort in agricultural production.

These approaches to dealing with household savings will work in this fashion as long as savers attempt to realize a return on savings. But as was pointed out in our discussion of national wealth, the relationship between wealth and productivity is a social rather than mechanical one. Customs, attitudes, and expectations can all affect the relationship. Suppose households expect a widespread layoff of workers or lose confidence in the stability of the banking system. There would be a tendency for them to delay consumption in preparation for that rainy day, and to simply "rathole" their cash. Any time large numbers of savers begin to "bury" funds rather than reinvest them, the gap in aggregate demand that results from savings will not be completely closed. Rather than enlarging the GNP pie, savings under these circumstances will cause it to shrink. (A real-world example of this situation

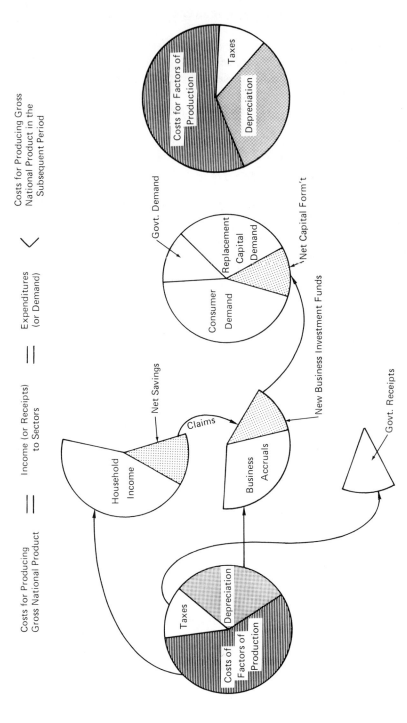

Costs for Producing = Income (or Receipts) = Expenditures = Costs for Producing Gross
Gross National Product   to Sectors   (or Demand)   National Product in the
                                                                   Subsequent Period

Figure 3.12 Impact of transferring household savings into investment and the subsequent increase in Gross National Product.

is found in India. When savings are generated, the Indian traditionally stores this savings in the form of gold jewelry. Thus, savings have not come back into the income stream and have enlarged the gap in demand that was created by the act of saving.) The total GNP cannot be sold at prices that will cover full costs of production, product inventories will begin to accumulate, and the downward spiral of recession and the increasing unemployment will begin.

Saving is crucial in the growth of an economy, but the schizoid nature of savings cannot be overemphasized. On the one hand, the decision to delay consumption in order to release resources to be directed into capital creation is the type of genuine saving that provides for economic growth. On the other hand, financial saving—the type of saving that we individually practice—really provides for nothing other than our individual goals unless those savings get into the hands of investors.

The difference in *genuine* savings and *financial* savings is perfectly illustrated by the difference in a savings account and a piggy bank. The funds in a savings account are loaned to various people for many purposes. In this fashion, savings re-enter the income stream and fill the demand gap. Piggy bank savings are for all intents and purposes buried. These savings add to the demand gap and (if they are large) can create problems in the economic system.

When we save, we are aware that we are not spending entire income for current consumption. However we seldom think of savings in terms of directing factors of production into the creation of capital resources for purposes of alternative employment. Savers and investors are typically two different groups of people. Because the savings and investment decisions are made by different individuals or groups, savings may not always be immediately converted into investment. Savers may begin to prepare for a rainy day by increasing savings at a time when investors share their pessimism and are in no mood to borrow money for purposes of investing in capital assets. On the other hand, business firms may frequently wish to invest at a time when savers are primarily interested in spending income in the purchase of such consumer goods as automobiles, and are therefore disinterested in savings. The separation of the savings-investment decision frequently gives rise to situations in which savings exceed investment (i.e., the gap in aggregate demand is enlarged) or in which investment plans exceed the householders' propensity to save (whereupon the total demand will exceed GNP and, rather than a deflationary demand gap, we have an inflationary excess of demand).

American Agriculture and Gross National Product • What does all of this discussion of national income, gross national product, and economic development have to do with agriculture? If Gross National Product is measured in terms of consumption, investment, government expenditures, and net exports, what difference could this possibly make to agriculture?

TABLE 3.3

ALLOCATION OF 1975 GROSS NATIONAL PRODUCT
TO AGRICULTURAL AND NON-AGRICULTURAL
SOURCES,
U.S., in Billions of Dollars

COMPONENT OF GNP	TOTAL	NON-AGRICULTURAL SOURCES	AGRICULTURAL SOURCES
Consumption	964	670	220 - Food
			74 - Clothing & shoes
Investment	197	?	?
Government	326	?	3[+]
Net exports	2	−10	+12
Total	1,489[1]	Less Than 1,180	390[+]

[1] Lack of agreement between GNP as expressed in table versus text due to rounding of figures.

Gross National Product in 1975 was $1,499 billion. Of this, gross farm income accounted for $99 billion, or only 6.6 percent. But when GNP for 1975 is broken down into its component flows of expenditures, it appears as in Table 3.3. Of the $964 billion in the consumption expenditures flow, 23 percent went for farm-produced food, and an additional 8 percent for the largely agricultural products of clothing and shoes. A full 30 percent of the crucial consumption expenditures flow, then, is made up of products that originate on farms and ranches.

The published statistics do not permit an estimate of the portion of investment expenditures that occurs on farms and ranches, nor of the portion that was made by agricultural processing firms and agricultural supply units. But these investment expenditures are substantial. A relatively minor portion of total government expenditure goes for agricultural purposes (less than 3 percent of federal outlays for goods and services, amounting to about $3 billion). Perhaps another $1 billion in state government expenditures was similarly allocated.

The Net Exports category shows the crucial importance of agriculture in maintaining a healthy economic relationship between the United States and other world economies. In the absence of trade in agricultural products, the United States would have experienced a $10 billion trade deficit in 1975. This would have had some grave consequences for the value of the American dollar in international markets and for the rate of inflation in consumer prices at home.

It is apparent that agriculture provides an enormous share of Gross

National Product. At least a fifth and more probably a fourth of America's GNP rests on the foundation of our tremendously productive agricultural sector. In 1966, $204 billion in production assets were used on farms and ranches. By 1976, this had increased to $492 billion. Since agriculture is such a large part of our national production, anything that affects the general level of American productivity will soon be felt in the agricultural sector.

The overall state of the general economy will determine the environment within which agriculture must live and operate. If 7 or 8 percent of the population is unemployed, it is highly unlikely that those people will be eating beef steak. If 7 or 8 percent of the demand for beef steak disappears, the impact will soon show up in the form of declining cattle prices.

It should be pointed out that not only is agriculture affected by the overall economic environment, but agriculture in turn helps determine that economic environment. If a major sector of agriculture is in economic difficulty, then agriculture's ability to buy the output of other economic sectors is hampered. Thus, agriculture and the rest of the American economy are married for better or for worse. Unfortunately, in this marriage of interests, American agriculture has only too frequently been the bride.

The study of an entire economy is known as *macroeconomics.* The national income analysis we have been discussing is only a part of the macroeconomics area. These same types of analyses can be applied to a state, a county, a city, a rural community, or to an entire economic sector such as agriculture or energy.

The study of an individual economic unit is known as *microeconomics.* Macroeconomic decisions fostered through public policy can frequently create some microeconomic problems to which individual firms must adjust. Most of the remainder of our study will be directed toward the microeconomics area. Chapter 5 briefly discusses some of the macroeconomic decisions that have generated needs for microeconomic adjustments.

Selected References

Boulding, Kenneth E., *Economic Analysis,* 3rd ed., Chapters 13 and 14. New York: Hayes and Brothers, 1955.

Heilbroner, Robert L., *Understanding Macroeconomics,* Chapters 2, 3, 4. Englewood Cliffs, N.J.: Prentice-Hall, 1965.

Leftwich, Richard H., *An Introduction to Economic Thinking,* Chapter 20. New York: Holt, Rinehart, and Winston, 1969.

4

Money and Agricultural Finance

Many forces have been credited for the revolutions of the earth. Physicists have long contended that gravity is responsible. Poets and song-writers say that love makes the world go 'round. Certain other libidinous individuals take the position that the motivating force is sex. From the economist's point of view, these are all convenient lies. Love and/or sex merely make man dizzy. Rather than causing the earth to turn, these factors throw man into a tailspin: hence, the reason for his loss of equilibrium. Gravity is simply the concept by which Sir Isaac Newton achieved immortality.

The economist thinks of the world in different terms. The force that allows our highly interdependent economic world of specialized economic units to operate smoothly—and the grease that lubricates the mechanism—is neither gravity nor love nor sex. It is money. During our discussion of national income, it was pointed out that there was a *flow* of production that resulted from the interaction between the *stocks* of wealth and labor. When the flow of production reached the final stage, it turned into a flow of *consumption,* whereby products were returned to the working force, to government, or to business firms for purposes of regenerating and increasing the original factors of production.

Throughout our discussion of the flows of production and consumption, we suggested that there was another, a flow of payments, that moved in a direction opposite to the movement of physical goods. As production occurred, the owners of the factors of production received payment for the use of their property. As consumption occurred, consumers traded income for the necessities and luxuries of life.

I am indebted to G. P. Collins, Professor Emeritus of Agricultural Economics at Oklahoma State University, for the materials relating to farm finance.

The lowest common denominator of the entire economic process, then—indeed the lowest common denominator of all human activity—is the dollar sign. Everything we have and everything we do is associated with a price. If the price is too high, we refrain from that particular purchase or that particular activity. In effect, we are saying that our dollars are worth more to us than the item or activity under consideration.

We have discussed the importance of savings and investment in the process of maintaining and expanding our economic system. Further, we have suggested that the people who save and the people who invest are often different groups of people. How, then, is savings turned into investment? The only way this can occur is for those who have engaged in *financial* saving to loan their *money* to investors to be used for the purpose of directing factors of production into the *genuine saving* of creating new or replacement capital items.

Our economy can operate because of *money*. Money commands the capital that is basic to growth. We have been very careful to point out that money is *not* wealth, even though it commands wealth. If money is so important in our existence, and if money is not wealth, then what *is* money and what are its functions?

Many items have been used as money throughout history, and some of these are still in use today. For example, some of the nomadic natives in Africa still use cattle as money. The Forty-Niners of the gold rush days used gold dust. The American Indians used beadwork (wampum) and tobacco. Tobacco was again used as money in Europe during and immediately following World War II. The price of the items that American occupation troops wanted to buy was often measured in cigarettes (and they occasionally got fringe benefits that they would have paid dearly to avoid!). The Chinese at one time used stone wheels; as a result they needed a wheelbarrow rather than a pocketbook. Many metals have been used in various societies. Regardless of the items used as money, all commonly serve several functions.

Money as a Medium of Exchange • In societies without money, the exchange of goods must be accomplished through barter. An economy such as ours, based on specialization and the division of labor, is impossible under a system of barter. Only the most primitive forms of production and exchange can exist without money. For example, under a barter system one good is traded directly for another. Imagine the multitude of transactions that go into the manufacture and sale of farm machinery being accomplished through barter. Or worse yet, imagine trying to give change under these circumstances. If you are trading cattle for the tractor and if the value of the tractor is not some exact number of cattle, how does one trade a piece of a cow? Or, does one accept a calf in change? The use of money as a medium of exchange removes problems of this nature. We trade our cattle for dollars and cents and then pay the dollars and cents price for the tractor, pocketing the amount left over from our cattle sale.

Money has probably done more for the freedom and welfare of mankind than all of the wars, churches, and legislation put together. Without money, men—all men—would be enslaved by possessions. Specialization and division of labor would be impossible. The economic efficiency that resulted from specialization could never have occurred. Without money, our modern interdependent industrial society could not exist. The best we could hope for in the absence of money would be a barter system.

A barter system forces people to become largely self-sufficient; self-sufficient in much the same way that each farm unit was self-sufficient in the colonial American society of the 1600s. Bartering would require so much time and effort that it would be more efficient simply to produce almost all of our own needs. With the presence of money as a medium of exchange, each man can specialize his efforts in the area where he performs best, sell his product, and then purchase his needs.

Characteristics of a Satisfactory Medium of Exchange • In order for money to serve as a medium of exchange, it must have several qualities.

1. It must be generally acceptable,

2. It must have a high value relative to its bulk and weight,

3. It must be easily divisible into small parts, and

4. It must *not* be easy to counterfeit.

The absence of any of these qualities would prevent any type of certificate or coin from functioning effectively as a medium of exchange. If it were not generally acceptable, no exchange could take place. Consider, for example, a trip that you may have made into Mexico or Canada. American dollars are generally acceptable in both of these nations and can be exchanged for goods with little difficulty. But any change received is typically in the local currency. If you should happen to bring back a pocket full of Mexican pesos, how satisfactory are they as a medium of exchange at the corner drug store? Most of us have seen foreign coins and currency, but few of us are willing to accept them in exchange for goods and services. Even most coin-operated vending machines are programmed to reject all coins other than those issued by the U.S. mint. Thus any foreign currency you hold is an interesting curiosity, but because of lack of general acceptability, it is considerably less than satisfactory as a medium of exchange.

If money did not have high value relative to its bulk and weight, carrying money for purposes of buying one's needs would be more trouble than it was worth. The ancient Chinese use of stone wheels discouraged exchange. The ancient Spartans' use of iron was intended to focus the public attention on the importance of defense rather than the accumulation of monetary wealth. During times of war, Spartan money was converted to armaments.

The need for divisibility of the monetary unit has already been mentioned. If money were not readily divisible, the only transactions that could be consummated would be those that were in exact multiples of the monetary unit. For example, if our smallest monetary unit were a thousand dollar bill, we would be forced to use barter for purchases of less than $1,000 and for those between $1,000 and $2,000. Conversely, if the economy is afflicted by *inflation*—that is, if the montary unit buys less than it bought in some previous period—some monetary units may go out of existence and other new units be created. For example, the lowest valued coin in the Mexican monetary system is the five-centavo piece. There is no one-centavo piece. (This is not surprising since the value of one centavo in the mid-1970s would be one-twelfth of a cent.) In our own system, the re-introduction of the two-dollar bill in the mid-1970s was the result of inflation's drastically reducing the numbers of items that could be purchased for a dollar or less.

If money were easy to counterfeit, no money would be generally acceptable. We have all seen swashbuckling movies of the pirate era. In most of them, there was a vivacious and volatile barmaid—usually a shapely redhead—who served drinks to all of the swashbucklers. When paid with a gold doubloon, her first response was to bite the coin in order to determine if it were in fact gold. If her evaluation were positive, that coin was stashed in her sock or some other convenient article of apparel. If her evaluation were negative, she read in sweet and dulcet tones the pedigree of the offending swashbuckler—or perhaps returned the coin to him in change when he bought the next round of drinks.

Money as a Store of Wealth • A second function that money performs is to serve as a *store of wealth.* With barter, you trade one good for another *at this moment.* With money, you can sell goods today and retain the money until you need some other good. Thus, you have a *claim* to physical goods or wealth when you have money. Money itself is not wealth, as we saw in our analysis of national wealth. Money merely commands wealth by giving us a claim on the available goods and services that are in fact wealth in our society. Money itself is valueless except in terms of what it will buy. A tubful of $100 bills themselves wouldn't even be satisfactory fuel in the winter, even though they could probably lay claim to more than enough fuel to heat a good-sized city. Without monetary status, dollar bills would probably be worth a bit less than an equivalent amount of toilet tissue.

For money to serve as a satisfactory store of wealth, it must be fairly constant in value. That is, a dollar must buy about the same goods today as it bought yesterday and it must buy about the same thing next week as it buys today. In other words, there must be an absence of *inflation;* or at least the *rate* of inflation must be fairly constant and predictable. The problem of inflation will be examined in some detail in Chapter 5. But those who must live on fixed dollar incomes and from savings are hurt badly by inflation.

Money as a Basis for Keeping Records • A third function of money is to provide a basis for accounting. When you write a check, no coin or currency changes hands. Your check is simply an instruction to the banking system to transfer so much money from your bank account to the account of some other individual. The entire transaction has occurred in the records of the banking system and has not involved actual coins or currency in any way. Still your ordinary business has been conducted by way of the monetary unit of account.

In recent years, the monetary unit of account has become of rapidly increasing importance in the American economy. The accelerated adoption and easy issuance of credit cards by untold numbers of business firms during the 1950s was the beginning of a "credit explosion." The emergence of the general bank credit card, such as BankAmericard and Master Charge, further enlarged this activity. The introduction of computers into banking has given rise to numerous programs in which many checks are no longer issued. For example, a business firm will program its payroll onto the firm's computer. The business firm's computer will then communicate with the computers of the various banks to transfer the funds from the firm into the personal accounts of the firm's employees. In this fashion, the firm will meet its payroll with no checks having been issued. Presumably, the frequency of lost checks and other errors will in this fashion be reduced.

What is Money? • We have defined the characteristics of money. What items in our system will qualify as *being* money (Table 4.1)? Obviously, coins and currency are money, since they meet all the qualifications. While checks are not quite as widely acceptable as cash (try cashing a check in a college town at the end of a semester), they are generally acceptable within very broad limits. Thus, the funds that are recorded on the books of banks as being in one's checking account may reasonably be defined as money. In 1975 the total supply of money amounted to $295 billion. Production assets used on U.S. farms amounted to $492 billion in 1975. Thus, farming alone had a value equal to more than the total supply of money available for the entire United States in 1975. How could this be? Does this mean that all of the other businesses in America operated without any money? Gross National Product amounted to almost $1.5 trillion in 1975—more than five times the amount of money we actually had available. How can this be?

Time deposits (or savings accounts), savings and loan shares, deposits in

TABLE 4.1

WHAT IS THE SUPPLY OF MONEY?

	APPROXIMATE AMOUNT U.S., JAN. 1976, SEASONALLY ADJUSTED (MILLIONS OF DOLLARS)
Money	
Coins and currency in circulation	$ 74,200
Private checking accounts	220,800
Total	$295,000
Selected near-monies	
Time deposits (savings accounts and certificates of deposit)	$430,100
Savings and loan shares, deposits in mutual savings banks, and shares in savings and loans and credit unions	433,500
Total	$863,600

Source: *Federal Reserve Statistical Release H.6,* Board of Governors, Federal Reserve System, Washington, D.C., May 27, 1976.

mutual savings banks, U.S. government securities, and the like are not immediately accessible, and technically are not money. These assets are not easily divided into small parts, nor are they necessarily readily acceptable. In practice, however, they may be converted to money on very short notice and are clearly very close to being money. But these totaled less than $900 billion in 1975–76, and if we add the money and the near monies, we still do not have enough to buy back our Gross National Product. How then do we come by the funds to do business day in and day out if we have more goods for sale than we have money to buy them?

In our discussion of money, we have ignored one very important factor: the *velocity* of money. We suggested earlier that money was the lubricant that greased the wheels of the economy. The fact that money does not necessarily stop moving when a single transaction is consummated is the reason that $295 billion in actual money could be used to cover more than five times that amount in transactions. For example, four different people may be selling meat, flour, housing, and clothing. The college professor spends a dollar at the meat market. The butcher spends this same dollar for flour. The miller uses this dollar to pay his rent, and the landlord uses it to buy a new shirt. The haberdasher's son needs an education and pays the college professor for his services. Thus, five dollars worth of business has been done with one dollar in cash. The professor has his steak and his dollar to spend again.

Everyone else has a dollar's worth of something he needs. This clearly illustrates the importance of college professors to the performance of an economy.

We have seen how money commands wealth, and how capital is wealth. We have also seen how savings is basic to investment, and how investment in capital is the heart of economic growth. Money is the vehicle by which we turn savings into investment. Thus, the supply of money available for lending will determine to a large degree how much investment and growth can occur at any given time.

Any discussion of the *supply* of money must necessarily involve a discussion of the banking system and credit. Since demand deposits (i.e., checking accounts) are a part of the money supply, the sizes of the private checking accounts in commercial banks must play a central role in the money supply. Further, most banking systems *create* money by means of lending against cash reserves. Thus, the credit of individuals and banks becomes a part of the basis for creating additional money.

How Banks Create Money • What do we mean when we say the banks *create* money? Counterfeiting is a penitentiary offense, but contrary to what we might wish to believe, very few bankers are in danger of a prison term. When banks "create" money, the "unit of account" characteristic of money is used.

Most economies have legal restrictions on the portion of a bank's deposits that must be backed by coins and currency. These restrictions are known as legal reserves. If the legal reserve level is set at 20 percent, then every dollar that is on the books in checking accounts must be "backed" by twenty cents in cash. Thus, if $100 in new reserves is deposited in commercial banks, then the banking system can "create" an additional $400 in deposit money on the basis of the $100 cash deposit. This $400 is created within the accounts of the banking system.

Let's suppose that a Mr. Schroeder emigrates from Germany with enough German marks to convert to $100 in U.S. dollars. He converts these funds before he leaves Germany and later deposits them with American banker Jones. Banker Jones will hold $20 for legal reserves and invest or loan the remaining $80. This $80 is placed in the borrower's account against which checks are written to be deposited in some other bank. The second bank now has $80 in new reserves, $16 of which will be held for legal reserves and $64 of which will be loaned or invested by the second bank. This process is repeated until a total of $400 in new money has been created by the banking system (Table 4.2). Mr. Schroeder still has a claim for $100 against which he can write checks, but the original $100 deposit in new reserves has actually enabled the banking system to increase the money supply by four times the amount of the deposit.

TABLE 4.2

HOW BANKS CREATE MONEY

TRANSACTIONS	DEPOSITED IN CHECKING ACCOUNTS	LOANED (NEW MONEY CREATED)	SET ASIDE AS RESERVES
Bank 1	$100.00	$80.00	$20.00
2	80.00	64.00	16.00
3	64.00	51.20	12.80
4	51.20	40.96	10.24
5	40.96	32.77	8.19
6	32.77	26.22	6.55
7	26.22	20.98	5.24
8	20.98	16.78	4.20
9	16.78	13.42	3.36
10	13.42	10.74	2.68
Total for 10 banks	$446.33	$357.07	$89.26
Additional banks	53.67	42.93[1]	10.74[1]
Grand total, all banks	$500.00[2]	$400.00[2]	$100.00[2]

Source: *The Federal Reserve System: Purposes and Functions,* Board of Governors of the Federal Reserve System, Washington, D.C., 1963, p. 73.
Note: Table assumes an average member reserve requirement of 20% of demand deposits.
[1] Adjusted to offset rounding in preceding figures.
[2] The total amount of *new* money that can be created can be calculated quickly and easily using the following formula

$$\text{New Money} = \frac{\text{excess reserves}}{\text{reserve requirement}}$$

Thus, in the example above, the $100 in new deposits creates an excess reserve of $80. The new money potential would be $80 ÷ .20 = $400.

Our discussion of money and its creation has admittedly been very, very basic and very, very sketchy. But the primary thing to remember is that money commands wealth and capital. Hence, since new capital formation is the key to economic growth, the monetary and banking system holds that key. The ability of the banking system to create—or to refuse to create—new money can be used as a very powerful tool in regulating the economy.

Let us suppose that savers are saving more than investors wish to invest. The demand gap that develops under these circumstances can potentially lead us into a downward spiral of national production and income. In order to close this gap, the central banking system (in our case the Federal Reserve

System) can take action that will lower the interest rate in order to encourage investment. This action would have the effect of enlarging the demand for new capital and would thus close the gap in demand. An alternative course of action would be for the government to increase government spending, thus expanding government demand and encouraging businesses to invest.

If, on the other hand, savers had decided that they were spending money only on themselves, and at the same time investors were demanding more and more capital items, total demand would exceed GNP. We would find ourselves in a situation in which prices would be rising in an inflationary spiral. Under these circumstances, the Federal Reserve System might take action to raise the rate of interest to discourage investment, and make certain types of loans more difficult to get. An alternative course of action under these circumstances might be for government to increase taxes, thus reducing the funds that consumers had to spend, or to reduce government spending. These reductions in spending would soon be evidenced in a reduction in total demand.

Manipulation of the money supply and the interest rate is known as *monetary* policy, and changes in taxation or government spending are called *fiscal* policy. Which of these two types of action is preferable depends on the particular situation of interest. Both are items in the economic policy maker's tool kit and the objective to be accomplished will determine the sort of action that should be taken.

Agricultural Finance

Why are we concerned about the monetary and banking system in agriculture? What earthly difference could changes in monetary policy make to a farmer, to a farm supply business, or to a processor of agricultural products? Why does agricultural economics concern itself with such subjects?

Agricultural economics is the science that is concerned with the *business* end of agriculture. How many farm businesses in today's world of increasing scale of agricultural operations could provide for the growth that is necessary for survival using only those funds that are generated internally to that business? How many farmers or ranchers can operate without ever borrowing money? How many farmers are completely free of debt? How many fertilizer or other farm supply businesses could operate on a strictly cash basis? How many cotton gins, flour mills, or meat packing plants could operate day-to-day without borrowing money or extending credit?

Credit is a way of life in today's world of specialization. It is essential to the maintenance of efficiency. This is true of farming—indeed, it is true of all agriculture—today more than at any time in history. Because technological growth has given rise to a situation in which farm businesses must get larger in order to remain competitive, the American commercial farmer is hungry for the money that will command the capital necessary for him to remain in business. Very few commercial farmers have the personal capital resources necessary for maintaining economic efficiency in an increasing size of operation. The need for monetary capital in modern farming is so great that it cannot be met unless farmers can acquire the use of other people's capital to add to their own.

The Extent of Farm Capital Needs • The extent of the capital needs in modern farming was emphasized in the early 1960s by the Director of Research for the Farm Credit Banks of Wichita, Kansas, when he predicted that the typical capital needs for a farm in the Plains region in 1975 would be between a quarter and a half million dollars. In support of this prediction, he added, "If you want to see the prototypes of these farms, look at the better ten percent of farms at the present time." If this same criterion is used to anticipate the capital needs of farmers in 1985, we can expect the average farm to use assets in excess of a half million dollars.

During the late 1950s and early 1960s, research in several Departments of Agricultural Economics across the southern United States showed that with then-current land values, the minimum capital needed to yield a labor and management income of $3,000 (the level of income that was at that time defined to be "abject poverty" by the Office of Economic Opportunity) ranged between $25,000 and $185,000 depending on soil type and the cropping alternatives available (Table 4.3). In the Southern Plains region, for example, the requirements ranged between $100,000 for farming and $185,000 for ranching.

The needs for financing in the farm sector of agriculture have continually increased, and they are large in all regions. However, there were some striking regional differences as shown in Figure 4.1. Generally, farmers in those regions having a broad array of production alternatives and a relatively dependable climatic pattern required less capital for earning a given return than did farmers in a high-risk, specialized farming area. While the high-risk Plains area had the greatest capital requirement, the capital needs in all regions were substantial.

But financial information for American agriculture in 1959 or in 1963 was very little more relevant in the 1970s than would have been similar information for the eighteenth century. The dramatic inflation of both farm costs and farm prices during the 1970s requires more recent information. Unfortunately, such information is not available for the regions specified in Table 4.3 and Figure 4.1. However, some generally comparable information for five types of farming areas within the Southern Plains is available for the 1970s (Table 4.4). The income target in this 1975 study was $7,000; considerably above the $3,000 target of 1959. However, when it is recognized

TABLE 4.3

ESTIMATED RESOURCE REQUIREMENTS TO EARN A $3,000 RETURN TO OPERATOR LABOR AND MANAGEMENT
Southern Plains, Mississippi River Delta, and Eastern Coastal Plains, 1959

ITEM	SOUTHERN PLAINS	DELTA	COASTAL PLAIN
	(S.w. Okla & N. Cent. Tex.)	(E. Ark & W. Miss, Cent. La.)	(E. N.C. & E. Va.)
Land (in acres)			
Cropland	466	107	27.6
Pasture	109	–	–
Total	596	187	27.6
Investment (in dollars)			
Land and building	$62,088	$46,750	$12,400
Livestock	17,619	–	–
Machinery & equipment	7,000	6,671	3,600
Miscellaneous	3,602	3,905	2,490
Total	$90,309	$57,326	$18,490
Labor (in hours)			
Operator	1,700	1,700	1,700
Hired	192	–	1,248
Gross Sales ($)	$15,503	$11,979	$ 9,416
Return to operator labor and management ($)	$ 3,000	$ 3,000	$ 3,000

Source: James S. Plaxico and John W. Goodwin, "Adjustments for Efficient Organization of Farms in Selected Areas of the South," in *Southern Agriculture—Its Problems and Policy Alternatives,* Agricultural Policy Institute, North Carolina State College, Raleigh, North Carolina, January, 1961.

Note: 1959 prices and costs are assumed.

that inflation reduced the value of the dollar by almost half between 1959 and 1975, this higher income target is not unreasonable.

In the early to mid-1970s, the total capital investment required for a $7,000 net income to an operator with 15 percent equity in the assets, and paying 8.75 percent interest, ranged from $112,000 for an irrigated farm to $370,000 for a crop-livestock operation in the various types of farming areas. In two of the five cases, this income target could not be achieved at market

TABLE 4.4

ESTIMATED RESOURCE REQUIREMENTS TO EARN A $7,000 RETURN
TO OPERATOR LABOR, MANAGEMENT, RISK AND OWNED CAPITAL

Selected Representative Farm Sizes

| | TYPE OF FARM AND AREA | | | | |
ITEM	Dry-Land Crop & Livestock N.e. Okla.	Dry-Land Crop & Livestock S.e. Okla.	Dry-Land Crop & Livestock S. cent. Okla.	Dry-Land Crop & Livestock N.w. Okla.	Irrigated Crop Farm Okla. High Plains
Land (in acres)					
Cropland, for crops	387	540	928	937	162
Rangeland	153	364	239	404	110
Improved pasture	232	2	26	5	0
Total land	772	906	1,193	1,346	272
Investment ($)					
Land and buildings	$258,620	$212,910	$298,183	$309,690	$ 95,036
Machinery and equip.	28,373	35,737	48,633	31,299	13,563
Livestock	41,556	7,873	—	—	—
Operating capital	19,634	8,495	23,644	11,578	3,758
Total capital need	$348,183	$265,015	$370,460	$352,567	$112,357

Labor (in hours)					
Operator	2,225	1,670	2,298	1,621	755
Hired	134	241	50	–	–
Equity Required (%)	38[1]	15	15	38[1]	15
Max. Feasible Interest Rate[2]	6.5%	9.5%	8.5%	7.0%	9.5%

Source: Dale L. Minnick, *Financial Alternatives and Minimum Resource Requirements for Low Resource, Beginning Farmers in Oklahoma,* unpublished M.S. thesis, Oklahoma State University, Stillwater, Okla., July 1975.

Note: Assumptions are 1973–74 prices for resources and farm commodities and interest rate at 8.75% per annum; five types of farming areas of Oklahoma.

[1] These units were incapable of earning returns to operator-owned resources at interest rates of 8.75% unless the operator's net worth was at least 38% of the total capital required.

[2] Maximum rate of interest the operator could pay on total capital required while still earning $7,000 return to operator labor, management, and risk – that is, this is the maximum interest rate that a beginning producer could pay if he had no equity. This does *not* assure that the cash flow will consistently service the debt.

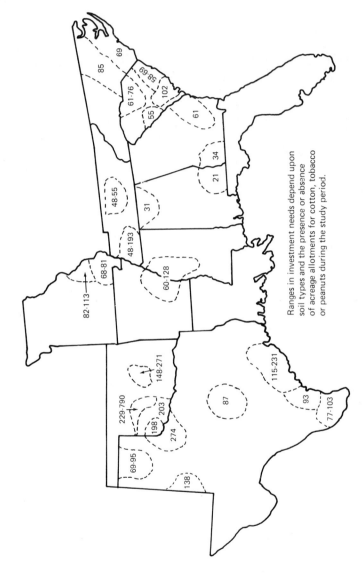

SOURCE: *Resource Requirements for $5,000 Operator's Income in Selected Cotton Producing Areas of the South*, Southern Cooperative Series Bulletin No. 140, Thirteen Southern State Experiment Stations and USDA, September, 1968.

Figure 4.1 Estimated investment (in thousands of dollars) required for $5,000 annual return to operator labor, management, and risk, selected farm situations in the southern U.S., 1958.

Ranges in investment needs depend upon soil types and the presence or absence of acreage allotments for cotton, tobacco or peanuts during the study period.

interest rates unless the operator owned at least 38 percent of the equity in the business. Indeed, there were only two cases in which the beginning farmer with no equity could expect any degree of success with the 8.75 percent market rate of interest.

When a balance sheet for the average American farm for the 1940–76 period is examined (Table 4.5), the increase in per farm capital needs is startling. Between 1940 and 1976, the average farm's assets increased from $8,350 per farm to $211,687—an increase of 2,435 percent! When it is recognized that the average value of farm land almost tripled during the 1960–74 period, the capital problem facing a beginning farmer appears even more difficult. There was a time when a young man could begin farming on a shoestring. All he needed was a team of horses, a walking plow and a girl who could raise chickens. In the last quarter of the twentieth century he can forget the team of horses and the walking plow. He can also forget about the girl who can raise chickens. He'd better be looking for a gal that can raise a quarter of a million dollars, since this is almost the minimum investment necessary for him to earn a "reasonable" living.

How Are Increasing Capital Needs for Farm Production Assets Being Met? • Where does a farmer find a shoestring that is a quarter of a million dollars long? We've already seen that the assets needed to generate minimum acceptable returns to operator labor, management, and risk approach this level. But how can he acquire the rights to these assets? There are basically two means that producers have for cornering the production assets necessary. They can acquire the *ownership* rights to those assets, or alternatively, they can acquire *use* rights. *Ownership* rights include the privileges of the right to sell an asset, the right to use it as collateral for borrowing money, indeed the right to destroy it if the owner so desires. *Use* rights are much more restrictive. *Use* rights are, of course, those rights that are acquired through rental (as of land or buildings), lease (as of machinery, silos, computers, or copying equipment), hiring (as of labor or custom harvesting crews and equipment), or through other devices such as vertical integration with manufacturers or processors. *Use* rights to assets are extremely important in modern agriculture since they tend to reduce total financial needs, although they may *increase* the flow of cash that must be generated in order to keep the business financially sound.

But whether the claim to production assets is to be via ownership right or use right, some financing is typically necessary. Financing of these assets can be of two general types. *Equity* financing (that is, the actual ownership of assets) can spring from several basic sources. Among the sources for equity financing are savings, gifts, inheritance, marriage, partnerships, incorporation, and the like. *Debt* financing, the acquisition of the use of other people's capital, occurs through the use of credit. Credit is simply the ability to

TABLE 4.5

BALANCE SHEET OF THE FARMING SECTOR

Average per Farm, Current Prices, January 1, Selected
Years, 1940–1976[1]

ITEM	1940	1945	1950	1955	1960[2]	1965[2]	1970[2]	1975[2]	1976[2,3]
Assets									
Physical assets									
Real estate	$5,297	$ 9,030	$13,324	$21,094	$32,945	$48,112	$70,026	$132,145	$151,580
Non-real estate									
Livestock & poultry	808	1,510	2,283	2,409	3,848	4,319	7,948	8,750	10,592
Machinery & motor vehicles	482	1,085	2,154	3,995	5,739	7,398	10,934	19,868	24,767
Crops stored on & off farms[4]	420	1,120	1,344	2,073	1,952	2,743	3,697	8,260	7,430
Household equipment & furnishings	663	936	1,524	2,147	2,419	2,569	3,295	5,494	6,102
Financial assets									
Deposits & currency	510	1,325	1,607	2,025	2,313	2,854	4,025	5,363	5,500
U.S. savings bonds	39	566	836	1,068	1,177	1,253	1,266	1,542	1,570
Investment in cooperatives	131	204	364	668	1,071	1,667	2,438	3,744	4,146
Total	$8,350	$15,776	$23,436	$35,479	$51,464	$70,915	$103,629	$185,166	$211,687

Claims

Liabilities									
Real estate debt	$1,037	$ 828	$ 988	$ 1,772	$ 3,049	$ 5,630	$ 9,879	$ 16,484	$ 18,629
Non-real estate debt:									
Excluding CCC loans	473	456	912	1,546	2,909	4,876	7,166	12,545	13,783
CCC loans[5]	70	114	305	477	294	460	906	114	128
Total liabilities	1,580	1,398	2,205	3,795	6,252	10,966	17,951	29,143	32,540
Proprietors' equities	6,770	14,378	21,231	31,684	45,212	59,949	85,678	156,023	179,147
Total	$8,350	$15,776	$23,436	$35,479	$51,464	$70,915	$103,629	$185,166	$211,687
Debt-to-asset ratio	18.9%	8.9%	9.4%	10.7%	12.2%	15.5%	17.3%	15.7%	15.4%

Source: *Balance Sheet of the Farming Sector*, Supplement No. 1, Agriculture Information Bulletin No. 389, Economic Research Service, U.S. Department of Agriculture, April 1976.

[1] Total values divided by total number of farms.

[2] Includes Alaska and Hawaii.

[3] Preliminary.

[4] All crops held on farms including crops under loan to CCC and crops held off farms as security for CCC loans.

[5] Nonrecourse CCC loans secured by crops owned by farmers. These crops are included as assets in this balance sheet.

command the present use of goods or services, commonly through the medium of money, in return for a promise to pay at some point in the future. Credit may result from a bank loan, a charge account with a farm supply agency, or an advance payment for a crop to be delivered at harvest time.

The Need for an Agricultural Credit System • If farm credit is to be dependable and generally available there must, of course, be some organized credit system capable of meeting the specialized needs of agriculture. Today in the United States we have such a system, but this is a relatively new development. From colonial times down to the early years of the twentieth century, the credit system was not well designed to meet the needs of agriculture. Many parts of the country had no credit institutions. Loans were made by individual lenders, usually at exorbitantly high rates of interest (15 to 20 percent per annum was not uncommon).[1] Other areas were served by commercial banks, but until the first national banking system was established in 1863, banking practices were often unsound. For example, in the mid-1800s one bank in Michigan was found to have $580,000 of its bank notes in circulation with only $86.46 in specie with which to redeem them.[2]

In some states, state-owned banks came into being, but many of these were among the worst offenders in the issue of unsound money. The name "wildcat banks" was applied to some of them because their notes could only be redeemed at the head offices of the banks, which often were located in the backwoods "where the only inhabitants were wildcats."[3] These inconvenient and out-of-the-way locations were for the specific purpose of making redemption of bank notes extremely difficult.

The effects of the depreciated currency, resulting from unsound banking practices with the concurrent inflation of prices, were not all bad. They did speed up development more rapidly than would have been possible without some institutional credit.

Even after the strengthening of the banking system under the National Banking and Currency Act of 1863, agriculture found itself poorly served because of certain provisions in the Act that impeded agricultural loans. It had been hoped that the National Banking System would create a flow of funds from those parts of the nation in which there was a surplus of money

---

[1] J. B. Mormon, *The Principles of Rural Credits as Applied in Europe and as Suggested for America* (New York: Macmillan, 1915), pp. 154–157.

[2] E. L. Bogart and D. L. Kemmerer, *Economic History of the American People,* Rev. Ed. New York: Longmans, Green and Co., 1942, p. 372. See also Alphene Welch, *Early Banks and Banking in Michigan.* Reprinted in Sen. Ex. Doc. No. 38, 52nd Cong. 2nd Sess.

[3] Bogart and Kemmerer, *Economic History of the American People.*

seeking investment opportunities to those other parts of the country where more investment funds were needed. This did not happen effectively until after many amendments to the Act of 1863.

During this period, there had been other attempts to establish institutions that would create a flow of funds from the investment markets of the East to the farms farther South and West. The property banks of the South in the middle 1800s attempted to sell bonds secured by real estate mortgages and to lend the proceeds of the bond sales to farmers and others on real estate security. The idea was sound, but mismanagement caused the banks to fail.[4] The farm mortgage banks of the Middle West tried essentially the same procedure by selling mortgages on western land to eastern investors. Again, although the idea was sound, mismanagement and fraud, coupled with a general financial crisis in the nation, caused most of them to fail.[5] In the later 1800s, life insurance companies became important suppliers of farm mortgage loans.

In 1908, the Country Life Commission, appointed by President Theodore Roosevelt to study rural conditions, reported that farm credit conditions were still unsatisfactory and recommended that something be done about it. A further study was made in 1909. In 1911, the American Bankers Association recommended that something be done by government to develop an improved farm mortgage banking system.

Prior to the presidential election of 1912, all political parties promised to work for the improvement of agricultural credit if elected. Even before the 1912 election, President Taft ordered a study of European agricultural credit systems, to be conducted by the American embassy and consular staffs. In 1913, two commissions were appointed to make two more thorough studies of European agricultural credit systems and to recommend action to improve the United States' system. In 1916, after many delays and much difference of opinion, a Federal Farm Loan Act was passed to provide for improved farm mortgage credit. This was the first federal legislation aimed specifically and solely at the improvement of farm credit.

Further modifications in commercial bank farm credit were embodied in the Federal Reserve Act of 1913. Subsequent legislation and further evolution in both the private- and government-sponsored sectors resulted in the comprehensive agricultural credit system that had developed by the mid-1970s. The system was not without imperfections, but it served the farmers of this country with amazing effectiveness.

---

[4] Earl L. Sparks, *History and Theory of Agricultural Credit in the United States* (New York: Thomas Y. Crowell Company, 1932), Chapter VI.

[5] Ivan Wright, *Farm Mortgage Financing,* (New York: McGraw-Hill, 1923), Chapter VI.

Sources of Agricultural Credit •   The agencies that go into the makeup of our present agricultural credit system may be divided into three broad types:

I.   Sources of Real Estate Loans to Farmers.

  A. Life insurance companies,

  B. Federal Land Banks,

  C. State agencies,

  D. Farmers Home Administration,

  E. Farm mortgage companies,

  F. Commercial banks, and

  G. Individual lenders

II.   Sources of Non-Real Estate Loans to Farmers.

  A. Commercial banks,

  B. Production credit associations and the federal intermediate credit banks,

  C. Farmers Home Administration,

  D. Livestock loan companies,

  E. Other agricultural credit corporations,

  F. Merchants and dealers,

  G. Credit unions, and

  H. Finance companies

III.   Sources of Credit to Farmers' Business Organizations (Farmer Cooperatives).

  A. Banks for cooperatives, and

  B. Rural Electrification Administration

The credit agencies that were serving agriculture in the early days of this century were supplemented by the cooperative farm credit system, which began in 1916 under the Federal Farm Loan Act of that year. During the 1930s, the independent agencies and the cooperative farm credit system were supplemented by government-owned and operated farm credit agencies. It may be convenient, therefore, to establish other classifications of farm credit agencies on the basis of whether the agency is part of the cooperative farm credit system, is a private agency outside of that system, or is governmental.

The Cooperative Farm Credit System • In the cooperative farm credit system, there are twelve Federal Land Banks, which make farm mortgage loans throughout the entire United States and Puerto Rico. These loans are made through local Federal Land Bank associations. These local associations are entirely owned by farmer-borrowers who, when they borrow from the Federal Land Bank, buy stock in their local association equal to approximately 5 percent of the amount of the loan. The local association in turn buys an equivalent amount of stock in the Federal Land Bank of its district. Thus, the Federal Land Banks are privately owned by the Federal Land Bank associations, which in turn are owned by the farmer-borrowers so that, indirectly, the farmer-borrowers own the Federal Land Banks from which they borrow.

Because the commercial banking system was found to be unable to meet the total needs of farmers for non-real estate credit during the agricultural depression of the 1920s, twelve federal intermediate credit banks were established by legislation in 1923. Originally they were entirely owned by the federal government. They were designed to provide funds to local banks and other agricultural credit corporations, which in turn would make these funds available to farmers. For a number of reasons, the commercial banks did not make significant use of these federal intermediate credit banks. When the great general depression struck in the 1930s, the commercial banks were again unable to meet the needs of farmers. The federal government was persuaded to set up a series of local lending agencies of a cooperative nature, known as production credit associations, through which the funds of the federal intermediate credit bank could be channeled to farmers. These production credit associations are now entirely owned by farmers. They obtain loan funds from the FICB in their district, with these loans secured by promissory notes from farmers who are borrowing from the PCA. Although the federal intermediate credit banks will provide funds to commercial banks, or to any other regularly incorporated lending agency that is making non-real estate loans to farmers, most of their funds are channeled to farmers through the production credit associations. Because of a developing sentiment that the federal government should no longer own the federal intermediate credit banks, legislation providing for purchase of the government's interest in the federal intermediate credit banks by the production credit associations was passed in the 1950s. This change of ownership was completed in the mid-1960s, and the federal intermediate credit banks are today owned entirely by the production credit associations, which in turn are owned by the farmer-borrowers.

The third segment in the cooperative farm credit system is the group of thirteen banks for cooperatives designed to make loans to farmers' cooperatives. There is a bank for cooperatives in each farm credit district, along with the Federal Land Bank and the federal intermediate credit bank. In addition there is a central bank for cooperatives in Denver, Colorado, which serves the needs of large cooperatives that are operating beyond the limits of any one district. This central bank for cooperatives cooperates with any district bank for cooperatives in supplying loans that are too large to be carried by the district bank alone.

Three questions might be asked about this cooperative credit system. Why did it come into being? Where do their loan funds come from? Who controls them? The first question has been answered in the earlier discussion. It may be said that the Federal Land Banks came into being as a result of a lack of adequate farm mortgage credit in many parts of the United States and in response to a demand for improved credit from a large segment of the agricultural, commercial, and financial world. At the time the Federal Land Banks came into being in 1916, it had been presumed that the commercial bank system and other agencies could meet the short-term non-real estate borrowing needs of farmers quite adequately. When such credit sometimes proved to be inadequate, farmers urged the development of some credit segment that would make them less dependent on commercial banks. Characteristically, commercial banks were unable to lend as much during poor times when deposits were small as they could in good times. It was often during bad times that farmers were unable to pay their existing debts and desperately needed continuing credit. Consequently, the federal intermediate credit banks were set up as an additional source of funds to commercial banks so that the banks would be able to meet the needs of farmers even though the volume of their bank deposits had decreased. If the commercial banks had in fact used the services of the federal intermediate credit banks extensively, it is unlikely that the government-sponsored production credit system would ever have come into being.

Characteristically, farmer cooperatives had found difficulty in finding adequate financing from conventional lenders. Therefore, in 1929 under the Agricultural Marketing Act, the federal government provided $500 million as a revolving fund administered by a Federal Farm Board out of which farmers' cooperatives could obtain loans. However, during the Great Depression of the 1930s, the Federal Farm Board was superseded by the Agricultural Adjustment Administration with much broader responsibilities in dealing with farm problems. The responsibility for providing loans to farmers' cooperatives was transferred to the banks for cooperatives, which were established in 1934.

Loan funds provided by these lenders in the cooperative farm credit system do *not* come from the federal government. Principally, they are acquired by selling bonds which are the joint and several obligations of the twelve Federal Land Banks, the twelve federal intermediate credit banks, and the thirteen banks for cooperatives, and in turn are secured by farm mortgages, notes, and other evidences of the loans made by the banks. These bonds are sold on the money market in New York City through a fiscal agent employed by the Federal Land Banks, the federal intermediate credit banks, and the banks for cooperatives. Law prohibits the government from assuming any responsibility, direct or indirect, for these bonds or other obligations issued by the banks. The Farm Credit Administration is a federal supervisory agency whose primary function is to see that the units in the system operate in accordance with the law. Within the system the emphasis is on farmer-borrower control. Twelve members of the Federal Farm Credit Board are appointed by the president of the United States from those nominated by the borrowers' representatives in the twelve farm credit districts. A thirteenth member is appointed to represent the U.S. Department of Agriculture. It is this Board that appoints the governor of the Farm Credit Administration and to which the Farm Credit Administration is responsible.

In each farm credit district a board of directors is elected by the farmer-borrowers through their Federal Land Bank associations, production credit associations, and the cooperatives which borrow from the bank for cooperatives. This district board is the policy-making body in the district to which the presidents of the district Federal Land Bank, the district federal intermediate credit bank, and the district bank for cooperatives are accountable.

Private Lenders that Are Not Part of the Cooperative Credit System • The second category of lenders embraces those nongovernmental lenders that are not part of the cooperative credit system. These include life insurance companies which use part of their reserves for making farm mortgage loans; state and national banks which use part of their funds for both real estate mortgage and production loans to farmers; and various agricultural credit corporations which make production loans to farmers and ranchers. Many of these agricultural credit corporations obtain much of their loan funds from the federal intermediate credit banks, although they are not part of the cooperative credit system. Some also obtain funds from the large commercial banks.

Just as the cooperative farm credit banks are under the general supervision of the Farm Credit Administration, so insurance companies come under the supervision of the insurance commissioners of the states in which they operate. The commercial banks, in turn, come under the supervision of the state banking commissioners in the case of state banks and the Comptroller of the Currency in the case of national banks.[6]

In addition to these institutional lenders, the merchants, dealers, and individual lenders who supply much credit to farmers and credit unions are important. Discussion of the structure of this group of lenders is omitted, not because they are less important than those in the cooperative credit system,

---

[6] Commercial banks may also come under supervision by the Federal Reserve System and the Federal Deposit Insurance Corporation.

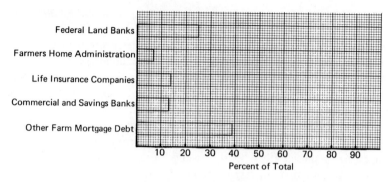

SOURCE: *Agricultural Statistics, 1975*, USDA, Table 663

Figure 4.2 Farm mortgage loans: percent held by selected lender groups, U.S., January 1, 1974.

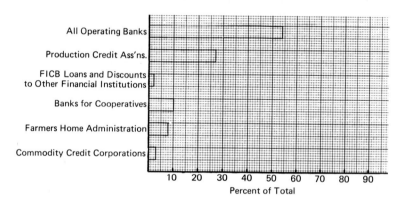

SOURCE: *Agricultural Statistics, 1975*, USDA, Table 666

Figure 4.3 Agricultural loans not secured by farm real estate: percent of amounts outstanding January 1, 1975, U.S.

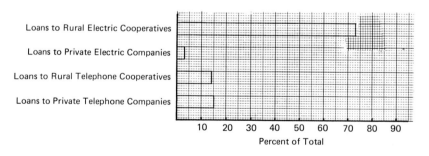

SOURCE: *Agricultural Statistics, 1975*, USDA, Table 666

Figure 4.4 Rural Electrification Administration: percent of loans outstanding, by type of loan and borrower, U.S., January 1, 1975.

but because people are more generally familiar with them. Relative volumes of loans by the various agencies are shown in Figures 4.2, 4.3, and 4.4.

Government Lending Agencies • A third category of lending agencies is that of government lenders. Some states have farm loans available from public funds. An important federal government lender to farmers is the Farmers Home Administration, which makes loans to farmers who cannot obtain adequate funds from other lenders at reasonable terms. Loans may be on real estate mortgages or for operating purposes. In addition, loans may be made for several other specialized purposes. Farmers Home Administration funds come from appropriations by the federal government except that much of the money for farm mortgage loans comes from private lenders who take over the loans on an insured basis. Much credit on certain harvested crops is also supplied by the Commodity Credit Corporation under federal agricultural programs. Also flowing into rural electric cooperatives are funds from the Rural Electrification Administration.

Selected References

Agricultural Banking Developments, 1962–1967. New York: Agricultural Committee, American Bankers Association.

The Federal Reserve System: Purposes and Functions. Washington, D.C.: Board of Governors, Federal Reserve System, 1963.

Financing Modern Agriculture. Wichita, Kan.: Farm Credit Banks of Wichita.

Fundamentals of Money and Banking. New York: Banking Education Committee, The American Bankers Association, 1963.

Nelson, A. G., and W. G. Murray, *Agricultural Finance,* 5th ed. Ames, Iowa: Iowa State University Press, 1967.

Swackhamer, G. L., and R. J. Doll, *Financing Modern Agriculture: Banking's Problems and Challenges.* Kansas City, Mo.: Research Department, Federal Reserve Bank of Kansas City, 1969.

5

The Problems of Agriculture and Macroeconomic Policy Decisions

There are probably no domestic issues as emotionally charged and as diversely viewed as those issues that deal with economic progress and government efforts to influence the outcome of these issues. One example of this was the federal declaration of war on poverty during the first half of the 1960s. As might have been expected, poverty steadfastly resisted the invasion. The different programs that were inaugurated in the 1960s were variously hailed as the first really significant progress in modern social legislation or the first American giant step toward socialism. These views still persist. But the so-called poverty programs such as Medicare, food stamps, and the Office of Economic Opportunity have become ingrained as a part of the government activity to which agriculture and all other economic sectors must adjust. The food stamp program, for example, has had a major impact on agriculture by increasing the markets for certain types of food, notably meats. The federal expenditure on this type of government activity increased from $200 million in fiscal 1966 to $5.9 *billion* in fiscal 1976. This represented about 2.7 percent of total consumer food expenditures in the calendar year 1975. By 1981, food stamp program funding is expected to increase to $10.4 billion.[1] Thus, agriculture, as well as the poor, is a major beneficiary of this program.

But agriculture is not always the beneficiary of macrodecisions—frequently it is the victim. Some cases in point are regulations promulgated by agencies such as the Environmental Protection Agency (EPA), the Occupational Safety and Health Administration (OSHA), and the Department of

---

[1] *Budget Options for Fiscal Year 1977: A Report to the Senate and House Committees on the Budget* (Washington, D.C.: Congress of the United States, Mar., 1976), p. 129.

State. The various EPA bans on pesticides and herbicides have forced in-creases in agricultural production costs and hence in consumer food prices. Bans on predator control efforts have had a similar impact. Safety regulations promulgated by OSHA have rendered much of the existing farm machinery and a number of farm buildings (notably dairy barns) obsolete. The expense of compliance has forced some farmers to incur higher production costs, and still others to cease operations altogether. As a result, food prices have been forced to rise. Department of State intervention in export grain sales during the middle 1970s generated enormous resentment among farmers and con-sumers alike—among consumers because the intervention was less than imme-diate, and among farmers because it occurred at all.

The Nature of Agricultural Problems

The economic problems that affect the agricultural sector can normally be classified into three general categories: endogenous, exogenous, and insti-tutional. Endogenous economic problems of agriculture are those that spring from internal sources. Exogenous problems spring from external sources, and institutional problems spring from human institutions such as government, social mores, custom, and various sorts of historical patterns.

Endogenous Economic Problems; Those Internal to Agriculture • In-cluded in the economic problems that are internal to agriculture are the problems that are internal to individual agricultural businesses. The avail-ability and adaptation of new technology creates all sorts of problems internally to individual businesses as well as to all of agriculture. The decision on the part of an individual to adopt new technology typically involves all sorts of decisions regarding the size of the business, the level of other technology (such as crop variety, fertilization rate, or machinery comple-ment) to use, or the product mix the business should adopt. As more and more farmers are faced with these decisions, and as the new technology begins to replace the old, a reorganization of the entire production sector must frequently occur.

Adaptation of a new technology (such as a higher yielding crop variety, for example) may lower the cost per unit of output. But as more and more producers adopt the new variety, the increase in the total output of that product may cause prices to fall by even more than costs have been reduced. Under these circumstances, consumers may actually get the product at less than the full cost of production. This would suggest that production should be reduced. But the problems of what to do with a resource such as the land that is displaced arises. If the land is diverted to another crop, the problem has been transferred, but it still exists. The fact that many agricultural resources can be adjusted out of agricultural uses only at great expense and agonizing pain has motivated government to intervene in an effort to ease the adjustment.

New technology (farm machinery, for example) frequently requires that a farm unit be enlarged in order to take advantage of the potential cost reduction. If most farm businesses must grow in acreage as a result of the new technology, there must necessarily be fewer farm businesses. If there are fewer farms, there must necessarily be fewer farmers. If there are fewer farmers, what is to be done with the people who have been displaced? This leads directly to the question of the "family farm." What has become and what is to become of the family farm? Will advances in technology expand the economically efficient size of the farm unit beyond the ability of a family to supply the majority of the labor and management? Will the advance in technology likely expand farm investment needs beyond the ability of the farm family to acquire control of enough capital to give them a majority interest in the business? Is technological advance in the agribusiness sector likely to change the marketing pattern such that the family farm will become extinct?

These questions are only a few of the economic problems that are endogenous to agriculture, but answers to all of them can be influenced by public policy decisions. Other questions deal with what sort of product mix an individual firm should strive toward, and government's role in that decision. For what sort of resource combination should managers plan? What sorts of growth plans should be made in order for the business to survive?

The lack of bargaining power of the farm sector of agriculture has always been a source of endogenous economic problems in agriculture. The structure of the farming sector is such that an individual farm provides only a minute part of the total volume of raw materials used by an agricultural processing firm. Unless farmers can get together and bargain collectively, they must continue to be "price takers." In other words, they will be unable to effectively negotiate price concessions. The area of agricultural cooperation to be examined in Chapter 15 is the portion of agricultural economics that is concerned with the problems of farm bargaining power.

Exogenous Economic Problems: Those External to Agriculture • In addition to the problems that are generated *internally,* agriculture also faces economic problems that come from outside the agricultural sector. For example, we have already suggested that technological growth causes farms to grow larger and results in fewer farms and hence fewer farmers. This problem is *internal* to agriculture. But consider the difficulty of achieving adjustment in agriculture because of the problems faced by farm workers who are displaced by increases in agricultural technology. How can production agriculture achieve the adjustment of reducing the numbers of people employed in the industry if there is no place for these people to go? What if the rest of the economy is not growing fast enough to absorb these people? Since World War II, the United States has experienced tremendous economic growth. But this growth has not generally been in the types of industries that could utilize displaced farm labor. In the absence of adequate adjustment either inside or outside the farm sector, these workers have swelled the ranks of the unemployed, creating the general economic problem of rapidly expanded welfare rolls that have affected the entire economy. Many of the farm programs of the 1950s and 1960s were designed in part to ameliorate this sort of problem by reducing farm to urban population movement to a rate more compatible with the entire economy's ability to absorb technologically-displaced farm people.

A second agricultural problem that has been generated outside the agricultural sector is the problem of an almost total depopulation of many rural areas. At the end of World War II, the United States faced the problem of providing jobs, housing, opportunity, etc., for several million young men returning from war. The time period over which these men were reinfused into the mainstream of the American economy was extended by the GI Bill, which encouraged many of these men to seek further education, thus delaying their re-entry into the job market. At the same time, we made it very easy to get financing for such things as housing, public utilities, and business development in communities of more than 50,000 people. The impact of these programs was that we met the immediate needs of our society following World War II, but we created some problems that were to become crucial twenty to thirty years later. The legislation that eased the financing problems for developing housing, utilities, and jobs in the metropolitan areas largely ignored the existence of rural America. As a result, the small towns and rural areas were stripped of the opportunity to participate fully in the tremendous economic growth of the 1950s and 1960s.

Farm youth, displaced by accelerating technological growth in agriculture, had no choice but to move to metropolitan areas in search of jobs and housing. Business opportunities in rural areas declined. The rural tax base for supporting such public services as roads, schools, and health care began to shrink. The availability of these services began to decline and become much more remote for rural Americans. At the same time, many of the rural migrants found themselves jammed into the least desirable of all metropolitan living situations. The economic and social problems that have resulted from this situation may well be the most critical of all the domestic national problems facing the United States in the latter quarter of the twentieth century.

Institutional Economic Problems Affecting the Agricultural Economy • Certain economic problems in agriculture flow from social mores, custom, legal restraints, and outmoded historical patterns. Many areas in the

United States have found it difficult to mechanize their farming operations because of the institutional restraint of land settlement patterns. Perhaps the land was settled in the long, narrow strips that not only were well adapted to horse-powered agriculture, but also gave a more equitable distribution of the different qualities of land. These long, narrow fields are almost impossible to farm efficiently with today's large-scale agricultural machinery. Thus, the cost of producing certain crops in some areas may be prohibitive because of the institutional restraints imposed by land settlement patterns of 150 years ago. The agricultural businesses normally associated with these crops will often face prohibitively high costs in such an area because of the expense of importing raw materials or because of the lower costs available to large units that can develop in competing areas which are free of such restraints.

It is within the context of institutional problems that agricultural people find themselves both collectively and individually forced to adjust to macroeconomic policy decisions promulgated by various government agencies. In Chapter 4, we discovered that there were two basic types of macroeconomic policy—*monetary* policy, which was concerned with the money supply and the rate of interest, and *fiscal* policy, which was concerned with taxation and government spending. In Chapter 2, we recognized that the basic economic problems concerned with economic growth and the intensity of resource use were the economic decisions most likely to be dominated by the public (or "institutional") sector. These public decisions of a macroeconomic nature have forced all sorts of difficulty on the individuals faced with making microadjustments.

Microeconomic Adjustment to Macroeconomic Decisions

Most of us individually can do the things we do primarily because most other people refrain from doing them. That is, if all Americans chose to live in New York City, the problems of the Big Apple would be even wormier than presently observed. But since most Americans refrain from living in New York (or indeed even going near it), the problems of the city are merely impossible.

One example of the problems that individual farm units, the entire industry, and society at large face as a result of general economic policy comes from tax laws governing inheritance and capital gains taxes. Much has been made of the fact that the most recent census of agriculture showed the median age of American farmers to be above the age of 50. That is, more than half of all farmers were approaching retirement age at the time of that census. This has led some analysts to believe that the United States may be running out of the producers of food and fiber. While a case can be built for that belief, an equally compelling case can be built for the proposition that substantial numbers of young people will embark on any career that promises an economic opportunity. But within this context, there is another problem that was suggested by the financial statistics for the average farm as presented in Chapter 4.

A large share of the *ownership* of farm land must necessarily be in the hands of people approaching retirement age. This land must change ownership either through sale or inheritance. Given the very high capital needs of modern farming, how is the intergenerational transfer of farm land assets to be accomplished without forcing these units to be broken up into units too small to achieve economically efficient production costs? The inheritance tax structure, for example, would make it extremely difficult for the heirs to assume operation of the unit, and the capital needs for an individual farm are too large for most young men to finance on a purchase basis. Yet, capital gains taxes discourage an elderly landowner from disposing of his land prior to his death. The problem is further complicated by existing legislation in some states and proposed legislation in still others that limits the degree to which devices such as incorporation may be used in the farm sector.

We recognized in our discussion of politico-economic systems in Chapter 2 that in a capitalistic society, decisions concerning the basic economic problems are theoretically made through the price system. We also recognized that, in practice, those decisions are made through the price system, but with a fair degree of public supervision of the basic economic forces. There are many economic problems that may be solved through the price system, but some segment or segments of the society will generally find any price-achieved solution to be unsatisfactory. This is because a price solution (or a solution achieved by any other means, for that matter) frequently will work to the advantage of some groups and to the disadvantage of others.

Because capitalist societies are governed by freely elected officials, these officials feel compelled to attempt to ameliorate and soften through public policy the impact of the adjustments made through the price system. But like the problem shown in the case of inheritance and capital gains taxes, public policy decisions regarding macroeconomic issues force some micro-adjustments within the agricultural sector. In the remainder of this chapter, we will briefly outline some of the microeconomic adjustments that these problems create for agriculture. No attempt will be made to suggest alternative solutions for these problems since we have not yet acquired the skills of economic analysis that will allow us to measure the impact of these adjustments. As we acquire these skills in subsequent chapters, we will re-examine the adjustments and specify some of their implications for the agricultural sector.

The Problem of Inflation • In the simplest of terms, inflation is the phenomenon observed when the monetary unit commands less in the way of goods and services than it commanded in some previous period. Inflation can spring from a variety of sources, including (but not necessarily restricted to):

1. Government spending in excess of tax receipts;

2. Government action aimed at increasing the money supply;

3. Sudden redistributions of income—either through government action or through collective bargaining, or both—that cause shifts in demand from investment goods to consumer goods;

4. Government regulations that force inefficiencies of resource use and reductions in productivity;

5. Alterations in foreign exchange rates that alter comparative values among commodities in both international and domestic markets; and

6. Either unilateral or multilateral action on the part of foreign governments that disrupts the price relationships for resources—such as energy.

In each of these cases, there are more dollars chasing goods than there are goods to be chased. As a result, the number of dollars required per unit of goods must necessarily increase.

During the 1950s and 1960s, inflation in the United States was at most a minor problem. Between 1950 and 1967, the annual rate of inflation averaged less than two percent per year. That is, the product that could be purchased for $1.00 in one year could generally be purchased at no more than $1.02 in the following year. However, beginning in 1968, prices for virtually all resources and for most products began to rise rapidly. During the 1974-75 period, the average annual rate of inflation reached 10 percent.

If the prices for all goods and all resources changed proportionally during an inflationary period, the problem of inflation would be limited to the problems faced by those who live on fixed dollar incomes, or who held large sums of cash at the beginning of the period. However, Figure 5.1 shows that prices do not inflate at the same rate for all products. The farm commodities that could have been purchased for $1.00 in 1950 cost $0.98 in 1967 and $1.77 in 1975. But the farm inputs that cost $1.00 in 1950 cost $1.33 in 1967 and $2.47 in 1975. It isn't difficult to understand why farm family incomes have typically lagged 20 to 30 percent behind those of non-farm families when it is recognized that farm costs have inflated much more rapidly than farm prices. It is also easy to understand why retail food prices have increased faster than farm prices when it is recognized that the non-farm labor that could have been purchased for $1.00 in 1950 had almost quadrupled in price by 1975. This increasingly expensive labor was the major ingredient added to farm products between the farm and retail levels.

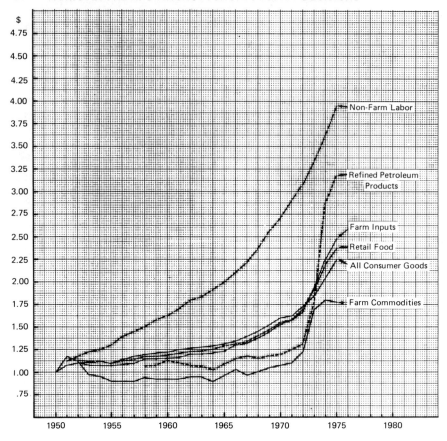

SOURCE: *Business Conditions Digest*, USDC, Bureau of Economic
Analysis, *Agricultural Prices*, CRB, SRS, USDA, and
Statistical Abstract of the United States, U.S. Depart-
ment of Commerce.

Figure 5.1 Purchasing power of one dollar in 1950 versus 1975, selected
commodity groups, U.S.

Prior to 1973, retail food prices had lagged behind the general rate of
inflation. But beginning in 1973, retail food costs, led by meat products,
began to rise at a rate that exceeded the general price increase. As a result, the
"freeze" that had been imposed in the summer of 1971 in an effort to retard
the increase in resource prices and wage rates was extended to retail food
prices. The result of this extension was a disruption of the domestic values of
farm products relative to international values. Concurrent with these developments there were short grain crops in Eastern Europe due to drought. Farm
exports began to accelerate, creating all sorts of unfounded consumer fears

about the probable availability of foodstuffs. This public concern led to export embargoes on farm products such as soybeans and grains.

But the worst was yet to come. The same forces that led to increased exports of farm products also caused increased exports of farm resources, particularly of agricultural chemicals such as fertilizers. Large fertilizer exports—because of the frozen domestic price—caused domestic fertilizer availability to be extremely limited, reducing agricultural production potential, hence further reducing the volume of agricultural goods potentially available. This added to the inflationary pressure. Thus, the government effort to control inflation via the Wage-Price Freeze actually aggravated rather than solved the problem.

The Balance of Payments Problem • At least a part of the inflationary problem was created through efforts to deal with a negative U.S. balance of payments. The balance of payments problem is concerned with the value of products exported as compared with the value of those imported. If imports exceed exports, citizens of other nations gain a claim upon a part of the assets in the American economy. In an effort to bring imports and exports into balance, there were two official devaluations of the American dollar in the 1970–71 period, and a third *de facto* devaluation when it was announced in 1972 that American dollars would no longer be redeemed in gold.

The intent of these devaluations was to cheapen American goods in the world market in order to encourage American export sales. This intent was achieved, but the American consumer was in no way prepared for the realities that went along with expanded export sales. When the sales (particularly of farm commodities and farm inputs) to overseas customers expanded, it left reduced volumes of these products in domestic markets. Reduced availability of these goods meant higher prices—a signal for expanded production. But that signal became garbled when the wage-price freeze was imposed in an effort to control the domestic inflation that resulted from these too-successful policies.

The Energy Problem • The so-called energy problem is related to both the problem of inflation and the U.S. balance of payments. By the mid-1970s, the United States was importing about half the petroleum used in fueling the American economy. During 1973, the Arab world awakened to the fact that Allah had seen fit to bestow upon them the lion's share of the world's crude oil reserves. Because of Arab displeasure with the distribution of the world's non-oil wealth (and just possibly because of displeasure regarding the industrialized nations' continuing close ties with Israel), the Arab nations agreed in late 1973 to begin redistributing the world's wealth through dramatic increases in the prices for crude oil. The impact of this decision upon the prices for

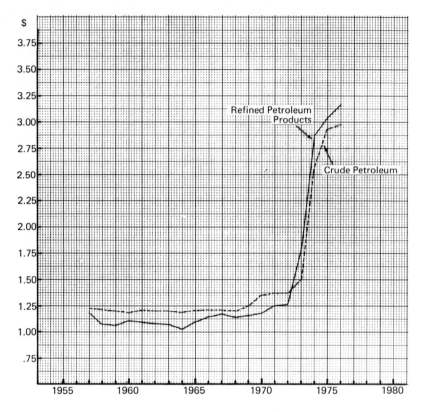

SOURCE: Statistical Abstract of the United States for all reported
years, U.S. Department of Commerce.

Figure 5.2 Current cost of the volume of petroleum products that could
have been purchased for $1 in 1950, U.S., 1957–1976.

crude petroleum and refined petroleum products in the United States is
shown in Figure 5.2.[2]

There can be little question that rapidly escalating oil prices added to
the fires of inflation in the U.S. economy. Fortunately, the expected adverse
effect upon the U.S. balance of payments was almost exactly offset by
expanded export sales of U.S. farm products. But government efforts to
prevent a price adjustment to this situation have had a serious impact on
many agricultural producers.

The immediate adjustment attempted by American industry was to
convert where possible to fuels other than oil. Even though Allah had given
the Arabs the lion's share of the world's oil reserves, Gichi Manitou had given

---

[2] Figures for 1976 are preliminary.

the North American Indians a major part of the coal and a substantial share of the natural gas. The European migrants to what was to become the United States had relieved the Indians of the responsibility for these resources (and most others) and had developed them to the fullest. Now that energy resources were short, the time had come to decide how the available supplies were to be distributed. Because of rapidly increasing prices for all energy, many people were apprehensive about assigning the price mechanism full responsibility for allocating these resources. The Federal Energy Office was established to administer refined petroleum fuel allocations at administered prices, the Federal Power Commission had responsibility for allocating natural gas, and the multi-faceted tug-of-war for energy allocations was underway.

Farmers in the spring of 1974 were assured by the President that he was not about "to let American agriculture run out of gas!" And agriculture did receive gasoline and diesel fuel allocations that would have allowed land to be prepared and crops to be planted. The attitude of the oil industry was that the Federal Energy Office was empowered to make petroleum fuel allocations as the Federal Energy Office saw fit. However, the Federal Energy Office was *not* empowered to force oil companies to *sell* that fuel. As a result, gasoline and diesel fuels simply were not available in adequate volumes in many rural areas until the price restraint was lifted. The potential impact of this situation on farm production is obvious.

Natural gas was a different matter. The Federal Power Commission had for many years enjoyed regulatory powers over prices and allocations of natural gas that moved across state boundaries; that is, over *inter*state gas. *Intra*state gas—that which was sold and used within the state in which it was produced—was unregulated. This meant that natural gas prices in the Plains states, which produced a major portion of the natural gas, increased sharply. But it also meant that industries in these states could get adequate volumes of the fuel, albeit at higher prices. Rapidly increasing demand for interstate gas meant that pressures would be brought to bear upon the Federal Power Commission to generate a distribution of natural gas more to the liking of the interstate users.

Irrigation farmers in the five-state South Plains region depended on natural gas to power irrigation pumps for 12.6 million acres of land in 1975. Prior to 1974, irrigation farmers in this area were classified as "non-interruptible" users of natural gas. That is, the service to an irrigation customer could not be curtailed should the available volumes of natural gas be short of the total demanded. Beginning in 1974 and 1975, the interstate gas companies began to petition the Federal Power Commission in an effort to reclassify irrigation users as "interruptible" customers.

At the time of this writing, some of these cases are still pending before the Federal Power Commission. If the Federal Power Commission should make the macrodecision in favor of an "interruptible" service category for irrigation farming, the microadjustment impact upon irrigation farming in the states of Texas, New Mexico, Colorado, Oklahoma and Kansas will be enormous. Alternative power sources do not exist in these areas. If irrigation gas service should be curtailed, the feed grain production in the area will likely be reduced by 75 percent as farmers restructure cropping patterns to conform with rainfall patterns. Farm incomes would drop precipitously, and the per capita incomes for all people in the area would be reduced substantially. While only about 7 percent of U.S. feed grain production is involved, this 7 percent of the feed grain involves about 40 percent of the nation's fed beef production.[3]

Public Policy: A Trap for Economists

There are a multitude of additional macroeconomic problem areas that could be outlined. Some additional examples include the environmental area (although this author confesses to a suspicion that the real problem may be with the environmentalist rather than the environment), and the matter of public health and safety. Virtually all of the public policy issues have their roots in the five basic economic questions of what, how, and for whom to produce, how fast is the economy to grow, and how intensively are resources to be used. Many of these public policy issues also are rooted in a basic public suspicion of the degree of equity provided by the capitalistic attitude that the price system is the most effective means for solving these basic problems.

The public controversy surrounding public policy issues dramatically illustrates why economics, and more specifically agricultural economics, is a social science. Public policy is concerned with people and the social systems in which they live. If the public objective is to stimulate economic growth in those areas that have lagged behind, the public must accept the fact that it will be necessary to induce some structural changes in the social systems of these areas. If the public objective is to recreate the pristine environment of 1850, then the public must accept the fact that the production of goods and services will become much more expensive and that average standards of living will most probably be reduced. If the public objective is that most Americans should drive private automobiles fueled by Arab oil, then Americans must accept the reality that American agricultural products must be traded for that oil and a part of the cost for driving an automobile will be

---

[3] For a complete analysis of the impact of irrigation natural gas curtailment in the five South Plains states, see the *Direct Testimony* of Dr. James S. Plaxico in *United States of America Before the Federal Power Commission in the Matter of Cities Service Gas Co.,* Docket No. PR75-62 (Washington, D.C.: Federal Power Commission, October, 1975).

paid at the supermarket checkout counter. Herein lies a trap for beginning students of economics. (In all fairness, it should be pointed out that this trap ensnares many who are *not* novices at the business of economics.)

The objectives of a society cannot be defined by economics. These objectives must be defined *outside* of economics. This is why economic analysis is equally applicable to capitalistic, socialistic, fascistic and communistic societies. Once the social objectives are defined, the economist can offer valuable advice and guidance about *how* the objectives may be achieved. Any time an economist says that the science of economics indicates that such and such an objective *should* be pursued, he is neither a scientist nor an economist. He is an advocate.

Economists have the same authority and the same rights as any other citizen so far as public policy is concerned. As a part of the public, they are entitled to an opinion as to what the objective of society should be. But no economist or group of economists can categorically state as economists what the public objective *is*. This is the function of some group—in our case, the Congress—which has been selected to represent all segments of society. Once a policy-making body has formulated the objectives, economics may be used to design the "road map" that defines the alternative routes by which we can move from the current situation toward the stated goal. As a part of that road map, the costs—time as well as money—must be defined. Once this function is performed, it is time for the economist to fade back into the woodwork. It is the responsibility of the body which represents the public to select the alternative that is most consistent with the capability and the objectives of the society in question.

Economic analysts can define alternatives and evaluate performance in terms of the goals that are set by society at large. Beyond this, the function of an economist is the same as the function of any other citizen. He is not endowed with any special omniscience nor with any special power. He is merely a man who can help an economic entity achieve its stated goals subject to some specified efficiency criteria.

Selected References

Cochrane, Willard W., *The City Man's Guide to the Farm Problem*, Chapters 11, 12 and 13. Minneapolis: University of Minnesota Press, 1965.

Goodwin, John W., "Community Impact of Population Shifts," *Rural America: Graveyard, Holding Pen, or Garden of Eden*, Proceedings of the American Country Life Association, Stillwater, Olka.: Oklahoma State University, July, 1969.

Hathaway, Dale E., *Government and Agriculture: Public Policy in a Democratic Society*, Chaps. 6 and 14. New York: The Macmillan Company, 1963.

Heady, Earl O., *A Primer on Food, Agriculture, and Public Policy,* Chapter 6. New York: Random House, 1967.

Keyserling, Leon H., *Progress or Poverty.* Washington, D.C.: Conference on Economic Progress, 1964.

Plaxico, James S., *Direct Testimony, United States of America Before the Federal Power Commission in the Matter of Cities Service Gas Co.,* Docket No. PR75-62, Washington, D.C.: Federal Power Commission, October 1975.

Ruttan, V. W., A. D. Waldo, and J. P. Houck, *Agricultural Policy in an Affluent Society,* Part 5. New York: W. W. Norton and Company, Inc., 1969.

Tolley, George S., "Combating Income Problems of Noncommercial Farmers and Other Rural Groups," *Good Goals, Future Structural Changes and Agricultural Policy: A National Basebook.* Ames, Iowa: Iowa State University Press, 1969.

Tweeten, Luther G., *Foundations of Farm Policy.* Lincoln, Nebraska: University of Nebraska Press, 1970.

6

The Economic Setting of American Agriculture

What is agriculture?

Any standard dictionary will define agriculture as "the art or science of cultivating the ground; the production of crops and livestock on a farm; farming." At one time, this definition was acceptable. However, the sweeping changes that have been evident in recent decades make such a definition obsolete. These standard dictionary definitions of agriculture are entirely too narrow when applied to today's agriculture. If *agriculture* ends when the crop or animal hits the farm gate, why do farmers become so concerned about off-farm issues such as imports and exports of farm products, packer feeding of cattle, or the trade practices of chain stores? If, during the time when our nation was young—say at the time of George Washington—agriculture ended when the crop or animal was grown, where would we be today? Well, let's consider this. Grain could not have been made into bread directly; it required *processing*. Animals had to be *slaughtered* for meat. Wool, cotton, and flax had to be *spun* and *woven*. All of these functions were carried out on the farm and the *finished* products were sold from the farm, if they were sold at all. If these processing functions had *not* been performed on the farm we would have had a nation of nudists that starved to death the first year they were in the New World. Just as the processing and marketing activities were a part of the *farm* life in the days of George Washington, they are a part of today's *agriculture*.

Farming is only a *part* of agriculture. In fact, there are more agricultural jobs *off* the farm than there are on the farm. About $1\frac{1}{3}$ workers are involved in farm supply for every worker engaged directly in farming. And more than two workers are involved in agricultural processing for every farm worker.

The U.S. Department of Agriculture definition of agriculture recognizes the extreme interdependence of the agricultural provisioning, producing, processing, marketing and consuming functions. The farm supply businesses that provide farm inputs such as fuel and machinery have replaced the on-farm activities of raising horses and mules and the feed for these animals. Chemical fertilizers have to a large degree replaced manure as the source of supplemental plant nutrients. These activities are as much a part of today's agriculture as were the horses and mules in the agriculture of yesteryear. The farm wife of 1900 skimmed the cream and made butter for sale in the local grocery store. The dairy manufacturing plant performing this function today has replaced the farm wife—who was unquestionably an integral part of farming. By the same token, the dairy processing plant cannot be separated from the farm industry of dairy production.

To say that farming is agriculture is the same as saying that the Corn Belt is the United States. Folks from the South and West would immediately disagree with Midwesterners, and people engaged in agricultural supply and processing *should* disagree with farmers. The welfare of farmers and the welfare of the rest of agriculture *cannot* be separated. While these segments do have some conflicting interests, they are still dependent on one another. The failure of the various segments to work together for the good of the entire industry is one reason for the inability of the agricultural sector to achieve the returns on investment that are considered minimal in other segments of the economy.

We will examine some of the changes that have occurred in American agriculture and in the farm phase of agriculture in Chapter 7. But it should be apparent that no industry, nor any segment of that industry, can be an economic island. The changes we have observed in agriculture are *not* independent of changes that occur throughout society, and cannot be completely separated. However, just as we constructed an economic model of the entire economy for purposes of discovering the relationships that define what made the entire economy tick, so can we construct an economic model of the agricultural economy for purposes of defining the setting of agriculture within the entire economy.

There can be no question that the farming sector of agriculture is the focal point for all of agriculture. Fertilizer companies depend almost exclusively on this sector for a market, and the agricultural processing industries such as meat packers must depend on the farm sector as a source of raw material supply. Even though farmers are less numerous than at any time in history, more off-farm jobs depend on farming than ever before.

The Pattern of Economic Development   •   When we examine the development of an economy, we generally can use adjustments in the three sectors of employment as a measure of that development. The first level of industrial development is the emergence of *primary* industries. Primary industries—

farming, forestry, fishing and mining—can exist in many cases where other industries cannot. Thus, when new areas have been opened, the first development has historically tended to be of an *extractive* nature; the raw materials are extracted from the area to be processed in other areas.

Farming, however, has become a special type of primary industry. It is true that, in times past, farmers have "mined" the soil. That is, the farmer attempted to use the land for production without investing any of the returns in maintaining the quality of the soil. When the soil was worn out, he simply moved west to new lands, leaving the mined and worn-out soil to the mercy of the elements. After World War I, there was no new land to which farmers could move. The available land was almost all tied up under some form of agricultural activity. Rather than moving to new land after the available nutrients had been extracted, farmers began to make a conscious effort to *maintain* and *improve* soil fertility. Agencies such as the Soil Conservation Service and the Bureau of Reclamation were established to aid in this effort.

Rather than being an extractive industry, the farming of today is a *generative* industry: Rather than depleting the soil resources by mining the land, today's farmer generates *better* soil resources through improved land management and scientific cropping and fertilization practices. In this fashion, each acre becomes *more* productive rather than less productive as it is farmed year after year. The agriculturally-related industry of forestry is in the process of adjusting from an extractive to a generative industry as scientific forest management practices of reseeding and selective logging are introduced on an ever broadening scale. Fishing and mining (including oil drilling) are still extractive, but there are some indications that the fishing industry will begin to exercise better harvesting practices in the future, thus ensuring that the sea will provide an even more abundant supply of food in the world of tomorrow. While the mining industries are not likely to outgrow their extractive stages (how does one "create" iron ore, petroleum, coal or copper desposits?), the further development of nuclear, solar or wind energy may relieve some of the drain on many of our mineral resources.

After the primary industries have been firmly established in an area, the second stage of development is possible. The *secondary* industries—generally the manufacturing and construction industries—which depend on the primary industries for raw materials and in many cases for markets begin to move in. Thus, a petroleum refinery would be dependent on, or secondary to, the primary industry of oil drilling for raw materials. That refinery would also depend to a large degree on the primary industry of farming for a market. A meat packing plant or cotton spinning mill would be secondary to or dependent on the primary industry of farming.

As secondary industries becomes established and as both primary and secondary industries begin to specialize to a greater and greater degree, *tertiary* or third stage types of industries begin to spring up. People employed in the tertiary industries service the needs of the other two employment sectors as well as many of the needs of the total economy.

So we have primary, secondary, and tertiary industries. So what? What difference does it make that farming is a primary industry? The point is that the primary industries provide the *basis* for all economic activity. It is from this concept that the term *basic industry* is derived. All other industries rest upon the foundation of basic or primary industries.

Figure 6.1 illustrates the pyramid type of growth that we have typically observed. The foundation of basic industries supports the pyramid of secondary and tertiary industries. It is true that the growth in the secondary and tertiary employment sectors may outrun the growth in the primary industries. When this happens the economy may continue to function, but there can be no question that a point of obvious weakness exists in that economy.

What might we expect to happen if tomorrow our economy should be deprived of the basic industry of farming? Less than 5 percent of our employment is involved in farming, so assuming that we could buy food from other countries, it might appear that we wouldn't be too badly hurt. But a moment of serious thought will expose the fallacy of this idea. A large portion of the foundation for our economy would be gone (Figure 6.2). Our high speed, modern economy would suddenly begin to operate as if it had square wheels. It would be so badly out of balance that at least a third of the employment in the secondary and tertiary industries would disappear. If this employment were to disappear, the people once employed in these activities would be unable to buy the goods produced in other segments and we could lose as much as a third to half the employment in these other non-agricultural industries. In short, our economy would virtually cease to operate. We could

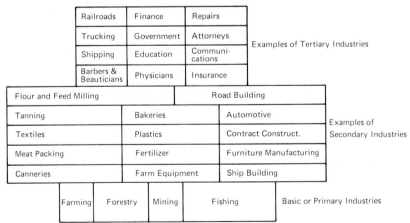

Figure 6.1   Secondary and tertiary industrial development rests on a foundation of primary industries.

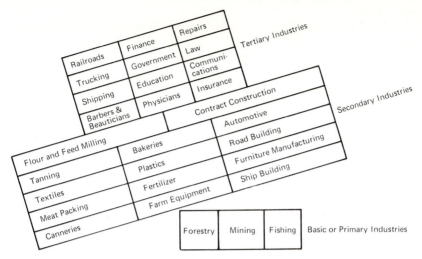

Figure 6.2 Loss or impairment of a primary industry throws the entire economy out of balance.

give up the basic industry of fishing with fairly minor overall consequences (even though local economic disturbances might be very severe). The loss of the basic industry of forestry would necessitate some major readjustments. Farming could make up most of the loss from fishing, and farming and mining together could absorb some of the loss from forestry. But nothing could replace either farming or mining.

Obviously, we are not suggesting that *any* basic industry should be given up. Each of the primary industries contributes heavily to our general economic welfare. But the point is that the soil and the products that are derived from tillage of the soil are fundamental to our very existence. The secondary and tertiary agricultural industries that depend on farming are a healthy chunk of our general economy and must be kept healthy by way of a strong farm economy. Our farm economy has maintained its strength to this point through technological development and internal adjustment to that technology. The development of labor-saving capital equipment has reduced the need for farm labor, and many people have adjusted *out* of farming into new occupations created by the developments in technical efficiency. With these developments have come the phenomena of *specialization* and *commercial farming*. The growth in commercial farming has separated the producers of food and fiber from the urban users of these products, hence creating a need for a marketing system to serve as a middleman between the two groups.

The problems of *any* marketing system—and particularly a marketing system that is concerned with the products of agriculture—are problems of location, form, and timing of both production and consumption. Differences in *locations* of production and consumption require that products be *trans-*

ported. Differences in *form* in which products originate and the form in which they are consumed require that they be *processed.* Differences in *timing* of production and consumption require that products be *stored.* Thus, the functions of the marketing systems—that mysterious region between production and consumption—are to get products to consumers *when* they are needed, *where* they are needed and *in the form* that is required, at *prices* that consumers can afford to pay.

If the basic problems that face every economy are *what, how,* and *for whom* to produce, the problems that face every marketing system are *when, where,* and *in what form* is the production of the entire economy to be produced and consumed. These *when, where* and *in what form* questions are not nearly so simple as they may appear. For example, wheat is produced primarily in the Great Plains, and is harvested as grain in the June through August period. Yet consumers need wheat in the form of *bread* in all parts of the nation at all times of the year. The storage of wheat is not a great problem, but in the absence of some agency that says, "We will release this much and no more wheat for processing into flour to be made into bread in August," how does the marketing system operate to insure that there will be an adequate supply of bread the year 'round?

Another problem is that wheat can be made into bread, it can be made into breakfast cereal, or it can be used as animal feeds to produce bacon, eggs and beef. How does the market system work to determine whether we eat our wheat in the form of bread, breakfast cereal, bacon, or beef?

A third problem is that New York City alone has about as many people as the entire Wheat Belt. Yet Kansas, with less than two million people, produces large volumes of wheat, while New York City produces none. Does this mean that Kansans eat a great deal of wheat bread while New Yorkers eat none? Obviously not. But how does the market system determine that people in New York as well as those in the Great Plains can eat wheat bread?

In order to approach an answer to our question of *how* the market system gets products from regions of production to regions of consumption, we need to take a look at exactly *what* the market system is and what it does. In 1976, there were about 2.8 million farms in the United States. These 2.8 million farms were the origin of the food and fiber that went into the mouths and onto the backs of about 215 million American consumers. The marketing system was the vehicle that served to transfer these food and fiber products from one group to the other.

The Functions of the Agricultural Marketing System   •   In getting products *where* they are needed, *when* they are needed, and in the *proper form,* the marketing system becomes involved in three types of functions. First, it is necessary to *concentrate* or *assemble* the basic agricultural products from all the 2.8 million farms that produce food and fiber for sale. Some examples of the businesses that are involved in the concentration activities are stockyards, grain elevators and cotton gins. There are about 15,000 of these businesses that are involved in assembling or concentrating products for purposes of moving them efficiently from the points of production to the points of consumption.

Once the products are assembled, it becomes necessary to *equalize* them. This equalization process involves sorting, grading, processing, packaging, and other activities that develop uniformity and consistency of product. The equalizing activities are designed to improve the ease of product handling, and generally increase their attractiveness to consumers. The equalizing activities may be, and often are, performed at a number of points throughout the marketing chain. A cotton gin, for example, will perform some processing activities after the seed cotton has been assembled and before the cotton lint is shipped to a cotton spinning mill and the cotton seed to a crusher for purposes of further processing into cottonseed oil and cottonseed meal.

There are about 30,000 firms that are involved primarily in the processing of agricultural products. Other equalizing activities are performed by the 32,000 food wholesalers and the 325,000 retail food stores. Some examples of businesses that are engaged in equalizing agricultural products might be meat packing, dairy processing, feed and flour milling operations. Further equalization occurs in the retail food store when the butcher breaks the beef carcass into the various cuts.

Equalization and concentration transform farm products into a condition and position such that they can be efficiently moved to the various locations in which they are most desired. This process of moving products forward to the consumer—that is, the step of *dispersion* of products—is the third type of activity involved in the marketing process. The transportation agencies that transfer products from one region to another during and after the equalizing process are all a part of the dispersion part of marketing. These agencies are the ones that distribute the products not only among the millions of domestic American consumers, but also among the millions of consumers in other parts of the world that are served through our export markets.

All right, we have some idea of what our marketing system *is* and what it does. But we have yet to answer the more fundamental questions of how the decisions are made as to whether we eat our wheat in the form of bread, breakfast cereal, bacon, or beef. Our definition of the problems of any marketing system gives a clue to the answers to these questions. That definition was that the problems of the marketing system are to get products to the consumer *where* they are needed, *when* they are needed, and in the *form required,* at *a price the consumer can afford to pay.* Thus, the factor of *price* must be something more than merely an unpleasant barrier to our securing all of the things in life that our little hearts may desire.

What is this factor of price? What is this unpleasant little five-letter word that bars us from many of the luxuries of life? Most of us have ingested prodigious quantities of soap as the result of having uttered four-letter words, but *price,* the dirtiest word of all, never raised an eyebrow in polite circles.

We pay a price for everything we have and everything we do. If one has an evening to spend and the alternative of going either to the movies or a ball game, the "price" of going to the movies is the cost of the tickets plus the pleasure you forego by *not* going to the ball game. That is, the cost of having chosen any activity involves the pleasure, satisfaction or *utility* that must be given up when you choose one alternative over another.

In our capitalistic society, we do not have a central planning agency that regulates every phase of economic activity. Our economy, as we have suggested, is regulated through the market system by way of prices. Those goods and services that are deemed highly desirable, and the resources that produce those goods and services, will be priced higher than will the less desirable items and the resources that produce them. Since the owners of resources are committed to maximizing profits they will transfer resources into the highest-paying alternative. In this fashion, the economic decisions made on the basis of market prices are the regulative force in our economy.

Profit has two sides; costs of production and prices received for the product. The primary function of the manager of any business is to make the decisions that permit the business to earn a profit. Price forecasting is a prerequisite to these decisions. Unless a manager has some idea of how much he will pay for the resources he uses and the price he can expect to receive for his product, on what basis can he make his managerial decisions? How can he *plan* for expanding the size of his business and reaping even greater profits in the future?

Price analysis is a major area of study in agricultural economics. This is the portion of agricultural economics that defines the forces that provide the basis for price formation. It also provides the basis for price forecasting. An interdependent economy composed of highly specialized economic units will be heavily dependent on the efficient performance of the market system and of the price mechanism. The history of the economic development of American agriculture in Chapter 7 provides some insight as to the importance of the exchange economy to the overall increases in economic efficiency.

7

The Economic History of American Agriculture

We've taken a hurried look at the American economy and at the procedure that is commonly used to measure its performance. We have suggested that the agricultural sector is of central importance in the total economic situation, accounting for about 30 percent of the value of the products that go into the satisfaction of consumer demand. In addition, substantial portions of investment demand come not only from farming but also from the agriculturally-dependent farm supply and agricultural-processing portions of the business sector. The share of government receipts that come from farming and its ancillary activities is widely disproportionate to the number of people directly engaged in the production of food and fiber.

So far, our examination of the economic role of agriculture has been entirely superficial. We have examined the role of agriculture only in the grossest of terms for purposes of orienting our discussion of the general economy. Now, let's narrow the scope of our discussion and focus more directly on the basis for human existence and economic progress.

The phrase *"The basis for human existence and economic progress"* is a pretty presumptuous name to use for the industry that many people look upon as the humblest of professions. Agricultural people are often portrayed as the crudest and most brutish segment of society. Farm people are the butt of many jokes and much derision. If agriculture and its people are held in such low esteem by the larger segments of our society (unfortunately, farm people all too often share this low opinion of themselves), what do we mean referring to agriculture as the "basis for human existence and progress"? Will Rogers gave us the clue when he said, "Lots of folks who ain't saying ain't, ain't eating!!"

Contrary to popular belief, farming and ranching are *not* humble professions nor is the agricultural industry a humble industry. Agriculture by

TABLE 7.1

PRODUCTIVITY OF THE AMERICAN FARM WORKER,
1949–1975

YEAR	TOTAL U.S. POPULATION (MILLIONS)	TOTAL FARM EMPLOYMENT (MILLIONS)	PERSONS SUPPLIED PER FARM WORKER		
			At Home	Abroad	Total
1949	149	10.0	—	—	14.9
1950	152	9.9	—	—	15.5
1951	154	9.5	—	—	15.8
1952	157	9.1	—	—	16.4
1953	159	8.9	—	—	17.2
1954	162	8.7	—	—	18.1
1955	165	8.4	—	—	19.5
1956	170	7.9	—	—	21.7
1957	171	7.6	—	—	22.8
1958	174	7.5	—	—	23.2
1959	177	7.3	21.4	3.1	24.5
1960	180	7.1	22.3	3.5	25.8
1961	183	6.9	23.6	4.0	27.6
1962	186	6.7	24.7	3.9	28.6
1963	189	6.5	25.8	4.9	30.7
1964	191	6.1	27.9	5.3	33.2
1965	194	5.6	30.8	6.2	37.0
1966	196	5.1	33.6	6.0	39.6
1967	198	4.9	36.0	6.1	42.1
1968	200	4.7	37.9	5.5	43.4
1969	202	4.6	39.0	6.1	45.1
1970	204	4.5	39.9	7.2	47.1
1971	206	4.4	41.7	7.5	49.2
1972	208	4.4	42.0	10.4	52.4
1973	210	4.3	48.5[2]	—[1]	—[1]
1974	213	4.4	48.3[2]	—[1]	—[1]
1975	214	4.4	49.0[2]	—[1]	—[1]

Source: *Agricultural Statistics, 1973*, U.S. Department of Agriculture, Washington, D.C.

[1] Not available; series discontinued.

[2] Estimated from total population and farm employment.

any measure other than profits represents the largest single industry in the United States. The farming portion alone is larger than any other industry. Thirteen percent of our 1968 stock of national wealth was tied up in farm real estate, farm inventories, and farm equipment. Yet less than ten percent of our population was on farms.

In the terms of many economic analysts, any industry that shows a declining employment is a sick industry. By this criterion, farming is inevitably, inherently, and invariably a "sick" industry in a growing and developing economy. Farming is the economic sector from which resources *must* be released if economic progress is to occur. As we saw earlier, the major portion of the population tends to be engaged in the production of food in an underdeveloped society. As the nation escapes from this starvation threshold, capital equipment will be substituted for labor, and people can begin to move out of farming into other activities that will produce some of the non-essential or luxury items.

Farm employment has declined in the United States for the past sixty years, but the efficiency of the American farmer has increased phenomenally (Table 7.1). In fact, since 1959—within the lifetime of virtually all of today's college students—the efficiency and productivity of farm labor has more than doubled. In 1959, the American farm worker produced enough to provide food and fiber for 24.5 people. In 1975, this rate of production supplied 49 people in the United States and an undetermined number abroad (Table 7.1). With our national commitment to supply food to other nations, and with the continuing rush of technological development, it is probable that the productivity of the American farm worker will continue to expand.

In order to grasp the importance of agriculture within the general economy, let's follow agriculture through the pages of history and see what has happened. The fundamental nature of agriculture cannot be questioned. *All* people must eat in order to exist. There are only two places that food can be produced; the earth and the sea. The American people have never eaten much fish; therefore, the source of the food that has permitted human existence and progress in America has been the soil.

For centuries, the most pressing problems of agriculture were problems of producing enough food and fiber to feed and clothe the farm family adequately. Most families were farm families—in 1790, during George Washington's second term as president, 95 of every 100 Americans lived on farms. These farm families produced almost every food item used at home. The farm wife manufactured her family's clothing from home grown wool and flax, and household furniture was made with hand tools in the farm shop.

About two hundred years ago, the invention of the spinning jenny (1767) in England suggested that a better life was yet to come. As the spinning jenny began to be used widely, the housewife was replaced as the spinner of wool. The English invention of the power loom in 1785 replaced her as the weaver of cloth, and by the early 1800s, large numbers of people moved from the land into urban areas for the jobs created by these machines.

During this period America was still largely agricultural, and until the mid-1800s many American farm products were shipped to England for processing. The American invention of the cotton gin had made cotton king in the southern states, but the ginned cotton was processed almost exclusively in English and French textile mills until the first textile mills were constructed in Massachusetts in the 1820s. The development of the railroads during the 1820s, 1830s, and 1840s enabled farmers to ship their products to more distant markets. The invention of the mowing machine and reaper in the 1830s released much farm labor from the chores of harvesting, and enabled one man to handle larger acreages of grain.

The development of the Colt Revolver during the 1830s not only enabled men to kill each other with much greater efficiency; it also allowed them to begin to expand American agriculture into the savage regions west of the Appalachian Chain and beyond. By 1850, enough of the labor-saving inventions were in general use that 15 percent of all Americans lived in cities and towns.

The three decades between 1850 and 1880 were a period of political, economic, and technological turmoil. The nation was torn with fratricidal strife, and the economic and political readjustments that followed the War Between the States created some very real hardships in many areas.

It has often been said that necessity is the mother of invention. Necessity must have been enormous during the 1850–1880 period. Our population more than doubled, and the number of people living in towns almost quadrupled. This meant that the farm labor force had to produce more efficiently in order to supply the tremendously increased urban population. The invention of the Mason jar helped to ensure an adequate year-around food supply, since garden products could be canned and stored against the needs of the long winter months. Steel was developed, and many iron farm implements and iron tools were replaced with the superior metal. The corn planter and grain drill improved the efficiency of crop planting.

It was also during the 1850–1880 period that westward expansion really got underway. The development of the repeating rifle enabled the pioneers to subdue the fierce Plains Indians. The Osage, the Cheyenne, and the Sioux were finally beaten; not by the Army, but by the buffalo. The Winchester rifle enabled men like William Cody to slaughter untold thousands of the beasts on which the Plains Indians depended for food, clothing and shelter.

The development of the refrigerated railway car permitted perishable products such as meats to be shipped for long distances, and this along with the development of barbed wire permitted crop farming to develop side by side with the cattle industry in the Great Plains. The gang plow and springtooth harrow were developed and used in the small grain production of the nation's breadbasket. The invention of the cream separator increased the efficiency of dairy farming and encouraged the production of butter and cheese in areas that were remote from the large central markets.

In the 1870s the first glimmer of real mechanization in agriculture was seen. The invention of the gasoline engine and the gasoline carburetor were the first steps toward replacing oxen, horses, and mules as the source of farm power. The establishment of the Land Grant College System in the 1860s was to form the basis for many improved crop varieties that were to increase farm productivity three-quarters of a century later.

During the period from 1880 to 1910, our population almost doubled again, and by 1910 almost half of all Americans lived in cities and towns. The lister plow, corn binder, disk harrow, and corn picker were all developed during this period, and the first gasoline-powered tractor was developed in 1905. The horse-drawn combine was used during the 1880s in California and Washington, and required 40 horses for power. This machine would cut a little more grain each day than was required to feed the horses that propelled it.

The decade from 1910 to 1920 included both the "golden age of agriculture" and World War I. The "golden age" (1910–1914) was the period in which farm prices as related to farm costs were the greatest in history, and it is this period that is often used as a benchmark by farm organizations when trying for higher farm price supports. During this period, the technology that had been developed was improved and widely adopted. By 1920, only 30 percent of our population was living on farms. Part of the relative decline in farm population during the 1910–1920 period is due to a change in the census definition of farm population, recognizing the emergence of an "agri-business" sector. A rural non-farm category was introduced in 1920 to account for those people who lived in rural areas and secured their livelihoods from other than farm sources.

During the 1920s a tractor-drawn combine was developed, thus further reducing the labor required for the harvest of small grains. Much of the horsepower used in farming was replaced with tractors during this period. This change released substantial acreages of land that could not be used to produce crops for *human* rather than animal needs.

By 1930, 75 percent of our population was living in urban areas. During the 1930s, hybrid corn and rust resistant wheat were developed and released through the land grant college system. These crops made each acre of land much more productive, but very few people moved from the farm. The reason was that the Great Depression of the 1930s limited opportunity to the point where there were no off-farm jobs to which youth could go. But World War II and the period of prosperity that followed provided ample opportunity. By 1950, only 17 percent of our population was farm population.

During the late 1940s and the 1950s, the investment that had been made in the land grant college system beginning in 1861 began to pay huge dividends. Agricultural research had developed crop varieties that were well adapted to specific climatic, topographic and soil conditions. We had learned a great deal more about the world in which we lived, and soil deficiencies in plant nutrients were corrected through the scientific use of chemically-produced fertilizers. Research in animal nutrition more than doubled the feed efficiency of poultry, and greatly reduced the feed requirements for all simple-stomached animals. Personnel trained in these Land Grant Colleges developed such mechanical devices as the cotton picker, the self-propelled combine, and the bulk fertilizer spreader. Farm labor requirements were further reduced by the development of pre-emergent herbicides that eliminated much of the labor formerly used for weed control.

By 1960, only 9 percent of our population resided on farms and ranches. But the rush of technology continued. Hybrid grain sorghum released in the mid-1960s increased grain sorghum yields by as much as 100 percent. Mechanical devices for harvesting the "stoop labor" crops of melons and certain fruits and vegetables were developed. The relative movement of people from farm into non-farm activities continued. By 1970, only 4.8 percent of our people were on the farm, and in 1975, only 4.2 percent.

Now why is all of this important? Is the inevitability of increasing farm productivity just common sense, or is it nonsense? As nations go, the United States is at the most a teenager. And yet this pimply-faced adolescent among nations has made phenomenal progress. Egypt, for example, has existed as a nation for thousands of years. And yet, the Egyptian economy is in about the same state as the United States was in 1875—a mere 100 years after the signing of the Declaration of Independence. The reason for this is, of course, the wealth of natural resources present on the North American continent and the quality of the human resources that came to develop what nature provided. Table 7.2 shows the pattern of growth in American agriculture.

In 1790, the economy of the United States was extremely primitive, being at about the same level as that of the newly emergent African nations of today. But as machinery was adopted in farming, large numbers of people were able to leave the land and engage in the production of items other than food and clothing. These developments created an entirely new economic structure. Rather than processing farm products at home, we have centralized these functions in a few strategic locations. Rather than having an economy in which each unit can produce most of its own needs and thus stand alone, we now have a highly complex economic system that is based on selling the output of specialized economic units (wheat farms, dairy farms, cattle ranches, meat packing plants, flour mills, etc.) and exchange of the money derived from these sales for the necessities and luxuries of life.

The development of the exchange economy has created all sorts of changes throughout our society. The actual production of farm products involves less than five of every hundred American workers. But an estimated additional 30 to 35 workers are directly dependent upon farm production for their livelihoods. These are the people who manufacture and sell farm machinery, fertilizer, and fuel, and the people who butcher the hogs, mill the flour, and spin the cotton.

The changes in the residences of our population that have been associated with the development of the exchange economy have brought tremendous changes in the political face of America. At the beginning of World War II, a quarter of our people were farm people. The size of the farm vote was a potent factor that had to be faced in the Congress. And to almost every congressman and senator, the political wrath of farmers was one and the same as the political wrath of God. The interests of agriculture were almost identical with the interests of the nation.

Since World War II, the size of the farm vote has declined not only relatively, but also absolutely. As late as 1940, almost a fourth of the vote was in the hands of farmers. And since rural people have always taken their voting responsibility seriously, a much better voting percentage was observed in the rural areas, thus making the power of the farm vote a factor with which to be reckoned. Even in 1950, almost a fifth of the votes were farm votes.

In the mid-1970s farmers and ranchers were outnumbered by other voters in a ratio of 23 to one. Thus, the group that influenced the American political scene so profoundly for so long had become buried in a sea of humanity. The American farmer produced himself into a position of political weakness. The agricultural production efficiency that has enabled the United States to achieve the world's highest standard of living has weakened the political power of those who created the major portion of that efficiency.

It must be accepted that the political muscle of agriculture is a thing of the past. But despite low farm profits, the economic muscle of the agriculturalist is stronger than ever in history. There were 50 Americans dependent on each farm worker for food in 1975. Of those 50 who were dependent for food, about 22 were in the working age groups. Almost a third of these depended on that farm worker for employment. It is in the area of economic efficiency that agriculture must concentrate if any of the problems faced by today's agriculture are to be solved.

The problems of agriculture were once problems of producing enough for home consumption. But the overriding problems of agriculture today are those of processing and distributing farm output, securing and financing the resources that go into production, combining those resources in a fashion that minimizes production costs, and marketing products in the place and form and at the time that will yield top returns. These problems are all economic in

TABLE 7.2

U.S. POPULATION, SELECTED YEARS, 1790–1975
By Place of Residence as Related to Selected Agriculturally
Important Events and Inventions

		U.S. POPULATION			
YEAR	INVENTION OR EVENT	Total (Mil.)	Farm (%)	Non-Farm (%)	Ratio of Farm:Non-Farm
1790		3.9	95	5	18.5:1.0
1791	Cotton gin, cast iron plow, steamboat, standard walking plow, Erie Canal				
1820		9.6	93	7	12.7:1.0
1821	Matches, railroad, mowing machine, reaper, six gun, telegraph, sewing machine, safety pin				
1850		23.2	85	15	5.6:1.0
1851	Evaporated milk, mason jars, steel, corn, drill Winchester rifle, oleo-margarine, refrigerated rail-road car, land grant college system, gasoline engine, gasoline carburetor, telephone, barbed wire, cream separator, cash register, gang plow, springtooth harrow				
1880		50.2	72	28	2.6:1.0
1881	Lister plow, horse-drawn com-bine, corn binder, disk harrow, gasoline tractor, corn picker				
1910		92.4	54	46	1.2:1.0
1911	Golden Age of Agriculture, World War I, tractor-drawn combine, introduction of hybrid corn and rust resistant wheat				
1940		132.1	23	77	1.0:3.3
1941–49	World War II, beginning of the "Cold War"				

1950		151.7	17	83	1.0:4.9
1950–59	Self-propelled combine, food freezers, mechanical cotton pickers, use of herbicides, bulk fertilizer spreaders, Sputnik 1, beginning of the Space Age			
1960		179.9	9	91	1.0:10.1
1960–69	Introduction of hybrid grain sorghum, U.S. space program, machinery for harvesting "stoop labor" crops			
1970		203.2	4.8	95.2	1.0:20.0
1971–75	Man on the moon, diplomatic recognition of Red China, expanded world markets for U.S. farm products, withdrawal of agricultural chemicals due to EPA bans, four-wheel-drive tractors introduced, energy crisis			
1975		212.8	4.2	95.8	1.0:22.8

nature and crucial in importance. These are the problems that the agricultural economist is uniquely equipped to solve. The long suit of agricultural economics, then, is *management*.

The managerial jobs open to the individual who is trained in agricultural economics are by no means restricted to the management of farm production units. The changing nature of agriculture has broadened the field of opportunity available to those with agricultural backgrounds. The agricultural marketing firms that were discussed in Chapter 6 are eager to employ those who understand the basic economic relationships that regulate the agricultural industry. The agricultural marketing firms—which employed more than 10 million Americans in 1970—are of the secondary and tertiary types that rest upon the foundation of the basic industry of farming. Employment opportunities with these marketing agencies are increasing rapidly and are expected to continue to increase. Since these firms are agriculturally dependent, the term *agribusiness* has been coined to describe them.

The agriculturally-dependent businesses are not limited to the agricultural marketing activities. About seven million American workers were employed in the farm supply industries in 1970. Some examples of the agribusinesses that supply goods and services to agricultural production units include feed, fertilizer, and seed dealers, farm equipment manufacturers and dealers, hatcheries, banks, drug firms, and the like. As in the case of the agricultural marketing firms, the personnel needs of the agribusinesses that provide supplies to production units are increasing rapidly. Because of the increasing scale of the average farm operation, more and more of the production activities will be customized and performed by individuals who specialize in these activities. Grain combining, hay baling, farm accounting, and tax management are examples of activities that are already dominated by custom operators. Also, more and more of the resources that are used in farm production are coming from off-farm sources. This means that we can expect still greater increases in employment in the farm supply types of agribusiness.

The economic history of American agriculture shows that this industry has become more and more business-oriented over the centuries of its existence. Solving many of the scientific problems of agricultural production over the years allowed all Americans to escape the threat of genuine food shortages. But solving these problems of production by way of technological improvement, specialization, and division of labor increased the interdependence between agriculture and other economic sectors. If agriculture sneezes, the rest of the economy gets pneumonia. But a mild digestive upset in the rest of the economy may frequently give agriculture amoebic dysentery. Thus the role of economic analysis in today's agriculture is of crucial and expanding importance. Chapter 8 examines the scope and nature of agricultural economics.

8

The Nature and Scope of Agricultural Economics

We saw in Chapter 7 how American agriculture originated as a system in which the self-sufficient, generalized types of farming units produced, processed, and consumed essentially finished products. Under this system, farm population greatly outnumbered urban population. Because non-farm people were interspersed with the farm population, the sales of farm products to non-farm customers could be accomplished through direct transactions. However, this system was also associated with rather severe limitations on the volume of production that was possible. With increasing numbers of people, increases in the volume of agricultural production were essential. Thus, we saw the beginnings of mechanization, urbanization and the division of labor. Today, agricultural production is widely separated from the centers of heavy urban consumption. This has created the need for the agricultural marketing system that transforms raw farm products into consumer goods and transfers them from points of production to points of consumption. These developments have created a broad array of changes in the locations at which various activities occur. The changes in the location at which the production and marketing functions are performed have in turn made it essential that all those people involved in the management of all the businesses in the production and marketing chain have an intimate acquaintance with the principles of agricultural economics.

In Chapter 1, we defined agricultural economics as *the science of allocating scarce resources among those uses associated with producing, processing, and consuming the products of farms and ranches.* We have traced the development of American agriculture and have seen that technical progress and related social changes have brought some sweeping changes in the agricultural industry. These changes have created new career opportunities and new responsibilities in the manner in which resources are allocated

Almost all of these new opportunities and responsibilities are in the business management area, so we might define agricultural economics to be the *business end of agriculture.* Such a definition would be absolutely correct. However, some further general discussion of what is involved in attending the "business end" of agriculture might improve our understanding of just what is involved in this field of agricultural economics.

Any agricultural enterprise in this day and age is a *business.* Farming and ranching are no longer a way of life, they are businesses just as surely as flour milling, meat packing, oil refining, or food merchandising. The affairs of all of these firms must be conducted in a businesslike fashion if they are to survive. The primary function of any business is to earn a profit. Profits are the difference between gross receipts (or sales) and costs. Thus, we can maximize profits by *minimizing* costs for producing some specified *output,* or by *maximizing output* from some specified *input.*

Four key ideas in economics have just been introduced: *maximize, minimize, input,* and *output.*

What do we mean by input? *Inputs* are the resources used in the process of production—that is, the land, labor, capital and management of Chapters 2 and 3. They may be measured in terms of physical units, in terms of costs, or in both terms. These items represent the *cost* side of the profit coin.

Output represents the sales side of the profit coin. This is the term used to describe the actual *production* of a business enterprise. Output may be either goods or services and may also be measured either in terms of physical units or dollars.

When we speak of *minimizing,* the idea is to reduce the quantity in question to the smallest possible amount. For example, if a student decides to earn an A in a course in agricultural economics, he wants to keep the time spent to the smallest possible amount that will still guarantee the A. Or, he can *maximize* his grade with a given time investment by using his time most efficiently. He *cannot* minimize and maximize at the same time. The minimum time investment, for example, would be zero. However, this almost surely would not earn the maximum grade. Minimizing and maximizing are the ends of the same two-headed snake. Unless at least one end of that snake is nailed down, there is no way one can safely operate on the other. If both ends are loose and wiggling, a bad case of snakebite is almost a certainty. *Minimization* and *maximization* are two of the most important ideas involved in the economizing process. One generally maximizes *returns* (or profits) or minimizes *costs.* This procedure is commonly called the *minimax* approach to economics.

All right, we have decided that agricultural economics is concerned with economizing through the minimax procedure. But this same concern is shared with the general economist. What makes agricultural economics different? We can find a clue to the answer to this question if we examine some of the problems to be solved.

Let's consider a problem that is typically faced by a farm businessman. Let's imagine that a combine that can be "programmed" to cut a field of wheat without an operator has been developed. The manufacturer says that this machine will reduce the cost of harvesting wheat by 8 cents per bushel. Let's assume that for some reason the farmer cannot *hire* a custom operator nor can he *become* a custom operator. In other words, he *must* harvest his own crop and *only* his own crop. Should our farmer friend purchase the new programmed combine?

If we believe the manufacturer's claim of a per-bushel cost reduction of 8 cents, we might be ahead to make the purchase. There is a decision to be made. Should we buy or should we not buy? How do we decide? Obviously, we need some more information.

What kind of information do we need if we are to advise this farmer adequately? Let's try these questions for openers:

1. How big an acreage (or volume) of wheat do we need before we can realize the cost reduction that the manufacturer claims can be achieved?

2. What volume of production do we currently have?

These questions are purely economic in nature. Figure 8.1 shows the average per bushel harvesting costs for using the new machine and for using a conventional combine. We discover that the volume at which an 8 cent per bushel savings is possible is 50,000 bushels. The average yield of wheat in the area is 25 bushels per acre, so this means our farm businessman would have to have 2,000 acres of wheat to achieve the per bushel savings of 8 cents. But suppose he only has 500 acres that produce 12,500 bushels each year. Should he buy the combine?

We still can't answer the question. We still need more information. What would be the cost of harvesting our 500 acres of wheat with a conventional combine as compared with the new machine? We discover that conventional equipment would cost 30.5 cents per bushel and the new machine would cost 32.5 cents. So for his volume of wheat, the farmer could not afford to purchase the new machine. If, however, he can discover some way to increase his volume of production, he may be able to use the new technology.

We read in some farm magazine that the agronomy department at the local state university is releasing a new crop variety that will increase yields by ten bushels per acre. The cost of the new seed is $3 more per acre than is the cost for standard seed. Thus, this new variety will increase our friend's

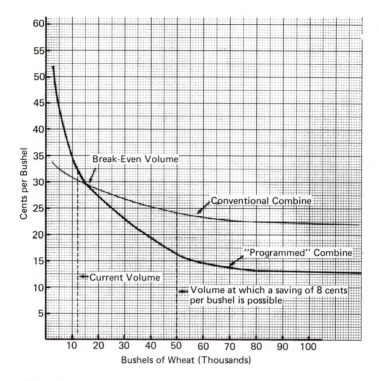

Figure 8.1 Comparison of costs per unit using alternative levels of machinery technology.

annual production to 17,500 bushels at a total added cost of $1,500. So we go back to our desk to re-examine our decision not to buy the new equipment. We discover that the harvest cost will now be 28.5 cents per bushel with the new machine and 29.5 cents with conventional equipment. Thus the purchase of the new combine would save 35 cents per acre or $175. Can he afford to take on a new investment for a saving of $175? Probably not. However, we also know that by increasing the fertilizer cost outlay by $12 per acre, we can increase the per-acre yield by an additional ten bushels. This cost includes the cost of application. Thus, the farmer will be harvesting 45 bushels of wheat per acre on 500 acres for a total volume of 22,500 bushels. Should he buy the new combine?

At 22,500 bushels of wheat per season, the new combine harvest cost is 25 cents per bushel compared with 28.25 cents for the conventional machine. We are saving 3.25 cents per bushel on harvest costs if we buy the new equipment. Thus, the expected annual increase in net income would be $731.25 for the total volume of output. The farmer could perhaps buy the · combine without reducing profits, and satisfy any desire he might have to "keep up with the Joneses." Also, if labor is generally short during the harvest period, he could afford to make the purchase purely for the sake of convenience. But the dollar and cents profitability of the change is so small that it would make very little difference which decision we made. The total profit would probably be changed very little.

Now let's imagine that the adjacent farm is for sale and that our farm businessman can get the money to buy it. The farm includes 300 acres of wheat land on which either the new variety of wheat or the heavier fertilization rate or both may be used. If our farmer buys this land, his pre-harvest costs per bushel will be reduced by 5 percent since existing equipment and labor can be utilized more efficiently. Should he buy both the land and the new combine? Should he plan to increase his fertilization rate?

The additional 300 acres of wheat will increase his total production to 28,000 bushels if he does not increase his rate of fertilization. This volume of production can be harvested at a cost of 27.25 cents per bushel conventionally and at a cost of 22.5 cents with a new electronic combine. Thus, he is getting into the volume of production where significant reductions in cost are possible. He is reducing his costs of harvest by almost 5 cents per bushel not only on the new land, but also on the land he presently operates. His net return would be increased by $1,330 annually if he used the new machine. He would therefore be wise to make the two purchases of land and new equipment at the same time.

As for the advisability of increasing the rate of fertilization, the increase in yield on the total 800 acres of wheat land would bring his total production to 36,000 bushels. This volume of production could be harvested conventionally at a cost of 26 cents per bushel and electronically at a cost of 19.5 cents. The increase in income that results from the additional fertilizer is about $16,500 but there is an additional $2,340 to be gained if he switches from conventional to programmed harvesting equipment.

Now let's review the analysis we have made (Table 8.1). Let's calculate the total profits our friend would have as he chose between the alternatives we have outlined. We can see that whether or not he chose to use the new electronically-programmed combine he would be smart to adopt the new variety of wheat and to use the heavier rate of fertilization. If he were to adopt the combine without making any other change, he would reduce his net return by $250. If he were to adopt the new variety, but not the heavier rate of fertilization, he would be making $175 more with the new combine than with conventional harvesting methods. The heavier fertilization rate would enable him to buy the new machine and to increase his income by $731.25, but the new combine doesn't really begin to pay until he has bought more land and has adopted both the new variety and the heavier rate of fertilization practice.

This example illustrates the type of problem with which agricultural

TABLE 8.1

EXAMPLES OF A FARM BUSINESS DECISION INVOLVING THE ADOPTION OF TECHNOLOGICAL PROGRESS

FARM SITUATION

ITEM	Initial	New Variety of Wheat Released	Additional Fertilizer & New Variety of Wheat	Additional Land & New Variety of Wheat; No Change in Fertilization	Additional Land, New Variety of Wheat & Additional Fertilizer
Acres of wheat	500	500	500	800	800
Yield/acre	25	35	45	35	45
Total bushels of wheat	12,500	17,500	22,500	28,000	36,000
Wheat price/bushel	$3.50	$3.50	$3.50	$3.50	$3.50
Total volume of sales	43,750.00	61,250.00	78,750.00	98,000.00	126,000.00
Pre-harvest cost:					
Per acre	60.00	63.00	75.00	59.85	71.85
Per bushel	2.40	1.80	1.56	1.71	1.60
Harvest cost per bushel					
Conventional machine	.305	.295	.2825	.2725	.260
Programmed machine	.325	.285	.250	.225	.195
Total cost per bushel					
Conventional harvest	2.705	2.095	1.8425	1.9825	1.860
Programmed harvest	2.725	2.085	1.8100	1.9350	1.795
Net return per bushel					
Conventional harvest	.7950	1.4050	1.6575	1.5175	1.6400
Programmed harvest	.7750	1.4150	1.6900	1.5650	1.7050
Total net return from wheat					
Conventional harvest	9,937.50	24,587.50	37,293.75	42,490.00	59,040.00
Programmed harvest	9,687.50	24,762.50	38,025.00	43,820.00	61,380.00
Difference in returns resulting from use of programmed combine	−$250	$175	$731.25	$1,330	$2,340

economists must deal. The basic scientific information provided by the technical agricultural sciences must be married to economic theory and sound business principles. The offspring of this union is agricultural economics. To demonstrate, let's review the fields of information that we drew on in order to reach our final decision.

First, we drew on work done by agricultural engineers and economists in cooperation in order to provide information concerning the per bushel costs of harvesting various volumes of grains with both conventional and electronically-programmed equipment. Using the economic criterion of profit maximization, we decided that it would be unwise to adopt the new machine. However, when we introduced the agronomic information concerning the productivity of a new variety and the soil science information of production response to fertilizer, we discovered that we could afford to adopt the new machine. Adding the economic principle concerning economies of size and growth and information from the area of finance, we discovered that we would be foolish *not* to adopt the new machine.

We drew upon these fields of information to make one economic decision in agriculture:

1. Economics,

2. Agronomy,

3. Soils Science,

4. Agricultural Engineering, and

5. Finance

In terms of the *input, output, minimize* and *maximize* concepts we discussed earlier, the agricultural economist must have worked with the agronomist and the soils scientist to get the input and output information for crop production. The engineer and the agricultural economist would have had to work together to define the cost functions for the two types of combines. Then the agricultural economist would have conducted the cost minimization or profit maximization analysis that would have determined the economic feasibility of adopting the new machine.

One point must be made clear. *No field in agriculture can stand alone.* The agricultural economist *must* have the advice of the technical scientists in order to define the input-output possibilities. The technical scientists *must* have the counsel of agricultural economists in order to determine the economic feasibility of technical practices. The animal or plant technician *must* be able to communicate with the economist, and the agricultural economist *must* know enough about technical agriculture to be able to ask the right questions and to frame answers in relevant terms.

How broad is this field of agricultural economics? With how many technical people must the aspiring economist be prepared to work? The field of agricultural economics is just as broad as the field of agriculture. The agricultural economist is concerned with and finds jobs in the *business* end of any industry that supplies the inputs used in agricultural production. This would include the oil industry, the fertilizer portions of the chemical industries, and the farm machinery portions of the automotive industry. Further, the agricultural economist is involved not only with actual farm production, but also with all of the industries that process, transport, or market products that originate on farms and ranches. In short, any time there is an economic problem that affects agriculture, the agricultural economist is automatically involved.

The Economic Functions of Agriculture • We have defined agricultural economics as the offspring of a marriage between the technical agricultural sciences and the social science of economics. The scope of agricultural economics includes all of the economic problems and situations that affect the processes of producing, processing, marketing, and consuming the products of farms and ranches.

The economic functions of agriculture have actually changed very little over the centuries, but the *locations* at which these functions are performed and the manner in which they are performed have changed a great deal. The functions of producing, processing, marketing, and distributing agricultural goods at one time were all centered on the farm. Today, the only one of these functions that is performed on the farm is that of actual production. The processing, marketing, and distributing activities are now specialized and centralized at strategic locations. A fifth function of agriculture—the resource-consuming function—is still farm-centered, but the type and form of resources has changed tremendously. In the past, most of the resources consumed on the farm were also produced on the farm. Today, more and more of these resources come from off-farm sources. Rather than oat-fueled horse power, we now use gas-powered tractors. Rather than organic fertilizers that came from animal manures, today we use chemical fertilizers that are by-products of the oil and chemical industries.

Let's take a systematic look at these economic functions and at some of the economic theory behind them. Obviously, the basic function of agriculture is that of production: the combining of the factors of production for the purpose of achieving some particular end result. It is this function that provides the basis for all other economic functions performed by agriculture.

The economic objective of most agricultural production is to achieve the maximum return from a given set of resources, or to reduce the resources needed to produce a given return to a minimum. In order for this objective to be achieved, the manager of a production unit must depend on the input-output information provided by technical research. The technical relationship between resource use (or the use of inputs) and the creation of products (outputs) is commonly called a *production function*. That is, resources are combined, and in this process they are *transformed* into some product different from the original inputs. (If we combine red and yellow pigments we *transform* them into an orange pigment.)

We'll learn more about production functions in the next chapter, but for the moment, think of a production function as being the information provided by the technical scientist. This is the sort of information produced by research concerning the production response to fertilizer or irrigation. The production function as such is *not* economics, although it does have economic implications and is basic to the theory of production economics. The physical production function raises an economic question when *prices* for inputs and outputs are introduced. It is at this point that *managers* can begin to use economic theory to make decisions about where to operate along a given production function, and about *which* production function to select for use in their productive effort. That is, managers can use economic theory based upon the physical production functions and price information in deciding *what* to produce and how to produce it.

Once the agricultural raw materials have been produced, the economic function of marketing must be fulfilled. As we discussed earlier, if the basic questions answered by all economies are *what, how* and *for whom* to produce, the basic questions facing the marketing systems within those economies are *when, where,* and *in what form* these products are to be provided.

The *form* of the product problem faced by the marketing system involves all of the processing activities. For example, who can use a hog as food in the form in which it comes from the farm? Obviously, it must first be *processed* in some fashion that will prevent its biting back when bitten. This means killing the hog, cleaning it, and chilling the carcass. But processing doesn't stop here. There is an economic decision to be made as to what parts of the carcass are to be sold as fresh pork and what parts should be further processed through curing and smoking. The shoulder can be sold as fresh pork or it can be cured and sold either as a smoked shoulder or as a picnic ham and a Boston butt. All of these decisions must be made daily by the processing firms engaged in meat packing.

How are these types of decisions made? Every hog has two hams, two shoulders, a loin, two sides of bacon, etc. How is a processor to decide whether to sell these as fresh items or as cured items? The meat scientist is concerned with formulating alternative methods for cutting up a pork carcass. But which of these methods is in the best interest of the pork processor?

When price information is combined with this technical data, the processor can begin to use economic analysis for purposes of making sound business decisions. If the value of a pork shoulder in the form of one Boston butt and one picnic ham exceeds the value of a fresh shoulder by more than the cost of converting the shoulder into these products, then obviously, the decision is in favor of further processing.

Now, the question of "in what form" seems to be a fairly simple problem to solve. But let's suppose that we are selling in both the Boston and Atlanta markets. Atlanta consumers prefer fresh pork shoulder, while Boston consumers prefer the picnic ham-Boston butt combination. This is reflected by the prices that they are willing to pay for these products. How, then, is a manager to go about deciding in what form he is to provide his product? Will he serve only one market, or will he attempt to sell in both? How is he to make this decision?

First of all, a demand curve for both types of product will be analyzed in both markets, and the price elasticity of demand will be estimated. We'll hear more about the demand curve and the price elasticity of demand in Chapters 10, 11, and 12, but for the moment we will define demand to be *the schedule of quantities that will be purchased in a given market at a given time at various prices, all other things being equal (ceteris paribus).* The price of elasticity of demand is simply an estimate of the consumer's *responsiveness* to a *price change.* You'll learn in Chapter 12 how to measure elasticity and more about the demand function and its use in determining the form in which production should be provided.

The question of *when* products should be provided is closely related to the question of *in what form.* Our processor friend not only has pork shoulders of which to dispose, but also pork bellies, the portion of the hog from which bacon is made. He needs to kill hogs the year around, since fresh pork chops are much in demand most of the year. But pork bellies are often stored as frozen "green" products, and then smoked and cured for sale at some later date. The Chicago Mercantile Exchange lists pork bellies as one of the commodities for futures trading. Should our processor friend cure and sell the bacon in the fall, or should he freeze and store bellies for sale at sometime in the future—say March of the next year?

Obviously, the answer to this question depends on whether bacon prices in March will be higher than fall prices by enough to pay the cost of storage and still earn a greater return than if the bacon were produced and sold immediately. How is the processor to *know* whether bacon prices will be higher in March than in October? Economic analysis can be used to *forecast* prices for some time in the future. We can find out how many pigs were born during the spring, and we can find out what size of fall crop is likely. We know from past experience that people demand and eat more bacon during cool weather than during hot weather. Using information of this sort, we can anticipate the price movements that are likely during the October–March period and help our processor friend plan his business on that basis.

In planning *where* we should market products, we can make both short-run and long-run decisions. In the long run, we want to be prepared to sell in the areas where population is growing rapidly. In the short run we will need to consider the differences in the composition of the various markets and the differences that this composition would make in the market demand curve at certain times of the year. For example, we aren't likely to find it very profitable to market pork in Brooklyn since the population is heavily Jewish and no one has yet been able to develop kosher hams. On the other hand, eggs and cheese would sell well in the Boston and Chicago areas during Lent since a large segment of the population in these markets is Catholic and hence faces certain restrictions on meat consumption during this period.

The problem of *where* goods should be sold involves the question of distribution and transportation. Obviously, this decision is going to be made on the basis of the *cost* of getting goods distributed in the various markets and on the prices that can be expected in these markets. Much of the econometric analysis conducted in industrial concerns is oriented toward this problem. Transportation models, spatial equilibrium models, and linear programming are some of the analytical tools that the econometrician will use in this activity.

The final economic function of agriculture is that of resource consumption. *Every productive activity requires resources.* These resources are *consumed* in the process of production. Agriculture competes with all other segments of our economy for the resources to be consumed in the production process. If the automotive industry is willing to pay a higher price for capital equipment in the resource market than is meat packing or flour milling, then grain companies and meat packers will have to be content to work with their present equipment. If the mining industry is willing to pay more for crawler tractors than is the farming industry, then farmers will have to be content to get along with what they have.

When industries (or individual farms or companies) go into the resource market to shop, they act very much like the housewife when she goes into the supermarket. These firms have a production budget within which they must live and operate. The housewife is going to shop for the particular combination of items that will provide the greatest possible satisfaction to her family within the limitations of her household budget. By the same token, agricultural business firms are going to shop for that particular combination that will produce the greatest returns to owned resources within the limits of the operating budget that they have. If new tractors are too expensive this year, we'll invest in the repairs and labor to keep our present equipment operating efficiently, or perhaps buy a used tractor, and use the remainder of our production budget on fertilizer and irrigation equipment.

Business managers face these sorts of decisions daily—not only on farms but in factories, grocery stores, and butcher shops. How are they to make these decisions? Obviously, if the *cost* of producing a given product is *minimized,* then the net returns to the operation will be the greatest possible for that level of production. Thus, the objective of agriculture in performing the economic functions of resource consumption *is to keep the cost of those resources consumed at a minimum level.*

In our discussion of the economic functions of agriculture, there are two ideas that have been used repeatedly. These two ideas are concerned with the managerial objective that is being pursued in each function. Further, these two ideas deal with the starting point of all economic analysis. These are the concepts of *minimum costs* and *maximum profits.* All rational managers attempt to maximize profits within their operations, subject to any non-economic restrictions they may face. In our discussion of the economic principles that govern the operation of business and industries, the assumption of profit maximization will be implicit. All of our economic analysis will deal with situations in which profit maximization is the motive for operation. In performing any of the commodity production, marketing, processing, distributing, or resource consuming functions, a rational businessman will attempt to keep costs to the minimum level possible for achieving some pre-specified objective, since this will move him closer to his total goal of profit.

Regardless of which economic function an individual performs, many of the same economic principles will apply to the analysis of his business. The price (or margin) that a processor receives for his services will be dependent on the supply of and demand for processing services. Likewise, the price that a trucker receives for transporting products depends on the supply of and the demand for transportation activities. The laws of supply and demand also govern the prices that resource owners and product producers receive for the items that they contribute to the economy.

The concepts of supply and demand provide many of the primary tools in the economic analyst's tool kit. Basic to these concepts are certain other principles. In the succeeding chapter, we will begin systematically to analyze the concept of supply and the production principles underlying this concept.

9

Production of Agricultural Goods and the Concept of Supply

As we look at a map of agricultural production in the United States it becomes immediately apparent that the various regions have tended to specialize in the production of the different agricultural products. Figure 9.1 shows the various types of farming regions as defined by the U.S. Department of Agriculture. Wheat is grown primarily in the Great Plains while corn is produced in the Midwest. Grain sorghums are produced in the Central and Southern Plains while soybeans are grown in the Corn Belt and the Mississippi Delta. Cotton is produced in the southern part of the United States while flax is grown in Minnesota and the Dakotas. Beef cattle are raised in the West and Southwest while dairy production is concentrated in the Great Lakes region and the Northeast. Cattle feeding is concentrated in the Corn Belt, the Southern Plains, and the Far West. Hog production is centered in the Corn Belt while poultry is centered in the southern hill areas and the Delmarva Peninsula.

These products are used in all parts of the United States. Further, the per capita levels of consumption do not vary greatly from region to region except as dictated by levels of income. If these products are used in fairly equal proportions in all regions, then why aren't they produced in fairly equal proportions in all regions?

Specialization in the production of agricultural goods cannot be discussed without consideration of the impact of geography. Economic life is inevitably bound up in physical environment. No one questions that the climate, soil type, and degree of slope will place limits on the productivity of farm resources. Some crops (cotton, for example) cannot be produced in regions that have growing seasons (i.e., numbers of consecutive days that are free of frost) less than 180 days. Certain fruit trees (citrus, for example) cannot withstand below-freezing temperatures for any appreciable length of

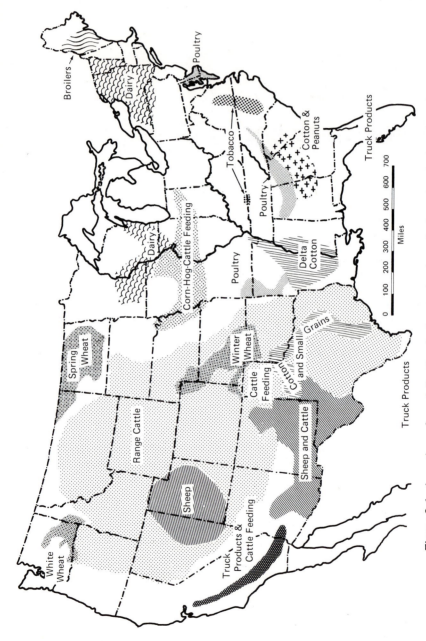

Figure 9.1 Location of specialization in the production of selected agricultural products.

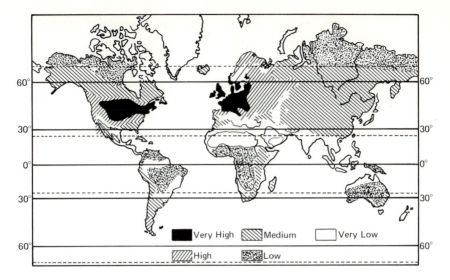

SOURCE: Huntington, Ellsworth, *Civilization and Climate*, Yale
University Press, 1923.

Figure 9.2   Work efficiency of factory personnel, by climatic zones, 1921.

time. Thus, it is apparent that climate places a limitation on the array of productive uses to which soil resources may be put.

Soil resources are not the only resources that face economic limitations imposed by geographic conditions. Human resources, likewise, are limited by extremes in climatic conditions. In 1921 the efficiency of factory workers was shown to be much higher in the temperate zones than in either the equatorial tropics or the Arctic wastes (Figure 9.2). Obviously the environmental control introduced by improved heating and air conditioning equipment has done a great deal to improve the efficiency of labor in the tropics and in the frigid zones since 1921, but little progress has been made in controlling the climatic environment for any substantial acreage of field crops.

Certain capital items, such as heavy machinery, are also impaired by work in certain climates. The uses for water-cooled motors in the Arctic are obviously quite limited, and the effects of heat and humidity on machinery in tropical regions can create situations in which the expense of repairs may be prohibitive.

The study of distribution of economic activities in relation to physical environment is known as economic geography. We are well aware that the costs of maintaining a given standard of living may vary widely from region to region. Because of the concentrated demand for living space in metropolitan areas, rents are likely to be higher in cities than in rural areas. Cold climates such as the Chicago area tend to be higher-cost areas because of the expense of heating. Mountainous areas such as Denver or Albuquerque tend to have high living costs because of the expense of transporting goods over this terrain.

When one enters the business world, the relationship between economic activities and the physical environment in which they are conducted first shows up in the form of costs. A businessman (say, a meat packer in Ohio or Pennsylvania) becomes concerned because his labor costs more than does that of his competitor in Texas. He likewise will discover that the differential is due in part to different physical surroundings. But this doesn't solve his problem. He is affected not only by the nature of his environment, but by the nature of other environments, inasmuch as those environments affect his competitors and customers. This differential in labor costs and other costs is one reason that meat packing rapidly shifted to the South and West during the 1960s and 1970s.

Economic geography is a powerful tool in business analysis and economic planning. The routes of railroads in the United States were chosen primarily by the physical nature of the country. These choices were based not only on the topographic features that determined the cost of construction, but on the resources of soil, climate and minerals. These resources not only provide freight in and of themselves; they attracted *people,* which in turn meant more freight.

The usefulness of the tool of economic geography has been illustrated repeatedly by big business. The Bell Telephone Companies have used geographic factors to plan the layout of their cables in the areas where high rates of population growth are probable. These same geographic factors have been involved in the movement of meat packing facilities from the Great Lakes to the Southwest. Steel foundries were located in the Gary, Indiana, area because of the iron ore and limestone deposits in the Upper Great Lakes and the coal deposits in southern Illinois, Kentucky, and West Virginia. Gary provided a location that was about midway between the sources of these all-important supplies of raw material. Lake barges could be used to bring iron ore and calcite to Gary at about a tenth the per-mile cost of rail transport, and railroads could bring in the coal for smelting. In this fashion, the costs of assembling the resources for steel production were minimized.

The Law of Comparative Advantage • The field of economic geography suggests to us that industries that might do well in a particular area because of the relationship between the productive resources available in that area and the location of the markets that can be served. But the *law of comparative advantage* will determine what particular phase of the industry will develop. The physical yields that can be achieved are *not* the only criterion for anticipating the development of a specialized farming industry in a region.

Even though these yields (which are based on climatic and topographic considerations) are important, the economic aspects must be included in order to get a true picture.

The law of comparative advantage illustrates the advantages of trade between regions and nations as well as between individuals. David Ricardo, a nineteenth-century English economist, illustrated the operation of comparative advantage in the case of international trade back in 1817. In the interest of simplicity, Ricardo assumed only two countries producing only two goods. All costs were measured in terms of the hours of labor required to produce these two goods. Ricardo showed how trade would still occur between the two nations, even though one of them was at an absolute disadvantage in the production of both products. Ricardo's analysis can also be applied to show why areas within a nation may specialize in the production of particular farm products, as follows.

The enterprise budgets constructed by the Commodity Economics Division of the U.S. Department of Agriculture showed that Central Kansas could produce both wheat and soybeans at lower cost per bushel than could east central Illinois in 1973 (Table 9.1). Let's assume that each of these areas needed a minimum of 100,000 bushels of each of the two commodities. In the absence of trade between the areas, Kansas would utilize 7,532 acres to produce these crops and Illinois would utilize 5,667 acres.

TABLE 9.1

COSTS INCURRED AND LAND REQUIRED TO
PRODUCE SPECIFIED QUANTITIES OF WHEAT AND
SOYBEANS
Central Kansas and East Central Illinois, 1973

PRODUCT	CENTRAL KANSAS	EAST CENTRAL ILLINOIS
100,000 bushels soybeans		
yield per acre	21.0 bu.	34.7 bu.
Total cost per bushel	$3.92	$4.32
Total land required	4,761.9 ac.	2,881.8 ac.
Total cost	$392,000	$432,000
100,000 bushels wheat		
yield per acre	36.1 bu.	35.9 bu.
Total cost per bushel	$2.34	$2.56
Total land required	2,770.0 ac.	2,785.5 ac.
Total cost	$234,000	$256,000

Source: *Firm Enterprise Data System,* CED, ERS, USDA, Unpublished Enterprise Budgets, 1973.

If Illinois could produce either wheat or soybeans at lower total cost than Kansas, it is obvious that trade between the areas would be beneficial. But with Illinois at an absolute disadvantage in the production of both crops, the advantages of trade are not nearly so clear. Illinois farmers confronted with this information would likely become very concerned that Kansas would undersell them in Illinois markets, forcing them into a loss position (ignoring costs of transportation). Their immediate reaction would be to attempt to erect some sort of artificial barrier to the importation of Kansas wheat and soybeans. (This sort of activity, incidentally, is not all that uncommon among agricultural production areas in the United States, despite the prohibitions of the Interstate Commerce Act. For example, Florida dealt with imported Georgia poultry products in the early 1960s by taxing all poultry products sold at retail in Florida—and then using the proceeds of this tax to promote and advertise Florida eggs! Georgia at least threatened retaliation through a tax on citrus sold at retail in Georgia. But since Georgia was not a citrus state, a citrus promotional effort would have been aimed at helping either Texas or California, both of which were even more repugnant to Georgians than were Floridians.)

The law of comparative advantage illustrates the fallacy of the antici- pated fears of Illinois farmers and the inherent good sense of the provision of the Interstate Commerce Act that prohibits restraints of trade within the borders of the United States. In Kansas, 100,000 bushels of wheat required 2,770 acres of land, while in Illinois it required 2,785 acres. On the other hand, 100,000 bushels of soybeans required 4,762 acres of Kansas land while it requires only 2,882 acres in Illinois. If Kansas consumers needed another 1,000 bushels of soybeans, it would be necessary for them to give up 47.6 acres or 1,719 bushels of wheat. If Illinois consumers needed another 1,000 bushels of soybeans, it would be necessary for them to give up 28.8 acres or 1,035 bushels of wheat. However, Kansas could trade for the 1,000 bushels of soybeans for something between 1,035 and 1,719 bushels of wheat—say, 1,350 bushels. Both Kansas and Illinois would benefit from the exchange. Kansas would get the extra 1,000 bushels of soybeans at 369 bushels of wheat below the cost of producing the beans in Kansas, and Illinois could get 315 bushels more wheat than they gave up to produce the extra 1,000 bushels of beans.

The end result of trade between the two areas would be that Illinois farmers would adjust away from wheat toward soybeans, and Kansas farmers would adjust more toward wheat production. This shift would continue as long as the cost ratios for wheat and soybean production were different in the two areas. If all 5,667 acres of the land utilized in Illinois were devoted to soybean production, it would replace 4,603 acres of the Kansas land so employed. Of the 4,603 acres of the Kansas soybean production replaced by the adjustment in Illinois, only 1,282 acres are required to replace the Illinois wheat production. This leaves 3,590 acres in Kansas to utilize in producing wheat and/or soybeans. Both areas are better off, since the total production of *both* wheat and soybeans can be increased and, through trade, both areas can enjoy more consumption of *both* goods.

The illustration of a two product world points out several facets of the law of comparative advantage. First of all, nations, regions, states, resources, and people will tend to specialize in production as long as the price and/or cost ratios between products vary. Second, the use of any protective tariffs must be very carefully designed if the protected industry or resource is to be truly protected rather than penalized. (The American National Cattleman's Association, for example, might profit from a careful analysis of the comparative advantage for grain-fed beef versus grass-fed beef versus aircraft and computer production in Australia and the United States.) Third, the specialization that results from the relative degrees of comparative advantage need not necessarily be complete. That is, an area merely increasing or reducing its production of a particular good in response to a change in the degree of comparative advantage is more likely than a total change in one direction or another.

The world of American agriculture is replete with cases of the operation of the law of comparative advantage. For example, in 1925, Wisconsin produced 11.6 percent of the milk in the United States and 4.1 percent of the beef. Oklahoma, on the other hand, produced 2 percent of the milk and 2.9 percent of the beef. By 1970, Wisconsin produced 15.6 percent of the milk and 2.6 percent of the beef, while Oklahoma produced only 1.1 percent of the milk and 5.0 percent of the beef. The implication of this change is that Wisconsin enjoys a comparative advantage for dairy production and that Oklahoma has a comparative advantage in the beef industry.

In context with the above examples, the law of comparative advantage has been stated: *In order to maximize profits, one should produce those items considering yields, costs and returns where the percentage return above cost is greatest.*[1] With the world's finest soil resources, the Corn Belt can produce many products efficiently. But by devoting her resources to those products that will earn the greatest total return over costs, Iowa leaves the wheat to be produced in the Great Plains, the fruits and nuts to be produced in California, and the potatoes to be produced in Maine and Idaho.

The principle or law of comparative advantage involves all of economic geography plus much of economic theory. Through this fundamental principle, we can explain why areas, regions, people, and resources tend to become specialized in the production of certain items. Money enables them to exchange their specialized products for the other items they require. The

---

[1] Milton M. Snodgrass and Luther T. Wallace, *Agriculture, Economics and Growth,* Second Edition. (New York: Appleton-Century-Crofts, 1970), p. 228.

process by which individual managers decide *what* product to specialize in involves our old friend, the allocation of scarce resources.

The Production Function

You will recall that in our discussion of the nature and scope of agricultural economics in Chapter 8, we carefully examined a decision typically faced by farmers when new technology increases the array of alternative means for production. In making that decision, information was drawn from the technical sciences, economic analysis was then applied, and finally the decision was made on the basis of the technical and economic information assembled. The technical scientist provided information concerning the relationship between the use of resources (or *inputs*) and the *output* of products. The term that defines this technical relationship of inputs and outputs is the *production function* or the *transformation function*. The technical rate at

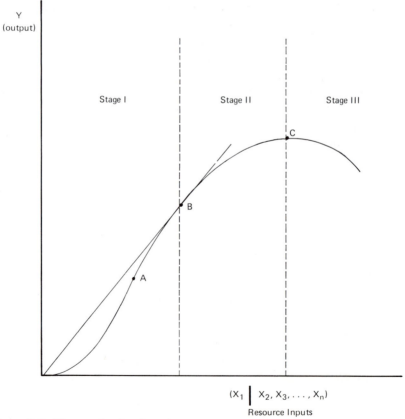

Figure 9.3 The production function.

which two or more inputs are transformed into products—as defined by the technical scientist—can be demonstrated graphically as shown in Figure 9.3.

You will notice that the inputs $(X_1|X_2,X_3,X_4,\ldots,X_n)$ are so defined that only one resource, X_1, is allowed to vary. (The inputs to the left of the vertical are variable, those to the right are fixed.) Think of this resource as being fertilizer, with the available quantities of land and labor and other capital being fixed. The product Y (think of this as corn, wheat, cotton, or whatever) then is observed to change as various amounts of fertilizer are used with our fixed resources of land and labor.

The production function normally performs such that, in the early stages, the second unit of fertilizer (or any other resource) injected will cause total production to increase *more* than did the first unit of the resource. The third unit will add more product than did the second, and so forth. This portion of the production function is known as the stage of *increasing marginal productivity* or *increasing marginal returns* (point 0 to point A in curve). Eventually some point is reached when the injection of an additional unit of the resource will add *less* to total product than did the previous unit (that is, point A on the curve defines the point of *diminishing marginal returns*). Total production will continue to increase as additional resources are used, but the *rate* of increase will continue to diminish until the maximum product that is possible to achieve with our *fixed* quantity of resources (other than the variable resource of fertilizer) is reached. Beyond this point (point C on the curve) the injection of additional fertilizer will actually reduce total production. (Beyond certain limits, added fertilizer will "burn" crops.)

The Stages of Production • The point at which the ratio of output to variable input is greatest (that is, the point at which *average product* per unit of variable input is greatest—point B on curve) marks the end of the first irrational stage of production (Stage I) and the beginning of the rational stage (Stage II). You will note that the point of diminishing marginal returns is in the irrational stage.

Why is Stage I on the production function irrational? In order to answer this question, it is necessary to define some more terms. The production function defines the total production that can be derived from combining various quantities of a resource X_1 with fixed quantities of other resources. But as we add each unit of X_1, the *change* in the total physical production of Y *increases* in the early stages as additional units of X_1 are injected (Figure 9.4). When the point of diminishing marginal returns is reached, each additional unit of X_1 injected still increases total production, *but by less than did the previous injection*. The *change* in total production that is associated with the addition of a unit of X_1 is known as *marginal physical product* (MPP) and can be plotted as in the lower part of the chart.

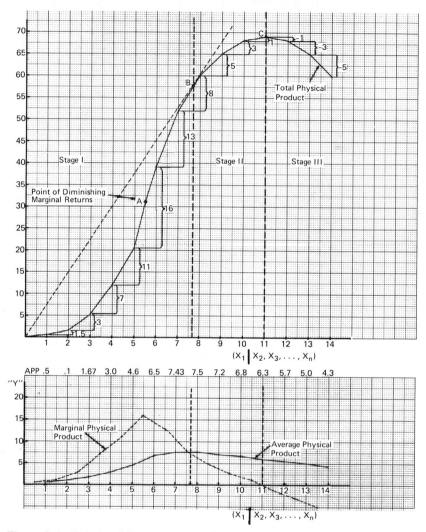

Figure 9.4 Relationship among total physical product, average physical product, and marginal physical product.

As we add units of X_1, the second unit is more productive than the first. However, if the first unit were not there, the productivity of the second unit would be reduced. Thus, the *first unit has contributed to the productivity of the second unit,* and therefore an *average physical productivity* (APP) measure is relevant. (Average physical product per unit of X_1 is simply the total physical product divided by the number of units of X_1 that have been used.)

As long as the marginal physical productivity of additional units of X_1

exceeds average physical productivity, the injection of additional X_1 will continue to increase average physical productivity. If it pays to produce at all, *it will pay to add inputs through Stage I,* since each additional unit of input in this stage contributes to increasing the average productivity of every unit of input used. If any point on the production function can be profitable, the point at which average physical product is maximum *will* be profitable. Thus, for the manager to plan to produce in Stage I with the average physical productivity increasing would be irrational. (That is, if a manager can make money producing an average of five bushels of corn per hundred pounds of nitrogen, he can certainly make money producing six bushels of corn per hundred pounds of nitrogen. *So long as average physical product per unit of variable resource is increasing, the rational manager will continue to add resources.*)

Since Stage III shows a situation in which total production is actually reduced by injecting additional units of X_1 into the production process (that is, marginal physical productivity becomes negative), it would be irrational for a manager to elect to operate in this stage of the production function.

Perhaps the details of calculating and charting average and marginal physical products can improve our understanding of these concepts. The first two columns of Table 9.2 are charted in the upper part of Figure 9.4. This information has been provided by the technical scientist. Both Table 9.2 and Figure 9.4 show the levels of product Y that can be produced when different levels of some variable resource have been combined with a body of fixed resources. But the economist can manipulate this information to gain still further information.

It should be pointed out that the information in Table 9.2 is provided only for certain *points* on the production function—that is, it is *discrete.* There is no information concerning the level of production associated with using 4.2 units of variable resource. An examination of the table tells us that 4.2 units of X_1 should produce between 12 and 23 units of product, and that production is probably closer to 12 units than to 23 units, since 4.2 units of input is closer to 4.0 than to 5.0. When the information is charted as in Figure 9.4, a straight line between points for 4.0 and 5.0 units of the resource X_1 will give an approximation of the output associated with 4.2 units of X_1, and the approximated level of 14 units of output may be read directly from the chart.

We defined marginal physical product as the *rate of change* in total physical product that is associated with a one-unit change in the level at which the variable resource is employed. Marginal physical product can be calculated simply by finding the *difference* in the level of output as the level of input is changed by one unit. Thus, as we go from four to five units of input, we increase output by eleven units. This is shown in the upper part of Figure 9.4 by the bracket that shows the product added when the fifth unit of X_1 is

TABLE 9.2

RELATIONSHIP AMONG TOTAL PHYSICAL PRODUCT, AVERAGE PHYSICAL PRODUCT, AND MARGINAL PHYSICAL PRODUCT

LEVEL OF X_1 COMBINED WITH FIXED RESOURCES (UNITS)	LEVEL OF TOTAL PHYSICAL PRODUCT (Y) (UNITS)	AVERAGE PHYSICAL PRODUCT (UNITS)	MARGINAL PHYSICAL PRODUCT (UNITS)
0	0	—	
1	½	.50	— ½
2	2	1.00	— 1½
3	5	1.67	— 3
4	12	3.00	— 7
5	23	4.60	— 11
6	39	6.50	— 16—A
7	52	7.43	— 13
8	60	B—7.50	— 8
9	65	7.22	— 5
10	68	6.80	— 3
11	69—C	6.27	— 1
12	68	5.67	— −1
13	65	5.00	— −3
14	60	4.28	— −5

employed. The sixth unit of X_1 adds sixteen units to total product, the seventh adds thirteen units, etc.

The rate of change in total product (i.e., the marginal physical product or MPP, as it is typically abbreviated) is greatest as we go from five units of X_1 to six units. Prior to the use of the sixth unit, each successive unit of X_1 adds progressively more to total product than did the previous one. Up to the sixth unit of X_1 employed, the production added by each unit (that is, the "return" to that unit of resource) is increasing. Units of X_1 subsequent to the sixth unit add progressively less. Thus, beyond the sixth unit, returns are *decreasing*. The rate of change (which is MPP) is *maximum* between five and six units of input, thus locating the point of diminishing marginal returns (the point labeled A in Table 9.2 and Figure 9.4).

We discussed the implications of discrete information above. But the fact that the information is discrete has some special implications for calculating, charting, and using the marginal physical product. In Table 9.2, when the level of X_1 is increased from eight to nine units, total product changes from

60 to 65, or by five units. If, on the other hand, the level at which X_1 is used should be reduced from nine to eight units, the change in production is still five units. That is, marginal physical product is the same, regardless of whether the change in the level of resource use is positive or negative. The rate of change in total product between eight and nine units is five units, whether it is increasing or decreasing. Therefore, the marginal physical product in Table 9.2 is posted between the lines associated with the two levels of input usage and is charted at the midpoint between eight and nine units (i.e., at 8.5 units) of input on Figure 9.4. Since the term marginal refers to a rate of change within some interval when working with discrete information, that rate of change applies to the *entire* interval. Thus, *all marginal functions should be posted and charted at the midpoint of the interval.* If this is not done, the approximations between the discrete points will be subject to substantial error.

The calculation of average physical product (APP) involves exactly what the name implies—the simple arithmetic average. It is calculated by dividing the total physical product at any given point by the level of resource use associated with that level of production, yielding the production *per unit* of variable resource. Since we only have discrete points along the production function, the average physical product that is calculated is associated with those discrete points and should be posted and charted as such. Thus, the average physical product at ten units of input is 6.8, at eleven units is 6.27, etc.

The Physical Production Function and Price Information as an Economic Tool

When we discussed the stages of production, we recognized that a manager would be irrational to stop adding resources, as long as average physical product was increasing. Thus, the rational stage of production began where average physical product was maximum (the point labeled *B* in Table 9.2 and Figure 9.4). That rational stage ended where total physical product was maximum (the point labeled *C* in Table 9.2 and Figure 9.4), since a manager would be irrational to use more resources when that usage reduced total output. It is in this second stage of production that profits can be maximized. But how does one know *where* within Stage II he should operate? It is obvious that the physical input-output information is inadequate for making this decision.

Back when we were making our decision with regard as to whether or not we were to adopt the electronically-programmed combine, we decided that we needed two types of price information in addition to the technical production information. We needed *product* price information as well as *resource* (or input) cost information. Thus, we can utilize the information in Table 9.2 and Figure 9.4 along with some price information to make the management decision as to where within the second stage of production we will achieve maximum profits.

If we say that the price of Y is set at some constant level—say $1 per unit—then our total, marginal, and average product curves can be converted to revenue curves measuring the value of the product created (Table 9.3 and Figure 9.5). Cost is a different matter. If X_1 is priced at a constant rate—say $5 per unit—then our total cost curve for the variable input X_1 appears as a straight line rising from the origin. (That is, each unit of X_1 has the same price regardless of its productivity.) Since each additional unit of X_1 adds the same amount ($5) to total costs, then *marginal* and *average* costs for the variable input are identical and fall in a horizontal line at the $5 level.

If we wish to maximize profits, we find the point where the difference in the *value of total product* (VTP) and the *total costs of the variable input* (TVIC) are greatest. In Figure 9.5, profits are maximum when 8.5 units of the X_1 input are combined with the rest of the resources at our disposal to create 66 units of the product Y. We see that this maximum profit point also occurs where marginal variable input costs (MVIC) and the value of the marginal product (VMP) of X_1 are exactly equal.

When we analyze the definitions of the *marginal* concepts, it is not surprising that profits should be maximum where value of the marginal product and marginal variable input cost are equal. Value of the marginal product X_1 is defined as the *change in the value of the total product as associated with a one-unit change in the use of variable input X_1*. The marginal variable input cost of X_1 is defined as the *change in total costs associated with a one-unit change in the use of the variable input X_1*. So long as an additional unit of X_1 adds more to receipts than it adds to costs, the use of that unit increases total profits. Thus, total profits are maximum when the revenue generated by the marginal unit of input is exactly equal to the cost added by that unit.

Figure 9.5 may be used to analyze the adjustment that a manager would make if the price of the resource X_1 should change. Suppose that X_1 is now priced at $3 per unit rather than $5. If the manager continued to use 8.5 units of X_1, his profit will increase to $36 from the $20 he earned when X_1 was priced at $5. But is this the maximum profit possible? All that is necessary to find the answer to this question is to redraw the MVIC at the $3 level in the lower part of Figure 9.5. We can see that at the old profit-maximizing position, the marginal increment of X_1 is adding revenue at a rate of $5 per unit while it is adding to cost at a rate of only $3 per unit. Another half unit of X_1 would add about $2–2.50 to revenue and only $1.50 to costs. Thus, it is clear that the usage of X_1 should be increased as long as the addition to total receipts (VMP) exceeds the addition to total cost (MVIC);

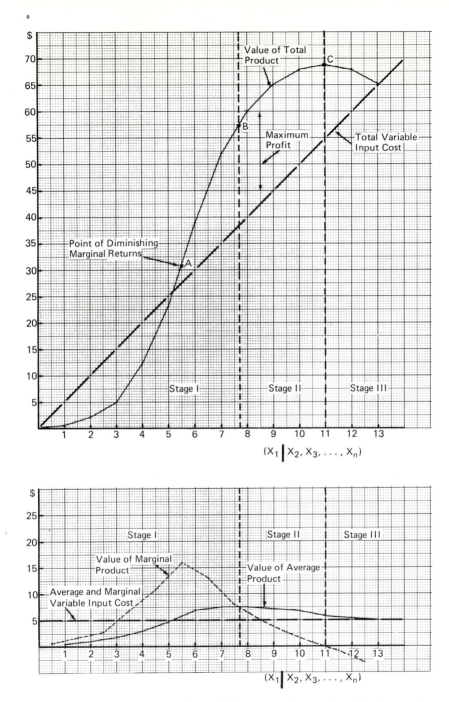

Figure 9.5 Example of conversion of the production relationships into value of product relationships, with comparisons to the cost of variable input.

TABLE 9.3

RELATIONSHIP AMONG TOTAL, AVERAGE, AND MARGINAL PRODUCT; VALUE OF PRODUCT FUNCTIONS; AND COST FUNCTIONS FOR THE VARIABLE INPUT

LEVEL OF X_1 COMBINED WITH FIXED RESOURCES (X_1)	LEVEL OF TOTAL PHYSICAL PRODUCT (Y)	AVERAGE PHYSICAL PRODUCT (APP)	MARGINAL PHYSICAL PRODUCT (MPP)	PRICE OF Y = $1 PER UNIT			PRICE OF X_1 = $5 PER UNIT		
				Value of TPP (VTP)	Value of APP (VAP)	Value of MPP (VMP)	Total Var. Input Cost (TVIC)	Average Var. Input Cost (AVIC)	Marginal Var. Input Cost (MVIC)
0	0	—	½	0	—	$.50	0	0	—
1	½	½	1½	$.50	$.50	1.50	$5.00	$5.00	$5.00
2	2	1.00	3	2.00	1.00	3.00	10.00	5.00	5.00
3	5	1.67	7	5.00	1.67	7.00	15.00	5.00	5.00
4	12	3.00	11	12.00	3.00	11.00	20.00	5.00	5.00

Stage I

5	23	4.60	16 ←A	23.00	4.60	16.00	25.00	5.00	5.00
6	39	6.50	13	39.00	6.50	13.00	30.00	5.00	5.00
7	52	7.43	8	52.00	7.43	8.00	35.00	5.00	5.00

--- B ---

Stage II									
8	60	7.50	5	60.00	7.50	5.00	40.00	5.00	5.00
9	65	7.22	3	65.00	7.22	3.00	45.00	5.00	5.00
10	68	6.8	1	68.00	6.80	1.00	50.00	5.00	5.00

maximum profit (at 40.00–45.00)

--- C ---

Stage III									
11	69	6.27	−1	69.00	6.27	−1.00	55.00	5.00	5.00
12	68	5.67		68.00	5.67		60.00	5.00	5.00

that is, the new profit-maximizing position would occur where VMP = MVIC, at 9.5 units of X_1.

The Production Function and Cost of Production

We have examined the production function and the cost and revenue functions that may be derived directly from the production function. However, our costs and revenues have all been measured in terms of resource inputs. Since we sell *output* rather than input, these cost and revenue functions must be translated into terms of costs and revenues per unit of production rather than per unit of input. Assume that we have the same production function that we have worked with throughout this chapter and as defined in Columns 1 and 2 of Table 9.4 and in the lower portion of Figure 9.6.

Economic charts are generally constructed so that the independent variable is measured along the horizontal axis and the dependent variable along the vertical axis. Since we wish to translate the cost and revenue curves derived from our production function into terms of output, we should measure output along the horizontal axis (as in the upper two charts in Figure 9.6). We are concerned with costs as they are associated with the various levels at which the variable input X_1 is used. Therefore, *variable* costs will be the costs that will be calculated. *Total variable costs* are simply the total costs associated with the use of X_1. We can calculate *average variable costs* by examining the table or the chart to find the level of output associated with each level of usage for X_1, and then dividing the total variable cost associated with any given level of input by the relevant level of output. That is, if the variable resource is used at a level of nine units and if those nine units cost $5 each and produce 65 units of output, then the total variable cost at 65 units of output is $45 or $0.692 per unit of output.[2]

Marginal costs would ordinarily be calculated by measuring the level of X_1 required to achieve each successive level of output, multiplying this level by the price paid for that resource (in order to measure total variable costs), and then calculating the change in total variable costs associated with each succeeding unit of production. But we have information only for the discrete intervals of whole units of the resource X_1. Since the ninth unit of X_1 increases total product from 60 to 65 units, or by 5 units, the cost added by

---

[2] An alternative method for calculating this relationship would be to divide the price of the resource X_1 by the average physical product for each level at which X_1 is used. The results of this calculation will trace out points along the average variable cost curve. That is, at nine units of input, the total output is 65 units and APP is 7.22 units of output per unit of X_1. Since X_1 is priced at $5, AVC per unit of output would be $5 ÷ 7.22 = $0.692. (See Table 9.4 and Figure 9.6.)

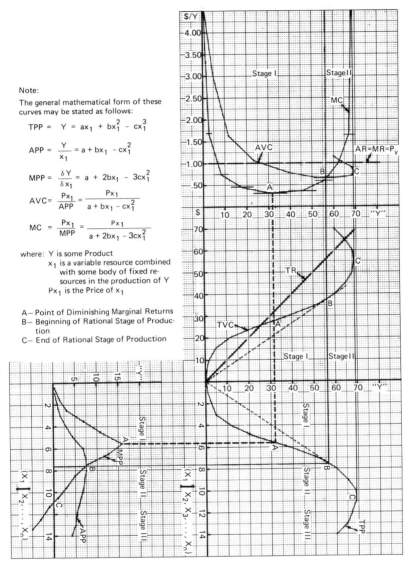

Note:

The general mathematical form of these curves may be stated as follows:

$$TPP = Y = ax_1 + bx_1^2 - cx_1^3$$

$$APP = \frac{Y}{x_1} = a + bx_1 - cx_1^2$$

$$MPP = \frac{\delta Y}{\delta x_1} = a + 2bx_1 - 3cx_1^2$$

$$AVC = \frac{Px_1}{APP} = \frac{Px_1}{a + bx_1 - cx_1^2}$$

$$MC = \frac{Px_1}{MPP} = \frac{Px_1}{a + 2bx_1 - 3cx_1^2}$$

where: Y is some Product
  x_1 is a variable resource combined with some body of fixed resources in the production of Y
  Px_1 is the Price of x_1

A— Point of Diminishing Marginal Returns
B— Beginning of Rational Stage of Production
C— End of Rational Stage of Production

Figure 9.6 Relationship between production function and costs of production.

that unit of resource must be distributed among these 5 units of product. Thus, within the interval from 60 to 65 units of output, the cost added is $5, or $1 per unit of product. Marginal cost per unit of product within the interval between 60 and 65 units then, is $1 per unit *at the midpoint of that interval* (that is, the marginal cost of $1 is charted at 62.5 units of Y in Figure 9.6). The marginal cost for units of product other than those occurring exactly

TABLE 9.4

RELATIONSHIP BETWEEN THE PRODUCTION FUNCTION AND COSTS OF PRODUCTION

	PRODUCTION FUNCTION					
Units of X_1	TPP from X_1 (Y)	APP from X_1	MPP from X_1	TOTAL VARIABLE COST ($P_{X_1}=\$5$) (TVC)	AVERAGE VARIABLE COST PER UNIT OF PRODUCT[1] (AVC)	MARGINAL COST FOR ADDING A UNIT OF PRODUCT[2] (MC)
0	0	—		$ 0	—	
			½			½ for $5 = $10/unit
1	½	½		5.00	$10.00	
			1½			1½ for $5 = $3.33/unit
2	2	1.0		10.00	5.00	
			3			3 for $5 = $1.67/unit
3	5	1.67		15.00	3.00	
			7			7 for $5 = $0.714/unit
4	12	3.0		20.00	1.66	
			11			11 for $5 = $0.455/unit
5	23	4.6		25.00	1.09	
			16←A			A→16 for $5 = $0.312/unit
6	39	6.5		30.00	.77	
			13			13 for $5 = $0.385/unit
7	52	7.43		35.00	.673	
			8			8 for $5 = $0.625/unit

Stage I of production (braces spanning rows 0 through 7)

B -

8	60	7.50	5	40.00	.666	5 for $5 = $1.00/unit
9	65	7.22	3	45.00	.692	3 for $5 = $1.67/unit
10	68	6.8	1	50.00	.735	1 for $5 = $5/unit
11	69	6.27		55.00	.80	
_C_						
12	68	5.67	−1	60.00	.88	At this level, marginal cost is mathematically negative, which suggests the manager is paying to get rid of product. This is irrational.
13	65	5.00	−3	65.00	1.00	
14	60	4.28	−5	70.00	1.17	

Stage II (rows 8–11)
Stage III (rows 12–14)

[1] Average cost per unit of Y may be computed by dividing the price of the resource X_1, here assumed to be $5, by the average physical product. It may also be computed by dividing the total variable cost by the level of output.

[2] Marginal cost, the cost for adding one unit of Y to total product, may be calculated for any given interval by dividing the price of the resource X_1 by the marginal physical product at that point. The marginal cost so calculated is the marginal cost for the unit of product at the midpoint of that interval.

A = Point of Diminishing Marginal Returns

B and C = limits of the Rational Stage of Production

147

at these charted levels may be approximated by a straight line connecting the midpoints.

Points *A, B,* and *C* in Table 9.4 and on all charts in Figure 9.6 refer to the point of diminishing marginal returns, to the point at which the rational stage of production begins, and to the point at which the rational stage ends.

The uppermost chart of Figure 9.6 includes most of the analytical information needed for making managerial decisions with regard to selecting the level of output that will return the greatest amount above variable costs. The only additional information needed is the price at which the product Y can be sold. If we assume that each unit of Y can be sold at $1.00, the total revenue function will be a straight line rising from the origin of the center chart in Figure 9.6. That is, each unit of product sold will generate $1.00 in total revenue. Marginal and average returns will be constant at $1.00: That is, the average price for all units sold is $1.00 and the change associated with a one-unit change in sales is also $1.00. Thus, marginal and average revenue would appear as a horizontal line at $1.00 on the upper chart in Figure 9.6.

To find the point at which the return above variable costs is greatest, the manager would simply locate the point at which the difference in the total cost function and the total revenue function is greatest. In the center chart of Figure 9.6, this occurs at 62 to 63 units of output. This level of output corresponds with the point at which marginal cost and marginal revenue are equal in the upper chart. Thus, every unit of Y that will add more to revenue than it adds to cost has been produced. Therefore, the returns above variable costs *must be maximum at that point.* In our example the manager would be wise to use 8.5 units of X_1 to produce 62 to 63 units of Y, thereby maximizing his returns above variable costs at $20.

The Impact of Fixed Costs • You will notice that we have been very careful to talk in terms of average *variable* costs and total *variable* costs, rather than in terms of simply average costs and total costs. In the lower part of Figure 9.6, which shows the production function, the input axis is labeled $(X_1 | X_2, X_3, \ldots X_n)$. This means that the only variable cost item we have in our analysis thus far is the input X_1. All the other inputs $(X_2, X_3, \ldots, X_n)$ are said to be *fixed.* This means that these inputs are present at some fixed level and that the costs of these items have been incurred whether or not they are used. Thus, the manager is already obligated for these costs and these costs *must* be paid, whether or not the business operates and without regard to the volume of output. (Examples of fixed cost items include such overhead items as rent, land taxes, and the interest on borrowed money.)

The presence of fixed costs affects the cost structure, since the amount of fixed costs must be added to total variable costs and must be allocated to the level of output produced. If, in our example, the fixed cost totaled $20, the total cost function would simply lie $20 above the total variable cost

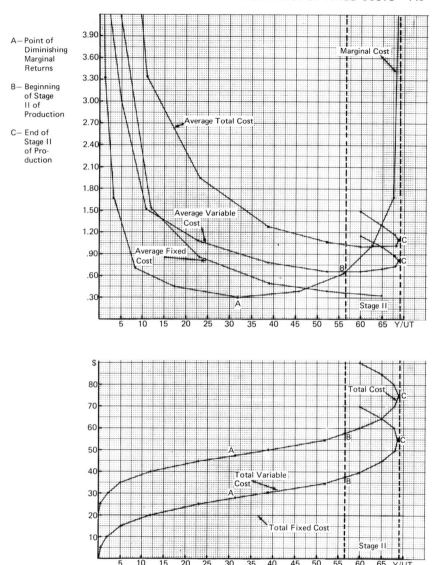

Figure 9.7 Relationship among fixed, variable, and total costs of production.

function for all possible levels of production (see Table 9.5 and Figure 9.7). In calculating *average total cost,* the $20 in fixed costs would be allocated to production so that at one unit of production, average total costs (ATC) would be $20 higher than average variable costs (AVC). At two units of output, ATC would be $10 higher than AVC. At five units of output, ATC would exceed AVC by $4. In other words, the more units of production we

TABLE 9.5

RELATIONSHIP AMONG FIXED, VARIABLE, AND TOTAL COSTS OF PRODUCTION

TOTAL PHYSICAL PRODUCT FROM X_1 (Y)	TOTAL VARIABLE COST FOR Y	AVERAGE VARIABLE COST FOR Y	MARGINAL COST FOR ADDING A UNIT OF Y	TOTAL FIXED COST	TOTAL COST OF PRODUCTION	AVERAGE FIXED COST PER UNIT OF Y	AVERAGE TOTAL COST PER UNIT OF Y	MARGINAL COST FOR ADDING A UNIT OF Y
0	$ 0	—		$20.00	$20.00	—	—	
½	5.00	$10.00	$10.00	20.00	25.00	$40.00	$50.00	$10.00
2	10.00	5.00	3.33	20.00	30.00	10.00	15.00	3.33
5	15.00	3.00	1.67	20.00	35.00	4.00	7.00	1.67
12	20.00	1.66	.714	20.00	40.00	1.67	3.33	.714
23	25.00	1.09	.455	20.00	45.00	.87	1.95	.455
39	30.00	.77	.312	20.00	50.00	.51	1.28	.312
52	35.00	.673	.385	20.00	55.00	.38	1.06	.385
60	40.00	.666	.625	20.00	60.00	.33	1.00	.625
65	45.00	.692	1.000	20.00	65.00	.31	1.00	1.000
68	50.00	.735	1.67	20.00	70.00	.294	1.02	1.67
69	55.00	.80	5.00	20.00	75.00	.290	1.09	5.00
68	60.00	.88	a	20.00	80.00	.294	1.18	a
65	65.00	1.00	a	20.00	85.00	.31	1.31	a
60	70.00	1.17	a	20.00	90.00	.33	1.50	a

aWithin these ranges, marginal cost is mathematically negative, suggesting that the manager would gladly pay in order to avoid producing product (that is, in order to reduce the level of production). This is obviously irrational.

spread our fixed costs over, the closer and closer ATC and AVC come to the same figure. Since marginal costs are defined to be the *change* in total cost resulting from one-unit change in production, and since fixed costs do not change regardless of the level of production, *marginal costs are not affected by fixed costs.*

We can see that the maximum profit position is still at 62 to 63 units of output where marginal revenue and marginal costs are equal. You will recall that the rational stage of production began where marginal physical productivity and average physical productivity were equal. This occurred in our example at 57 to 58 units of output. This point corresponds with the point at which marginal costs and average variable cost cross (i.e., where the two are equal). Thus, the *rational stage of production includes that portion of output in which marginal cost is above average variable costs.* So long as marginal cost per unit of production is less than average variable cost, increasing the volume of production will *reduce* average variable costs. Thus, if it is good business to produce at all, it will be good business to produce at least up to the point where marginal and average variable costs are equal, since this is the point at which average cost per unit of production is minimum.

The point that is important in our discussion is that the *production function and price information concerning the cost of inputs will define the cost of producing the output or product in question.* Further, the only *relevant portion of the various cost functions derived is that portion where the cost added by the marginal unit of output exceeds average variable costs of production,* since this is the portion of the cost function that describes the cost structure for the rational stage of production.

Production Cost and the Concept of Supply • Since the only relevant portions of the cost functions (or, for that matter, of the production function) are those portions within the rational stage of production, let's focus our attention on the cost structure within that range. We have established that the firm will be wise to produce as long as the addition to total revenues resulting from a unit of production *exceeds or equals* the amount of added to total costs resulting from that unit (i.e., as long as marginal revenue exceeds marginal costs). In the case of individual farmers, the price doesn't change perceptibly regardless of how much that farmer produces. Thus, we can treat product price as a constant (that is, farmers are *price takers* rather than price makers).

If prices should fall *below* the low point on the average variable cost curve in Figure 9.8 (price *A*), what happens? Since we have said that prices received are constant, average revenue and marginal revenue are both constant at the price level. Thus, if marginal revenue is below the minimum point on the average variable cost curve, what is the situation we face? Obviously, if you can't recover the costs of using the variable resource, X_1, you wouldn't

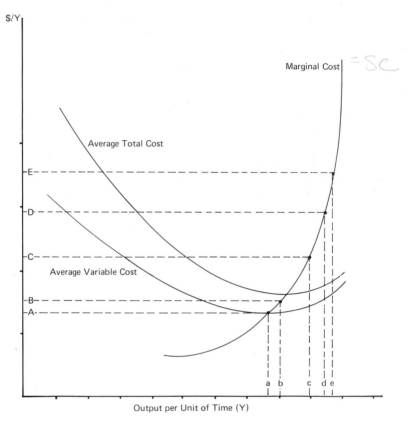

Figure 9.8 The cost structure related to the concept of supply.

operate at prices below this level. The resources at your command would be rechanneled into other sorts of employment.

Let's say that prices are above this point. Since we are now in the rational range, what do we have? How much would be produced if the price were to fall at *A, B, C, D,* or *E*? How much would the manager be willing to produce? How much would he be able to produce? If the manager could *not* cover the cost added by producing the additional output *c-d* at price *C* (and he could not), then obviously he would not produce beyond output level *c*. From this analysis, you can see that *the marginal cost curve associated with a particular production function for the individual firm traces out the quantities of product that the firm will be willing and able to offer for sale at the various prices.*

The *supply curve* for an individual firm may be defined as the *schedule of quantities that a producer is willing and able to make available at a specified series of prices, in a given market, at a given time, other things being* equal (*certeris paribus* is the Latin term used to mean "other factors being equal.") Thus, a firm's marginal cost curve represents a supply curve for that firm.

The firm's supply function has two elements—willingness and ability. The firm must be *able* to produce the quantity that it is willing to sell and it must be *willing* to sell what it can produce. In the case of agriculture, weather variability may cause the quantity supplied for a specified price to differ from what was intended. However, this does not invalidate the concept of supply. The producer tried for the production function that would normally give him the quantity he would be willing and able to sell at the expected price. Nature either withheld the weather resource or bestowed it in abundance, causing the producer to be either on a higher or lower production function that he had originally intended. (Weather in this case was one of the *ceteris paribus* conditions that was *not,* in fact, constant.)

The time-dimension term in the definition of firm supply functions can be extremely important. There are two time dimensions that we normally consider: short run and long run. The difference in these two dimensions rests upon how many of the factors of production can be varied. In agriculture, the production period for most crops and livestock is generally several months to several years in length. A price change today isn't going to make much difference in what is available for sale in the market tomorrow or next week. Our resources are already committed to production. But after this crop is laid by, if wheat prices have been favorable for some time, we are likely to devote more resources to wheat production than we have in the past.

In the immediate period, many resources are fixed—machinery, land, and in many cases, labor. But as the length of time is extended, the firm can buy or sell both land and machinery and can hire labor. Thus, the time dimension of the *"length of run" consideration depends on how many resources are fixed.* In the "market" period (the very short run), no adjustments in production can be made. A very few adjustments can be made during a single production period. Numerous adjustments can be made over a time that includes several production periods, and *total* adjustment can be made during a truly long-run period. A given production function is associated with the short run, since the firm can change production functions over long periods of time.

We'll revisit the time dimension portion of the concept of supply in Chapter 16, but regardless of the time dimension, the *law of supply* is operative. The law of supply states that *the higher the price of a commodity the greater will be the quantity that a producer or a group of producers will be willing to produce or offer for sale in a given market at a given time.* The primary reason for the operation of the law of supply is the fact that the increased profits associated with higher levels of price provide an incentive for an existing production unit to expand and for new production units to be

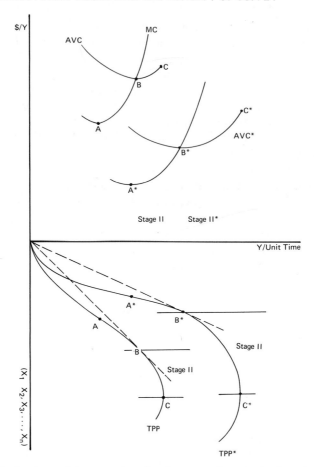

Figure 9.9 Impact of improved technology on the supply function for the individual producer.

created. Further, the increasing nature of marginal and average costs in the rational stage of production suggests that prices *must* increase if producers are to be induced to produce more. (Increased prices will cover the increased cost liability incurred by increased production.)

The important point of this analysis is that the short-run supply function for an individual firm is defined by that firm's marginal cost curve. If in a longer-run period the firm should adopt a new technology that causes resources to be more productive, then the production function shifts upward. This shift will tend to *broaden* the range of production within which the manager can rationally produce, and will cause the firm's average and marginal cost functions shift downward and to the right (Figure 9.9). Thus, with the new technology that can be adopted in the long run, a producer would generally be willing and able to offer more product for sale at every possible price. The *shift in the production function by way of new technology has shifted the short-run supply function for the firm.*

The Market Supply Function

We have discussed the production function as it related to the short-run functions for the individual firms, and how the short-run marginal cost curve defined the supply curve for the firm in the short run. We saw how the firm could select the level of the production function to be used in the short run (the selection being made, in our example, on the basis of deciding whether or not to adopt new technology). Since not all firms would be able to adopt new technology at the same time, there will be a "family" of production functions, and hence a family of individual firm supply curves for any given short-run period. The fixity of resources in the short run will affect the firm's selection of a production function: a firm that has just invested in new equipment would be unlikely to reinvest in new technology immediately. Thus, a lower (or suboptimal) production function would have been selected because the firm has not yet been able to amortize the fixed investment in items such as machinery or equipment. The cost per unit of production associated with the suboptimal production function would therefore tend to be higher.

With almost three million farms present in the economy, and with thousands of farms producing each agricultural commodity, it is apparent that no single farm can satisfy the total market needs for a given product at any given time. Thus, some method must be devised for combining the individual firm supply relationships that describe the information derived from the various production functions into a single short-run supply relationship that describes the aggregate production information for the entire market.

Earlier, we defined the individual firm's supply functions as the *quantity that an individual firm would be willing and able to produce and offer for sale at a given schedule of prices, in a given market and at a given time, ceteris paribus.* This same definition applies to the market supply relationship.

The term "given market" can be extremely important in the market supply relationship. Consider, for example, the impact of a change in the price for Class I milk in the markets of Madison, Wisconsin, and Little Rock, Arkansas. The law of supply states that an increase in price will call forth an increase in the quantity available in the market. How could milk producers in the Little Rock market go about increasing the sales of Class I milk at the higher price? Basically four possibilities are open:

1. Some increase could be generated by a change in feeding programs, hence increasing per-cow production (i.e., Class I milk producers

would move further out on their production functions by combining more feed with their other resources, thus increasing the
average costs and producing where marginal costs were equal to the
new price).

2. Class I producers could add a few cows, increasing total production
   in this fashion (i.e., the producers would be moving out along a
   new production function, combining more feed and more cows
   with their fixed resources of barns, equipment, labor and the like.
   Again, producers would be incurring increasing average costs of
   production and producing where marginal costs were equal to the
   new price).

3. Manufacturing milk producers would tend to become Grade A
   producers, hence transferring the resources from their old activity
   to the newly more attractive enterprise. (We thus *increase the
   numbers* of producing units or production functions involved.)

4. New producers go into the dairy business. (This, like number 3
   above, represents an increase in the number of producing units.)

The chances are that producers in both markets would employ all four
methods of increasing Class I milk production. But the possibility for increase
in the Madison area resulting from the manufacturing milk producers shifting
into Grade A production is enormous because of the tremendous numbers of
manufacturing milk producers present in the environs of Madison. Because
there are relatively few manufacturing milk producers in the Little Rock
milkshed, the response to such a price change would likely be quite limited in
the short run. Thus, the production of Class I milk in the Madison milkshed
would probably be by far the more responsive to price changes.

How are the individual farm supply functions (i.e., the individual
short-run marginal cost curves) to be combined to describe the short-run
market supply function? This is really a pretty simple matter. To accomplish
this combination, we merely add up the quantities that each firm would
provide for sale at each of the possible prices; that is, *the short-run market
supply function is the horizontal summation of all the short-run marginal cost
curves for all firms in the industry.*

Imagine that the product Y is produced by only three firms—that is, the
output of these three firms (Firm A, Firm B, and Firm C) makes up the total
short-run market supply for the product Y. Each of these three firms has its
own production function and the associated cost curves (Figure 9.10). Some
firms are more efficient than others, and therefore their cost structure is such
that they can profitably produce at lower prices than can their less efficient

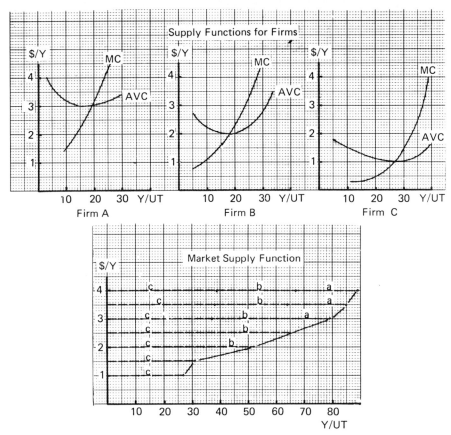

Figure 9.10 Relationship between the supply function for the individual firm and the market supply function.

competitors. Thus, at very low prices, only the most efficient (that is, the low-cost firms) will be willing and able to produce and sell in the market. In the case of our example, Firm C is the lowest cost firm and the only one of the three that can operate at prices below $2. When the price Y gets to $2, Firm B can start producing and selling, and at a price of $3, Firm A can enter the market. At prices above $3, all firms expand production along their individual short-run marginal cost curves, and the market supply function for Y takes on the shape that we see in Figure 9.10. In reality, the numbers of firms producing any agricultural product are large enough that the market supply function would most probably be a smooth curve, since producers would be entering at all price levels. But the nature of the market supply function is illustrated in Figure 9.10: as prices rise, the availability of the product will expand.

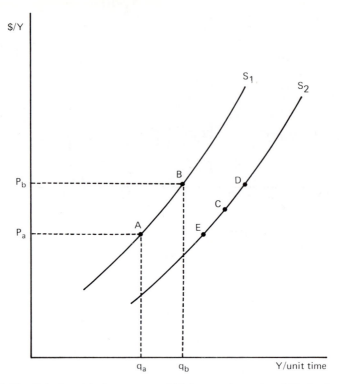

Figure 9.11 Relationship between a shift in supply and a shift in the quantity supplied.

Conclusion

Our analysis of the concept of supply is just about complete. The
concept of supply is based on the production function and the cost of
resources. It suggests the manner in which producers can be expected to
adjust to various sorts of change. But *supply* is probably one of the two most
misused words in the English language. Supply refers to the *entire curve*. A
movement from point *A* to point *B* in Figure 9.11 does *not* constitute a
change in supply; it merely represents a change in the *quantity supplied*. The
movement observed has merely been from one point to another along a given
supply curve *in response to a change in price*. On the other hand, a movement
from *A* or *B* to *C, D,* or *E* would represent a shift in the entire curve and
would constitute a change in supply. The difference between a change in
supply and a change in the quantity supplied is an extremely important
difference in economics. This difference must be clearly understood, since it

denotes the difference in a producer's adjustment to a change in price and his adjustment to a change in one of the *ceteris paribus* conditions of supply.

There are several key things that should be remembered about the concept of supply:

1. Short-run market supply is simply the total of all the short-run supply functions for the individual firms included in the industry. The short-run supply function for the individual firm is defined by that portion of marginal cost that lies above average variable cost. Marginal cost and average variable cost for the individual firm are both derived from the production function and the input or resource price information.

2. The supply curve will normally slope upward and to the right because of the law of supply, which states that the quantity available for sale will be directly related to the level of price; that is, as price is increased, the quantity that producers are willing and able to produce and sell will increase.

3. A *shift in supply* involves a movement of the entire supply function. In the case of an individual firm, this will normally be associated with a change such as an improvement in technology or a change in resource prices. In the case of the market supply function, the shift in supply is associated with the total reaction of all firms in the industry.

Selected References

Boulding, Kenneth E., *Economic Analysis,* 3rd ed., Chapter 28. New York: Harper and Brothers, 1955.

Brokken, Ray F., and Earl O. Heady, *Interregional Adjustments in Crop and Livestock Production, A Linear Programming Analysis,* Technical Bulletin 1396, Center for Agricultural and Economic Development, Iowa Agricultural Experiment Station and Economic Research Service, U.S. Department of Agriculture, July, 1968.

Crom, Richard J., *Simulated Interregional Models of the Livestock-Meat Economy,* Agricultural Economic Report No. 117, Economic Research Service, U.S. Department of Agriculture, June, 1967.

Dietrick, Raymond E., *An Interregional Analysis of the Fed Beef Economy,* Unpublished Ph.D. Dissertation, Oklahoma State University, Stillwater, Oklahoma, August, 1964.

Heady, Earl O., *Economics of Agricultural Production and Resource Use,* Chapters 2 and 3. Englewood Cliffs, N.J.: Prentice-Hall, Inc., 1952.

Klimm, Lester E., and Otis P. Starkey, *Introductory Economic Geography,* Chapters 1, 2, and 3. New York: Harcourt, Brace and Company, 1940.

Leftwich, Richard H., *An Introduction to Economic Thinking,* Chapters 7 and 8. New York: Holt, Rinehart and Winston, Inc., 1969.

Snodgrass, Milton M. and Luther T. Wallace, *Agriculture, Economics and Growth,* 2nd ed., p. 228. New York: Appleton-Century-Crofts, 1970.

10

Consumption of Agricultural Products and the Concept of Demand

The laws of supply and demand are to a large degree the forces that cause our economy to operate. We have discussed the concept of *supply* and the factors underlying this concept in some detail. But production and supply of any good is meaningless unless that good is ultimately to be utilized in the satisfaction of some of the needs and wants of humanity. These needs and wants may exist *within* the American economy or *outside* the American economy, but the fact that they *do* exist creates some purpose for the productive activities to which our resources are put.

Our definition of economics—the science that deals with the allocation of scarce resources among unlimited and competing ends—can be restated to include a statement of *purpose.* Economics is the *science that deals with the allocation of scarce resources among unlimited and competing ends for the purpose of maximizing the satisfaction of human wants.* This restatement implies that the focal point of the economizing process is the *consuming* activities of *people.* Wants are satisfied through consumption, and the nature of the human animal is to *desire* the material things that may be created through the production process.

Population as a Basis for Consumption • If *people* are the key to the process of consumption, then some study of the group which generates human wants seems to be warranted. If we look at what has happened to total U.S. population since 1790, we see that the most striking thing is the steady pattern of growth (Figure 10.1). The growth occurred at a fairly steady rate until the large European migrations began in the early 1800s. The rate of growth increased throughout the European migration and then tapered off in the early 1900s. This growth rate came almost to a standstill during World War I and then picked up in the 1920s. During the Great

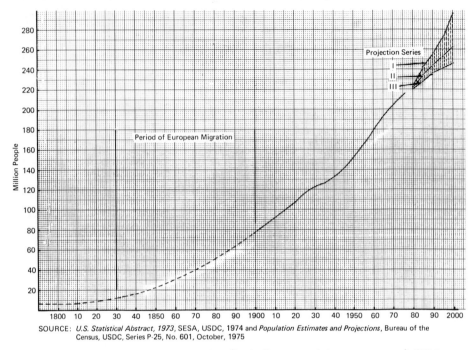

SOURCE: *U.S. Statistical Abstract, 1973*, SESA, USDC, 1974 and *Population Estimates and Projections*, Bureau of the Census, USDC, Series P-25, No. 601, October, 1975

Figure 10.1   Total U.S. population (including armed forces overseas) 1790–1976 with projections.

Depression it slowed down again, and then accelerated following World War II. There appears to be a reduction in the rate of growth that began in the 1960s. Whether this reduction is real or merely the result of relatively low birth rates during the Great Depression and World War II remains yet to be seen. The population projections formulated by the Bureau of the Census suggest that U.S. population for the latter fourth of the twentieth century could go either way.

The information in Figure 10.1 very graphically portrays the much publicized population explosion in the United States. The interesting thing is that birth rate and the natural population increase portion of the population explosion didn't really begin until the early 1900s. The termination of major European migration did not slow the rate of population increase. Natural population increase maintained the rate of expansion. Paradoxically this occurred at about the same time that the general availability of contraceptives permitted people to consciously limit family size. This paradox vividly illustrates the fact that we have not yet discovered what makes people decide to have or refuse to have families. We do know that in times of war or economic stress, the rate of population growth has characteristically dropped, and that periods of economic expansion have often been accompanied by rapid expansion in population.

Our total population unquestionably provides the basis for the consumption of all products. The fact that our population has grown and is growing very rapidly suggests that the basis for business activity is increasing steadily. Therefore, some detailed study of our population may give some indication of things that are yet to come. We know that not all people want the same things; the tastes and preferences for various consumption goods vary among individuals. But we also know that certain *groups* of people tend to want some items, while certain other groups would prefer that these items were not produced at all. For example, many people in the college-age group derive a great deal of satisfaction from today's popular music. Their parents, on the other hand, are of the firm opinion that this musical profanity should be outlawed. Most wives appear to derive a great deal of satisfaction from the possession of china and crystal while most husbands could not care less about these items.

The *composition* of population then will give us some idea about the types of products that will be in demand. *Population trees* define the composition of the population by age and sex. As we look at a population tree for 1930 (Figure 10.2), we see an almost perfect pyramid. The only deviations were in the zero to five age group and in the 30 to 35 age group. The 1925–30 period (which supplied the 0–5 age group) saw depression in agriculture and a decrease in the historically-larger rural families, along with the age of the feminists who felt that women should be emancipated from the burden of child bearing. These forces, along with other factors, reduced the number of children born during this period. The other group, 30–35 years old, would have included those persons born during 1895–1900. This was the group that fought World War I and was also the group that seems to have been the hardest hit by the flu epidemic of 1917–1919.

As we look at the population tree for 1940, we can see the full impact of the Great Depression on the birth rate. The population groups of zero to five and five to ten years of age are the smallest of the groups under 35.

The 1950 and 1960 population trees show basically the same information as the 1930 and 1940 trees. However, the composition of America's 1960 population has some striking characteristics. The short baby crops during the period of 1930–39 joined the junior executive age group during the 1960s. Because of the low birth rate during the depression, and the rapid economic expansion following World War II, there simply were not enough of these people to fill all the jobs available in the junior executive category. As a result businesses were forced to drop the age level at which they were willing to hire people for these jobs. As a result they simply skimmed the top off this younger group to fill the really fine jobs that were available. This was one reason for the tremendously competitive pressure for good grades among college students in the 1950s and early 1960s. The really fine jobs went to people who were being accelerated into the jobs that would normally have been filled by people born during the 1930s.

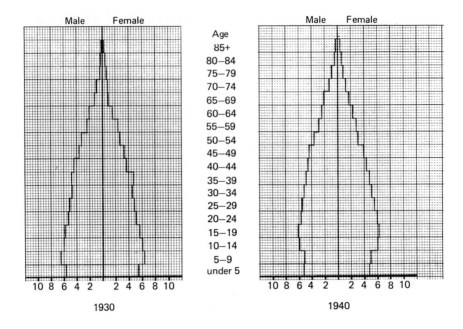

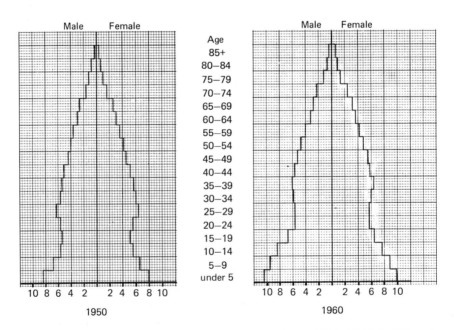

Figure 10.2 United States population by age and sex, 1930, 1940, 1950, and 1960, in millions of people.

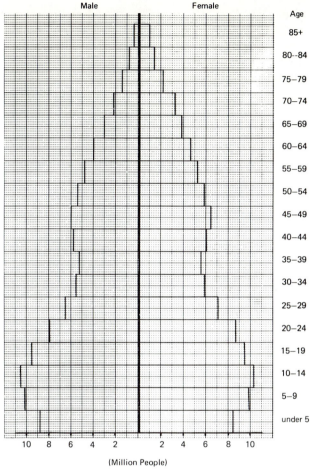

Figure 10.3 United States population by age and sex, 1970.

The 1970 population tree (Figure 10.3) sheds some light on a number of social problems that began in the late 1960s and on some that are yet to come. The post-World War II baby boom got to college in the late 1960s (these are the 20 to 24 and 15 to 19 year age groups in Figure 10.3). The dramatically expanded numbers of these people had created stress on the availability of the relevant public services from the time of their birth. Because of the lag in school construction, for example, many of them had been forced into half-day sessions in the early 1950s when they began to reach school age. By the mid-to-late 1960s when they began to reach college age, this group found that the available college facilities were inadequate to accommodate their numbers. When they entered the job market, they found that there weren't enough jobs to go around. Small wonder that the college students of the late '60s and early '70s should finally get a bellyful of frustration. Throughout their lives, these people had been confronted with a society that wasn't quite ready to absorb them. Thus, while it is regrettable, the alienation among the young people of the 1960s and 1970s was understandable and predictable.

In looking at the 1970 population tree, there are three strong influences:

1. The proportion of people beyond the age of 50 in 1970 was at an all-time high. This meant that those products that are normally associated with post-middle-age maturity were likely to find a more receptive market than at any time in history. And this was indeed true. Nursing homes to care for the aged, for example, became a major new industry across the country during the 1960s.

2. Among this 50-plus age group, there was a disproportionate number of women. This was a change. Prior to 1960, older men had outnumbered older women. This reflected the reality that the "good old days" may have been all right for men and dogs, but they were hell on women and horses! But with improved medicine, particularly for obstetrical care, women began to live longer than men in the middle part of the twentieth century. This meant that the products that older women use (blue hair rinse, for example) would face a lush market, and that there would be many older women without husbands.

3. The people born since 1945 were present in almost frightening numbers. In 1970, there were 93 million Americans—46 percent of our population—under the age of 25. This meant several things, both good and bad. First and foremost, the competition for the better jobs during the latter fourth of the 1900s was to be absolutely murderous. Second, the political power potentially in the hands of young voters meant that the vote power of young people was enormous and was increasing. Third, and probably most important, large numbers of people in this group would be entering the work force and establishing new families in the immediate future. This meant that the economic activity in the 1970s and 1980s had to be accelerated to a high degree. The demand for the items needed by young families (milk, baby food, clothing, housing, etc., etc.), would expand very rapidly. This created a challenge to our economy's productivity and at the same time provided the means for meeting that challenge. The means for meeting *any* challenge is well-trained young people with guts.

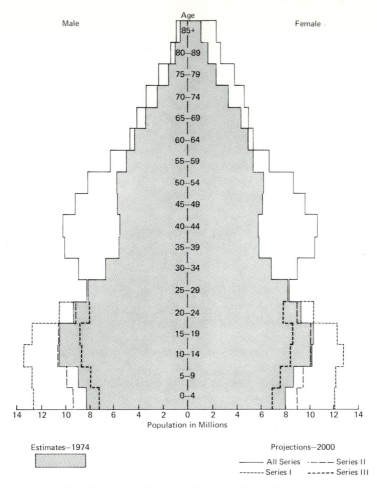

Figure 10.4 Estimated U.S. population by age and sex, 1974, with projections to 2000.

But the expected age and sex distribution of U.S. population in the year 2000 (Figure 10.4) gives a glimmer of things that are yet to come. Those people born in the post-World War II baby boom will be in their forties and fifties, and will be far more numerous than their offspring, should the reduced birth rate observed in the '60s and '70s persist through the remainder of this century (Population Projection Series III in Figure 10.4). But regardless of which population projection should happen to be most nearly accurate, the children born during the latter 1970s and 1980s are likely to enjoy some very fine employment opportunities. The "waist" in the population distribution that results from reduced numbers of births during the 1965–74 period will likely create a situation in the year 2000 similar to that observed in the 1950s and 1960s. The presence of very large numbers of middle aged suggests that the products associated with maturity will be much in demand. The numbers of older people relative to the young may force a revision in the retirement policies of both public and private institutions in the early part of the twenty-first century. The younger work force simply may not be large enough to produce enough goods and services to meet the needs of an American population approaching or exceeding a quarter of a billion people.

Income as a Basis for Consumption   •   We've seen the tremendous increase in population in the United States. This gives us some clue to the *magnitude* of desire for the goods that our economy can produce (i.e., *how much* of the goods will be needed). The structural components of our population (i.e., the age and sex distribution) suggest some of the *types* of products that will be needed. But as we saw earlier, the *need* for products is not enough to create *demand* for products. The other part of demand is *purchasing power.* What has happened to the purchasing power of the average person in recent years?

Between 1950 and 1975, the "current" dollar estimate of per capita disposable income consistently increased (Figure 10.5). When the "current"

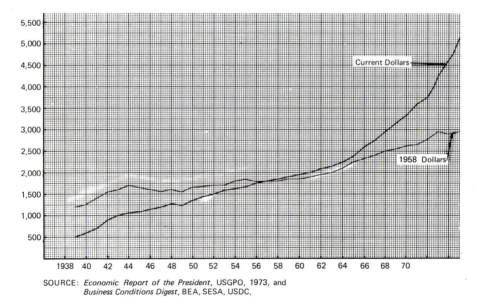

SOURCE: *Economic Report of the President,* USGPO, 1973, and
Business Conditions Digest, BEA, SESA, USDC,
February, 1976

Figure 10.5   United States disposable personal income per capita, 1939–75, in current dollars and in 1959 dollars.

dollar estimate is adjusted to 1958 dollars to correct for inflation, the magnitude of the increase in per capita income is somewhat smaller, and the periods of economic recessions become apparent. Nevertheless, even after adjustment for inflation, the purchasing power of the average American almost doubled between 1950 and 1975! This means that we not only have more people to *need and want* products, but we also have a dramatically increased ability to pay for those goods and services. Thus, the demand for goods and services has increased at an unparalleled rate since World War II. Another important feature of income is that an ever increasing *proportion* of the families have been moving into the upper income brackets. Thus, the wealth is becoming more evenly distributed among our population.

Consumption and Demand • All right, we know that the *desires* for products are increasing because the numbers of people are increasing. We know that the average ability to pay for products is increasing because per capita income is increasing. These two facts tell us that consumption of all products, agricultural as well as non-agricultural, is potentially at the greatest volume in history. But what causes consumers to buy a particular product or group of products? In other words, what is the motivating force or forces in consumption? Why do consumers behave as they do?

We as consumers engage in the act of consumption because in some fashion we derive *satisfaction* or *utility* from consumption. This satisfaction may spring from having satisfied either a physical or emotional need. For example, we all achieve gratification or satisfaction from eating when we are hungry. But many people also receive gratification from eating when they are angry or upset. Thus, food can fill both a physical and an emotional need. We may buy a new car because we need dependable transportation, or we may buy a new car because we derive pleasure simply from *possessing* a new automobile. Regardless of whether the satisfaction we achieve from consumption is physical or psychic in nature, the fact remains that *it is satisfaction.* We as consumers will often sacrifice physical gratification in favor of psychic pleasures. The source of motivation for consumption is really not too important. The important thing is that consumers *are* motivated by the *utility* that they derive from the act of consuming.

Another reason that consumers behave as they do is *habit.* We may like fish perfectly well. But we simply aren't in the habit of including fish in our menu planning. Or we may habitually serve steak on Monday night, hamburger on Tuesday and chicken on Sunday. If one were to check the menu in a university dining hall over a period of several weeks or months, he would likely find a pattern in the frequency with which certain dishes are served. Meat loaf, for example, is likely to be served with disgusting regularity. This is because dieticians are people, and like most people, university dieticians fall into habitual patterns of performing their duties.

The *ceteris paribus* conditions of supply and demand that we assume to be constant are held constant because they are important. These *ceteris paribus* conditions in the case of demand include the influences discussed above. Some behavioral factors that will have an impact on the consumption relationships are:

1. Consumer tastes and preferences for products,

2. The number of consumers (population),

3. Consumer habits, and

4. Consumer incomes.

As we discuss demand, we will initially be assuming that all of these factors remain constant. Once we get the relationships defined in a static sense, then we will begin to relax some of the assumptions and observe the dynamic changes that are introduced as these *ceteris paribus* conditions are permitted to change.

In our discussion of national income we defined consumption to be a *flow*. A flow of production was created as the result of an interaction between the *stock* of national wealth and the *stock* of labor at any particular time. As the flow production reached the finished stage, it became a *flow of consumption.*

It is important that we keep in mind the "flowing" characteristic of production and consumption as we discuss these subjects in relation to supply and demand. Because of the flow characteristic, when we speak of supply and demand, we must think of the demand or supply for some *particular unit of time.* Thus, we will expect a certain quantity of goods and services to be produced or consumed at a certain price, during some specified time interval.

Also in our discussion of national income, we defined *consumer demand* to flow from the household sector and the *demand for resources* to flow primarily from the business sector. These are the two sectors with which we will be primarily concerned during the remainder of this book.

In agriculture, we are dependent on the household consumption sector as a place to ultimately *market* most of the products that originate on the farm. The resource-consuming function of the agricultural sector provides a part of the demand for many resources. The resource consumption occurs because *production* results from the combination of the resources. *Productivity* provides the basis for the demand for resources just as *utility* provides the basis for the demand for consumer goods. Thus, *utility* plays the same role in the consumer product market that *productivity* plays in the resource (or factor) market.

The Relationship Between Desire For Goods
and Purchasing Power

We have defined *utility* as the satisfaction that consumers derive from the consumption or possession of goods. Utility can also be derived from services such as medical care, dental care, or police protection, since these services also fulfill human wants and needs. The idea behind the entire concept of demand is that every rational consumer selects that combination of goods and services that will permit him to *maximize* his utility within the limits imposed by his budget. This idea of maximum consumer satisfaction implies that consumers *know* the relative amounts of utility that they individually can derive from the consumption of all the items available to them.

Can consumers in fact define the relative amounts of utility that they derive from consuming the various items available in our society? Obviously, we can't say that a steak dinner gives us a specified number of units of satisfaction (or "utils"), while a chicken dinner gives us so many less units of satisfaction. But we *can* say whether we would rather have a steak or a chicken dinner. All of us can *rank* goods and services in the order of our preference. This ranking, along with our income restraint, is all that is necessary for us to begin to analyze our individual demand for products.

Let's imagine that there are only two items available in our economy—food, representing the necessities of life, and clothing, representing the luxury items. We know that we can derive satisfaction from the consumption of each of these goods.

How do we know what the levels of satisfaction are? The utility we can derive from a new article of clothing will depend to some degree on how much clothing we already have. Likewise, the satisfaction we derive from additional food will depend on how much food we already have. If a person has just eaten three hamburgers, another hamburger doesn't hold much value to him. This situation is known as the *law of diminishing marginal utility.* Stated in the simplest of terms, the law of diminishing marginal utility is that *as additional units of a good or service are consumed, the satisfaction derived from the consumption of each additional unit is reduced.*

We can agree that the marginal utility of additional units of a good declines as the number of units increases. It follows that if we have a great deal of clothing and very little food, we would be willing to give up perhaps ten units of clothing to get an additional unit of food. We would, however, be willing to give up something less than ten units of clothing for the next unit of food. The third additional unit of food would be worth still less to us in terms of the clothing than was the second, and so on. This situation represents *the principle of diminishing marginal rates of substitution: suc-*

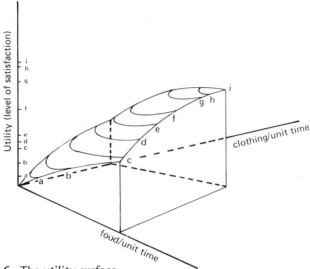

Figure 10.6   The utility surface.

cessive units of one good will be worth progressively less, when measured in terms of a second good.

Now that we have the law of diminishing marginal utility and the related principle of the diminishing marginal rates of substitution firmly in mind, let's imagine that satisfaction or utility is a hill (the common term for this is a utility surface) as shown in Figure 10.6. As we move up that hill, we achieve progressively elevated levels of satisfaction. If, however, we walk *around* the hill, we are merely staying on the *same* level of satisfaction (in exactly the same sense that a terrace on a hillside field maintains a given level of elevation). Thus, each line or terrace going around the hill defines some

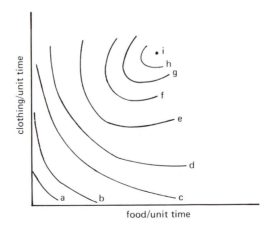

Figure 10.7   The utility map or the indifference map of the utility surface.

level of utility. The various combinations of food and clothing that will give us that particular level of satisfaction are defined by the line around the utility surface. Therefore, we are indifferent as to *where* we are on that line because our level of satisfaction is unchanged.

Now let's imagine that we are in an airplane looking straight down at the hill or utility surface. All we see is the lines or the terraces that define the various levels of satisfaction (Figure 10.7). This type of illustration is the same as a military contour map or a topographic map—the lines indicate the elevation or level of satisfaction. This type of diagram is known as a *utility map*. As we move northeast on the utility map, we are going up the hill, increasing the level of satisfaction.

The lines defining the levels of satisfaction are known as *indifference curves,* since we are indifferent as to where we are along any single curve. There are several characteristics of indifference curves that should be specified. First of all, indifference curves slope downward and to the right. Second, they are convex to the origin with the "bow" of the curve pointing toward the origin or corner of the diagram. Third, they cannot intersect.

The curve slopes downward and to the right because in order for a consumer to give up some of one commodity and still remain on the same level of satisfaction, he must be compensated with additional units of another product. Figure 10.8 illustrates the principle of diminishing marginal rates of

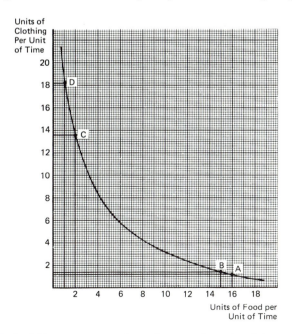

Figure 10.8 Indifference curves slope down and to the right and are convex to the origin.

substitution. As successive units of one product are lost, it will take progressively more and more of the substitute commodity to adequately compensate for the loss of satisfaction. When the consumer has lots of food and not much clothing, it doesn't take much clothing to compensate for the loss of one unit of food (as from point *A* to point *B*). But before many units of food are given up, the consumer's stomach begins to growl and he becomes a much more demanding trader. Between point *C* and point *D,* it takes a great many clothes to compensate for a unit of food since this consumer suffers from an empty belly.

The reason that indifference curves cannot intersect is that an intersection would mean that the same combination of goods would give two different levels of satisfaction. This is the same as saying that you could be 20 feet aloft and 50 feet aloft at the same time. The only way this could happen would be for you to be 31 feet tall.

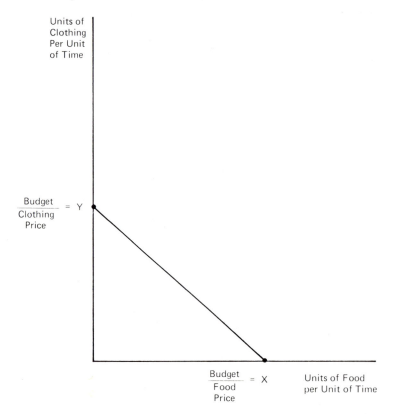

Figure 10.9 Construction of the budget line using the consumer's budget and the prices of the alternative commodities.

We now have our two-product world, and we know the satisfaction that these products can yield from the indifference map of the utility surface. We also know the rates at which those products will substitute for one another in maintaining any given level of satisfaction. All we need to determine the quantities of food and clothing that our sample consumer will buy is information concerning the prices of these commodities and the consumer's purchasing power or budget for these items. If the consumer should spend *all* of his budget on food, there is some maximum amount of food that he can buy. That is, if we divide his budget by the price of food, he can buy *X* units of food in Figure 10.9.

Likewise, if all of our income is spent on clothing, the consumer can buy *Y* units of clothing. A straight line connecting these two points shows his *income restraint*—that is, his income will permit him to consume any combination of food and clothing that falls on or below his "budget line." His objective is to *maximize* his total satisfaction (or utility) *within the limits of this budget line.* Therefore, he is going to attempt to get the highest possible level of satisfaction that this budget permits.

In a very real sense, a consumer's budget (or income) does the same thing to him on his utility surface that a fence does to livestock on a hillside pasture (Figure 10.10). No matter how badly the consumer might wish to graze the tender grasses available at higher elevations, he is prevented from

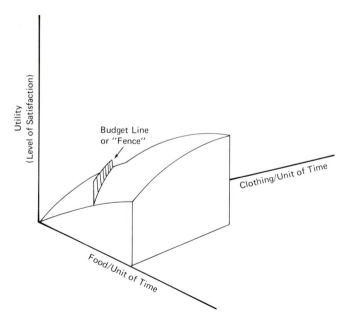

Figure 10.10 Budgetary limit on the utility surface.

doing so by the unpleasant fact that there is a budget fence between him and his heart's desire.

Now, let's combine the indifference map with the budget line that defines the range of combinations that may be obtained with the particular income restriction we have postulated (Figure 10.11). The objective of our analysis is to determine what combination of items the consumer is going to select for consumption, given his income, the prices of the items, and a map of his preference order.

First, let's ask a question. Which level of satisfaction is our friend the consumer going to select? Obviously, he is going to get the greatest amount of satisfaction his income will permit. Any point *on* or *below* his budget line restriction is attainable, but we have already said that we are going to assume that consumers are *rational*. If a consumer is rational, he will *not* select a combination of goods below his budgetary constraint since he can increase his satisfaction by moving out to the budget limit. He will not select combination *A* since he will have a higher level of satisfaction at any of the combinations *B, C,* or *D*. Since combination *C* is on the indifference curve that just touches (or is *tangent* to) his budget line, this is the highest possible level of satisfaction that the consumer can achieve, given his income restriction and the product prices. Combination *C* is the point at which the rational consumer will choose to operate.

We know that the tremendous range of commodities available in our society gives the consumer a wide range of consumption alternatives. If beef

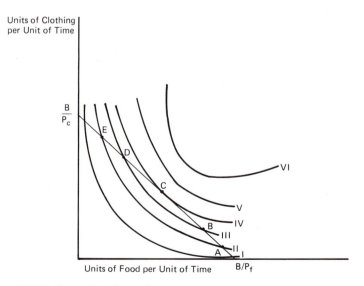

Figure 10.11 Determination of consumption using indifference curves, commodity prices, and budget restraint.

becomes too expensive, the consumer has the option of shifting to pork. If both beef and pork are too expensive, the consumer can meet protein needs with poultry, fish, cheese, or vegetable sources such as dry beans. For any particular consumer, these products all possess varying degrees of substitutability.

The relationships between commodities can be classified into two broad categories. Products such as beef, pork, poultry, fish, cheese, and dry beans are generally considered to be *substitutes*. Quantities of any of these products can to a large degree replace quantities of another. The rate of substitution may not be, and probably is not, a one-to-one relationship. But if you eat pork chops for lunch, you aren't likely to be eating roast beef also. Thus, an increase in the consumption of pork will likely be associated with a *decrease* in the consumption of the substitute products, other things being equal.

The counterpart of the substitute commodities is that group of items that are *complementary* in nature. Shoes and shoe laces, tractors and tractor tires, or ham and eggs are examples of commodities that tend to be *complements*. Complementary types of products tend to be consumed together. If everyone wore cowboy boots or loafers, there wouldn't be much use for shoe laces. Thus, an increase in the use of one complementary item would most likely be associated with an increase in the use of the other.

The shape (or degree of convexity) exhibited by the indifference curves indicates the type of relationship that exists between products (Figure 10.12). Products that are perfectly substitutable—two brands of aspirin, for example—will be associated with an indifference map that shows the curves to be perfectly straight. This means that the loss of one unit of one brand of aspirin

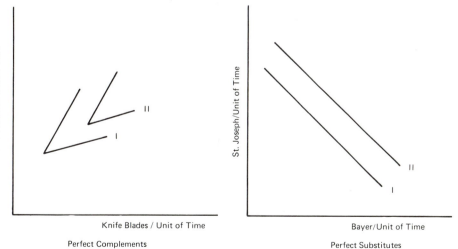

Perfect Complements   Perfect Substitutes

Figure 10.12 Indifference maps for perfect complements and perfect substitutes.

could be fully compensated by one unit of the other brand at any point on the curve. Perfect complements (two products that must be consumed in exact proportions—knife blades and knife handles, for example) would be shown on an indifference map whose curves have such an extreme degree of convexity that they really become points. Thus, the loss of a knife blade would render the handle virtually useless.

The Concept of Demand

Several factors have been illustrated thus far in our discussion of the consumption of agricultural products. First, the total consumption of agricultural goods in our society rests largely on the numbers of consumers present. An analysis of the *composition* of the population can suggest the types of products that will be consumed, and can also suggest what we might expect in terms of future trends in population growth. Individual consumption is determined by a combination of several factors:

1. Price for the product in question,

2. Prices for substitute products,

3. Individual income, and

4. The taste and preference pattern as shown by the individual's utility surface or indifference map.

An individual's demand function for products is largely determined by these same four factors, but exactly what is demand? *Demand may be defined as the schedule of quantities that a buyer (or group of buyers) is willing to purchase at a specified series of prices, in a given market, at a given time, ceteris paribus.* Demand is based on the desirability of goods and services to consumers, backed up with purchasing power. Thus, demand, like supply, represents both willingness and ability.

We have suggested that our indifference analysis could be used for purposes of defining the demand curve for an individual. Let's return to our example of the world in which there are only two products, food and clothing, and attach some numbers to the diagram. We'll specify a price for clothing, a price for food, and a level of income. Within the context of the definition of demand, if the individual's demand for food is to be estimated, the only things that can be permitted to change are the price of food and the combinations of products purchased as prices change. The consumer's income, the price for the alternative commodity of clothing, and the consumer's state of tastes and preferences as defined by his indifference map are all a part of the *ceteris paribus* conditions that do not change.

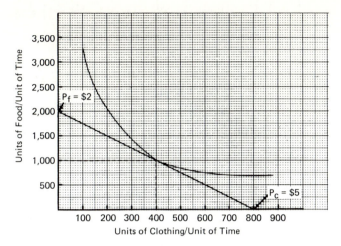

Figure 10.13 Construction of budget line with income of $4,000, food priced at $2, and clothing priced at $5.

Let's assume that our sample consumer has $4,000 to spend each year. The price of food is $2 per unit, and the price of clothing is $5 per unit. Thus, if he spends all his income on food, he can buy 2,000 units of food. If all income is spent on clothing, he can buy 800 units of clothing. So the budget restriction in Figure 10.13 is defined by a straight line between these points. Given his preference order as defined by the indifference curve in Figure 10.13, he will buy 400 units of clothing and 1,000 units of food, spending $2,000 for clothing and $2,000 for food during the time interval in question. Within our definition of demand, we know that our consumer will purchase 1,000 units of food at a price of $2 per unit, other things remaining constant at the levels we have specified.

Now, suppose that the price of food drops to $1.60 per unit. The budgetary restriction the consumer faces with his $4,000 income and with a clothing price of $5 per unit is changed. (Figure 10.14). His maximum attainable clothing purchase is still 800 units, but he can now purchase a maximum of 2,500 units of foods. With this new budget line, he can increase his consumption of food and still have money left over to spend on more clothing. In this fashion, he has been able to move out to a higher level of satisfaction. He is now buying 1,100 units of food at $1.60 per unit, spending a total of $1,760 on food. This leaves $2,240 for clothing expenditure, enabling him to buy 448 units of clothing.

As the price of food declines, the consumer purchases more and more food (Figure 10.15 and Tables 10.1 and 10.2). This illustrates the *law of demand: the lower the price at which a product is offered for sale in a given market at a given time, the greater will be the quantity purchased, ceteris*

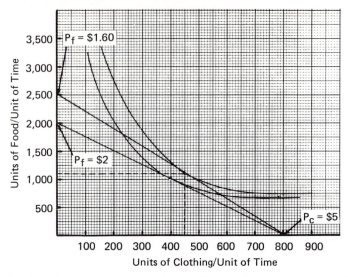

Figure 10.14 Construction of the budget line with income of $4,000, food priced at $1.60, clothing priced at $5.

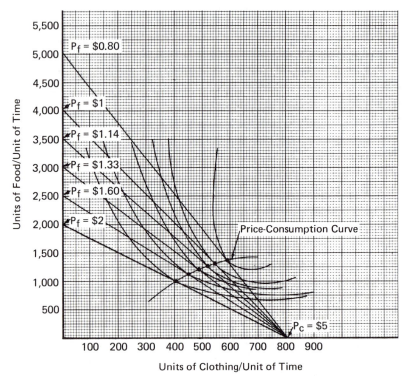

Figure 10.15 The price-consumption curve.

TABLE 10.1

BUDGET RESTRAINTS FOR FIGURE 10.15

INCOME	PRICE OF CLOTHING PER UNIT	MAXIMUM ATTAINABLE CLOTHING PURCHASE	PRICE OF FOOD PER UNIT	MAXIMUM ATTAINABLE FOOD PURCHASE
$4,000	$5.00	800	$2.00	2,000
4,000	5.00	800	1.60	2,500
4,000	5.00	800	1.33	3,000
4,000	5.00	800	1.14	3,500
4,000	5.00	800	1.00	4,000
4,000	5.00	800	.80	5,000

paribus. (An alternative way of stating the law of demand is *the greater the amount of a commodity offered for sale in a given market at a given time, the lower will be the price per unit at which the entire quantity can be sold.*) In either case, the main point in the law of demand is that as prices change, the quantity purchased will change in the opposite direction.

So far, we do not have a demand curve as such. What we have at this point is a *price-consumption* curve. However, the demand curve is just one simple step further. All that we do is transfer the information derived from

TABLE 10.2

QUANTITIES OF FOOD AND CLOTHING PURCHASED
AS FOOD PRICES CHANGE AS SHOWN IN FIGURE
10.15

PRICE OF FOOD PER UNIT	QUANTITY OF FOOD PURCHASED[1]	TOTAL FOOD EXPENDITURE	QUANTITY OF CLOTHING PURCHASED	TOTAL CLOTHING EXPENDITURES
$2.00	1,000	$2,000	400.0	$2,000
1.60	1,100	1,760	448.0	2,240
1.33	1,200	1,596	480.8	2,404
1.14	1,250	1,425	515.0	2,575
1.00	1,300	1,300	540.0	2,700
.80	1,350	1,080	584.0	2,920

[1] Quantity purchased with income fixed at $4,000 per year, price for clothing fixed at $5 per unit, and consumer tastes and preferences constant at levels shown by the indifference maps.

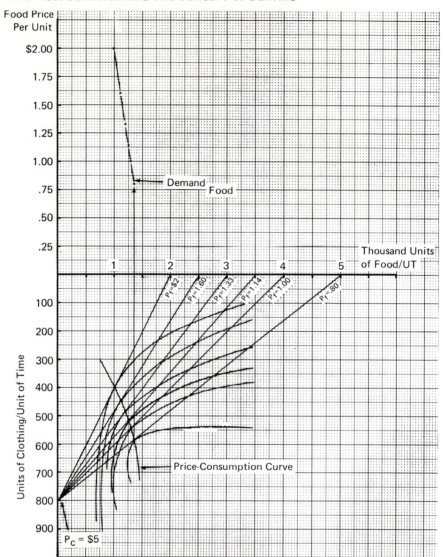

Figure 10.16 Relationship between the price-consumption curve and the demand curve.

our indifference analysis in Figure 10.15 to a chart that shows the quantities of food that our sample consumer purchased under the various price conditions, plotted against the levels at which food was priced. The lower part of Figure 10.16 is identical with Figure 10.15, turned on its side. From this, we can move directly to the demand curve shown in the upper part of Figure

10.16. For example, the indifference curve analysis in the lower chart shows 1,000 units of food purchased when food is priced at $2. The upper chart shows exactly the same information.

When the chart showing the demand curve is constructed, the definition for the concept of demand becomes clearer. The definition of demand was stated to be that schedule of quantities that a buyer is willing and able to purchase at a given series of prices in a given market at a given time, *ceteris paribus*. The concept of demand is a *schedule*: it presents the alternative price-quantity combination at which a buyer is both willing and able to operate in a given market at a given time, other conditions being *equal*.

The Impact of Changes in Ceteris Paribus Conditions • The time dimension is an important element in the concept of demand because of the *ceteris paribus* conditions. These conditions are *not* in fact constant. We merely assume them to be constant (or we *hold* them constant) so that we can sort out the effects of various types of changes. The *ceteris paribus* conditions do change over time, and when they change, they cause changes in the demand schedule. In the case of an individual consumer's demand curve, the *ceteris paribus* conditions include income, prices for substitute and complementary goods, and the preference pattern for the individual.

Consider for example the impact on the demand for food of a change in price of alternative goods. Let's assume that we are still in our two-product world and are analyzing the behavior of our sample consumer. His income is still $4,000 annually, and his preference pattern is unchanged. When the price of clothing was $5 per unit and price of food was $2 per unit, he was willing to purchase 1,375 units of food per year at the $2 price. Let's assume that the price of clothing declines from the $5 per unit level to $4 per unit. What happens to the consumer's willingness to purchase food at the price of $2 per unit under these conditions is shown in Figure 10.17.

The decline in the price of clothing increases the total number of units of clothing that the sample consumer's income can buy from 800 units to 1,000 units. This gives the consumer a new budget line along which he can operate. A larger portion of the indifference map is now within the range of his income. He increases his food expenditure from $2,000 per year to $2,200 per year as a result of the change in the price of the alternative product of clothing.

The increase in food purchases at the $2 price represents a shift in the demand for food, resulting from the change in the price of the other product (Figure 10.18). The thing that must be pointed out is that a *change in demand means that the entire demand schedule has shifted as a result of a change in one of the ceteris paribus conditions*. A change in demand for a given commodity *cannot* result from a change in the *quantity* demanded. *The*

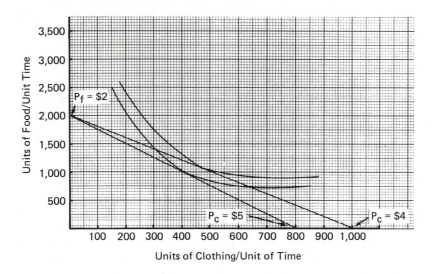

Figure 10.17 Effect of a change in the *ceteris paribus* condition of the price of alternative goods on the combination of goods purchased.

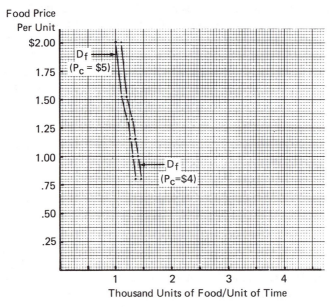

Figure 10.18 Effect of a change in the *ceteris paribus* condition of the price of alternative goods upon the demand for a good.

only means by which a change in demand can occur (i.e., a shift in the entire schedule) *is by way of a change in the ceteris paribus* conditions.

A change in income would move the budget line out such that the new budget line would be parallel with the old. Thus, with a given preference structure (as shown by the indifference map), the consumer would be able to increase his level of satisfaction by purchasing more of both commodities at the same prices. The entire demand schedule would have shifted to the right as a result of such a change in the *ceteris paribus* condition in consumer income.

Suppose that the sample consumer gets on his scales one morning and discovers that he weighs 627 pounds. He goes to his doctor and is told in sweet and dulcet tones that he is risking a severe coronary thrombosis unless he loses 400 pounds. A discovery of this sort might very well alter the structure of his utility surface. As a result, the shape of his indifference curves would be altered *away* from food and toward the alternative product. This type of development in the consumer's state of tastes and preferences would have the effect of reducing his demand for food.

Our discussion of the individual's demand function has been greatly oversimplified. The idea of a two-product world is admittedly unrealistic, but it is convenient for purposes of illustration. The indifference analysis can be conducted for individual demand using any two products. As long as the individual can state a preference between two combinations, there are two or more indifference curves involved. When the consumer is indifferent between two combinations, then two points on the same level of satisfaction have been defined—that is, we have located two points on a single indifference curve.

Obviously, we aren't going to go out and construct an indifference map for every possible individual in order to define his individual demand curve. However, the indifference map is an effective tool for understanding the concept of demand. The fact that the *ceteris paribus* conditions are held constant while price and quantity are varied is illustrated by the manipulation of the budget line as it is associated with a given level of income. The manner in which a change in the *ceteris paribus* conditions shifts the demand function is illustrated again by means of manipulating the budget line. The movement along a given demand function is shown when the prices of the product under examination are changed and the consumer reacts to the new price situation by altering the combinations in which he purchases goods.

The utility surface may be different among consumers and, if so, the indifference map for one consumer may be completely different from the indifference map for another consumer. In any case, every person has some schedule of prices that he is willing to pay for the various quantities of a product. This schedule represents the demand curve for that individual.

The Market Demand Function

We've seen how consumers behave in their efforts to achieve the maximum level of satisfaction possible within the limits of their income restraint. In the process of maximizing utility, individual consumers reveal their preference patterns. From this revealed preference, individual demand curves can be specified. The market demand schedule can be derived by simply adding the quantities of product that each consumer was willing to purchase at each specified level of price. Thus, as in the case of supply, market demand is simply the horizontal summation of all the demand curves for all the individuals who are buying in a given market at a given time.

Let's assume that Consumers *A, B,* and *C* are the only buyers trading in our market for food (Figure 10.19). Each of them has revealed through his preference patterns that price that he is willing to pay for given quantities of food. At $2 per unit, Consumer *A* buys 100 units of food and Consumer *C* buys 150 units. Consumer *B* buys no food at all at the $2 price—in fact,

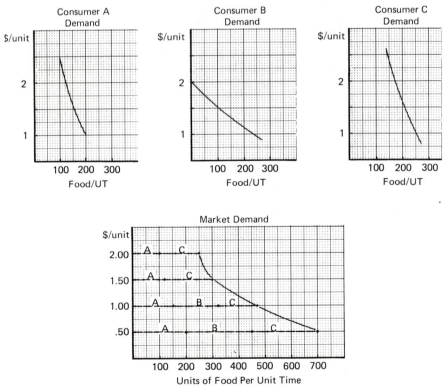

Figure 10.19 Derivation of market demand from individual demand functions for a product.

Consumer *B* doesn't start buying until the price gets below $1.50. (This does not necessarily mean that *B* doesn't eat. It may mean that he either has access to some alternative market or produces his own food when prices in our market are above the level that he is willing to pay.)

At a price of $2 per unit, then, the demand for food in our market is 250 units. As the price comes down, each consumer buys more and more food. Our market demand schedule is illustrated at the extreme right of Figure 10.19. As Consumer *B* enters the market, the slope of the curve is reduced (i.e., the response to price reduction is greater after prices have declined to the level where *B* decides to enter the market).

Several characteristics of the market demand schedule should be specified at this point. First of all, there are more *ceteris paribus* conditions that are specified in the case of market demand. The factors of income, prices of alternative products, and tastes and preferences are defined to be constant within each of the individual demand curves. But the market curve includes some additional factors that must be held constant. We have defined our market to include only three consumers. If we introduce another consumer, the market demand curve will shift. Thus, the population must be held constant when we talk in terms of the other things that are held constant in the market demand function.

We know that population is not in fact constant. It has increased at a rate of about 1.0–1.7 percent per year during the 1950–1975 period. But at a given instant in time, population changes very little. Thus, we can hold the population constant for analytical purposes. An alternative to holding population constant when measuring demand is to measure demand in terms of the *per capita* quantity that is purchased as prices change. In this fashion, since demand per person is the factor under scrutiny, we are not too concerned about how many people are involved.

Other *ceteris paribus* conditions that are present in the market demand might include:

1. Distribution of income,

2. The general price level (the overall state of the entire economy), and

3. International trade agreements.

If the income is distributed such that most people are very, very poor, the types of products most in demand will be different from those demanded when income is more evenly distributed. For example, if the top 5 percent of the families controlled only 15 percent of the income, then some of the luxuries of life could be enjoyed by larger numbers of people, and the market for these items would be much larger than under a situation in which 5 percent of the families controlled half the income.

We've already suggested that the general state of the whole economy affects the demand for almost all items. We saw how a situation in which there was a gap in demand could potentially send an economy into the downward spiral of depression, and how the reverse of this situation could create inflation. Both of these situations are reflected by the general price level. Inflation or deflation will alter the value of the dollar, but since some items will tend to inflate or deflate more rapidly than others, the quantities of individual goods demanded at the various prices will very likely be changed.

Because of international and governmental trade arrangements, many products that are available, or potentially available, face market demand schedules different from those that might be faced under a different set of these arrangements. Tariff structures, for example, can change the demand patterns. Import quotas or prohibitions will alter the market demand patterns. The government agreement to sell wheat to Russia in the early 1970s, for example, increased the quantity of wheat that could be sold at (and below) the price at which the Russian wheat was contracted. The ban on shipping cattle into the United States from areas infested with hoof and mouth disease has certainly affected the demand for some of the exotic breeds of cattle. Some potential customers have tended to ignore some of these breeds because of fear of disease.

The law of demand in the case of the individual consumer indicated that the quantity taken from the market changed in a direction opposite to changes in price—that is, as price increased, the quantity purchased by the individual was reduced, and *vice versa*. This principle applies to the market demand function as well. There are several reasons for the operation of the law of demand in the case of the market demand function. First of all, different consumers have different patterns of tastes and preferences. At high prices, only those consumers with intense desires for the product (Consumers A and C in Figure 10.19) would be interested in purchasing. As the price declines, those with a less intense desire for the product (Consumer B in the diagram) would become interested and enter the market. Imagine, for example, that our diagram is concerned with the demand for wheat. Consumers A and C are purchasing wheat for milling into flour. Consumer B, however, is purchasing wheat for use in cattle feeding. Since people demand wheat bread, the millers will pay high prices for wheat. But the cattle feeder can easily substitute corn or grain sorghums for wheat when wheat prices are too high. Thus, the cattle feeder's desire for wheat is less intense than is the desire (or demand) exhibited by the millers (that is, the cattle feeder is less eager to purchase wheat than are millers).

A second reason for the operation of the law of demand in the case of the market demand schedule is that individual consumers have differing levels of purchasing power. Demand involves not only the desire for the product, but also the ability to pay. At high prices, only those with adequate pur-chasing power can purchase. At lower prices, lower income individuals or families can buy. This explains why one sees more Chevrolets on the road than Cadillacs, and why there are more rowboats than yachts.

A third factor in the operation of the law of demand is that individual consumers experience differing levels of marginal utility from the use or possession of products. Intense desires, backed with purchasing power, are reflected in high levels of marginal utility and hence in high prices. Low prices mean that the utility to be derived from adding an additional unit to consumption doesn't increase the total satisfaction very much.

The things to remember about a market demand function include:

1. Demand is a schedule.

2. It presents the alternative price-quantity combinations.

3. At any given point on the market demand curve, all individual buyers pay the same price and take as much or as little as they want, *at that price.*

4. The *least eager* buyer determines the price for all the others. This is the person whose purchase is necessary to move the last unit of the quantity made available. Until price gets to the level that he is willing to pay, not all of the product offered for sale can be sold and the market price will not be established.

Changes in demand, like changes in supply, involve a shift in the entire demand schedule. If the price of a T-bone steak was $4.50 per pound at this time three years ago and if the price for T-bone steak is $2.50 today, does this mean that the demand for T-bone has declined? The answer is probably negative. What is more likely is that the move has been a change such as the move from point A to point B in Figure 10.20. The amount of T-bone offered for sale has increased enough that the less eager buyers have come into the market and the price has moved downward *along a given demand curve.*

Let's examine some of the possible changes that might be observed in the case of market demand curves and the sources of such changes. Suppose we observe changes in the prices of substitutes and/or complements for a given product. What would be the impact on the price for the product in question and the quantity taken from the market?

Suppose we are interested in the demand for bacon. What would be the impact of an increase in the price of the substitute good of ham? Figure 10.21 illustrates this situation. If the price of ham increased from P_{h1} to P_{h2} (a move from A to B on the diagram), what happens to the demand for

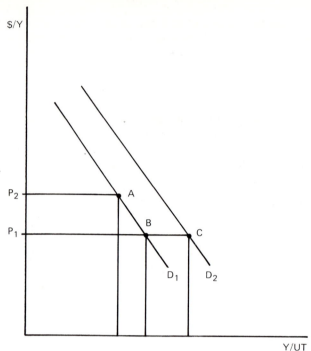

Figure 10.20 Difference between a change in demand and a change in the quantity demanded.

bacon? Well, the ham price increase means that less ham will be taken from the market at the new higher price. This suggests that consumers are going to try to compensate for the resulting loss in satisfaction by trying to buy more of the relatively lower cost substitute product of bacon. If there is no change

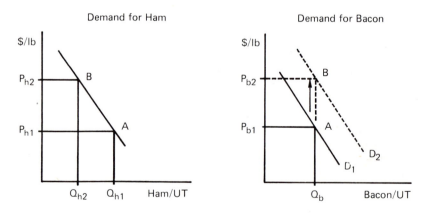

Figure 10.21 Relationship between substitute goods.

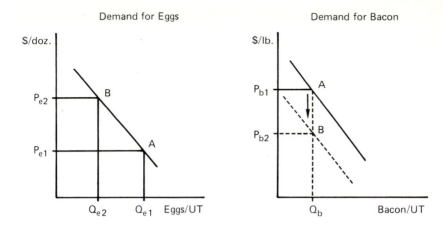

Figure 10.22   Relationship between complementary goods.

in the quantity of bacon offered for sale, the price for bacon will be bid up as the demand curve for bacon shifts. A downward movement in the price of ham would have the opposite effect on the demand for bacon.

Suppose on the other hand we observe a change in the price for the complementary product of eggs. Since bacon and eggs might tend to be consumed together, a price increase for eggs would tend to reduce the *quantity* of eggs purchased and hence to reduce the *demand* for bacon. That is, a *movement along the demand curve* for eggs would tend to generate a *shift in the entire demand curve* for bacon as in Figure 10.22. Consumers would reduce the price they are willing to pay for a given quantity of bacon (or, alternatively, they would reduce the quantity of bacon they were willing to purchase at a given price) as the result of the change in the price of eggs.

The changes introduced by shifts in other types of conditions can be analyzed in the same fashion. Increases in consumer income or in population would tend to shift the demand curve to the right. Changes in tastes and preferences could shift the demand curve in any fashion, depending on what type of change was observed. Government regulations can alter the demand curve in many ways, depending on what sort of regulation is introduced.

We examined production functions and their role in the generation of supply functions in Chapter 9. We have examined utility surfaces and indifference maps as they operate in the generation of demand functions in this chapter. We have seen that demand typically slopes downward and to the right and that supply characteristically slopes upward and to the right. We have stated repeatedly that price is determined by the forces of supply and demand. In Chapter 11, we will examine supply and demand and their roles as market price determinants.

Selected References

Hicks, J. R., *Value and Capital,* 2nd ed., Chapters 1 and 2. London: Oxford University Press, 1957.

Leftwich, Richard H., *The Price System and Resource Allocation,* Chapters 4 and 5. New York: Rinehart and Co., Inc., 1956.

Marshall, Alfred, *Principles of Economics,* 8th ed., Book III, Chapter III. London: Macmillan and Co., Ltd., 1959.

Samuelson, Paul A., *Economics, An Introductory Analysis,* 7th ed., Chapter 22 and Appendix. New York: McGraw-Hill Book Co., 1967.

11

Supply, Demand, and the Role of Market Price

In Chapter 9, we analyzed the production of agricultural goods and the production function that determines the levels at which those goods are produced. We translated this information into the cost of producing goods, and showed how the marginal cost function defined the supply function for an individual firm. We then saw how we could simply add up the individual supply functions to get a market supply function. Because of the increasing nature of the marginal cost function, the market supply function will typically slope upward and to the right. That is, producers can be induced to increase production only if prices rise enough to cover the increasing marginal cost. It is apparent that this sort of information may be used by individual producers in organizing their operations for maximum profits. Thus, the concept of market supply will be one of the determinants of market prices with which producers must cope and to which they must adjust.

Chapter 10 was devoted to an analysis of the consumption of the products of farms and ranches. We saw that people consumed products because they derived *utility* or *satisfaction* from that consumption. We analyzed the individual consumer's utility surface, since this surface reveals the individual consumer's state of tastes and preferences. We mapped that utility surface through the use of indifference curves, and discovered that we could derive an individual consumer's demand function for a product by holding everything constant except the prices of that product and the quantity that the consumer purchased at the various prices. Because of the law of diminishing marginal utility and the related principle of diminishing marginal rates of substitution, we found that the demand function typically slopes downward and to the right. This reflects the consumer's unwillingness to increase purchases unless prices decline. As with supply, we discovered that a market demand function could be defined by simply adding up the individual demand functions.

Market Price Determination

We now have the market demand function and the market supply function. But what is the significance of these two functions? Demand and supply are the forces in our economy that work to determine the market price level, but how do we combine the pictures of the market demand and market supply functions into a composite picture of market price determination?

As you may suspect from the time we have devoted to defining not only the forces of supply and demand, but also the principles that go into making up these forces, the supply and demand concepts provide us with some very powerful tools of analysis. We've stated that the supply and demand curves will determine price. Price, however, is not the *only* economic phenomenon determined by the forces of supply and demand. The *volume of transactions* consummated in our market place (i.e., the quantity exchanged) is determined at the same time as price.

In order for any of a product to be exchanged in the market place, there must be a difference of opinion (i.e., a divergence of attitudes) on the part of the potential buyers and sellers. If someone offers a dollar for a ticket to the Army–Navy football game and you accept that offer, then we have an example of a difference of opinion about the excellence of at least one of the two football teams in question. One individual has said, in effect, that seeing the game is worth more than the dollar. You have said, in effect, that the dollar is worth more than seeing the game.

A difference of opinion on the parts of buyers and sellers is not enough to *ensure* exchange in the market place. The opinions of sellers (as expressed by the market supply function) must differ from the opinions of buyers (as expressed by the market demand function) *within the same price range* (see Figure 11.1). If there is no overlap in these price ranges, exchange cannot occur.

We have seen how supply is determined by the cost structures of the producing agencies. We have further seen how demand is determined by the tastes and incomes of consumers, and the prices of alternative products. If the cost structures of the producers were such that none of the product in question would be produced and sold at prices below p_1, and if consumers were faced with a situation in which they would pay no more than p_2, then the divergence of opinion would be so wide that no exchange could possibly occur.

You may feel that this example is not relevant since you can't visualize a setting in which this situation would prevail. However, during World War II, the American optics industry was in very much this sort of situation. American optical producers were unwilling (and unable because of costs) to produce certain types of lenses at the prices at which the Dutch optical

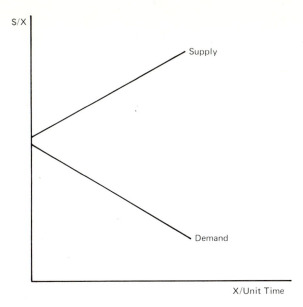

Figure 11.1 Divergence of attitude among buyers and sellers can prevent exchange from occurring.

industry was selling these lenses. Gun sights required this particular type of optical equipment. The German occupation of the Netherlands had curtailed our supply of these lenses. Therefore, it was necessary to devise some method that would lower the producer's cost curve in order that some production and exchange could occur. This was accomplished by means of subsidies paid directly to the optical industry.

The case of the optical industry occurred before most of today's college students were born. But immediately prior to the emergence of the energy crisis, which improved the outlook for natural fibers in the early 1970s, cotton was a commodity that was approaching this same situation. If all government programs for cotton had been removed, many areas that were at that time producing cotton would have been unwilling and unable to produce and sell at the prices that would have very likely prevailed. This was evidenced by the necessity to steadily reduce cotton acreage allotments in order to maintain the prices that were considered to have been acceptable. During the wage-price freeze in the early 1970s, numerous products virtually disappeared because producers were unwilling and unable to sell at the frozen price levels.

Tariffs have been erected in many nations to guard against the situation in which consumers would refuse to pay the price necessary to support certain industries locally. Subsidies are another technique that has been used. In these cases, it generally was not a case of an industry ceasing to exist—

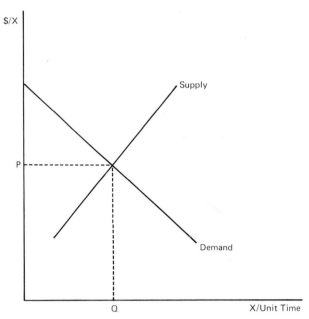

Figure 11.2 Interaction of supply and demand in determining prices and volumes of transactions.

more often, the situation was one in which free market prices were lower than was deemed to be socially acceptable or one in which the volume of domestic transactions was less than was deemed to be safe for purposes of national security.

The more common situation is, of course, one in which buyers and sellers can find an area to express their opinion through exchange. This occurs where the market demand and supply functions intersect, as illustrated in Figure 11.2. At that point, both the market price and the volume of transactions are determined. If some distrubance (i.e., a change in the *ceteris paribus* conditions) should occur, then either the demand schedule, the supply schedule, or both will shift. If only one of the schedules shifts, a change in both the price and the quantity exchanged will occur. In the case of a shift in both schedules, unless the shift in the two curves is exactly proportional, both the quantity exchanged and the price will change.

The demand-supply diagram (or model) is one that will be seen many times and one that you will use frequently for purposes of analysis. Let's postulate some changes in the *ceteris paribus* conditions that will cause changes in this model, and analyze the impact. Consider first what happens to the supply, demand, and market price under circumstances in which the price for an alternative product is changed.

Suppose that increased grain exports have reduced domestic availability

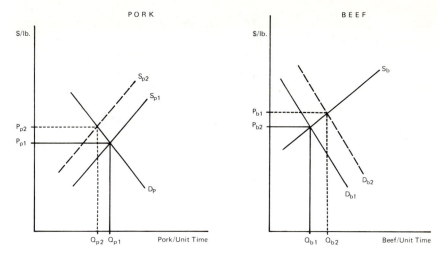

Figure 11.3 Changes in supply or demand for one good may generate changes in supply or demand for an alternative good.

of feed grains. The resulting increase in grain prices causes hog producers to decide that they can no longer produce as much pork at the market price of P_{p_1}. Their individual supply functions, and hence the market supply curve, have shifted upward and to the left as a result of such a cost increase as illustrated in the left half of Figure 11.3. What will be the impact on meat prices and the quantities exchanged? As a result of the shift in the supply curve for pork (pork producers are willing to sell reduced quantities of pork at all the alternative prices), the market price for pork has increased while the quantity exchanged has been reduced. Each individual customer looks at the budget and realizes that if he is to achieve maximum utility, he will have to alter the combination of products that he buys. Since beef can be produced using forage rather than grain, beef is now relatively less expensive when compared to pork. The consumer can increase his satisfaction (or limit the reduction in his satisfaction) by substituting some beef for some pork in his meat consumption. He is now willing to purchase more beef at each alternative price than previously. As a result, the market demand function for beef is shifted, and both the price and quantity exchanged increase.

Once we understand the bases for the market demand and supply curves, the impact of changes in the *ceteris paribus* conditions is fairly easy to analyze. Increases in average incomes or population will tend to increase demand for most products. A change in the prices of other products may either reduce or increase demand, depending on whether these products are substitutes or complements and on the direction of the change. Supply can be changed by the advance of new technology, by a shift in the relative profitability of one enterprise, or by changes in the cost of resources. The shifts in these functions will, of course, define the change in quantities exchanged and in the market prices.

In a later chapter, we'll examine in some depth the relationships between these types of changes and the shifts in supply and demand. For the moment, however, let's consider the relationship between market supply and market demand and the management of an individual business operation. When we were studying the individual firm supply function as defined by the marginal cost curve, we always took prices as given or constant. In the case of many agricultural business enterprises (particularly farm businesses) this is a completely realistic assumption.

Farms operate in what is termed a purely competitive market. Almost every farm product is produced by large numbers of producers. Further, if prices for a particular product should increase steadily over a period of time, there are a great many additional farmers who can *potentially* become producers. No individual producer can produce enough to affect the market price—that is, each individual operator controls such a small share of the total supply that he cannot appreciably affect the quantity available in the market.

If an individual firm cannot affect the market supply function, then that firm cannot affect market price. Therefore, the demand curve as faced by the individual firm is identical with the marginal revenue function and the average revenue function *at the market price level* (Figure 11.4). This means that the individual firm under conditions of pure competition will maximize profits at the output at which marginal costs are exactly equal to the market price. If market supply should increase (shift to the right), the market price would decline and the individual firm would be faced with the necessity of reducing production to the point at which the market price just equals the cost of *producing the final unit* (that is, where marginal cost and marginal revenue are equal).

As we saw in the case of national income analysis, most of us can afford to do the things we do only because most other people refrain from doing them. This is particularly true in agriculture. If large numbers of farmers decide to do the same thing at the same time, the market supply function will reflect these decisions. If all farmers simultaneously decide to increase marketings of cattle, depressed cattle prices will be the result. If all farmers decide to withhold wheat from the market, prices will increase. When the wheat price gets to the levels that sellers have decided to accept, then the volume of wheat that is exchanged will increase and the chances are that wheat prices will decline. All of these changes can be analyzed through the use of the supply and demand model.

The impact of market prices and the adjustments that managers must make to changes in those prices are the guts of a large part of the study of economics. Because of its highly fragmented nature, with nearly three million independent production units, production agriculture is especially sensitive to

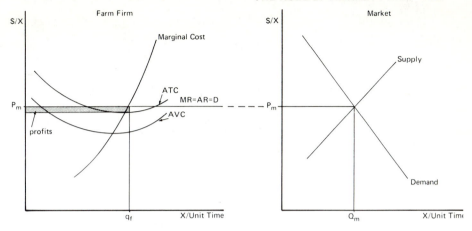

Figure 11.4 Relationship between supply and demand at the market level and at the farm firm.

price movements. Agricultural producers, perhaps more than any other economic sector, depend on the market prices as determined by the forces of supply and demand to signal the necessary business adjustments.

The Role of Market Price

We have suggested that price plays a key role in regulating the functions of a free enterprise capitalistic economy. This regulation is accomplished in a number of ways, but there are five specific functions that are performed by the price system. These functions are:

1. Fixing standards of value,

2. Organizing production,

3. Distributing production,

4. Rationing products in the short run, and

5. Providing for maintenance and growth in the economy.

In the process of maximizing their satisfaction, consumers cast their dollar votes in the form of prices they are willing to pay in the market place. In this fashion, prices have determined the relative values (or "fixed the standards of value") among commodities. These votes are counted by producers who are committed to maximizing the profit (or return) to the resources they control. On the basis of the apparent consumers' desires, producers organize (or allocate) these resources in such a manner that they produce the products

High Prices

High Income Consumers

Lower Income Consumers

Low   Prices

Figure 11.5 How prices distribute goods.

that maximize profits. In other words, the standards of value as fixed by the price system provide the information necessary for the managerial decisions made by producers.

After resources have been allocated and the production process completed, the product must be distributed among the various consumers of that product. Since demand involves purchasing power as well as desire for products, the decisions as to who gets what are made on the basis of who is willing to pay the necessary price. To a very significant degree, the income at the consumer's disposal will determine how much he will buy.

At very high prices, only a few people with high levels of income will be either willing or able to purchase goods. However, as the production of a good increases, the price falls and the consumption of the good is spread over a larger and larger group. This is very much like the flow of water through the various levels of basins shown in Figure 11.5. As prices decline to the levels that lower income consumers can afford, more and more people participate in consumption, and most people can increase the level of consumption in which they indulge. Thus, the product-distributing function of price is shown. Also, at the very high prices, only those few persons who derive a large degree of satisfaction from consuming the product will be willing to purchase. As price declines, the numbers of people in the market grow larger.

The short-run rationing of the product as performed by the price system simply means that the use of the product is spread over a longer period of time. This price function is particularly important in the case of agricultural commodities, since the production of many of these goods tends to be highly seasonal in nature. Wheat, for example, is harvested in the early summer months. The use of the wheat harvested each summer must be spread over the months until the next crop is harvested. The general price pattern is that wheat price will normally be low at harvest time and then increase through the fall until about mid-October when export commitments are generally completed (Figure 11.6). Prices generally taper off through November, when the corn harvest increases availability of all grains. In December, wheat producers begin to make plans to hold a part of their wheat inventories until after January 1 in order to spread their incomes over two tax years. This action reduces the volume of wheat going to market. The price will normally

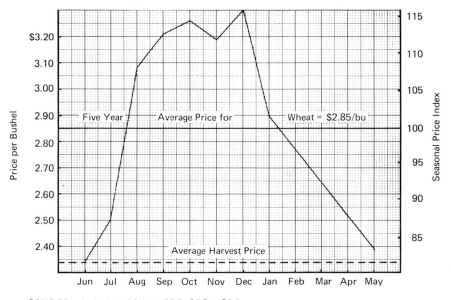

SOURCE: *Agricultural Prices*, CRB, SRS, USDA

Figure 11.6 Wheat: average price received by farmers at mid-month, U.S., 1971–75.

rise fairly rapidly during this period, and then fall rapidly after the first of January as producers release wheat to generate the cash needed for spring farming operations. Wheat prices will generally continue to decline until the new harvest in June.

Seasonal corn prices perform in a fashion similar to that observed for wheat (Figure 11.7). Corn producers are harvesting the crop in the September-December period, and prices reflect the increased availability of grain as the harvest progresses. But as producers begin to plan for tax management, the grain available in December is reduced and prices rise. After the first of the year, corn prices generally decline into April, and then rise through the summer until the new harvest begins.

People in the grain trade are well acquainted with these seasonal price patterns. The difference between the price at harvest time and the cash price paid in the market place during the rest of the year represents the payment to the owners of grain storage facilities and to those persons who assume the risk of price changes. Those producers who own or have access to storage facilities often hold wheat in anticipation of higher prices later in the year. Hence, they ration or allocate the sale of grain throughout the year.

Another example of price rationing the product in the short run may be seen in the case of feeder calves. Most calves are born in the late winter and early spring to be marketed in the late fall. The price pattern is such that seasonal lows in price normally come in October-November and seasonal highs come in April-May. Thus, some producers have shifted from spring calving to fall calving in order to take advantage of the normal spring high in price. Also, the purchase of steers to go on wheat pasture delays the placing of the animal on grain feed until the spring period, thus insuring a year-round supply of beef.

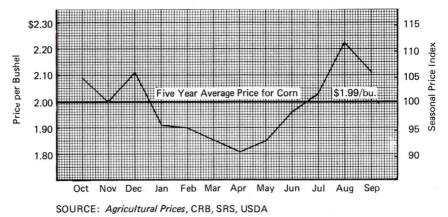

SOURCE: *Agricultural Prices*, CRB, SRS, USDA

Figure 11.7 Corn: average price received by farmers at mid-month, U.S., 1971–75.

The fifth function performed by price is that of providing for economic maintenance and growth. If prices are not high enough for the replacement cost of capital equipment to be covered, then the products produced by that capital equipment will gradually disappear. If costs are just barely being covered, then there will be no funds to plow back into the business for purposes of expansion. Thus, the dollar votes that consumers cast in the form of prices are the determining factor in what products are to be available and in what quantities.

Throughout our discussion, the various roles of price have had two things in common: first, price is the regulatory force in our economy, and second, price regulates by communicating the desires of consumers to producers. The regulating and controlling mechanisms are inventories and prices. As inventories build up, prices begin to decline, thus sending the message to producers that they are overdoing a good thing. The reduced price has the dual effect not only of blocking the flow of resources into the production process, but also of opening the gates for increased consumption. The resources that are blocked from this particular enterprise will overflow into the now more attractive (and more profitable) production alternatives. When consumption is accelerated and production is reduced, inventories begin to decline. As a result, the price rises and the flow of resources into the production of the good in question is increased. But the higher price discourages consumption and inventories begin to build up and price falls. This process is repeated until the point is reached where the price causes the flow of production to be just equal to the flow of consumption. At this point, the price is stable and inventories are maintained at a stable level. It is at this point of stability that *economic equilibrium* is achieved.

The state of economic equilibrium can be disturbed by a variety of factors. A change in the price of some alternative product may cause consumers to change their buying habits. A new substitute good can have the same impact. A change in resource prices or a change in the profitability of producing one good relative to another can disturb the state of equilibrium. When this disturbance occurs, it is reflected in the reaction of price, and the equilibrating process is activated. Price and inventories will stabilize at new levels, and the production (supply) and consumption (demand) flows will again be equalized.

You will immediately recognize the factors that disturbed our economic equilibrium to be the *ceteris paribus* conditions that we have defined as being constant. As these conditions are relaxed and allowed to change, they cause the demand or supply to shift. As you may have guessed, the process we have described is nothing more than a description of the standard line graph model showing market supply and market demand. The point at which the demand and supply curves intersect represents the point of economic equilibrium. This is the point where the price comes to rest, where the production and consumption flows are equated, and where the volume of inventories is stabilized. As changes in the *ceteris paribus* conditions occur, they activate an adjustment process whereby a new equilibrium is achieved.

An example of the relationship between five functions of price and the line graph model in supply and demand might be shown by the developments in the broiler industry during the 1950s and early 1960s. Improved nutrition and improved strains of birds reduced the feed requirement per pound of bird from more than five pounds of feed to less than two. This situation resulted in a phenomenal increase in the production of broilers and a corresponding decline in the farm price of chicken. The reduction of the value of poultry relative to other meats increased broiler sales and per capita poultry consumption enormously.

As a result of the reduction in the volume of feed required to produce a broiler, large volumes of resources were organized into the production of these birds. Even though prices dropped sharply, the technological improvement was rapid enough to permit the broiler industry to absorb this loss in price and still continue growing rapidly.

It is important to point out that in our static world where both producers and consumers are assumed to have perfect and complete knowledge, the adjustment from one point of equilibrium to another is immediate and direct. In the real world, however, the state of knowledge is something less than perfect. Thus, once a disturbing factor is introduced, the adjustment occurs through a series of successive approximations. If no further disturbances are introduced, economic equilibrium will be achieved. In reality, ours is a dynamic and changing world. The forces that disturb the equilibrium positions for most commodities often follow close on the heels of one another. Because of the imperfections in the knowledge of both consumers and producers, the series of adjustments to one disturbance is rarely completed before a new disturbance occurs. Thus, the target of economic equilibrium is steadily moving. Rather than *achieving* an equilibrium, we are constantly *chasing* one.

Consider the situation in which an epidemic of some fungus disease has drastically reduced the production of corn. Grain sorghum producers would find themselves in the situation in which the quantity of grain sorghum they had planned to produce for the price of P_A would now command a price of P_2 as illustrated in Figure 11.8. This change would be the result of a sudden change in the demand for grain sorghum resulting from the reduced availability of corn.

If producers had perfect knowledge of the market demand function, when the price of Q_A of grain sorghum rose, the adjustment would be for them to move directly from point A to point B. However, in the absence of perfect knowledge, the first adjustment would probably be to plan production at point D on the basis of P_2. This would result in a price at point E,

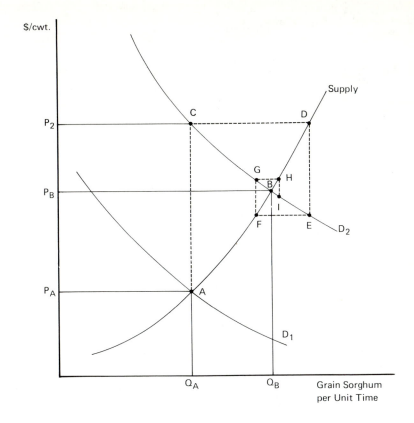

Figure 11.8 Pattern of adjustment to changes in demand.

which in turn would cause producers to move to point *F,* and so forth. In this fashion, producers would "bracket" the new equilibrium and then through a series of successive approximations make the necessary adjustments.

Occasionally, it has been deemed desirable by those who formulate economic policy to deliberately prevent an economic equilibrium from being achieved. Some notable examples of this have been in cases of certain farm products. The reasons for this decision have generally resulted from rapid technological growth in agriculture. The larger sizes of producing units are the ones that can most readily adopt the cost-reducing technology. Since the new technology lowers the cost structure for the adopting firms (Firm *B* in Figure 11.9), these firms will be willing and able to supply more at each price. This causes a shift to the right in the market supply schedule. The shift in the market supply schedule lowers the market price, and those firms that are unable to adopt the new technology (Firm *A* in Figure 11.9) find themselves in a loss position. In the absence of outside restraints, these firms will

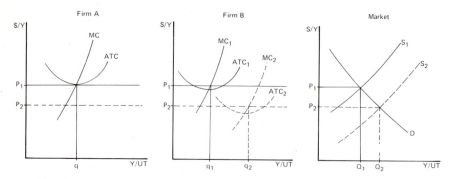

Figure 11.9 Impact of new technology on firms in the production agriculture sector.

ultimately be forced to phase out of the business and their resources will be absorbed by other firms as equilibrium is achieved.

The nut of the problem illustrated in Figure 11.9 is that the rest of the economy may be unable to absorb all the people that will be displaced by the economic adjustments that will potentially result from the new technology. This was the situation in which the United States found itself immediately following World War II. Therefore, prices were supported at P_1. Rather than immediately attempting to adjust to the new equilibrium, the adjustments were spread out over a 20–25 year period.

The price support programs created a variety of associated problems. As prices were held above the normal equilibrium level, producers had an incentive to produce more than could be sold at the support price. The agency that has responsibility for administering any price support program is faced with the problem of what to do with the surplus. Basically four alternatives are available.

1. The product can be sold on the open market and the difference in the market price and the support price can be paid in the form of a direct subsidy. The subsidy necessary is shown by the bracket A in Figure 11.10.

2. The production or sale of the commodity can be restricted to the level at which the market price and the support price coincide (point B in Figure 11.10).

3. The surplus can be bought and either stored, dumped in the export market, or destroyed. (The surplus is shown by bracket C in Figure 11.10.)

4. The support price can be paid on the volume of product that will clear the market at market prices, the remainder of the product

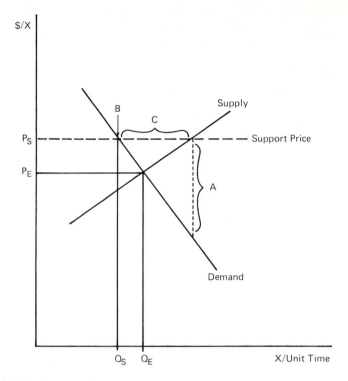

Figure 11.10 Impact of price supports.

allowed to sell at whatever value the market allows. (This is the case, for example, of Class *A* fluid milk versus the manufacturing grades.)

The back side of price supports occurs when for some reason society decides that the price of some good (or of some group of goods) is higher than is socially acceptable. This was the case in the wage-price freeze in the early 1970s. The problems created by such an action are illustrated in Figure 11.11.

At the administered price (P_A in Figure 11.11), consumers want to buy even more product than they would want at the equilibrium price. But the quantity that producers are willing to produce and sell at the administered price is *less* than they would ordinarily offer. As a result, there is a *shortage* of product (shown by bracket *A* in Figure 11.11). That is, when prices are administered at levels below the equilibrium price, the price system cannot perform to distribute products among consumers. Even worse, consumers are willing to pay a price above the equilibrium level (P_B in Figure 11.11) for the quantity that is available. Thus, there is an enormous incentive (bracket *B* in

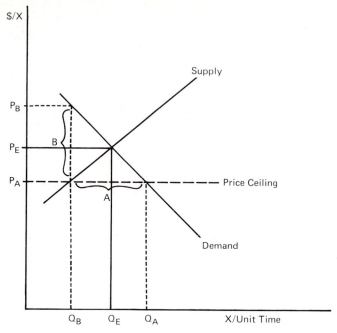

Figure 11.11   Impact of ceiling prices.

Figure 11.11) for businessmen and consumers to circumvent the administered price through illicit black market activity.

We have recognized that consumers normally react to changes in the quantities of the various products available to them by bidding prices either up or down. If the quantities in the market are reduced, prices rise. If the quantities available are increased, the prices fall. This is the means by which the price system conveys information concerning the opinions of consumers to producers. If consumers want less saturated fats and more of the poly-unsaturates, the price system will express this desire through higher prices for the unsaturated fats and lower prices for the saturates. As a result, the profitability of producing the two items is changed and resources are either attracted into or released from production as producers get the message conveyed by the price system.

When society acts to repeal the ancient laws of supply and demand, market prices can no longer perform their fivefold function of regulating the economy. In the absence of economic regulation via the price system, some extra-market means of getting these regulatory functions performed must be designed and implemented. During the wage-price freeze of the 1970s, for example, the Cost of Living Council (the agency empowered to administer the wage-price freeze) simply froze certain prices at their levels of August, 1971. No effective effort was made to provide for non-price means of fixing standards of value, organizing production, etc. Problems began to surface as the result of an absence of the regulatory force provided by non-administered prices. Rather than abandoning the original regulation, the Cost of Living Council saw the problem as an obvious need for still further regulation that would render the original regulation effective. All sorts of additional controls, such as export embargoes, were proliferated through the three-year duration of the wage-price freeze. Some examples of the ultimate results of the wage-price freeze includes shortages of a host of goods ranging from beef to binder twine, ultimately higher costs for many items resulting from inefficiencies that came from attempts to make price-motivated adjustments to problems that were induced from non-price sources, and gross inefficiencies throughout the economic system.

The message conveyed by the problems that arise from attempting to administer prices—whether higher or lower than equilibrium levels—(and the author confesses to a personal bias in this statement) is that until human ingenuity and computer technology achieve a level of sophistication that will permit moment-to-moment monitoring of the literally billions of messages conveyed daily by the price system, direct price intervention is a damn fool policy for any government to contemplate.

Selected References

Boulding, Kenneth E., *Economic Analysis,* 3rd ed., Chapter 5. New York: Harper and Brothers, 1955.

Hicks, J. R., *Value and Capital,* 2nd ed., Chapters 4 and 5. London: Oxford University Press, 1957.

Leftwich, Richard H., *The Price System and Resource Allocation,* Chapter II. New York: Rinehart & Co. Inc., 1956.

Marshall, Alfred, *Principles of Economics,* 8th ed., Book V, Chapters I, II, and III. London: Macmillan and Co. Ltd., 1959.

Shepherd, Geoffrey S., *Agricultural Price Analysis,* 5th ed., Chapter 3. Ames, Iowa: Iowa State University Press, 1963.

Stigler, George J., *The Theory of Price,* Chapter I. New York: The Macmillan Co., 1952.

Thomsen, Frederick L., and Richard J. Forte, *Agricultural Prices,* 2nd ed., Chapter 5. New York: McGraw-Hill Book Co. Inc., 1952.

12

The Concept of Elasticity

We know (some of us from sad experience) that the price system will merely whisper about a change in the availability of one good while it will positively scream about a change in the availability of another. On the other side of this coin, consumers will accept an increase in the price of one product without too much reaction. But an increase in the price of another good will be met with stubborn resistance and a refusal to purchase.

We also know that a strong price increase for some commodities will induce large numbers of producers to increase production and will further interest other people in becoming producers of that commodity. Yet there are other products that will absorb a price increase with little reaction on the part of producers. Still a third situation is that an increase in consumer income will be associated with a reduction in the use of one commodity, an increase in the use of another, and no change in the use of a third.

The means that has been devised to measure the sensitivity of consumers and producers to changes in prices and incomes is known as *elasticity*. Elasticity may be defined as the *percentage change in the quantity of a good that is purchased* (in the case of demand) *or sold* (in the case of supply) *associated with a 1 percent change in some other factor.* Thus, the elasticity of demand with respect to price would be concerned with the percentage change in the quantity purchased in response to a 1 percent change in price.

A leading agricultural economist has been quoted as saying that the primary use for the elasticity concept is to scare the hell out of sophomore students in economics. While this statement may have some merit, it is not quite fair. The concept of elasticity helps students to understand *why* certain things happen. Further, an understanding of the elasticity concept indicates to managers *how* to make adjustments in response to some of the changes that affect their business.

Through the use of elasticity estimates, a manager can anticipate the probable direction of the market impact of various sorts of changes. Further, the elasticity estimate can help him to predict the degree of the impact. For example, if the borders of the United States are opened to unlimited imports of beef, and if Australia and New Zealand should ship enough product to increase the beef available in American markets by 3 percent, the price elasticity of demand for beef can be used to anticipate how much beef price could be expected to change.

Price Elasticity of Demand

We have defined price elasticity as the responsiveness of the quantity of a product to changes in price along a given supply or demand curve. If the quantity is changed by more than 1 percent as a result of a 1 percent change in price, then we say that the relationship is relatively *elastic*. Conversely, if a 1 percent change in price evokes a change of less than 1 percent, the relationship is said to be relatively *inelastic*.

Probably the most common use of the elasticity measurements is the price elasticity of demand. This estimate measures the responsiveness of the quantity of a product consumers are willing to buy to changes in the price for that product, given the demand curve for that product. If the quantity taken is very responsive to price changes, a reduction in price may increase the total amount of money spent on the product. But if the quantity taken is not particularly sensitive to price changes, a reduction in price may reduce total expenditures on the commodity. The measurement of the various elasticity relationships may be accomplished by exactly the same procedure. Therefore, we will measure the price elasticity of demand in several ways, and then use these same procedures in analyzing the other elasticity relationships.

Arc Elasticity •   We can measure price elasticity of demand by dividing the percentage change in the amount purchased by the percentage change in price for a small segment or arc along a given demand curve, when the change in price is small.[1] Algebraically, the relationship may be expressed as:

$$\epsilon = \frac{\dfrac{\Delta Q}{Q}}{\dfrac{\Delta P}{P}} \tag{12.1}$$

Where: Q is quantity purchased
         P is price of the product.

---

[1] Alfred Marshall, *Principles of Economics*, 8th ed. (London: Macmillan and Company, Ltd., 1920), Book III, Chapter IV.

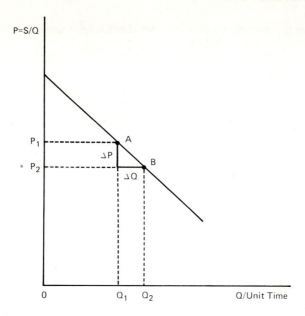

Figure 12.1 Geometric representation of the arc for calculating price elasticity of demand.

The mathematical symbol Δ(Delta) may be interpreted to mean "the change in." The algebraic formulation is shown geometrically in Figure 12.1. The change from point A to point B along the demand curve is the arc for which we measure the elasticity. The change from Q_1 to Q_2 represents ΔQ in our formula and the change from P_1 to P_2 represents ΔP. If our initial situation were at point A, and if the values of Q_1, Q_2, P_1, and P_2 were as shown below,

POINT A	POINT B
$Q_1 = 20$	$Q_2 = 25$
$P_1 = \$8$	$P_2 = \$7.50$

then our calculation of the elasticity of demand with respect to price for moving from point A to point B would be:

$$\frac{\dfrac{Q_1 - Q_2}{Q_1}}{\dfrac{P_1 - P_2}{P_1}} = \frac{\dfrac{\Delta Q}{Q_1}}{\dfrac{\Delta P}{P_1}} = \frac{\dfrac{20-25}{8-7.50}}{\dfrac{-5}{8}} = \frac{\dfrac{-5}{20}}{\dfrac{.50}{8}} = -1/4 \times \frac{8}{.50} = \frac{-8}{2} = -4 \qquad (12.2)$$

If however, we were to calculate the elasticity for moving from point B to point A, the estimate would be:

$$\frac{\dfrac{Q_2 - Q_1}{Q_2}}{\dfrac{P_2 - P_1}{P_2}} = \frac{\dfrac{\Delta Q}{Q_2}}{\dfrac{\Delta P}{P_2}} = \frac{\dfrac{25-20}{25}}{\dfrac{7.50-8}{7.50}} = \frac{\dfrac{5}{25}}{\dfrac{-.50}{7.50}} = 1/5 \times \frac{7.50}{-.50} = \frac{7.50}{-2.50} = -3.0 \tag{12.3}$$

Obviously, there is something amiss when we get two different estimates of elasticity for the same arc. The key to our difficulty lies in the fact that our percentages are different depending on the point we select as our initial situation. This shows that our calculation of the elasticity for the arc between A and B is merely an approximation. The greater the size of the arc between A and B, the greater will be the difference in our two estimates, and the less will be the confidence that may be attached to either. Therefore, *it is imperative that the arc be small* (or as Marshall says, that the change in price be small) if the resulting estimate of elasticity is to have any degree of reliability.

We can modify our basic elasticity formula to eliminate the discrepancy that arises from selecting either of the two end points of the arc A-B as the initial situation. This modification is accomplished by including both Q_1 and Q_2 and P_1 and P_2 in the calculation of the percentages, such that

$$\epsilon = \frac{\dfrac{Q_1 - Q_2}{Q_1 + Q_2}}{\dfrac{P_1 - P_2}{P_1 + P_2}} \tag{12.4}$$

Thus, our calculation for our example would be:

$$\epsilon = \frac{\dfrac{20-25}{20+25}}{\dfrac{8-7.50}{8+7.50}} = \frac{\dfrac{-5}{45}}{\dfrac{.50}{15.50}} = \frac{-5}{45} \times \frac{15.50}{.50} = \frac{-77.50}{22.50} = -3.44 \tag{12.5}$$

The modified formula gives us an approximation of the elasticity within the arc from A to B in Figure 12.1. This represents an average of sorts of the two estimates that result from the basic formula. Further, the modification eliminates the problem of the discrepancy that arises from that formula: no matter which end of the arc is selected as the initial situation, the resulting estimate of elasticity is the same.

It should be pointed out that both the numerator and the denominator in the elasticity formula represent percentages. Thus, the elasticity estimate itself is a pure number. The algebraic sign of the elasticity estimate tells nothing more than the *direction* of the relationship. In our example, the sign is negative because the slope of the demand function in Figure 12.1 is negative. That is, within the arc between points *A* and *B,* if price is *increased* by 1 percent, we would expect the quantity taken to *decline* by approximately 3.44 percent. Since a 1 percent change in price is associated with more than 1 percent change in quantity taken, demand is relatively elastic with respect to price *within that arc.*

If the absolute value (that is, the value without regard to algebraic sign) of the elasticity coefficient is between zero and one, it is relatively inelastic. If the absolute value is greater than one, it is relatively elastic. The absolute value of the elasticity coefficient can range between zero and infinity for any given demand curve, *but it cannot pass through zero unless the curve exhibits a U shape* (that is, unless the curve reverses direction, such as sloping downward and to the right, then leveling out and beginning to increase). Thus, we might visualize the elasticity coefficient to lie along two continua as illustrated below:

For Curves of Negative Slope	For Curves of Positive Slope

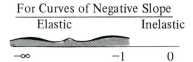
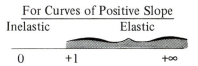

Elastic	Inelastic	Inelastic	Elastic
$-\infty$	-1 $\quad$ 0	0 $\quad$ $+1$	$+\infty$

If the elasticity coefficient should be exactly equal to one, elasticity is said to be *unitary.* That is, a 1 percent change in price will be associated with exactly 1 percent change in the quantity taken.

Demand curves will often exhibit all three ranges of elasticity (elastic, inelastic, and unitary) within a single curve. This is always true in situations where demand is a straight line. The selection of an arc along a given demand curve will frequently determine the value of the elasticity coefficient. Most demand curves are elastic with respect to price at relatively high prices and inelastic at relatively low prices (see Figure 12.2). This suggests that as the price of a product falls, sales will increase to some saturation point at which consumers are virtually "filled up" on the product. When this is the case, further price cuts will not induce buyers to increase purchases by relatively as much as the price has been cut (i.e., demand is inelastic). Conversely, when prices are already high, further price increases will induce buyers to either seek out substitute goods or to do without the product, causing the reduction

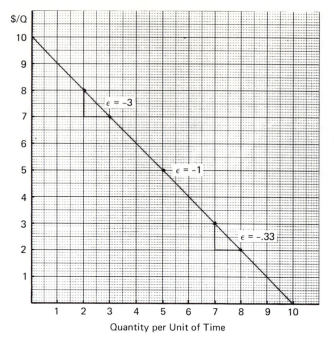

Figure 12.2   Elasticity measurements at various points on a market demand
curve.

in sales to be relatively greater than was the increase in price (in this case,
demand is elastic).

Since both the elastic and inelastic ranges can occur within a single
demand curve, it is obvious that as consumers pass from the elastic into the
inelastic range, they must pass through some point (or range) of unitary
elasticity.

Price Elasticity of Demand Related to Total Revenue •   The elasticity
concept involves a definition of the impact of price changes on the total
revenue that is generated by product sales at all the possible levels of price.
The demand curve shown in Figure 12.2, along with the total revenue
generated by the various levels of sales, is shown in Table 12.1. Price
reductions in the *elastic* range of the demand curve are associated with
increases in the total revenue. Price reductions in the *inelastic* range are
associated with *reductions* in total revenue. When total revenue is maximum,
elasticity is unitary. This may be shown graphically as in Figure 12.3.

It will be noted that elasticity is unitary at the midpoint of the relevant
range along the quantity axis. Thus, that portion of a straight line demand
curve which lies to the left of the midpoint of the quantity that would be

TABLE 12.1

RELATIONSHIP BETWEEN ELASTICITY AND TOTAL REVENUE

PRICE	QUANTITY SOLD	ELASTICITY	TOTAL REVENUE $(P)(Q)$	CHANGE IN TOTAL REVENUE AS PRICE DECLINES (MARGINAL REVENUE)
10	0	-19.00	0	9
9	1	-5.66	9	7
8	2	-3.00 } Elastic	16	5 } Total Revenue Increasing
7	3	-1.86	21	3
6	4	-1.22	24	1 } Total Revenue
5	5	$-.82$ ⌐ Unitary	25	-1 — Unchanged
4	6	$-.54$	24	-3 } Total Revenue
3	7	$-.33$ { Inelastic	21	-5 Decreasing
2	8	$-.18$	16	-7
1	9	$-.05$	9	-9
0	10		0	

taken by consumers if the product were free (i.e., that would be sold at a price of zero) is elastic with respect to price. The portion to the right of this point is inelastic. At this midpoint, demand is unitarily elastic. Another way of stating these relationships is illustrated in Table 12.1. If the change in total revenue that is associated with a one-unit change in sales (that is, the marginal revenue) is positive, demand is elastic with regard to price. If marginal revenue is negative, demand is inelastic. If marginal revenue is zero, demand is unitarily elastic.

Point Elasticity   •   In our analysis of the arc computation of elasticity, we saw the importance of keeping the arc small. Since we have seen how a straight line demand curve includes all three ranges of elasticity, we know that the elasticity on the two ends of the arc must necessarily be different. It follows that there is a unique elasticity associated with every individual point within the arc. The arc elasticity computation, as modified, results in an average elasticity estimate that approximates the elasticity for all points within the arc. By keeping the arc small, the distortions that result from this averaging are minimized. If however, we make the arc so small that it is

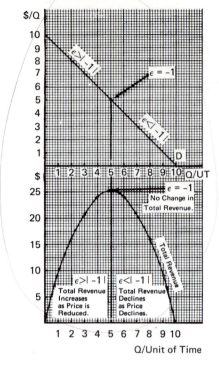

Figure 12.3   Relationship among total revenue, demand, and elasticity.

impossible to distinguish point *A* from point *B,* we have in effect reduced our arc to a single point and can make a much more precise estimate of the elasticity coefficient.

The arc for which elasticity is to be calculated has been made so small in Figure 12.4 that the end points of the arc have become a single point. The quantity that consumers would consume if the product were free (i.e., if the price were zero) is measured by *ON* along the quantity axis. The level that price would need to reach before consumers would forego all consumption of the commodity is measured by *OD* along the price axis. Our straight-line demand curve, then, passes through points *D* and *N,* and has a negative slope of −*OD/ON* (the mathematical formula for calculating slope is rise over run). The problem we face is calculating the elasticity at some point along the demand curve such as at point *A*.

Our basic formula for calculating elasticity relates the percentage change in quantity to the percentage change in price such that:

$$\epsilon = \frac{\frac{\Delta Q}{Q}}{\frac{\Delta P}{P}} \qquad (12.6)$$

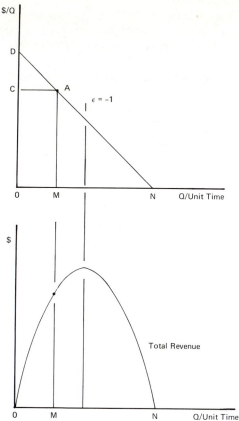

Figure 12.4 Calculation of point elasticity.

Where: Q is the quantity purchased
      P is the price of the product.

which may be rewritten:

$$\epsilon = \frac{\Delta Q}{Q} \cdot \frac{P}{\Delta P} = \frac{\Delta Q}{\Delta P} \cdot \frac{P}{Q} \qquad (12.7)$$

Since our demand curve is a straight line, any segment of that line has the same slope. But the final fraction in this identity is the inverse of the ratio in our rewritten elasticity formulation. Thus,

$$\frac{OD}{ON} = \frac{MA}{MN} = \frac{\Delta P}{\Delta Q} \qquad (12.8)$$

If we invert all of the fractions in equation 12.8, we get $ON/OD = MN/MA = \Delta Q/\Delta P$. We can now substitute MN/MA for $\Delta Q/\Delta P$ in our elasticity formula. Since the slope of the demand function is negative, we know that the sign of MN/MA must be negative.

$$\epsilon = \frac{\Delta Q}{\Delta P} \cdot \frac{P}{Q} = -\frac{MN}{MA} \cdot \frac{P}{Q} \qquad (12.9)$$

Our original price, measured by MA, and our original quantity, measured by OM, may now be substituted into our elasticity formula such that:

$$\epsilon = \frac{\Delta Q}{\Delta P} \cdot \frac{P}{Q} = -\frac{MN}{MA} \cdot \frac{MA}{QM} \qquad (12.10)$$

We can rid ourselves of the two MAs through cancellation and find that the elasticity for any point along a linear demand function may be calculated by:

$$\epsilon = MN/OM \qquad (12.11)$$

If the distance from M to N exceeds that from O to M, we can safely say that we are in the elastic range of the curve within which the total revenue is increasing and marginal revenue is positive. Conversely, if OM is greater than

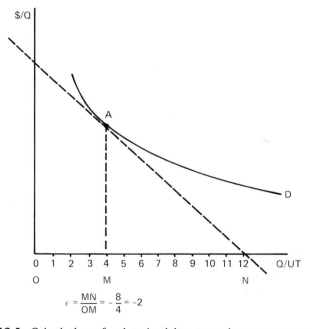

$$\epsilon = \frac{MN}{OM} = -\frac{8}{4} = -2$$

Figure 12.5 Calculation of point elasticity at a point on a curve.

MN, we are in the inelastic range within which total revenue is declining and marginal revenue is negative. If the two are equal, then we are at the point of unitary elasticity where total revenue is maximum and marginal revenue is zero.

The point elasticity calculation may be made for a curvalinear demand function as easily as for a linear one. All that is necessary is to draw a straight line tangent to the curve at the point where elasticity is to be measured (Figure 12.5). The ends of the tangent are extended until they intersect both the price and the quantity axes. Then the elasticity computation is made from the tangent in precisely the same fashion as for the linear demand curve; that is, by dividing *MN* by *OM.*

Some Special Cases   •   There are three special cases of price elasticity of demand that should be mentioned. Or more precisely, there is one special case that should be mentioned, and two extremes. The two extremes are shown in Figure 12.6. These are the cases in which elasticity is equal to zero

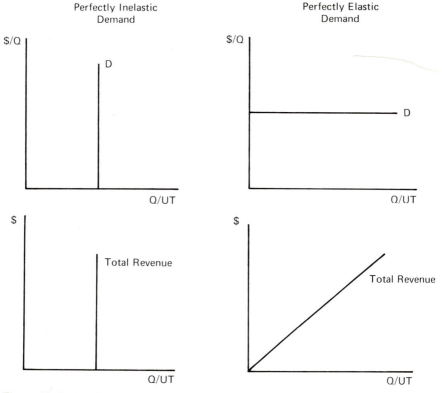

Figure 12.6 Configuration of demand and total revenue functions when demand is perfectly elastic or perfectly inelastic.

(or *perfectly inelastic*) at all points on the function, and in which elasticity is infinite (or *perfectly elastic*) at all points of the function. When demand is perfectly inelastic, the same quantity will be demanded no matter what the price happens to be—that is, the demand function is perfectly vertical. This sort of demand function is largely theoretical, but the demand for an item that normally represents a small part of the total budget and is an absolute necessity, such as table salt, will approach this situation.

The perfectly elastic demand function is one you have already seen in Chapter 9. This is the situation that is faced by the individual firm operating under conditions in which he cannot affect the price he receives, no matter how much he sells. That is, the market will absorb any quantity offered, and at the prevailing price. This situation approximates the conditions under which most farmers sell their products. Therefore, the perfectly elastic demand function is an important concept in agricultural economics, of which we will see more in later chapters.

The special case of a demand curve that is unitarily elastic throughout its range is rare. However, there are occasional examples of empirical demand curves for commodities that approach a unitarily elastic situation. One case in point is the demand for live broilers during the early 1960s.

The demand curve that has an elasticity of one at all points on the function is a rectangular hyperbola. Its basic characteristic is that total revenue is constant, regardless of what price is charged, and regardless of how much is sold (Figure 12.7). That is, a price reduction is exactly offset by the increase in sales, such that the total revenue generated is unchanged.

What Determines Price Elasticity of Demand?   •   We have seen that many demand functions include all three ranges of elasticity. What, then, determines whether business is to be transacted in the elastic or inelastic range of the demand function? Of course, business will ultimately be transacted at the market equilibrium, and to find that equilibrium we must confront our market demand function with a market supply function. However, there are a number of factors that will help determine this point of intersection. In general, the price elasticity of demand for any product will be greater as the number of good substitutes available is greater. It will normally be greater if expenditure on this product represents a large item in the consumer's total budget. Also, demand is likely to be more elastic with respect to price for luxuries as opposed to necessities, since consumers can do very nicely without luxuries.

Let's discuss these determinants to see if they make sense logically. Can we think of an item that has no good substitutes? Salt was the example mentioned earlier. There are simply no good substitutes to which the consumer can turn if the price of salt goes from 15 cents to 20 cents per pound. Furthermore, a household's expenditure on salt is such a small part of a

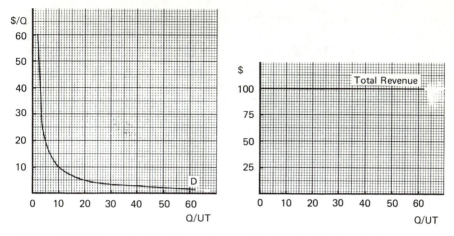

Figure 12.7 Example of a demand curve that is unitarily elastic throughout.

family's total weekly, monthly, or annual budget that the total impact of this price increase is negligible. Finally, the product is looked upon as a necessity. Most people consider unsalted food to be extremely unpleasant. As we might expect, the elasticity of demand for salt is extremely low. Brandow found this to be true for most food items at both retail and farm levels.[2] Hence, agricultural economics is often concerned with products for which the price elasticity of demand is very low.

On the other hand, the demand for Magnavox stereophonic record players might be expected to be relatively elastic. There are a good many substitutes available in the form of Philco, General Electric, Motorola, Webcor, and other competing brands of stereo, not to mention FM radio and other forms of entertainment. The price of the Magnavox record player is large in relation to the average consumer's budget, and a given percentage change in price will generally have a very significant impact on that budget. Further, to most families, a stereo is a luxury and therefore an expendable item in their budgets.

There are numerous other factors that can affect elasticity. Consumers are creatures of habit. It is only over a period of time that they alter their customary patterns of expenditure in response to price changes. Demand therefore tends to be more elastic as the length of time period in question is extended. Further, the durability of some products will affect the elasticity of demand for them. Few consumers actually face the choice of doing

---

[2] G. E. Brandow, *Interrelations among Demands for Farm Products and Implications for Control of Market Supply* (University Park, Pennsylvania: Pennsylvania Agricultural Experiment Station, August, 1961), Bulletin 680. This publication is generally recognized as the "Bible" of elasticity for agricultural products.

without a refrigerator, washing machine, or automobile. Rather, the choice is more likely to be among repairing one's old automobile, buying a used car, or buying a new one. Repairing older durable goods is very frequently a good substitute for buying a new model. Durability therefore tends to make demand more elastic than might otherwise be the case.

These factors that we have mentioned as affecting the elasticity of demand will immediately be recognized as some of the *ceteris paribus* conditions of the concept of demand. As you will recall from our discussion of the concept of demand in Chapter 10, we saw how a shift in the demand function came about if and only if there was a change in one of the *ceteris paribus* conditions. Since these conditions affect the position of the demand function, they will certainly affect the point at which the market demand and supply functions intersect. It is at this point of intersection that market transactions occur and that market prices are formed. Within the immediate neighborhood of these market prices, we become concerned about elasticity.

Cross-Price Elasticity of Demand

In our study of the demand function we began to relax some of the *ceteris paribus* assumptions in order to see what happened to the demand function as a result of these changes. We know that the demand function responds to these changes, and there are related elasticity estimates that are designed to measure the sensitivity of the demand for a product to changes in the *ceteris paribus* conditions. One of these estimates is the cross-price elasticity of demand, which measures the adjustment that consumers make in their consumption of one product in response to a change in the price of another. Another way of saying this is that cross-price elasticity of demand measures the extent to which the demands for various commodities are related.

Cross-price elasticity may be calculated in very much the same fashion as own-price elasticity. Only a slight alteration in the basic elasticity formula is required. If we are interested in what happens to the consumption of beef as the price of pork is changed, for example, we simply divide the percentage change in the quantity of beef purchased by the percentage change in pork price. In terms of our basic elasticity formula, this would be:

$$\epsilon_C = \frac{\dfrac{\Delta Q_B}{Q_B}}{\dfrac{\Delta B_P}{P_P}} \qquad (12.12)$$

Where: Q_B is the quantity of one good purchased (beef in this example)
P_P is the price of another good (pork in this example.)

which may be modified to eliminate the problem of discrepancy

$$\epsilon_C = \frac{\dfrac{Q_{1B} - Q_{2B}}{Q_{1B} + Q_{2B}}}{\dfrac{P_{1P} - P_{2P}}{P_{1P} + P_{2P}}}$$

The relationships with which we are most concerned are the degree of substitutability or complementarity between commodities. When commodities are *substitutes* for each other, the algebraic sign of the cross elasticity between them will be positive. That is, if the price of one increases, the quantity of the other commodity purchased will also increase. Beef and pork, for example, tend to be substitutes. As the price of pork rises, consumers respond by reducing consumption of pork substituting beef in an effort to maximize their satisfaction within the limitations of their budgets (i.e., they begin to move *around* their indifference surface as a result of the altered price ratio).

Commodities that are *complementary* to each other have *negative* cross elasticities. Dress shirts and neckties serve as an illustration. An increase in the price of dress shirts would likely cut dress shirt consumption and hopefully the consumption of neckties (which are useless and archaic articles of apparel to begin with). A decrease in the price of dress shirts would be expected to increase shirt consumption and, regrettably, the consumption of neckties as well. The change in the price of dress shirts is accompanied by a change in quantity of neckties consumed, with the change in necktie consumption being opposite in direction to the change in shirt price. Therefore, the cross elasticity of demand will be negative.

It should be recognized that the cross elasticity between the price of one product and the consumption of another may be quite different when the direction is reversed. For example, Brandow found the elasticity of demand for lamb with respect to the price of beef to be .62, but the elasticity of demand for beef with respect to the price of lamb was only .04.[3] This may be interpreted to mean that beef may be substituted for lamb rather readily, but that lamb is in no way a satisfactory substitute for beef.

---

[3] G. E. Brandow, *op. cit.* Brandow's results are in general agreement with those of P. S. George and L. A. King in *Consumer Demand for Food Commodities in the United States with Projection for 1980* (California Agricultural Experiment Station, Giannini Foundation, March 1971), Monograph Number 26.

Income Elasticity

A second *ceteris paribus* condition that, if allowed to change, will cause a shift in the demand curve is that of consumer income. Here again, we have an elasticity measure that will indicate the degree of sensitivity that consumers show in response to changes in income. Income elasticity of demand shows the manner in which consumers alter the purchases of any good as a result of changes in income. (That is, if the consumer's budget restraint is changed, to what position on his utility surface does he adjust?) Income elasticity is a quick way of estimating this change. With slight alterations, our basic arc elasticity formula can be used to estimate income elasticity:

$$\epsilon_I = \frac{\dfrac{\Delta Q}{Q}}{\dfrac{\Delta I}{I}} \qquad (12.14)$$

Where: Q is quantity purchased
         I is income.

which may be modified into the standard arc formula:

$$\epsilon_I = \frac{\dfrac{Q_1 - Q_2}{Q_1 + Q_2}}{\dfrac{I_1 - I_2}{I_1 + I_2}} \qquad (12.15)$$

This formula simply relates the percentage change in the quantity of some good that is purchased to the percentage change in consumer income. If consumer demand for a particular good is inelastic with respect to income, then a 1 percent change in income would be associated with a less than 1 percent change in the quantity taken. Conversely, if demand were elastic with respect to income, then a 1 percent change in income would be associated with a more than 1 percent change in the quantity purchased.

Normally, we expect the algebraic sign of the income elasticity coefficient to be positive. That is, as a consumer has more purchasing power, his consumption of the good in question will be increased. However, there are a limited number of goods—lard, for example—that will exhibit negative income elasticities.[4] As consumers have higher incomes, they will tend to reduce their consumption of these inferior goods; that is, if they can afford to substitute

---

[4] Brandow found in 1961 that of 24 food products, only lard exhibited a negative income elasticity. George and King analyzed the demand for 48 products in 1971, and again found lard to be the only one that exhibited a negative income elasticity.

vegetable shortening for hog lard, they will do so. There are a number of goods that saw increases in the levels of per capita consumption when real consumer income was reduced in 1974 and early 1975. These included the starches, dry beans, and cheese. This phenomenon suggests that consumers are entirely capable of substituting lower cost foods for high cost foods when confronted with reductions in their income.

If the income elasticity of demand for a particular good is zero, the demand for that good is not affected by income. This would normally be the case for items such as salt and other condiments. Brandow found margarine, baking products, and evaporated milk to fit in this category in 1961. George and King added sweet potatoes, beans and bread to this list in 1971. These items are such a small part of the normal consumer's total budget that they are generally insignificant as an expense item. Further, while some minimum level of these items is highly desirable, even essential in some cases, anything much above this minimum level is to be avoided. (In the case of sweet potatoes, for example, any consumption level above zero is too much for this consumer.) Thus, the demand for these sorts of products is largely independent of income changes.

It is difficult to say what are the most important numerical values of income elasticity of demand. However, there are several that might be useful as bench marks. First, in the case when income elasticity is zero, as discussed above, we can conclude that demand is independent of income. A second interesting value of income elasticity is positively unitary. This means that the proportion of the consumer's income spent on the good in question is exactly the same both before and after income rises. This seems to be a useful dividing line. If the income elasticity of demand for any good is greater than one, it means that an increasing proportion of the consumer's income is spent on the good as his income increases. It seems reasonable to think that a good with an income elasticity greater than one, on which a consumer therefore spends a greater proportion of his income as he becomes richer, is in some sense a luxury. A second car would fall in this category for most families. A good with an income elasticity of less than one, on which the proportion of income spent falls as he becomes richer, is in some sense a necessity. Most foods fall in this classification. One cannot, of course, give a precise definition of necessities or luxuries in terms of income elasticities of demand, but the notion that goods with income elasticities greater and less than one are in a general sense luxuries and necessities respectively seems a useful one.

Price Elasticity of Supply

The idea of price elasticity of supply is almost identical with the concept of price elasticity of demand. The formula for measurement is identical, but whereas the algebraic sign for price elasticity of demand is normally negative, that for price elasticity of supply is generally positive. That is, since the quantity supplied increases as price increases, the supply function slopes upward to the right, a positive slope. Hence the positive elasticity of supply with respect to price.

Elasticity and the Cobweb Theorem

The relationship between the elasticity of demand and supply with respect to price gives rise to the Cobweb Theorem. The Cobweb Theorem was alluded to in Chapter 11 when the path of adjustment to changes in market supply and market demand was discussed. When some disturbance causing the market equilibrium position to change was introduced, the market reacted in a series of successive adjustments, the path of which suggested a cobweb.

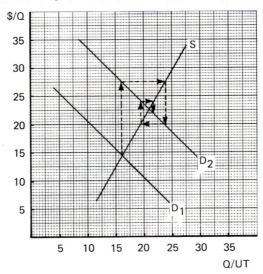

Price Elasticity of Demand Around New Equilibrium		Price Elasticity of Supply Around New Equilibrium	
P_1 = \$22.00	P_2 = \$23.00	P_1 = \$22.00	P_2 = \$23.00
Q_1 = 21.5	Q_2 = 20.5	Q_1 = 20.5	Q_2 = 21.0

$$\epsilon_D = \frac{\dfrac{Q_1 - Q_2}{Q_1 + Q_2}}{\dfrac{P_1 - P_2}{P_1 + P_2}} = \frac{\dfrac{21.5 - 20.5}{42}}{\dfrac{22 - 23}{45}} = -1.02$$

$$\epsilon_S = \frac{\dfrac{Q_1 - Q_2}{Q_1 + Q_2}}{\dfrac{P_1 - P_2}{P_1 + P_2}} = \frac{\dfrac{20.5 - 21.0}{41.5}}{\dfrac{22 - 23}{45}} = .54$$

Figure 12.8   The convergent cobweb: demand is more elastic than supply.

Figure 12.8 indicates the necessity for the suppliers of a product to make adjustments in response to a change in market demand. If we calculate the price elasticities of demand and supply in the immediate neighborhood of the new equilibrium, we can show demand to be relatively more elastic with respect to price than is supply in the neighborhood of this new equilibrium point. As a result, the successive adjustments will ultimately converge on the new equilibrium. This convergent cobweb is the type of adjustment path that was described in Chapter 11.

There are occasions, however, when an equilibrium position in the market place is hard to come by. Consider, for example, the situation in Figure 12.9 in which the absolute values of the price elasticities of demand and supply are exactly equal. The result of this situation is a *continuous* or *stable* cobweb, in which prices and quantities regularly oscillate between two levels in successive production periods. This situation gives rise to a year-to-year (or more precisely, a production period-to-production period) cycle of

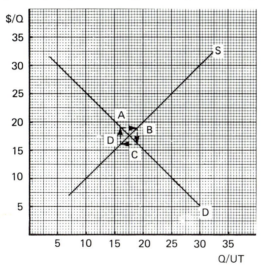

Price Elasticity of Demand

Point A	Point C
$Q_1 = 19$	$Q_2 = 16$
$P_1 = 16$	$P_2 = 19$

Price Elasticity of Supply

Point B	Point D
$Q_1 = 16$	$Q_2 = 19$
$P_1 = 16$	$P_2 = 19$

$$\epsilon_D = \dfrac{\dfrac{Q_1 - Q_2}{Q_1 + Q_2}}{\dfrac{P_1 - P_2}{P_1 + P_2}} = \dfrac{\dfrac{19 - 16}{35}}{\dfrac{16 - 19}{35}} = -1.0 \qquad \epsilon_S = \dfrac{\dfrac{Q_1 - Q_2}{Q_1 + Q_2}}{\dfrac{P_1 - P_2}{P_1 + P_2}} = \dfrac{\dfrac{16 - 19}{35}}{\dfrac{16 - 19}{35}} = 1.0$$

Figure 12.9 The stable cobweb: supply and demand are equally elastic.

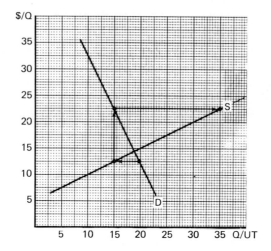

Price Elasticity of Demand		Price Elasticity of Supply	
$Q_1 = 19$	$Q_2 = 18.5$	$Q_1 = 18$	$Q_2 = 20$
$P_1 = \$14$	$P_2 = \$15$	$P_1 = \$14$	$P_2 = \$15$

$$\epsilon_D = \frac{\frac{Q_1 - Q_2}{Q_1 + Q_2}}{\frac{P_1 - P_2}{P_1 + P_2}} = \frac{\frac{19 - 18.5}{37.5}}{\frac{14 - 15}{29}} = -.387 \qquad \epsilon_S = \frac{\frac{Q_1 - Q_2}{Q_1 + Q_2}}{\frac{P_1 - P_2}{P_1 + P_2}} = \frac{\frac{18 - 20}{38}}{\frac{14 - 15}{29}} = 1.52$$

Figure 12.10 The divergent (or explosive) cobweb: supply is more elastic than demand.

prices and production. There are numerous examples of agricultural products that exhibit some of these cyclical traits. These cycles are not necessarily only one or two production periods in length, however. Often, more than one production period will be necessary for complete adjustment. And frequently, a second disequilibrating force will be introduced before complete adjustment can be made.

A third type of cobweb, and by far the most common so far as agriculture is concerned, is the *divergent* or *explosive* cobweb. This is also the most difficult with which to deal. The divergent cobweb occurs under circumstances in which the price elasticity of supply exceeds the price elasticity of demand in the neighborhood of the equilibrium point (Figure 12.10). This means that if the production sector, with less than perfect knowledge, should mis-guess by a very small amount what the price at the point of equilibrium will be, and should then produce in harmony with that miscalculation, the result may well be disastrous.

Suppose in Figure 12.10 that producers figured that the equilibrium price would be $16 rather than $15.50. This represents an error in price expectation of only three percent. In response to this expected price, they produce 15.5 units of Q. However, consumers are willing to pay a price of no more than $14.50 for 15.5 units of Q. Thus, the producer gets a price nine percent lower than he had expected as a result of a three percent error in his expectations.

The worst thing about the divergent cobweb is that once the disequili-brating force is introduced, the market alone cannot possibly restore equilib-rium. When producers adjust along the supply curve, they overreact to what the consumer is trying to tell them, and the situation goes from bad to worse. Unfortunately, the supply for almost every farm product is more elastic with respect to price, at least in the short run, than is the demand for that product. Therefore, those who advocate permitting market forces to meet all of the needs for regulating the agricultural industry are victims of self-delusion. If price stability is of any value at all to a farmer in planning his business, or to society at large, such *stability cannot be achieved using market forces only.* This requires some extra-market regulation, and it is to this end that much of our agricultural policy regulation has been directed.

A case in point, in which the nature of the market supply function precludes stability achieved on the basis of market forces alone, is the situation that faced cotton producers in the Rolling Plains sections of the southwestern United States during the early 1960s. The shape of the supply function was of an inverted S type, similar to the total cost function observed in Chapter 9 (see Figure 12.11). At prices below 21 cents per pound of lint and at prices above 30 cents per pound, the supply function for cotton was fairly inelastic with respect to price. But at prices between 21 and 30 cents per pound, producers were highly responsive to price changes. For example, an expected price of 22 cents per pound would have generated an output of 320 million pounds of lint (Point M in Figure 12.11), assuming that pro-ducers were free to plant all the cotton they wished. But an expected price of 23.5 cents per pound—a price difference of 6.8 percent—would have gener-ated an output of 650 million pounds (Point N in Figure 12.11)—an output difference of 103 percent! If the market demand had been such that some point such as R was the actual equilibrium point, the supply function for cotton in the Plains area was so sensitive to price changes that a highly explosive cobweb function would have been inevitable in the face of free market pricing.

The forces of inflation, the energy crisis, and changing prices for wheat, grain sorghums, and livestock have altered the level and perhaps the shape of the cotton supply function since 1960. But the general form of that function is not changed. Basically, there are certain critical price levels below which only those land resources adapted only to the production of cotton will be so employed. Once these price levels have been achieved, other lands that may

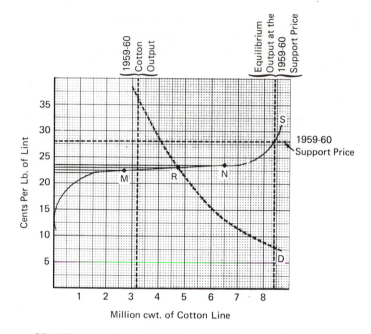

SOURCE: John W. Goodwin, James S. Plaxico and W. F. Lagrone,
Aggregation of Normative Microsupply Relationships for
Dryland Crop Farms in the Rolling Plains of Oklahoma
and Texas, Technical Bulletin T-103, Oklahoma Agricultural Experiment Station and FPED, ERS, USDA, Stillwater, Oklahoma, August, 1963.

Figure 12.11 Estimated supply function for cotton, rolling plains of the
southwestern United States, 1959–60.

feasibly be utilized for cotton will be shifted very rapidly in response to very
small price incentives. This accounts for the general shape of the cotton
supply functions, which tend to be rather inelastic at the extremes and highly
elastic in the middle. If cotton demand intersects supply toward either
extreme of the supply function, the problems are normal. But if the intersection occurs in the highly elastic center portion of the cotton supply function,
the market instability is awesome. The adjustments in the 1972–75 cotton
markets, when cotton prices were up and down like a bride's nightgown,
demonstrated this instability.

Price Flexibility

The elasticity coefficient is concerned with estimating the percentage
change in the quantity purchased (or sold) as related to a 1 percent change in

price. Agricultural producers, however, are generally far more concerned with anticipating the changes in *price* as related to changes in the availability of goods. The elasticity coefficient may be utilized for this purpose simply by conversion to *price flexibility.*

Price flexibility is the inverse of elasticity. That is, price flexibility can be calculated by either of the following:

$$\text{Price flexibility} = \frac{1}{\epsilon} \tag{12.16}$$

or

$$\text{Price flexibility} = \frac{\dfrac{P_1 - P_2}{P_1 + P_2}}{\dfrac{Q_1 - Q_2}{Q_1 + Q_2}} \tag{12.17}$$

In the introductory paragraphs to this chapter, it was pointed out that we could anticipate the probable price impact of various sorts of changes through the use of elasticity estimates. The example was that if beef imports should increase the quantities of beef available in American markets by 3 percent, we could use the price elasticity of demand for beef to anticipate the probable price impact of these expanded imports. George and King estimated the price elasticity of demand for beef to be −0.6438 at retail and to be −0.416485 at the producer level.[5]

George and King's elasticity estimates suggest that the quantity demanded would change by .64 percent at retail and by .42 percent at the farm level for each 1 percent change in price. But a beef producer isn't terribly concerned with that information. The producer's concern is with the probable price impact of this increased beef availability. Converting George and King's elasticity estimates into price flexibilities for beef can help solve this problem.

$$\text{Expected change in} = \left(\frac{1}{-.6438}\right)\left(3\%\right) = -4.66 \text{ percent} \tag{12.18}$$

$$\begin{array}{l}\text{Expected change in} \\ \text{beef price at farm}\end{array} = \left(\frac{1}{-.4165}\right)\left(3\%\right) = -7.20 \text{ percent} \tag{12.19}$$

---

[5] P. S. George and G. A. King, *Consumer Demand for Food Commodities in the United States, op cit.,* Tables 1 and 2.

That is, the expected increase in beef availability could be expected to reduce retail beef prices by nearly 5 percent and live slaughter cattle prices by a bit more than 7 percent. Thus, a 45¢ live cattle market would be expected to be reduced to 41.75¢ per pound as the result of a 3 percent increase in beef availability.

Selected References

Brandow, G. E., *Interrelations Among Demand for Farm Products and Implications for Control of Market Supply,* Bulletin 680. University Park, Pennsylvania: Pennsylvania Agricultural Experiment Station, August, 1961.

George, P. S. and G. A. King, *Consumer Demand for Food Commodities in the United States with Projections for 1980,* Giannini Foundation Monograph Number 26. Davis: California Agricultural Experiment Station, March 1971.

Marshall, Alfred, *Principles of Economics,* 8th ed., Book III, Chapter IV. London: Macmillan and Co., Ltd., 1959.

Shepherd, Geoffrey, S., *Agricultural Price Analysis,* 5th ed., Chapters 4, 5, and 6. Ames, Iowa: Iowa State University Press, 1963.

13

Market Structure: The Conditions of Competition

In Chapter 12 we discussed the concept of elasticity of demand with respect to price, with respect to income, and with respect to the prices of alternative goods on which consumers might choose to spend their incomes. We also discussed the elasticity of supply and the relationship between supply and demand elasticity as they relate to the Cobweb Theorem.

We saw how a straight line market demand curve will have ranges within which demand is relatively elastic and relatively inelastic and a point at which elasticity is unitary. If demand is relatively inelastic, the quantity purchased will be reduced by less than price is increased. Thus, as prices are reduced the total expenditure of funds for a particular product will be increased, *up to the point of unitary elasticity.*

A rational producer will always produce and sell *within the elastic range of the demand curve he faces.* By reducing production in order to get out of the inelastic range, he will reduce his costs. At the same time, he will be increasing his revenues. Thus, he will unquestionably be increasing his profits if he moves out of the range of inelastic demand.

The elasticity of the demand curve as faced by the individual firm can tell much about the market structure within which the firm operates. For example, a firm operating under conditions of pure competition faces a demand curve that is *perfectly elastic*; that is, no matter how much it produces, the market will absorb its product at the market price.

Pure Competition

In reference to our discussion of market structure, we should first define what we mean by "competition." In our everyday conversation, we normally think of competition in the sense of rivalry—every competitor is attempting to outdo his rivals. In the economic sense, competition simply refers to the degree of importance of the individual consuming or producing unit in relation to the total industry or market within which that unit operates. As we saw in the case of the individual farmer, the individual unit provides such a minute portion of the total supply (or demand, as the case may be) that the individual cannot influence the market price of the product he sells (or buys). If the individual drops out of the market completely, his absence will not change the total demand or supply enough to affect the market price. Thus, that individual is unimportant or insignificant so far as the market is concerned.

The conditions necessary for the existence of pure competition include:

1. The insignificance of the individual producing or consuming unit in relation to the total market,

2. Homogeneity of product, and

3. Absence of artificial limitations on entry to or exit from the market.

We have already discussed the insignificance of the individual economic unit. The condition of homogeneity of product is concerned simply with the uniformity of the product bought and sold. One bushel of wheat, for example, is pretty much like another bushel of wheat. One chicken is pretty much like another. One choice grade 1,000-pound slaughter steer is very much like another. In other words, when we are concerned with homogeneity, a product cannot be identified as to source or destination once it gets into the market place. Buyers will be about as satisfied with one unit of a product as with another. (Grain-finished beef would thus be a different product from grass-fat beef, since the two types are not homogeneous. An Arkansas Razorback would be quite a different product than an Iowa hog. Different grades of wheat or corn would likewise be different products.)

The third condition of the absence of artificial limitations on entry to or exit from the market is concerned largely with the freedom of choice on the parts of both producers and consumers, and with the mobility of resources and products. Prices are assumed to be free to move in response to changes in market supply and market demand. Neither market supply nor market demand is subject to the forces of organized pressure groups such as labor unions, trade associations, or government agencies. Resources are free to move into those alternative employments that pay the highest returns to the resources. Goods and services are free to move to those consumers and into those areas that are willing to pay the highest prices.

Competition in the economic sense is without emotion. Adjacent cattle ranchers are unlikely to be antagonistic over the fact that one sells cattle at a reduced price. The lower price accepted by one will in no way affect the price (and hence the income) received by the other. In fact, the neighbor is far more likely to feel compassion toward a stupid man who accepts a low price than he is to be resentful of cutthroat pricing practices. On the other hand, a blood rivalry will often exist between the dairies providing door-to-door deliveries, since price cutting by Borden's will unquestionably affect the size of the market served by Carnation. Thus, the rancher or wheat farmer operates under conditions approaching pure competition, while the milk processor operates under something less than a purely competitive situation.

The situation defined by the assumptions of the purely competitive market do not in fact exist in any important degree in the American economy. Most farm products are produced and marketed under conditions that *approach* pure competition. But the agribusiness firms that process and distribute farm products can in most cases affect the incomes and profits earned by their competitors. Also, the agricultural supply firms normally operate under circumstances other than those defined by the purely competitive criteria.

As we constructed a model to describe the national economy in Chapter 3, so will we now construct models to describe the different market structures with which we must deal. Our discussion of the purely competitive model will provide a starting point for analyzing the farming sector of the agricultural economy, and will further provide a standard of comparison against which the less perfectly competitive sectors may be evaluated. The model of pure competition provides a model of the most efficient type of economic organization. That is, resources will flow into those uses that will pay the highest prices and the total satisfaction realized by people in the economy will be maximized within the constraints of limited resources and technology.

We've already seen how under conditions of pure competition the firm's marginal cost curve defines the firm's supply curve. We've seen how the demand curve faced by the firm appears as a horizontal line *at the price level.* This line defines the marginal and average revenue curves for the individual firms, as well as the demand function faced by the individual firm (see Figure 13.1). You will notice that the quantity axis for the market is measured in much larger units than is the quantity axis for the firm. Thus, the individual firm provides only an infinitesimally small part of the market supply. If Farmer Bellmon hauls a load of wheat to town and asks more than the market price, the man at the wheat elevator will simply grin and punch Farmer Bellmon's TS card. About the only thing Farmer Bellmon can do is to haul his wheat back home. This illustrates that the demand for wheat, so far as Farmer Bellmon is concerned, is defined by the point at which market supply and market demand intersect. If this point of equilibrium is changed, it represents a change in the price at which Farmer Bellmon can sell his

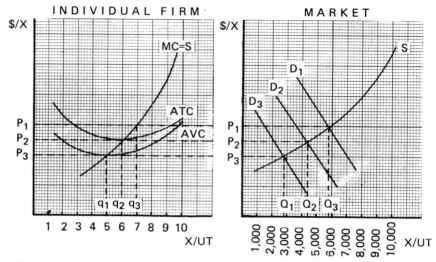

Figure 13.1   Relationship between the pure competitor and the market.

wheat, and hence represents a change in the demand for the wheat *belonging to any particular producer.*

You will recognize the demand curve as faced by an individual farmer under the conditions of pure competition as being *perfectly elastic*: no matter how much or how little that individual sells, the price is unchanged. Thus, our friends who maximize profits by producing where marginal costs and marginal revenue are equal under the conditions of pure competition are completely rational. They are operating within the elastic portion of the demand curve they *individually* face, even though *market* demand may be inelastic with respect to price. Any individual seller who insists upon a price above the market level will have a sales volume of zero.

At this point in our discussion, we need to digress for a moment and talk about economic profits. In an accounting sense, when we speak of profits, we think in terms of gross sales and total operating expenses. The difference in these two items is what the accountant calls profits. However, in the sense of economics, the accountant's estimate of operating expenses does not include all the costs of doing business. When we discussed the cost of a college education in the foreword, we included the money which a student could be making from a job as a part of the cost of his education. This opportunity cost also applies in the case of the world of economics. Included in the total costs are the return that all the resources used could earn if employed in the highest-paying alternative use. Thus, the farm businessman (or any other businessman) should include as a part of the cost of doing business the price that he could get for his labor in the best alternative job available to him, and the interest he could get in the best alternative investment for his capital. If there is anything left after these costs have been paid, then economic profits have been earned.

In the highly imaginary spirit world of pure competition, we have said that resources are free to move into those industries in which returns are the greatest. What does this mean in the case of economic profits? If average total costs (including the opportunity costs for all resources used) are less than average revenue per unit of a particular product, as at price P_1 in Figure 13.1, in what direction would resources be expected to flow? Obviously, since the returns in this business are greater than "normal"—that is, since resources are earning returns above their opportunity costs—resource owners could be expected to attempt to cut themselves in for a piece of the action. As a result, resources would be expected to flow into the industry where economic profits were being realized. As resources came into the production of the good in question, the market supply curve for that product would shift to the right, and the price would be reduced, shifting downward the demand curve faced by each individual firm, causing the economic profits to disappear ultimately.

We have seen many examples of resources flowing out of an industry in which returns did not match those returns possible from another form of employment. We can also think of situations in which resources have flowed into a high-profit industry. For example, very little cotton farming currently occurs in many of the Southeastern states where cotton was originally king, because the returns to land, labor, capital, and management from cotton in these areas will not cover the opportunity costs of using these resources in some alternative form of employment. On the other hand, large volumes of these same resources have gone into the production of beef cattle, soybeans, and pine trees in recent years. Because of the rapidly expanding demand for beef, beans, and wood, economic profits were being realized and the owners of resources located in these Southeastern areas began to cash in on the profits possible in other industries.

We stated earlier that the purely competitive model would provide us with a standard for comparing the efficiency of the various types of market structures that do in fact prevail in our economy. We've examined the world of pure competition. What then, is the impact of pure competition on the economy? Since resources are mobile in this situation, resources will move into an industry until the returns from the industry are just equal to the average total costs (including opportunity costs). That is, products will be priced at the minimum point on the average total cost curve. *Consumers will therefore be buying at the lowest possible price. The product will be produced at the least possible cost per unit of production.* Each firm will be operating at an optimum scale of plant and at an optimum rate of output so *economic efficiency will be maximum* and total costs of production will be minimum. Since no single firm can affect product price, and since all firms in the industry are producing a homogeneous product, *there is no incentive for sales promotion and advertising.* Consumers can't tell the difference between Colorado corn-fed beef and the beef that comes from feedlots in West Texas or the Corn Belt. Advertising on the part of Colorado feeders will not, therefore, make one iota of difference in the price received by Colorado feedlots for such beef.

We have briefly defined the conditions for the purely competitive market structure. Included in those conditions were a number of buyers and sellers large enough that no single buyer or seller could affect the market price. That is, both buyers and sellers accept the price as an accomplished fact, and make their plans for production and consumption on the basis of that price with no thought of attempting to negotiate the price. Under conditions of pure competition, both resources and products are free to move to the highest paying user and the product produced by a particular industry is completely homogeneous. The impact of the purely competitive model on the economy is that consumers get products at the lowest possible price, producers produce at the lowest possible cost, and sales promotional activities are nonexistent. No seller under the conditions of pure competition can affect the prices paid nor the prices received by any other seller in the market.

We have admitted that the existence of the purely competitive market situation was rare in the real world. However, we have suggested that the purely competitive market model provides us with a very convenient standard for comparing the impacts of various types of market structure. Further we do have certain important segments of our economy, notably farming, in which the situation *approaches* the purely competitive model.

Pure Monopoly

Now, using our purely competitive standard for comparison, let's examine a market structure at the other extreme: Pure monopoly. The conditions necessary for the existence of pure monopoly include:

1. There is one and only one seller of a given product in a given market. Thus, the individual seller is *totally* significant, and the market demand function *is* the demand function faced by that individual firm.

2. There are no close substitute goods for the product. Hence, the changes in the prices and outputs of alternative goods have no direct impact on the monopolist, and changes in pricing and output on the part of the monopolist will not directly affect other producers in the economy.

3. Entry of other firms into the market for this product is blocked.

Like pure competition, the incidence of pure monopoly is rare in the real world. One example of pure monopoly is the American postal system as far as first class mail is concerned. Many public utility systems approach the purely monopolistic case at least in a local sense. For example, most communities will grant a franchise to a single seller of electricity and another to a single seller of natural gas. Electricity and natural gas will substitute for one another to some degree, so while the monopolistic character of these examples is not "pure," it unquestionably approaches purity.

Let's compare the analytical concepts of pure monopoly with their counterparts under the conditions of pure competition. For purposes of simplicity, let's assume that our friend the monopolist buys his resources in a purely competitive market. Since the basic difference in monopoly and pure competition lies in the manner in which the product is sold, we can treat the monopolist's cost curves as if they were derived in exactly the same manner as are the cost curves for the purely competitive firm.

The pure competitor can sell all he wishes at the price set by the forces of market supply and market demand. Since the monopolist is the only seller of the product, the demand curve he faces *is* the market demand curve. Thus, the more product the monopolist sells during any given time interval, the lower must be the price at which this product is sold. If an increase in sales volume means that the price at which the entire volume sells is going to be reduced, then the marginal revenue curve for the firm is no longer identical with the demand function.

The market demand function *is* an average revenue function—that is, the total volume of sales (i.e., total revenue) can be calculated for any point on the demand function simply by multiplying the price at that point by the quantity that would be taken at that price. When the change in total revenue associated with a one-unit change in the quantity sold (that is, the marginal revenue) is measured, it becomes apparent that as the quantity taken is increased, marginal revenue falls twice as fast as does average revenue (or demand). (See Table 13.1 and Figure 13.2.) This is because as the quantity taken per unit of time is increased, the price received for *every* unit sold is reduced. That is, if one unit were to sell for $12.80, and two units for $11.65 per unit, the $12.80 unit is reduced in value by $1.15 when the volume is expanded from one to two units. Thus, the marginal revenue per unit sold is less than the price at which the product is sold (i.e., $11.65 - $1.50 = $10.50 marginal revenue or the amount by which total revenue has changed as a result of a one-unit change in the volume of sales).

Since the monopolist faces the market demand curve rather than producing where his marginal cost curve crosses the demand curve, he will produce at that point where marginal revenue and marginal costs are equal

TABLE 13.1

MONOPOLY RELATIONSHIP BETWEEN DEMAND (AVERAGE REVENUE), TOTAL REVENUE, AND MARGINAL REVENUE AS SHOWN IN FIGURE 13.2

AVERAGE REVENUE OR DEMAND CURVE		TOTAL REVENUE (PRICE × QUANTITY)	MARGINAL REVENUE (CH. IN *TR*)
Price	Quantity		
13.95	0	0	
12.80	1	12.80	12.80
11.65	2	23.30	10.50
10.50	3	31.50	8.20
9.35	4	37.40	5.90
8.20	5	41.00	3.60
7.05	6	42.30	1.30
5.90	7	41.30	−1.00
4.75	8	38.00	−3.30
3.60	9	32.40	−5.60
2.45	10	24.50	−7.90
1.30	11	14.30	−10.20
.15	12	1.80	−12.50

(Figure 13.3). We have already defined "total costs" to include the opportunity costs of paying resources the same return that those resources could earn in their best alternative employment. Therefore, it is apparent that the monopolist is extracting "pure" profits—or economic profits—from his business activity. Also, since he will produce at that point where marginal costs and marginal revenues are equal, and since marginal revenue is negative beyond the point of unitary elasticity, a monopolist will produce only in the elastic portion of the demand curve. If costs were zero, he would produce at the point of unitary elasticity (where marginal revenue is zero and where the total revenue is maximum). The only way that a monopolist (or any other rational businessman, for that matter) could be induced to produce in the inelastic portion of the demand curve he faces would be either through legislative coercion or through the heavy subsidies that would cause costs to be negative in that portion of the curve.

The existence of economic profits in a monopolistic industry will provide the incentive for other owners of resources to attempt to enter the market through becoming producers of the good currently being sold only by the monopolist. Unless the monopolist is capable of effectively blocking entry into his field when profits are being realized, he will not long *be* a

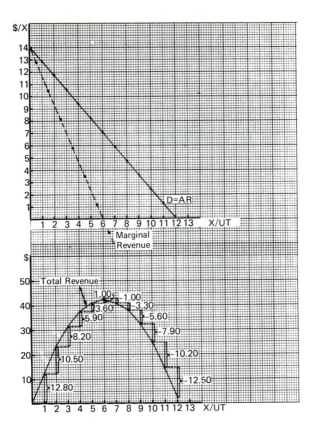

Figure 13.2 Monopoly: relationship among demand, total revenue, and marginal revenue.

monopolist. Several factors may be present that will prevent competition. These include:

1. Almost complete control by one firm of at least one of the resources necessary for the production of a particular good;

2. Government patents and copyrights that may prevent the production of a good substitute product; and

3. The size of the market to be served may be such that the existence of another firm would drive prices so low that both firms would be forced into bankruptcy.

Probably the most common of these barriers to entry are the patent barrier and the limitation of market size. For a number of years, International Business Machines was popularly believed to control enough of the patents

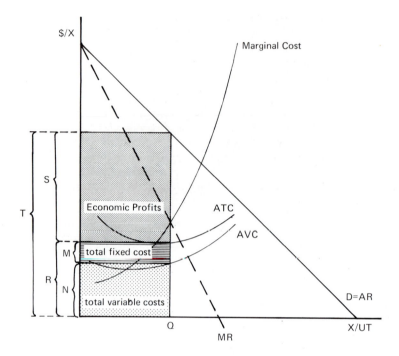

The letters on the vertical axis refer to per unit levels of:

M — Fixed Cost (i.e., Average Fixed Cost)
N — Variable Cost (i.e., Average Variable Cost)
R — Total Cost (i.e., Average Total Cost)
S — Economic Profit
T — Average Revenue (i.e., Price)

Figure 13.3 Pricing and output under conditions of monopoly.

for electronic computing equipment that they enjoyed what amounted to monopolistic control of the industry. Another example of a government-sponsored barrier may be found historically in the case of the machinery used in the manufacturing of shoes.

The barrier to entry into a business that probably has more effect on agriculture than any other is a limitation on the size of the market to be served. Many farming communities, for example, are forced to patronize a particular feed or fertilizer dealer because the local market cannot support more than one such business. The nearest alternative source of these products is distant enough that cost prohibits an effective transfer of this patronage. Another example may be found in the case of a physician or a hospital in a sparsely populated area. By the time a patient gets to an alternative source of medical care, he may no longer require such attention.

As we have suggested in our discussion of the market size limitation to competitive firms entering the market, monopolistic firms are *not* necessarily always profitable. Examples of this may be found in abundance in the rural areas of America. The rapid consolidation of farm assets and the consequent out-migration of rural people have caused many communities that were once thriving rural trade centers to become virtual ghost towns. A community that once boasted six grocery stores may now have only one. Or a community that once had three dry goods stores may now have none. What has happened is that the shrinking market has forced some of these businesses into non-existence, and if the empty and deserted stores along Main Street are any indication, the town may soon follow. In the case where a single grocery store remains in a community, if the building were to burn down, the business would often cease to exist since the returns that can be generated are so limited that investment in a new building would be unlikely to pay for itself.

This situation may be illustrated by the case in which the monopolist is making some contribution to his fixed costs, but is not completely covering the expense necessary to provide for replacing all of the capital equipment used in his business (see Figure 13.4). If some contribution to overhead is

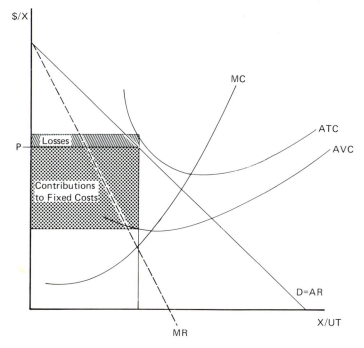

Figure 13.4 Monopolies aren't always profitable.

possible, he will continue to do business until he has depleted (or used up) the investment in fixed equipment. Once it becomes necessary to replace the building (for example, in the case of a rural grocery store) or, what more frequently occurs, once the returns drop below the operating expense (average variable cost in Figure 13.4), the business will cease to be.

A local market of limited size will often lead to the granting of an exclusive franchise by a local government unit. This locational monopoly is, as we have suggested, particularly common in the case of public utilities. Periodically, the voters in most communities will vote to renew the franchise held by some public utility company. Since the fixed expense of laying gas mains or stringing electric wires is so great, and since the presence of more than one firm would mean that these high fixed costs would be duplicated for every firm in the market, a single firm can provide these services much less expensively than can two or more. A franchise agreement will normally specify the price at which the utility is to be provided, and the agreed-upon price will generally be a limited percentage above the level at which all costs are expected to be covered. Should operating costs increase such that the percentage return is not being generated, most franchise agreements contain a clause that provides for re-negotiation of rates.

What, then, are the effects of monopoly? Is monopoly necessarily *bad*? If the market is of the nature where pure competition *could feasibly exist,* consumers would pay a higher price under monopoly conditions than they would pay under conditions of pure competition. We know that in pure competition, the market supply curve is simply the horizontal summation of the marginal cost curves for the individual firms. Thus, under pure competition in a market such as described by Figure 13.5, consumers would pay P_{pc} per unit of the product and would buy Q_{pc}. Under monopoly, they get less product (only Q_m) and pay a higher price (P_m) to get it. There are no economic profits under pure competition once enough time has elapsed to permit economic adjustment to occur. But the economic profits extracted by the monopolist are still being ripped out of the consumer's hide. Thus, the effects of monopoly in a market that is large enough to support pure competition are:

1. Higher prices,

2. Reduced availability of product, and

3. A transfer of wealth from consumers to the monopolist through the economic profits above and beyond the opportunity cost return to all resources.

If, however, the monopoly is of the locational type due to a market of limited size, consumers are very likely to be in a more favorable position

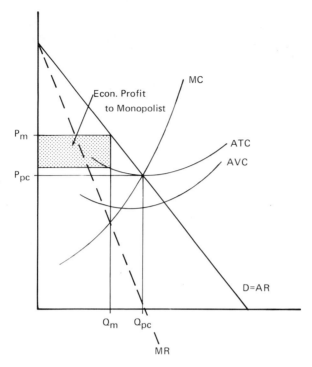

Figure 13.5 Comparison of the impacts of monopoly versus pure competition.

under monopoly since without it they would be forced to pay more to get the product to the locations where it is needed (to their homes in the case of electricity or natural gas). If a new source for some product such as natural gas were to enter the market and serve every second house in town, then individual consumers would be faced with paying twice as large a share of the fixed costs for gas mains, office overhead, etc., as they pay under monopoly conditions.

Imperfect Competition

We've discussed the two extremes of market structure—pure competition and pure monopoly—and some of the circumstances surrounding the existence of these two types of markets. We have recognized that these two types of market structure rarely exist in the purest form in the real world, but certain industries do in fact approach pure competition and in a locational sense we often encounter what amounts to pure monopoly. The demand curve facing the pure competitor is infinitely elastic, while the demand curve facing the monopolist will generally include all three degrees of elasticity. The rational businessman will *always* operate in the elastic portion of the demand curve he faces, provided that there are no legislative or other institutional restraints to prevent his doing so.

Between the two extremes lies a broad area that includes much of the non-farm agricultural businesses. For purposes of convenience, we will call this area "imperfect competition" and lump all the duopolistic, oligopolistic and monopolistically competitive types of business into this category. (Technically, pure monopoly also would fit in the category of imperfect competition, since monopoly constitutes the ultimate in imperfection in the degree of competition. However, for purposes of clarity, monopoly has been treated separately.) The situation that will probably be most familiar, and most important in terms of the volume of business, is the oligopoly type of business arrangement. Under conditions of oligopoly, there are but a few sellers of a good. The decisions as to pricing and output on the part of one firm will have a definite impact on the volume of sales and incomes realized by all other firms in the industry. Thus, any time one oligopolist changes his pattern of operations, it is a pretty good bet that the competing oligopolists who share that market are going to retaliate.

In our discussion of pure competition, we pointed out that in the economic sense, competition is completely unemotional. Intense personal rivalry between competing businessmen on the basis of business operations is rare. Not so in the case of oligopoly. The drivers of rival home-delivery milk trucks, for example, will do some pretty distasteful things to acquire the business of a new resident in the neighborhoods served by their routes.

Probably the classic example of oligopoly is provided by the petroleum industry. Almost every community has at least two service stations that are affiliated with different oil companies. Often, there are ten or more stations. If one should attempt to increase his volume of sales by cutting the price of gasoline by one cent per gallon, what happens? We all know from experience (pleasant experience, unless you happen to own a filling station) that a full-scale price war may well be in the making. Price wars are characteristic of the oligopolistic industries.

Managers who know they face an oligopolistic industry are apt to be very, very cautious about reducing prices. They must consider the impact that their actions will have on their rivals and the retaliatory measures that those rivals may adopt. Rather than competing on the basis of price, firms operating under oligopolistic conditions are more likely to rely on advertising and devices such as trading stamps, since the reaction to these techniques is generally less immediate and less disastrous than is the reaction to a price reduction.

So far, we have devoted our discussion of market structure exclusively to the structural differences on the product-selling side. However, there are a number of differences on the resource-buying side that merit attention. For

TABLE 13.2

RELATIONSHIPS BETWEEN NUMBERS OF BUYERS
AND SELLERS UNDER SELECTED TYPES OF
MARKET STRUCTURES

NUMBERS OF PEOPLE IN THE MARKET	MARKET STRUCTURE TYPE	
	Selling	Buying
One	Monopoly	Monopsony
Two	Duopoly	Duopsony
Few	Oligopoly	Oligopsony
Many	Pure[1] Competition (Polyopoly) or Monopolistic Competition[1]	Pure Competition (Polyopsony)

[1] Monopolistic competition differs from pure competition primarily in that while the products of monopolistic competitors are very near to being the same product, there is enough difference in the minds of consumers that a brand name on the product may cause the demand curve for the product to be somewhat less than perfectly elastic. An example of this type of market structure is seen in the case of the multiplicity of small sausage kitchens found in almost every area of the United States. Acclimating consumers to the particular blend of spices in *Whole Hawg Sausage* may create a slight consumer preference for this product over alternative products, even though the rest of the formula may be identical to any one of a hundred other brands.

example, a single firm may dominate the market for livestock or cotton in a given area. If producers want to sell to some other business organization they must leave the area (and accept a transportation charge) to do so. Since there is a substantial cost for shipping cattle from Fort Worth to Omaha, it is unlikely that a producer finding the market in Fort Worth dominated by a particular packer at a given time is likely to ship his cattle to Omaha.

Structural conditions of the markets in which farmers sell are more often than not imperfectly competitive. The agricultural processing firms tend to be oligopolistic on the selling side. Most agricultural processing firms tend to be fairly specialized toward particular types of farm products. Therefore, it follows that the conditions under which these firms purchase resources are likely to be something less than perfectly competitive.

The suffix "-opoly" in economics denotes the manner in which a product is sold (see Table 13.2). Hence, *mon-opoly* suggests that there is one and only one seller of the good in question. The suffix "-opsony" denotes the conditions under which a product or resources is purchased. Thus, an industry that is said to be a *mon-opsony* would be an industry in which there was one and only one buyer for a good. To be consistent, pure competitors on the

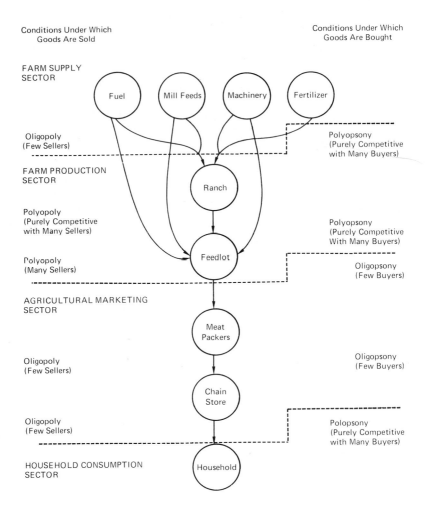

Figure 13.6 Conditions of competition throughout the production-marketing chain for beef cattle.

selling side (farmers, for example) would be called *polyopolists* and pure competitors on the buying side (housewives doing their grocery shopping, for example) would be called *polyopsonists.*

So much for the Latin roots of words and our English lesson. What meaning does all this have for agriculture? What earthly difference does it make to a farmer whether or not he sells as a pure competitor to an agency that buys as an oligopsonist? Why should we be concerned about the conditions under which a meat packer buys and sells? What difference could it make that farmers face something other than pure competition when they buy machinery, fuel, fertilizers, or other productive resources?

Let's trace the market structures involved in the transactions that occur in the production of beef from the moment a calf is conceived until the roast beef appears by some miracle on the dining table (Figure 13.6). As we trace this product through the various phases of the agricultural industry, we find that an individual rancher has only a few sources from which he can buy the machinery, the fertilizer, the mill feeds, or the protein supplement he must have to carry a mother cow through the winter. At best he is buying from an oligopolist, and in some cases he may in a locational sense be obliged to purchase from a monopolist. When the calf goes to market in the fall, the rancher sells competitively to a cattle feeder who buys competitively. When the cattle feeder has fed the animal to the desired weight, he sells as a pure competitor to a firm that is most likely to be buying as an oligopsonist. After the packer has dressed and processed the animal, he sells the carcass to a chain store. Since there are only a few packers that can meet the needs of chain stores, the packer is operating as an oligopolist, but since there are relatively few food chains, the chain store is operating as an oligopsonist. The chain store in turn oligopolistically sells the beef roast to the housewife who is buying as a pure competitor and can in no way affect the market price.

This involved chain of transactions and terminology may not be too important, but what is significant is that *there are only two segments throughout the chain that operate under conditions of pure competition* on either the selling or the buying side. These segments are the farm production sector and the household consumption sector. Every other agency has some bargaining power as far as price is concerned.

We hear a great deal about the small share of the consumer's dollar that eventually gets back to the farmer. For example, if wheat prices were $6 per bushel, the value of wheat in a one-pound loaf of bread would be only 8.5 cents. At $3 a bushel, the value is a bit above 4 cents per loaf. Yet the price of a loaf of bread has moved continuously upward, and 39 to 45¢ per loaf was a common price in the mid-1970s. It is apparent that the businesses that handle farm products between the time the farmer markets them and the housewife prepares and serves them must operate on something more than an insignificant margin. This margin is known as the "marketing margin." The size of the marketing margin will be one of the determinants in how much the housewife pays for food and in what prices are paid for farm commodities. This marketing margin and the firms that operate this area of marketing will be our point of discussion in Chapter 14.

Selected References

Boulding, Kenneth E., *Economic Analysis,* 3rd ed., Chapters 4, 29, 30, and 31. New York: Harper and Brothers, 1955.

Leftwich, Richard H., *The Price System and Resource Allocation,* Chapters 9 and 10. New York: Rinehart and Co., Inc., 1955.

Marshall, Alfred, *Principle of Economics,* 8th ed., Book V. Chapters IV, V and XIV. London: Macmillan and Co., Ltd., 1920.

Robinson, Joan, *The Economics of Imperfect Competition,* Chapters 2, 3, 15 and 16. London: Macmillan and Co., Ltd., 1933.

14

Price Spreads, Market Levels, and Marketing Margins

During the first half of the 1970s, rapidly escalating food prices generated enormous public concern. While some of the increase in food costs resulted from rapidly escalating farm costs, a substantial share was related to increases in the costs of the marketing services that were added to basic farm production between the time raw farm products left the farm and finished goods reached the consumer. In early 1974, for example, increased exports of American wheat took wheat prices above $6 per bushel. The average American consumer was frightened witless when a press release issued by the president of the American Bakers Association predicted that the price for bread would rise to $1 per loaf if the export of wheat were not curtailed.

The American public may someday learn that there are three types of people who issue press releases: liars, damn liars, and folk who just don't tell the truth. While this statement is not entirely fair, it must be recognized that the general objective for a press release is to lead the public to believe whatever the agency issuing the release finds *convenient* for the public to believe. This is illustrated in Figure 14.1. The president of the American Bakers Association was correct in his contention that bread prices would rise as wheat prices rose. But he was very careful to avoid pointing out that bread prices would also rise as wheat prices declined. The major source of increase in bread prices—not only in 1974, but indeed since the end of World War II—has been in the margin required by the baking industry. Generally, less than 20 percent of the cost of bread has been embodied in the cost of wheat, while well above half of that cost has been added by the baking industry.

There is no question that retail food costs escalated very rapidly in the early part of the 1970s. During the 1950–1970 period, increases in retail food prices had lagged substantially behind the general rate of inflation. But during the early 1970s, the inflation in food costs equaled, and in some cases

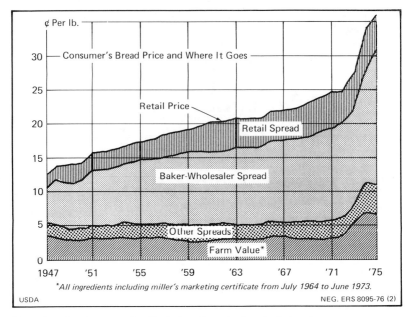

SOURCE: *Developments in Marketing Spreads for Agricultural Products in 1975,* Economic Research Service, U.S.D.A., Agricultural Economic Report No. 328, March, 1976.

Figure 14.1 Allocation of the consumer's expenditure for bread, U.S., 1947–75.

exceeded, the general rate of inflation. Part of this increase was due to increased farm prices.

In the 1970–1972 period, there were two official devaluations of the American dollar. In 1972, the president announced that the U.S. Treasury would no longer settle international accounts in gold. Thus, the value of the American dollar was allowed to "float" as far as its value in terms of other currencies was concerned. This action in fact amounted to a *third* devaluation of the dollar in less than two years. The result of these three devaluations was to substantially lower the cost of American products in international markets. Lower values in international markets meant that international sales of American products were dramatically expanded. Since weather had reduced crop yields in Eastern Europe, much of the expansion in foreign trade was made up of U.S. farm products and farm inputs such as fertilizer and other agriculture chemicals. The reduced domestic availability of U.S. farm commodities drove domestic farm prices up very rapidly during late 1972 and 1973. But the expansion in export sales of items such as fertilizer also drove farm production costs to unprecedented levels.

The sources of increase in U.S. retail food costs in the first part of the

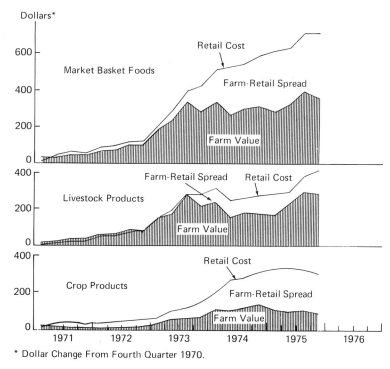

Figure 14.2   Sources of increase in U.S. retail food prices, 1971–75.

1970s are compared in Figure 14.2. Just about half of the increase in retail prices for all foods may be attributed to increased farm prices. But the inflationary impact was not restricted to the farm sector. When we examine the increase in retail prices of livestock products, we see that about a quarter of the increase results from increased charges for marketing services. Since a major input in the production of livestock products is feed grains (the cost of which was more than doubled between 1972 and 1974), it is not surprising that the farm value of livestock products should absorb much of the increase in retail price. But in the case of crop products, at least two-thirds of the increase in retail food cost was made up of increased marketing charges.

An examination of the distribution of the total retail values of beef and pork (Figures 14.3 and 14.4) reveals that the price margin added by the marketing agencies expanded substantially in the early 1970s. The farm-retail price spread for both beef and pork expanded by half over this period. The

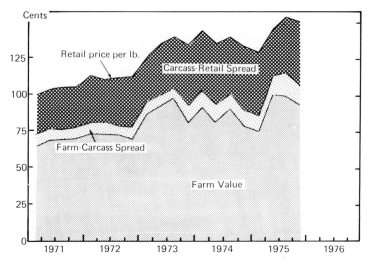

Figure 14.3 Price spreads for choice beef, U.S., 1971–75.

farmer's share of the consumer's food dollar is obviously something less than overwhelming. In 1974, the producer received more than half of the consumer expenditure for most animal products (Figure 14.5). But his share moved steadily downhill as other commodities were considered. Overall, the farm producer has historically realized 40–42 percent of total retail food expenditures.

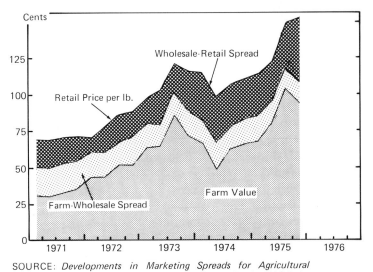

SOURCE: *Developments in Marketing Spreads for Agricultural Products in 1975*, Economic Research Service, U.S.D.A., Agricultural Economic Report No. 328, March, 1976.

Figure 14.4 Price spreads for pork, U.S., 1971–75.

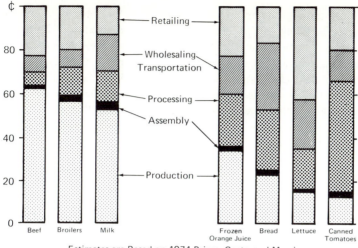

Figure 14.5   Who gets the American food dollar?

Price Spreads   •   What we have been examining above has been the change in farm-to-retail price spreads for farm products. This farm-retail price spread is simply the difference between the average retail price per unit sold and the farm value of the equivalent quantity sold by farmers, with credit given for the value of any by-products. A price spread does *not* provide information concerning the *profitability* of any of the businesses between the farm and retail market levels. The price spread simply compares the total value of the product that comes in the back door of the business with the total value of that which goes out the front door. It does not in any way include the costs that are incurred through added services while the product is being moved from the back to the front of the store.

Different Market Levels Involve Different Products

In Chapter 13, we saw how farm products typically pass through a marketing chain and are marketed at several different levels. Our example was the beef animal that passed from the rancher, to the feeder, to the packer, to the chain store, and finally to the consumer. Transactions are consummated and prices are established at each market level. It shall be our task in this chapter to examine just how these events occur.

Most farm products require the addition of some of the marketing services before they can be used in the direct satisfaction of human wants. These services may be in the form of further processing, transportation, grading, packaging, storage, or any one of a number of other services. The fact remains that these services must be performed to some degree prior to the time that the item is consumed. Thus, the product in demand by the consumer at the retail level is a *different* product than that which is available at the farm. This difference may be a difference of time, place, or form. That is, fresh peaches in an orchard in Georgia are not the same product as canned peaches in light syrup in a supermarket in the District of Columbia. For that matter, fresh peaches in a Georgia orchard are a different product than fresh peaches in a supermarket in Atlanta. In each case, marketing services have been added to change the time, place and/or form in which the product was available. As a result, costs have been added.

Derived Demand and Supply   •   Baked ham provides an immediate satisfaction of some want or need. But to get that ham, a live hog must first be *processed* to prevent its biting back when bitten, *transported* in some fashion from the point of production to the point of consumption, and very probably *stored* for some period of time before consumer satisfaction can occur. The services of labor, a packing plant, a smoke house, and transportation and storage facilities must be added to the live hog if a cured ham is to be the result. Thus, the satisfaction to be realized from a live hog is *indirect.* The demand function for live hogs, therefore, is *derived* from all the demand functions for ham, fresh pork, lard, and the other products that are derived from live hogs.

We've already seen how the forces of supply and demand determine prices, and how the price mechanism serves as the messenger boy that informs producers concerning the desires of consumers. Price also informs consumers concerning what producers can and will do, and informs the middle man about the situations facing *both* producers and consumers. Both demand and supply may be observed at several levels. However, the *basic demand* function *is* the *ultimate* or *final demand*; that is, the demand for finished products at the retail level. That retail demand includes the demand for the processing and other marketing services, for transportation, for packaging materials, and the like, *as well as* the demand for the farm-produced raw material. The problem we face in dealing with the marketing margin is that of separating the demand for the processing, packaging, etc., from the demand for the raw farm product.

Demand at wholesale under conditions of pure competition would be the demand at retail less the margin that a retailer requires for handling the various volumes of product that are defined along the quantity axis. Demand at the basic source of production (at the farm in the case of agricultural products) would be demand at wholesale less the margin for processing, packaging, and all the other services that are performed between the farm and the wholesale levels. Under conditions of pure competition, these margins would be comprised of the costs for adding the marketing services. These costs, of course, would include the opportunity cost of the return that all resources used could earn in their best alternative use.

Supply can also be observed at several levels, but in contrast to demand, the *basic* and fundamental *supply function is* the supply schedule observed *at the* basic *source of production.* In the case of agricultural products, the basic supply schedule is observed at the farm and is simply the sum of the marginal cost functions for all farms presently producing or potentially producing the product in question. The supply at wholesale may be estimated by simply adding the cost of processing, packaging, etc., to the supply schedule at the farm level. Likewise, the supply schedule at retail may be similarly estimated.

The Marketing Margin

The difference between the price at which some quantity of product would sell at the farm level and the price at which that same quantity of product would sell at some other level is called the *marketing margin.* Basically, the marketing margin is jointly determined by the demand for and the supply of the various marketing services. Agricultural processors normally are not eager to operate under circumstances in which they are not covering their total costs of operations. Nor are the agencies that buy and sell the processed items likely to tolerate exorbitant processing costs for very long. Thus, payments to processors (which are a part of the marketing margin) are likely to be kept fairly near the average total cost (including opportunity costs for all resources) for processing, most particularly if the processing agencies operate under conditions approaching pure competition.

We have already recognized that most processors do not in fact operate under conditions of pure competition. A single processor will often handle the output of many farms, buying as an oligopsonist or even as a monopsonist, and will generally sell under conditions of oligopoly. The price he charges will often reflect his marginal cost curve for processing. Since the market in which he sells is more often than not limited to a few buyers, however, there is a process of bargaining that will have a considerable impact on the ultimate price that the processor receives. The location of market power will play a major role in determining who gets what part of the difference in the price that a consumer pays for a loaf of bread and the price that the producer receives for wheat.

We are concerned with the performance of the agricultural economy at all levels. Therefore, we must necessarily separate the demand for the farm-produced raw material from the demand for the processed consumer goods which include these raw materials plus a great many services. How are we to go about this? A careful examination of the basic forces that underlie the supply and demand functions can give us the clue. Even though we have recognized that agricultural marketing agencies typically do not operate under conditions of pure competition, for purposes of understanding let's assume that we are dealing in a purely competitive world. We are interested in some product at the farm level and that same product as it progresses through the marketing chain toward the consumer.

The Constant-Cost-Per-Unit Marketing Margin   •   The constant marketing margin is commonly observed for products such as fresh fruits and vegetables. For purposes of illustration, let's use the hypothetical example of purple eggplant. From our analysis of the supply function, we know that the supply for an individual firm is the marginal cost curve, and that the market supply curve is simply the summation of all the individual supply curves in the market. Thus, our basic individual supply function would be the marginal cost curve for producing purple eggplant at the farm. The market supply function at the farm level would be the horizontal summation of all these individual supply functions (the greek letter Σ is used to denote summation), as shown in Figure 14.6. Since the product as sold at retail is the product that ultimately satisfies human wants, the demand at retail is the basic demand function with which we will be concerned.

Our immediate response to an examination of Figure 14.6 would be to anticipate a market volume of eight million pounds of purple eggplant at a price of ten cents per pound. But a question arises. Who gets that ten cents per pound? If the eggplant producer were dealing directly with the consumer, there would be no problem. But few consumers have ever encountered an eggplant farmer. The retail market demand for eggplant is in reality a demand for transportation, labor, and packaging materials, as well as for eggplant. The farm supply function, on the other hand, is the market supply for eggplant alone. The apparent market equilibrium in Figure 14.6 is no equilibrium at all, since the retail market demand function is really measuring the demand for a product that is different from the product measured by the farm supply function.

It is obvious that some manipulation of Figure 14.6 must be accomplished before any conclusion can be drawn concerning the eggplant market. That is, the demand for marketing services and materials must be stripped from the retail demand for eggplant in order to *derive* the demand for the product that is supplied at the farm level. The marketing services involved in the sale of fresh fruits and vegetables tend to cost the same per unit sold, regardless of the volume involved. That is, the costs for marketing these items tend to be almost exclusively variable costs. There is essentially no invest-

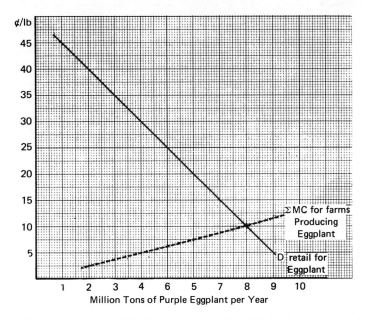

Figure 14.6   Basic demand is observed at retail while basic supply is observed at the farm.

ment in processing facilities utilized to change the form of the product, so fixed costs for marketing tend to be very close to zero.

Since there are no fixed costs, the eggplant marketing bill might appear as below:

Labor, Harvesting	$0.0050/lb.
Labor, Sorting and Grading	.0045/lb.
Labor, Packing for Shipment	.0025/lb.
Employee Benefits (5.85% of Wages)	.0007/lb.
Packaging Materials	.0268/lb.
Transportation	.0605/lb.
Total	$0.1000/lb.

At any given time, any of these items could normally be purchased by a truck-product marketing firm at a given cost per unit without regard to the volume. That is, most of the labor would generally be hired on a piece-work basis. The employee benefits (basically FICA—Social Security) would depend on the volume of labor hired. Packaging materials would consist largely of boxes or crates and a limited amount of padding, and transportation would normally be contracted at some set rate per ton. The absence of any significant fixed cost would suggest that the marketing agencies would require

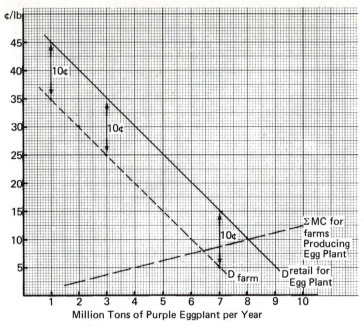

Figure 14.7   Farm demand is derived from retail demand by deducting the constant marketing margin.

a total return of ten cents per pound of product to get purple eggplant from field to food store, regardless of the volume of product involved.

Marketing costs must be paid in order to get the product from producers to consumers. Therefore, in our example, the retail price per pound that consumers are willing to pay for any quantity of eggplant includes ten cents to cover the consumer demand for marketing services. Thus, we can deduct ten cents per pound from the basic demand observed at retail in order to *derive* the farm demand for eggplant (Figure 14.7).

The retail supply function can be derived from the basic farm supply in a fashion similar to that shown for deriving farm demand. The farm supply function reveals the eggplant prices that are necessary to get various quantities produced at the farm. However, if the product is to be made available at retail, an additional cost of 10 cents per pound must be disbursed to cover the marketing costs. Thus, the retail supply function is simply the basic farm supply added to the marketing margin (Figure 14.8).

We can now find an equilibrium quantity exchanged and an equilibrium price for eggplant at the two market levels. As would be expected, the equilibrium quantity is the same at both market levels. Obviously the product cannot be sold at retail until it has first been produced and marketed from the farm. Our equilibrium output in Figure 14.8 is 6.4 million pounds of eggplant that sells for 18 cents per pound at retail and 8 cents per pound at

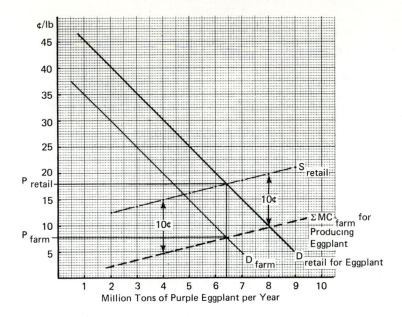

¢/lb

Million Tons of Purple Eggplant per Year

Figure 14.8 Retail supply derived from farm supply using the constant marketing margin, compared with retail demand and farm demand, showing the market prices at different market levels.

the farm level. It should be pointed out that these curves have the greatest relevance in the immediate neighborhood of the equilibrium position, and that the normal *ceteris paribus* assumptions associated with both demand and supply must necessarily hold in this case.[1]

The Increasing Cost Marketing Margin • So far, our analysis has assumed that the marketing services are provided at a constant cost per unit without regard to the numbers of units involved. As it happens, empirical research has suggested that this is true for agricultural products for which the marketing activities are largely restricted to services affecting the "time" and "place" phases of marketing activity. Time and place marketing problems typically involve variable rather than fixed resources. However, the addition of processing services that alter the form of the product between farm and retail levels involves rather large fixed investments in plant and equipment. Therefore, the marketing agency involved in this sort of activity faces quite a different situation than was the case with the constant-per-unit-cost marketing margin.

---

[1] Alfred Marshall, *Principles of Economics,* 8th ed., (London: Macmillan and Company, Ltd., 1920), Book V, Chapter VI.

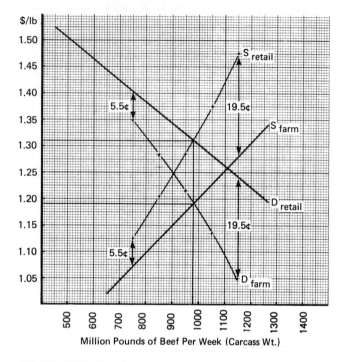

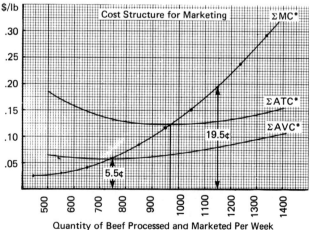

*The Greek symbol Σ means that the cost curves for all firms have been added and that these curves represent aggregate cost curves for all firms.

Figure 14.9 Derived demand and derived supply using the increasing-cost-per-unit marketing margin.

The average and marginal cost curves for marketing services in the case in which all costs were variable costs would appear as a horizontal line at the per unit cost level. But the marketing firm that does in fact have large, fixed investments in plant and equipment will face the normal cost structure that we derived in Chapter 9. This is the case with the meat packing industry, for example. Under these circumstances, both the derived demand curve and the derived supply curves will reflect the impact of the cost structure for processing, which includes a marginal cost curve that increases as volume of product increases.

In our analysis of supply, we learned that the supply curve for the individual firm operating under conditions of pure competition in the short run was defined by that portion of the marginal cost function that lay above the average variable cost curve. The market supply function was derived simply by adding the individual firm supply functions. Let's continue with our assumption of pure competition among the marketing firms. Thus, the aggregate marginal cost curve in the lower part of Figure 14.9 defines a supply function for marketing services. The prices at which the various quantities of a product—beef in the example in Figure 14.9—can and will be processed and marketed are defined along the aggregate marginal cost curve for those firms that provide these services. Thus, in Figure 14.9, 750 million pounds of beef will be processed each week at a cost of 5.5 cents per pound. But as the volume of processing increases, so must the marginal cost. At 1,150 million pounds, the processor must receive 19.5 cents per pound to cover the cost of handling the marginal unit. In the first case, the marketing sector would barely be covering the average variable costs for doing business. That is, they would be losing 8 cents per pound of beef processed, since the average total cost per pound at this volume is 13.5 cents per pound. This 750 million point level is, of course, the minimum volume the industry would handle since variable costs would not be covered at lower volumes. At a volume of 1,150 million pounds per week, the industry would be realizing economic profits of 6.5 cents per pound of beef processed. The presence of these profits would, of course, attract resources into the industry.

The supply curve for the processed goods will be defined by adding the marginal cost at which each volume of raw materials will be processed and marketed to the price at which that volume of raw materials will be supplied, as in the upper part of Figure 14.9 and Table 14.2. The demand curve for the raw product—cattle in the case of our example—will be derived by deducting the marketing margin (that is, by deducting the cost of processing) from the retail demand, as in Table 14.1 and Figure 14.9. This is the same analytical procedure as was followed in the case of the constant-cost-per-unit marketing margin. The only difference is in the form of the marketing margin itself. The equilibrium quantity and the equilibrium price at each market level will be defined, and if the price for marketing services should exceed the average

TABLE 14.1

EXAMPLE OF THE DERIVATION OF FARM DEMAND FROM RETAIL DEMAND, ASSUMING AN INCREASING-COST-PER-UNIT TYPE OF MARKETING MARGIN

QUANTITY OF CARCASS BEEF PER WEEK (MIL. LB.)	RETAIL PRICE OFFERED FOR THAT QUANTITY ($/LB)	LESS	MARG. COST FOR PROCS'G AND MKTG. ($/LB)	=	FARM PRICE OFFERED FOR THAT Q OF BEEF ($/LB)
550	$1.48		$-^1$		$ -
650	1.445		$-^1$		-
750	1.405		.05.5		1.35
850	1.365		.08.0		1.285
950	1.325		.11.0		1.215
1,050	1.285		.15.0		1.135
1,150	1.245		.195		1.050
1,250	1.205		.240		.965
1,350	1.165		.295		.870

Note: Same data as used in Figure 14.9.

[1] Since the processor will not operate at levels below his average variable costs, these figures are irrelevant.

Market Equilibrum at Retail Level

total cost curve for providing those services, then there will be an incentive for new firms to enter the business of processing.

In the very real world of meat packing, we know that packers make large profits during periods in which volume is high. They are fortunate to break even during periods in which volumes are limited. The demand for live cattle, which is derived on the basis of an increasing marginal cost of processing, illustrates why this happens. The marketing margin is fairly narrow at 800 million pounds of carcass beef per week in Figure 14.9, and if we look at the cost situation for the packer, we can see that he is not in fact covering all the fixed costs of his operation at this volume (fixed cost as measured by the difference in the aggregate average variable cost curve and the aggregate average total cost curve). At the equilibrium quantity of 980 million pounds, however, the marketing margin is just large enough that all costs are being covered.[2] Since no economic profits or economic losses are

---

[2] It must be remembered that the *farm* supply must be compared with *farm demand* and *retail supply* must be compared with *retail demand* in finding the equilibrium position.

TABLE 14.2

EXAMPLE OF THE DERIVATION OF RETAIL SUPPLY, ASSUMING AN INCREASING-COST-PER-UNIT TYPE OF MARKETING MARGIN

RETAIL PRICE AT WHICH THAT Q OF CARCASS BEEF WILL BE OFFERED ($/LB)	=	MARG. COST FOR PROCS'SING AND MKTG. ($/LB)	PLUS	FARM PRICE AT WHICH Q WILL BE SUPPLIED ($/LB)	QUANTITY OF CARCASS BEEF PER WEEK (MIL. LB.)
$ –	=	$ –		$.97	550
–		–		1.02	650
1.125		.055		1.07	750
1.205		.080		1.125	850
1.285		.110		1.175	950
1.375		.150		1.225	1,050
1.470		.195		1.275	1,150
1.56		.240		1.32	1,250
1.665		.295		1.37	1,350

Note: Same data as used in Figure 14.9.

[1] Since the processor will not operate at levels below his average variable costs, these figures are irrelevant.

⬡ Market Equilibrium at Farm Level

being realized at the equilibrium quantity in our example, there is no incentive for resources to enter or leave the beef marketing sector. Thus, we have a stable equilibrium.

The Constant-Percentage-Of-Price Marketing Margin • We have suggested that there are several possible types of marketing margins. We first saw a constant- price -per–unit type of margin in which the demand for the raw product as derived from the consumer demand function was parallel with the parent function. Second, we saw an increasing cost marketing margin in which the margin reflected the increasing nature of the marginal cost for processing. As the volume of marketing increased so did the margin between the price of the raw and finished products. Under these circumstances, the demand for the raw product declined at a faster rate than did the demand for the finished product. A third type of marketing margin that we observe in the real world (for example, in the case of dairy processing) is the constant percentage of finished product price.

Under conditions of the constant percentage marketing margin, the price at which a given quantity of the raw material will be purchased by the marketing firms will be based on some constant percentage reduction from the price at which the product can be sold at retail. This situation can arise from situations in which marketing firms have relatively high fixed costs, but in which relatively small increases in investments can significantly reduce the per unit costs of marketing services within the rational stage of production (i.e., in those firms that can achieve economies of scale).

Figure 14.10 iilustrates a situation in which a 20 percent increase in fixed investment (and hence in total fixed costs) significantly reduces average costs of operation. The larger scale of facility (cost structure 2 in Figure 14.10) can handle all volumes of processing at lower average costs than can the smaller facility. But the minimum average total cost per unit for the large facility occurs at 6,000 units of product rather than the 4,600 units observed with the smaller unit. At the optimum volume of output with the smaller unit

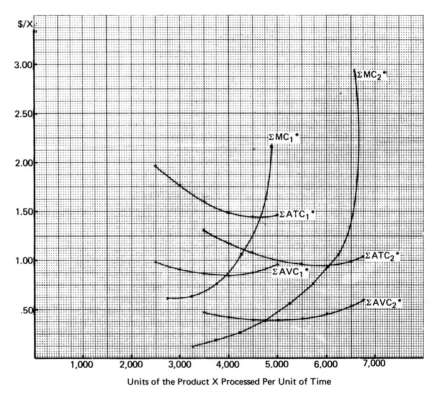

Units of the Product X Processed Per Unit of Time

*The Greek symbol Σ means that the cost curves for all firms have been added and that these curves represent aggregate cost structures for all firms supplying marketing services.

Figure 14.10   Hypothetical cost structures for alternative scales of processing plants.

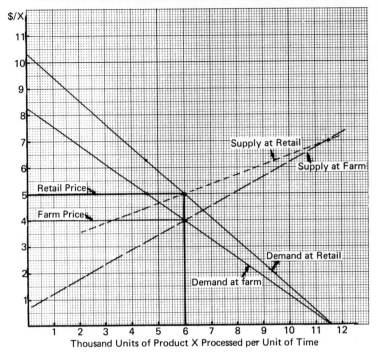

Figure 14.11 Derived demand and derived supply using the constant-percentage-of-retail price marketing margin.

(4,600 units) the average total cost of operations is $1.44 per unit. The larger unit can process this same volume at an average total cost of $1.07. Thus, even though the available volume of product to be processed may be optimum for the smaller, less expensive unit, the operating cost reductions available from the larger, more costly unit force processors to overbuild for the available volume of product. But this volume of product is in the irrational first stage of production for the large-scale unit. If processors can induce raw material suppliers to increase raw material availability such that they can process 6,000 rather than 4,600 units, the average total cost per unit can be reduced from $1.07 to $0.95 per unit. So the incentive is present for processors to pay the highest possible price for raw materials in order to encourage the increased production of those raw materials. (Or more specifically, they try to refrain from *discouraging* increased raw material production insofar as possible by limiting the price cuts for increased levels of output. That is, the processor under these conditions will absorb some of the increases in marginal costs in order to gain the advantage of reduced average total costs.)

The impact of alternative cost structures such as those of Figure 14.10 is shown in Figure 14.11, which assumes that the marketing margin is 20 percent of retail price. As we saw in Figure 14.10, with the larger scale of processing unit, the cost for processing the final unit (i.e., the marginal cost) increased from $0.25 to $0.95 as processing volume was expanded from 4,600 to 6,000 units. However, average total costs for processing were *reduced* from $1.07 to $0.95 per unit. In Figure 14.11, we see that retail market price falls from $6.25 per unit to $5.00 per unit as the quantity available is increased from 4,600 to 6,000 units. But rather than reducing the farm price by $1.25 (the reduction in retail prices associated with this increase in volume) to $3.75, as would be the case with the constant-cost-per-unit marketing margin, or increasing the marketing margin from $1.25 to $1.95 (since marginal cost has increased by $0.70) such that the farm price would be only $3.05 as with the increasing-cost-per-unit marketing margin, the farm price is reduced by only 80 percent of the retail price reduction—or by $1.00 per unit—to $4.00 per unit for 6,000 units.

As with other marketing margins, the retail supply and farm demand functions that are derived in Figure 14.11 have no real meaning except in the immediate neighborhood of the market equilibrium. This is illustrated in the case of the derived retail supply function. As in the other cases, the derivations of demand and supply are accomplished by deducting the marketing margin from retail demand to derive farm demand, and by adding the marketing margin to farm supply to derive retail supply. But since retail price is zero at 11,600 units, and since the farm price is 80 percent of the retail price, the farm price and the marketing margin are also zero at the extreme of 11,600 units. Thus, the farm and retail supply functions must also intersect at this level of market output. Obviously, it is nonsensical to give much credence to this sort of relationship. Hence the reason for the observation that these derivations are to be given credence only in the neighborhood of the market equilibrium.

When fixed costs are very high relative to variable costs in the operation of processing firms, those organizations can operate at a reduced marketing margin as the volume of product handled is increased. Another condition under which a marketing firm (or a group of firms, in the case of a cooperative) might elect to accept this sort of marketing margin would be an imperfectly competitive market, in which the firm would want to eliminate the threat of other competing firms entering the market.

Price Elasticity of Demand Related to Market Level

The three types of marketing margins we have discussed have some rather definite implications for the planning and management of agricultural marketing. The constant-price-per-unit type of marketing margin is typical of industries in which fixed costs are relatively unimportant as a part of total costs, and in which the bulk of marketing costs are paid to variable factors such as labor. If all foods are considered as a single product, the marketing margin as observed since World War II tends to be of this type. Prior to World War II, the marketing margin for all food tended to be set on the basis of a constant percentage of the retail price. The increasing-cost marketing margin that reflects the marginal cost of the marketing firm is typical of those industries that incur substantial fixed costs, but in which scale economies are not totally overwhelming. Meat packing is an example of such an industry, and the marketing margin for meat packing has been of the increasing-cost type throughout the range of the available data.

Policy decisions concerning agriculture are often related to these marketing margins. For example, the prices at the retail level often react quite differently to an increase in the quantity supplied than do farm prices subjected to the same stimulus. All of these relationships are related to the differences in the price elasticity of demand (and to the price flexibility of demand) at the various market levels.

We know that the price elasticity of consumer demand (i.e., the demand at retail) for most foods is relatively inelastic. Consumers must have a certain level of caloric intake in order to exist. Once that level has been met, the consumer's need or desire for additional food drops off quite rapidly. When the consumer achieves adequate caloric intake, rather than demanding *more* food, he begins to pick and choose on a quality basis. The decline of starches and vegetable proteins in the diet of the average American and the increase in the per capita consumption of animal proteins such as beef may be explained in these terms.

We have suggested that some conclusions about the performance of the price mechanism may be drawn on the basis of price elasticity of demand. What exactly are these conclusions? The capacity of the human stomach is limited (unless one happens to be feeding teenagers). Further, while total food expenditures account for a substantial share of total expenditures, the cost of an individual unit of food is a relatively small share of the average consumer's budget. Further, a certain level of food intake is an absolute necessity for the maintenance of life. Therefore, the retail demand for food items would be expected to be quite inelastic with respect to price.

Empirical research has shown that the demand for all food, as well as the demand for most individual food items, tends to be inelastic at the retail level. From our discussion of elasticity, we know that when the equilibrium point occurs in the inelastic range of the demand curve, a one-percent increase in the price will be associated with a less than one-percent reduction in the quantity that consumers are willing to purchase. Thus, in the inelastic range of demand, a price increase will generate an increase in total revenues. Conversely, a one-percent change in the quantity available in the market will be associated with a more than one-percent change in the price at which that quantity will be sold. Thus, a one-percent increase in production will be accompanied by more than a one-percent decrease in price, and the total revenues will be reduced.

We know that the demand at retail is the basic demand function in our economy. Demand at all other levels must be derived from this basic function. Since basic agricultural production occurs at the farm level, and since the bulk of the agricultural marketing activities occur between the farm and retail levels, the demand functions that are of direct and immediate concern to agricultural businesses are most often the demand functions at the farm and intermediate levels, as derived from retail demand.

Let's consider first the situation faced by the agricultural businesses when confronted with a constant marketing margin as in Figure 14.12. We can see that, as marketing services are added, the range of quantities within which the demand is elastic with respect to price is enlarged. For example,

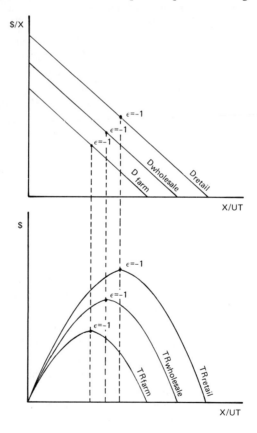

Figure 14.12 Demand, elasticity, and total revenue at selected market levels with the constant-cost-per-unit marketing margin.

when the demand at the farm level has unitary elasticity, demand at wholesale and retail are both in the elastic range. The total revenue to farmers is maximum at that quantity, but the total revenues for both wholesalers and retailers are still increasing. We know that prices above the point at which elasticity is unitary fall in the elastic portion of the demand schedule and that prices below that point fall in the inelastic portion. Therefore, we can readily see that when the marketing margin is constant, *the demand at the farm for any given quantity of a product is less elastic with respect to price than is the demand at any succeeding market level.*

The graphic method for measuring the price elasticity of demand at a given point along the demand curve can be used to analyze the elasticity of demand at the various market levels under conditions of constant marketing margins. It is readily apparent in Figure 14.13 that the elasticity for any given

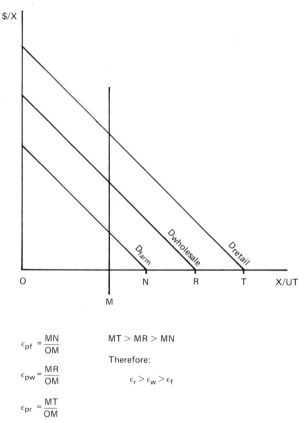

$$\epsilon_{pf} = \frac{MN}{OM}$$

$$\epsilon_{pw} = \frac{MR}{OM}$$

$$\epsilon_{pr} = \frac{MT}{OM}$$

MT > MR > MN

Therefore:

$$\epsilon_r > \epsilon_w > \epsilon_f$$

Figure 14.13 Comparison of price elasticities for a given quantity of product at various market levels using the constant-cost-per-unit marketing margin.

quantity of product declines as the sale of that product moves progressively nearer the point of production. Another way of saying this is that the price elasticity of demand increases as the magnitude of the constant marketing margin increases. As more and more marketing services are added to the product, the marketing margin must increase, and therefore, the elasticity of demand is increased directly.

What does this mean for farmers and firms that provide the processing and other marketing services for agricultural products? If the marketing margin is in fact constant, and if consumers are in fact buying within the range of quantities where demand is inelastic, then an increase in the production of a good will mean that the total receipts at retail will decline. This is

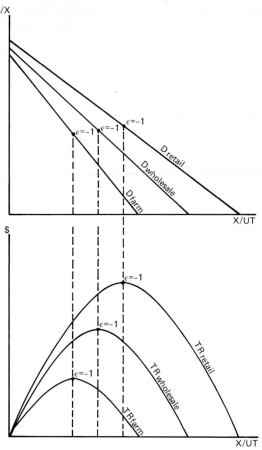

Figure 14.14 Demand, elasticity, and total revenue at selected market levels with the increasing-cost-per-unit marketing margin.

because the consumer (or retail) prices will decline faster than the quantity taken by consumers is increased. More important, the price and total revenues at the wholesale and farm levels will decline even faster. This is because a quantity that falls within the inelastic range of the retail demand function will fall within an even *more* inelastic range of the demand function at lower market levels. This is why a reduction in the farm prices for products such as fruits and vegetables is rarely reflected proportionally in the produce counters of retail food outlets.

Even more striking than the difference in elasticity of demand with respect to price at different market levels with a constant marketing margin is the difference seen between market levels in the case of the increasing margin (Figure 14.14). We can see that the general form of the demand and total revenue functions are the same as in the case of the constant marketing margin. However, as the quantity taken is increased, the margin required to pay for the marketing services is also increased. This means that the total revenue function at retail will increase over a *much* larger range of quantities than will the total revenue function at wholesale or at the farm level.

When we consider the elasticity of demand for any given level of output under conditions in which an increasing-cost type of marketing margin is present, the differences between marketing levels is striking (Figure 14.15). This type of marketing margin is typical of the meat packing industry. As may be seen from our illustration, the elasticity of demand for a particular product may be very near to unity, or even relatively elastic, at the retail level and yet highly inelastic at the farm level. Because of the increasing costs associated with processing, distributing, and marketing larger and larger quantities of the products, the drastically reduced prices at the farm level are to a large degree washed out before the product ever reaches the retail level. This is the reason cattle prices may decline by 30 percent at the farm level, while the change in retail prices for fresh beef cuts may be almost imperceptible. Another way of saying this is that the reduction in price resulting from an increase in the available quantity is absorbed totally at the farm level. Further, the marginal cost increases incurred by the marketing agencies as the result of increased volumes must likewise be absorbed by the farms. Thus, in the case of farm products such as livestock, the burden of both reduced prices and increased marginal costs for marketing resulting from increased output is borne totally by the producer. The marketing agencies must have the increased marketing margin in order to cover the increased marginal costs, and these are reflected in the farmer's or rancher's paycheck when he ships his livestock to market. (It should be pointed out that the process works in reverse when output is reduced. The adjustment comes out of the hide of the marketing agencies under these conditions.)

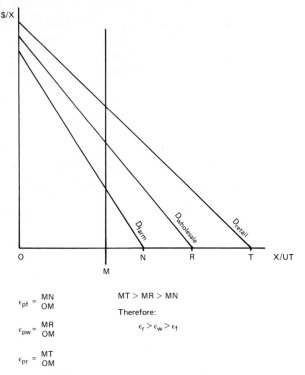

Figure 14.15 Comparison of price elasticities for a given quantity of product at various market levels using the increasing-cost-per-unit marketing margin.

    In the constant-percentage-of-price type of marketing margin that seems to have been represented in the demand for all foods prior to World War II, a given quantity will be in the same elasticity range on either demand curve (Figure 14.16). This appears to be the case for dairy products in today's world of agriculture. As the quantity available for sale is changed, the percentage change in price seems to be about the same at the various levels.

    These three types of marketing margins can, and do, appear in various and sundry combinations. For example, the marketing margin for some product moving from the farm to retail level may be a constant-price-per-unit type of margin. The margin from the farm to the wholesale level, however, may be of the increasing-cost type, and the wholesale to retail margin of the constant percentage of price nature (Figure 14.17). Under circumstances such as these, the sensitivity of price to changes in quantity would be much greater at the farm than at either wholesale or retail. Wholesalers and retailers would be affected in about the same manner by a change in quantity, but the farmer would experience a boom or bust type of business.

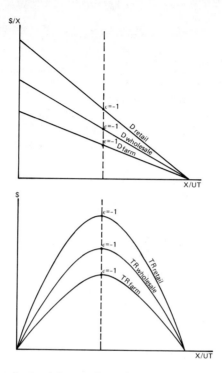

Figure 14.16 Demand, elasticity, and total revenue at selected market levels with the constant-percentage-of-retail-price marketing margin.

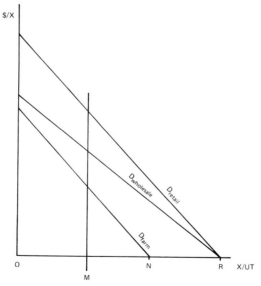

Figure 14.17 Marketing margins may appear in various combinations among various market levels.

Summary and Implications

What is the interest of the agricultural industry, and particularly of the producing and processing segments of agriculture, in this whole gamut of marketing margins? Producer associations concerned with the products that are confronted with either the constant marketing margin or the increasing-cost type of margin must be careful to point out to their memberships the penalities of rapidly expanding production. In the 1973–75 period, the beef cattle industry incurred the economic wrath of God by increasing beef slaughter tonnage by 15 percent. This brought disastrously low prices to the producing sectors of the beef industry. With a price elasticity of farm demand of about −.4, the 15 percent increase in production would be expected to be associated with farm prices reduced by about 35 percent. However, sharp reductions in the availability of pork during this period held the cattle price reduction to only 25 percent—quite sufficient to generate economic disaster and shipwreck in the cattle business.

Packers during this period earned unprecedented profits from their beef operations. The economic facts of life are that even though average costs per unit of beef processed may increase as the volume processed increases, marginal costs increase much faster. And it is the *marginal* cost that determines the packer marketing margin. Thus, a larger spread between average costs per unit and average revenue per unit, combined with a larger volume, means rapidly expanding profits.

Food retailers also earned some handsome profits from their meat departments during the 1973–75 period. These profits came not only from the direct sale of meats, but also from the use of meat as a leader to get people into the store. Consumers were, of course, delighted. In fact, the only people in the producing-processing-marketing chain of events that were unhappy about the state of affairs were the producers of beef. This was the sector that bore the entire brunt of the economic problems created by the expanded production. When beef slaughter was reduced and prices were forced to move upward toward more normal levels, consumers reacted with boycotts of chain stores and political pressures on the Congress. In the end, the people who got credit for the increases in food prices were the producers—primarily those who were producers of meats. These uncooperative souls had been so audacious as to refuse to continue to produce at the level that put them in a loss position that would ultimately force them into bankruptcy! Therefore, they were responsible for the inflationary increase in food prices.

The story we have just told, and the esoteric bit of logic that accompanies it, represents but one of the problems that arises from the differing elasticities at the various market levels. Obviously, our specialized economy cannot operate without marketing agencies, and marketing agencies cannot exist without marketing margins. What, then, is to be done about problems such as these? Should we outlaw marketing agencies as we know them? Should we nationalize the marketing agencies? Or should we merely let consumers and politicians scream and continue to do what the economic facts of life dictate that we must? These questions obviously are political rather than economic in nature. Many people feel that the economic forces require some pretty stringent regulation. But in the absence of such regulation, what avenues are open to those who earn their livings from agriculture?

In cases where the marketing margin is constant or increasing in nature, there are several implications that should be drawn. First of all, the closer the product gets to the consumer, the less inelastic the demand for that product is going to be and the better is the bargaining power of the basic producer. Herein lies the case for vertical integration in agriculture. If the producing, processing, and marketing activities can all be consolidated under one level of management, then profits can be taken at any one point in the chain and distributed back to the various segments of the business.

A second implication is that if producers can bargain collectively with the marketing agencies, the marketing agencies might be induced to re-evaluate their requirements for the various levels of volumes handled. Herein lies the case for agricultural cooperation. Cooperatives operate not only in the area of marketing, but also in the area of farm supply. However, a major contribution has been made by co-ops in the marketing of agricultural goods. Cooperative marketing is one field of specialization in agricultural economics in which the opportunities are highly satisfying and highly profitable. Chapter 15 deals with some of the problems that can be solved through cooperation.

15

Agricultural Cooperation

In Chapter 13, we saw how the agricultural producer and the consumer of agricultural products stood alone in the production and marketing chain as the only segments of that chain that operated under conditions approximating pure competition. We saw how, as pure competitors, these individuals had virtually no bargaining power when dealing with firms that operate under less perfectly competitive conditions. In Chapter 14, we saw how the marketing margin relationship caused farm producers to be extremely vulnerable to changes in price, since the demand at the farm level was typically less elastic with respect to price than was demand at market levels closer to the consumer.

We suggested that some degree of bargaining power might be achieved by farmers through cooperative association. This objective of bargaining power is a primary reason for the establishment of agricultural cooperatives.

The economic environment within which the agricultural producer and his cooperative association must operate is a world of large scale enterprises. Agricultural processing and farm supply businesses are characteristically operated by large centralized business agencies that have a high degree of concentration and control over the activities they perform. This concentration and control have in turn generated a considerable degree of bargaining power for these businesses. The economic environment of agriculture is also one in which there are large market imperfections. We saw in Chapter 12 how the market price mechanism could fail to efficiently perform its function of getting the right products produced in the right quantities, at the right time,

I am indebted to a colleague, the late Dr. Nellis A. Briscoe, for many of the materials in this chapter.

and at the right places, particularly in situations in which the retail demand for goods was inelastic. The farm demand for the ingredients that go into making up the finished food and fiber items is even less elastic than is the demand for these products at retail because of the nature of the marketing margin. Thus, we might expect substantial market imperfections in the case of agricultural goods.

The market power of some business concerns that process and market agricultural goods and of those that provide farm inputs is tremendous as a result of their ability to control procurement and selling policies. For example, the refiners of crude oil have frequently integrated forward into the filling station business. Feed and fertilizer manufacturers have frequently maintained control and market power through a system of franchised dealers. This economic environment has created an incentive for agricultural producers to focus their attention on cooperatives—most especially on the degree of horizontal and/or vertical integration that can be achieved through cooperative associations.

What Is A Cooperative?   •   In order to discuss agricultural cooperation, we must define some terms. First of all, just what is a cooperative? In the simplest of terms, a cooperative is nothing more and nothing less than an organizational method for doing business. Various forms of business organizations are compared in Table 15.1. The only real difference between a cooperative and any other corporation is that the cooperative is designed to do business with its member-patrons rather than with the public at large and that corporate earnings are distributed to the owners on the basis of stock ownership. An agricultural cooperative is a form of business organization set up by a group of individuals in the agricultural industry for purposes of performing a service for themselves. The service they perform cooperatively may be one that was formerly purchased individually from some other organization or it may be one that the members of the cooperative formerly did without.

The cooperative association is *voluntarily* owned and controlled by its member patrons and is operated by them on a cost basis. No individual is coerced into joining or doing business with a cooperative. Even as a member of a cooperative, he may not necessarily transact all of any type of his business through the association. Almost any group of individuals, agencies, or businesses that have a common need for some service can combine into a cooperative association. Individual farm producers can form a cooperative for the purpose of providing the services of a local grain elevator, a cotton gin, or electrical power services to themselves. Frequently, these associations will combine in order to provide the services of a terminal elevator or a cotton compress to the member associations. The world's largest grain storage

TABLE 15.1

COMPARISON OF ALTERNATIVE TYPES OF
BUSINESS ORGANIZATION

QUESTION	TYPE OF BUSINESS ORGANIZATION				
	Single Proprietorship	Partnership	Limited Partnership	Non-Cooperative Corporation	Cooperative
Who owns the business?	The proprietor	The partners	The partners	The stockholders	The members who buy stock as they do business with the firm
How is the business managed?	By the proprietor	By the partners	By a manager hired by the partners	By management hired by a Board of Directors	By management hired by a Board of Directors
With whom does the firm do business?	The general public	The general public	The general public	The general public	The member—patrons
What is the extent of the owner's personal liability for unpaid debts of the firm?	Total	Total (both partners are liable for all debts)	Limited to the partner's share of the ownership	None	None
How are earnings distributed?	To the proprietor	To the partners as per the partnership agreement	To the partners as per the partnership agreement	To the stockholders on the basis of share of ownership	To the members on the basis of patronage
What taxes are paid?	Property tax plus personal income tax on proprietor's earnings	Property tax plus personal income tax on partners' earnings	Property tax plus personal income tax on partners' earnings	Property tax plus corporate income tax on corporate earnings not refunded on patronage basis	Property tax plus corporate income tax on corporate earnings not refunded on patronage basis

facilities (located at Enid, Oklahoma) and the port facilities at Houston, Texas, are examples of some assets owned by a cooperative whose membership is made up of other cooperative associations. Other examples of "cooperatively-owned" cooperatives include Farmland Industries, Inc., of Kansas City—a federated farm supply cooperative that owns and operates installations such as oil refineries, packing plants, a tire factor, a battery manufacturing installation, fertilizer plants, and feed mills.

There are numerous cooperatives owned by independent businesses that will likely be familiar to most people. Examples of these include the Railway Express Agency, owned and operated cooperatively by a group of railroad companies; Allied Van Lines, whose membership is made up of a large group of independent local movers across the nation; the Florists' Telegraph Delivery Association; Associated Press, owned and operated by independent newspapers; and the Equitable Life Insurance Society of the United States. Some of the brand name items that may be found in any grocery store are processed, packaged, and marketed by cooperatives. These include Sunkist Oranges, Welch's Grape Juice, Ocean Spray Cranberry products, Sunmaid Raisins, and Sunsweet Prunes.

A cooperative exists for the purpose of giving greater economic returns to the members of the organization than could otherwise be achieved. Cooperatives are often spoken of as "nonprofit" organizations. Nothing could be further from the truth. Cooperatives are profit seeking, as *any* business must be profit seeking. The difference is that the profits pursued are the profits that accrue to the member-patrons.

As the above examples suggest, there are three basic types of cooperative associations. Probably the most familiar is the *marketing* cooperative, whose function is to improve the efficiency of the marketing process and to reduce the marketing margin. The returns to the members of such a cooperative are thus increased. A second type of cooperative is the *purchasing* cooperative—an example of which is the Independent Grocer's Association (IGA. Food Stores)—whose purpose is to take advantage of the bulk lot discounts offered by many manufacturers, and otherwise minimize the cost of procuring materials used in the member-patrons' business. A third type of cooperative is the *service* cooperative, whose objective is to provide some service to its members at minimal cost. Examples of service cooperatives include community hospitals, certain funeral parlors, the rural electric cooperative, and the insurance companies operated by organizations such as the Farmer's Union and Farm Bureau. Frequently, a single cooperative association may operate in all three areas. A cooperative grain elevator that serves as a marketing agency will often mix and sell fertilizer to its members and may also provide a service such as hail insurance or fertilizer application.

Economic Integration

A second term that should be defined is that of economic integration. When we speak of economic integration, we mean the tying together of two or more economic activities under some sort of unified control. Economic integration may be thought of as a fusion or coordination of business units. There are two main types of economic integration; *horizontal* and *vertical.* The terms horizontal and vertical integration are used to convey the characteristics of the type of business coordination. Integration as such is *not* a form of organization. Rather, it is a term used to designate a type of organizational or structural growth. We might think of economic integration as a process of "knitting" business units together.

Horizontal integration refers to the general grouping of similar business units under one administrative control. These businesses will be performing the same production or marketing functions at exactly the same point in the marketing sequence. Food chains represent an example of horizontal integration. In a food chain, there are a series of stores brought under one management, all of which are performing exactly the same function.

A second example of horizontal integration is provided by an organization such as Continental Grain Company, in which many individual grain elevators have been consolidated under one management. The federation of local grain marketing cooperatives into a regional grain marketing organization provides still a third example of horizontal integration. The main point to remember about *horizontal integration* is that *a single management gains control either through voluntary contract or through ownership over a series of firms performing similar activities at the same level in the production or marketing sequence.*

Vertical integration refers to the knitting together of two or more stages of the production and/or marketing sequence under a single managerial control. It occurs when *a firm combines activities which are unlike but are sequentially related to those that it currently performs.* An example of vertical integration is provided by the oil industry, where refiners frequently own their own retail outlets. A second example is the food retailer who processes his own dairy or meat products.

It should be pointed out that horizontal integration at some level within the production and marketing chain is typically prerequisite to vertical integration. If vertical integration is to be accomplished, the volume of product moving through the integrated sequence must be the same. The most completely integrated segment of agriculture is probably the poultry industry. The economically efficient sizes of units at the various levels in the broiler production marketing sequence are shown in Figure 15.1. It is obvious

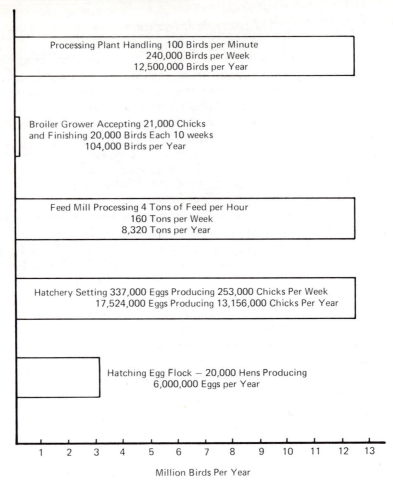

Figure 15.1   Product flows present from each unit at each level in a typical integrated broiler operation.

that a substantial degree of horizontal integration must be accomplished at the levels of the hatching egg flock and broiler growing to generate the volume of product necessary for vertically integrating into other phases of this chain. A representative organization for an integrated broiler firm is shown in Figure 15.2. A hatchery operation of a size sufficient for operating efficiently will require the hatching egg output of about four efficient hatching egg producers. Likewise, an economically efficient feed mill will process enough feed to satisfy the needs of a multiplicity of broiler growers as well as the needs of the hatching egg producers. Since most broiler processing plants kill and process about a hundred birds per *minute,* it is apparent that the processing plant will require the output of many growers. Thus, we have

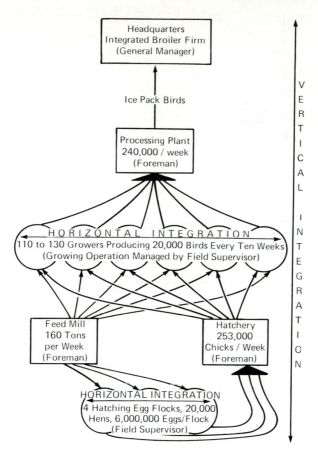

Figure 15.2   Representative organization of integrated broiler firm.

horizontal integration of hatching egg production and broiler growing that are prerequisite to vertically integrating throughout the rest of the business.

Horizontal integration of a single function such as the growing and egg operations in the broiler industry can occur in many ways. As it happens, in the broiler industry the integrating force has generally been centered at the feed mill. Following World War II the numbers of farms that had egg flocks and milk cows declined rapidly. With the reduction in the market for bagged feeds, feed processors found themselves with large processing capacities that were unused. As a result, they were not covering all the fixed costs. From our cost curves in Figure 15.3 we can see that the average total costs per unit are relatively high when a firm operates at less than full capacity. (Full capacity occurs where average total costs are minimum; that is, where marginal costs and average total costs are equal.) An increase in output will reduce the

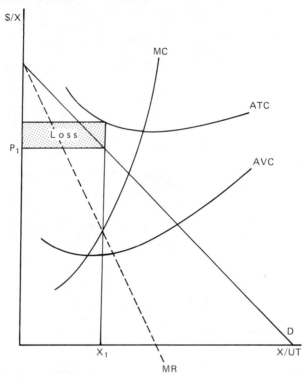

Figure 15.3 Market expansion through integration offers one way of adjusting to losses that result from declining demand.

average total costs of producing. But since feed processors did not operate under conditions of pure competition, and since their market had grown smaller, an increase in output would have lowered the price at which the product sold. Therefore, a feed processor would be foolish to expand his production in order to take advantage of a potential cost reduction unless he can devise some means by which the market can be expanded (that is, if he can shift the demand curve he faces upward and to the right). If he can expand his market, perhaps he can take advantage of the cost reduction, avoiding the normal attendant reduction in price, and thus get himself out of a loss position.

This is the situation that faced the feed millers. The technique that they used for demand expansion was to negotiate a series of contracts with a large number of individual farmers for purposes of horizontally integrating the broiler growing operation. In this manner, they assured themselves of a captive outlet for their mill feed output. From this point, they began to integrate both backward toward the hatchery and forward toward the consumer. By the early 1970s, almost all of the broilers produced in the United

States were produced in completely integrated operations. Indeed the industry was so thoroughly integrated by the mid-1960s that the Del-Mar-Va Poultry Exchange ceased operations. This was the last major organized market where the prices for live broilers could be discovered and reported. Subsequent to the closing of the Del-Mar-Va Poultry Exchange, broiler prices were reported only on an ice-packed, table-ready basis. This has essentially forced the remaining independent broiler producers either to cease operations or to become absorbed by integrators, whereby the product never changes ownership from the time the hatchery flock pullet is placed until the ice-packed, table-ready bird is sold to the supermarket buyer. Through vertical integration, six production and marketing activities (hatching egg flock, hatchery, feed mill, growing, processing, and wholesaling) have been consolidated under a single management that takes its profits at a single point. Under this arrangement, the efficiency of broiler production and marketing has been dramatically streamlined. The cost of producing and marketing broilers in 1970 was less than half the cost in the mid-1950s.

As would be expected, the phenomena of horizontal and vertical integration in the broiler industry have altered the market power structure in that industry. There are perhaps three companies that can have an enormous impact on the broiler market. However, this same integrating activity could have been started at some point in the production-marketing chain other than at the feed mill level. In the case of some products such as oranges, prunes, raisins, pork, beef, and wheat, the integration that has occurred has come about through the activities of the producers themselves. In most cases, this integration has occurred through cooperatives. This "cooperative integration" has given these producers some degree of bargaining power.

When farmers have banded together in a cooperative association for purposes of marketing their products, of purchasing, or of performing some other service for themselves, we have an example of *both* horizontal and vertical integration. The act of banding together in an association represents *horizontal* integration, and the association going into the related but unlike activity of marketing, purchasing, or service, represents *vertical* integration.

This idea of farmers banding together in cooperative associations for purposes of achieving market power through horizontal and vertical integration is the basis behind the farm cooperative movement. Because of the extreme economic competition present in the agricultural industry, the market power that could be achieved by the individual associations working independently was neglibile. If a grain marketing association in western Kansas, for example, attempted to bargain with one of the major millers, that miller was not in the least reluctant to shift his attention from Kansas to South Dakota, Nebraska, or Oklahoma. The miller had many alternative sources of grain supply. Further, there were a number of problems inherent in the agricultural industry that individual cooperative associations were ill equipped to solve. While an individual marketing association could regulate the quantities of product that flowed through its facilities into the market place, it could not regulate the flow from other associations or from non-association producers. That is, the agricultural industry was so big that even the individual cooperative marketing associations operated essentially as pure competitors. Control of product quality and utilization of by-products were problems that the management of individual associations could not afford to undertake. Other problems included:

1. Standardization of production,

2. Stabilization of production,

3. Distribution,

4. Inspection,

5. Financing,

6. Improvement of business practices, and

7. Research

All of the "problems" provided an incentive and an opportunity for still further horizontal integration. While a single association could not afford a massive research program, for example, an association of associations could make this investment. While a single association did not have enough volume and hence could scarcely afford to invest in an installation to process certain by-products, an association of associations could benefit from such an action.

Because of such problems, federations of cooperative associations were formed. Examples of such federations include organizations such as the Cooperative Grange League Federation, Eastern States Cooperatives, Farm Land Industries (formerly Consumers Cooperative Association), and Union Equity Grain Marketing Cooperative. Further, federations of federations expanded the degree of horizontal integration. Examples of federations of federations include the National Federation of Grain Producers and the National Association of Cooperative Manufacturing. These expansions of horizontal integration permitted the expansion of vertical integration into such areas as export selling.

We have seen how farm cooperatives have achieved horizontal integration through *federation.* With federation, the members of the federation retain their individual identities and operate more or less independently of the other members. A second way in which cooperatives have integrated horizontally (and vertically) is through *merger,* whereby the assets of the businesses are combined and they are operated as a single business under a single management. For example, three state-wide purchasing associations in the northeastern states merged to form the Cooperative Grange League Federation. The GLF merged with Eastern States Cooperatives to form AGWAY. AGWAY then absorbed the Pennsylvania State Farm Bureau Federation and now covers the entire northeastern section of the country.

There are a number of reasons *why* farm producers integrate through cooperatives. The general objective is to maximize the returns from their business operations. The purely competitive economic framework within which the farm operates, and the fact that not only those to whom he sells but also those from whom he buys operate under oligopolistic (or even monopolistic) conditions leaves the farmer at the mercy of these people in the market place. His small scale business unit is such a small portion of the total market that he individually has no bargaining power. If he were to attempt to vertically integrate on an individual basis, the specialized training and equipment would be prohibitively costly. The optimum scale of operation could not be achieved at all respective levels. For example, an individual farmer could hardly afford to use the entire output of an economically efficient fertilizer plant. Through joining together in cooperatively horizontal integration, individual farmers can often gain some control in these matters.

Further gains can come through vertically integrating, since the successive selling costs normally incurred in transferring the product from firm to firm can be eliminated. In our example of the broiler integrator, an unintegrated industry would have at least six such costs of transfer, while the integrator has only one. Also, specialized personnel, equipment, plants, management, etc., can be used because a more efficient division of labor is possible. The vertically-integrated cooperative can buy farm inputs in large lots, and often gain price concessions in the process. The cooperative has the opportunity to absorb the middlemen's profits (or their losses!), but it must also assume their functions.

How far a cooperative can feasibly go in vertical integration depends on a number of factors. First and foremost, unless there is a broad enough horizontal base of producers to support an economically efficient scale of operation that will keep costs minimum, a cooperative would be foolish to embark on a new function or activity. This is why regional federations of associations have often been formed; the broader base will support the proposed new function.

The managerial capacity of present and potential managerial personnel may limit the degree to which an association may vertically integrate. The present management may not be able to assume the additional function because of lack of time or ability. As the number of functions performed is increased, the ability of the manager to coordinate all of these activities must also increase. Frequently, mergers have provided the managerial ability for vertically-expanded activity. Financial limitations may prevent further vertical integration by a cooperative. The more stages through which an organization vertically integrates, the more capital is required. Merger is a technique that may also solve problems for financing further integration.

As we stated at the beginning of this chapter, agricultural cooperation represents nothing more and nothing less than a way of doing business. There is nothing sacred and nothing mystic about the function of a cooperative. Cooperatives are merely organizations that are established by groups for purposes of increasing their returns by way of increased efficiency and increased bargaining power. Cooperatives seek to earn profits just as any business seeks to earn profits. The analytical framework for the business problems of a cooperative is identical with the analytical framework for any other corporate business organization. The rules concerning marginal costs and marginal returns apply regardless of whether the business is a single proprietorship, a partnership, a cooperative, or a publicly-held corporation. All of these organizations are subject to the same economic forces.

16

Production Management

In Chapter 8, we defined the three basic functions of agriculture to be production, marketing (which includes the functions of processing and distributing the production of farms and ranches), and consumption of resources. We discussed the marketing activities and some of the managerial problems associated with these marketing activities in a very general way in Chapter 14. We learned that the managerial problems could be expected to vary with the type of marketing margin faced, and with the structure of the market within which the marketing firm operated. The economic models for analyzing both market structure and the marketing margins were introduced and explained.

The reverse side of the coin of marketing management involves the principles of production management. Regardless of whether the firm under scrutiny is a farm, a farm supply business, or a processing or distributing agency that adds services to the product prior to the time it reaches the ultimate consumer, these production principles can and should be applied. In our discussion of the concept of supply in Chapter 9, you were introduced to the production function. This function defined the technical relationship between resource inputs (or factors) as they were transformed into outputs (or products). When we added price information to the information concerning the technical transformation of factors into products, we discovered that the cost curves could be specified. The individual firm's supply function was defined by the marginal cost function as derived from the production function. Under conditions in which the firm sold in a purely competitive market, the price for the product defined the marginal revenue curve and we could then say where the firm should operate. If the firm equates marginal revenue with marginal cost, profits are maximized and the firm has achieved an economic optimum. As we constructed models for describing the marketing activities that occur between the basic producer and the ultimate consumer, so can we construct models for analyzing the means by which production efficiency can be maximized. It is with these production management models that we are concerned in this chapter.

The Factor-Product Model

Let's quickly review our production function as combined with the price and cost information. You will recall that we said the production function as such was *not* economics, even though it had strong economic implications. When information concerning the prices paid for factors of production and the prices received for products was added to the technical production function, we had an *economic* model. The technical name for this model is the *factor-product* model.

The factor-product model simply defines the economic relationships brought about by combining variable quantities of one factor of production with fixed quantities of one or more other factors in the production of a particular product (Figure 16.1). When we multiply the price of a product by the levels of production associated with the differing levels at which the variable resource X_1 is used, the total revenue function is defined. Total cost may be similarly calculated by multiplying each level of usage of X_1 by the price paid for X_1. The level of factor input that maximizes the difference in total cost and total revenue will maximize the returns that can be achieved from producing the product in question. These returns represent the earnings of the bundle of fixed resources. The point at which returns to these resources (or profits in the accounting sense) will be maximum can be defined by drawing a line tangent to the total revenue function and parallel to the total cost function. The point of tangency will define the profit-maximizing level of factor usage as well as the profit-maximizing level of product output.

It should be pointed out that marginal variable input cost (or marginal factor cost) and the value of marginal product are by definition the rate of change in total variable input cost and value of total product. The slope (or change) associated with the total cost of the variable input is defined by the price of the variable resource, and therefore the marginal variable input cost (or marginal factor cost) is also defined by the price of this variable resource. The slope of the line tangent to the value of total product function defines the slope (or rate of change) in total receipts at the point of tangency and hence defines value of marginal product. When the tangent to the value of total product function is drawn parallel with the total variable input cost function, total cost has the same rate of change as does the total revenue at that point. Thus, the profit maximizing level of output or of factor use (point

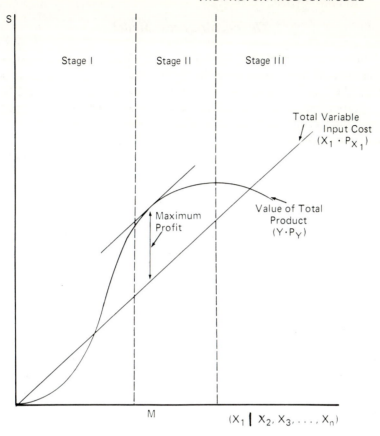

Figure 16.1 The factor-product model.

M in Figure 16.1) occurs where the value of marginal product is equal to the marginal factor cost as measured by the price of that variable input.

The factor-product model showing the economic relationship between factor inputs and product outputs is basic to the entire study of production management. In our earlier discussion of the factor-product model and the production function, we showed how maximum profits would always occur within the second stage of production. If it is profitable to produce at all, it will be profitable to produce at least up to the point where average productivity per unit of variable input is maximum—i.e., the beginning of Stage II. Thus, the part of the model that is really relevant is the second stage. In this second stage of production, the marginal return is declining (i.e., each successive injection of a unit of the resource X_1 adds less to total product and total revenue than did the previous unit).

The Factor-Factor Model

Situations in which only one variable factor is used in the production of a good are rare. More often, there will be two, three, or half a dozen variable factors, the level at which any one factor may be profitably used being dependent on not only the quantities of the other variable factors employed but also the level of fixed resources. Thus, our factor-product model must be modified and generalized to take into account the impact of more than one variable factor. If the product Y can be produced with some bundle of fixed resources (including some fixed level of X_2) with the factor X_1 allowed to vary, then we have a simple production function that can be diagrammed on a two-dimensional chart. Likewise, if X_2 is the only factor allowed to vary, we have a simple production function. But when we permit *both* X_1 and X_2 to vary at the same time, we are immediately in the situation of a three-dimensional diagram, such as that shown in Figure 16.2. Rather than being concerned with a simple production function, we are now concerned with a production *surface*.

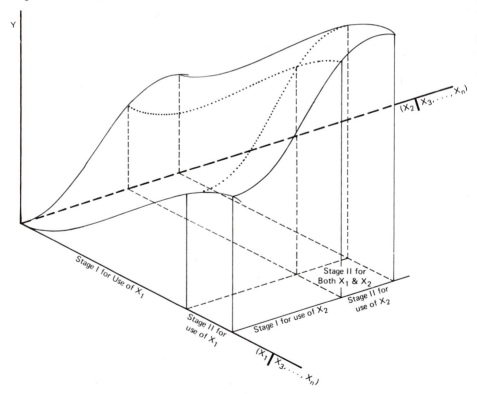

Figure 16.2 Production surface with two variable inputs.

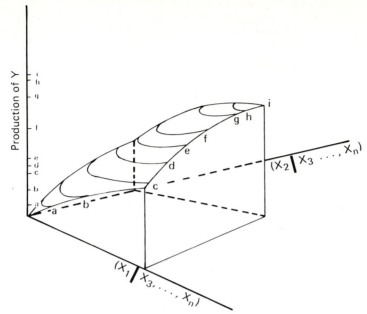

Figure 16.3 The production surface in the second stage of production for both variable resources with production levels shown.

We have recognized that the only rational part of a simple production function is that portion in the second stage of production. It follows that the only relevant portion of a production surface using two variable factors would be that portion of the surface in which the second stage of production prevails for *both* variable inputs. For purposes of clarity, we can redraw the diagram in Figure 16.2 to include only the rational portion of the production surface (Figure 16.3). As in the case in which we had the entire production surface, the rational portion of the surface looks like a hill whose sides have been blasted off. The sheer cliffs on the two sides most distant from the axes represent the beginning of the third stages of production for each of the two variable factors. Those sheer cliffs on the sides immediately next to the axes represent the end of the first stage of production for each of the variable resources. All that remains is the rational second stage of production for both factors.

We can measure contours around the surface that specify the combinations of variable resources which, when combined with the fixed resources, will yield given levels of production. These production contours can then be mapped on a two-dimensional isoproduct map as in Figure 16.4. By this time, you should have recognized our analysis of the production surface as being a near relative of the analysis of the utility surface that we made in Chapter 10. (In point of fact, Figures 16.3 and 16.4 are identical with Figures 10.6 and

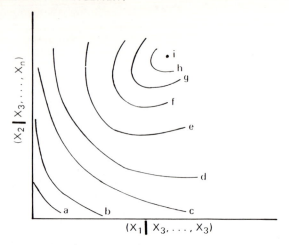

Figure 16.4   Isoproduct (or isoquant) map of the production surface.

10.7.) The production surface is a hill. We can increase production by climbing *up* that hill (i.e., by increasing the use of *both* X_1 and X_2) to point *i,* which represents the absolute maximum production possible with our given level of fixed resources. We can maintain a given level of production by moving around the hill (thus, by substituting one variable resource for the other). When we move around the hill, we are varying the combinations of X_1 and X_2 that we are combining with the fixed factors $(X_3, \ldots, X_n)$ for the purpose of producing a given quantity of Y.

While our isoproduct map of the production surface is perfectly analogous to the indifference map, rather than measuring levels of satifaction the curves measure either levels of production or levels of revenue, depending on whether we are measuring units of product or dollars worth of product along the vertical axis. If the curves measure physical units of the product, all that is necessary to convert them into measures of total revenue is to multiply each level of product by the price received for that product.

From your experience with indifference curves, how do you suppose this production surface can be used? We know that both X_1 and X_2 can be used in producing the product Y. But how are we to decide which combination of X_1 and X_2 is to be used in the production of some particular quantity of Y? Obviously, we need more information than we currently have to answer these questions.

Up to this point, our factor-factor model is purely technical in nature. A particular *isoproduct curve* (or *isoquant*[1]) shows simply the technical rate

---

[1] The Latin term which means "the same" is *iso-*. Any time the prefix *iso* appears in a word, the reference is to something that is unchanged. Thus, an isoproduct curve as we have in our illustration shows the various combinations of variable factors which may be used in producing a given level of product.

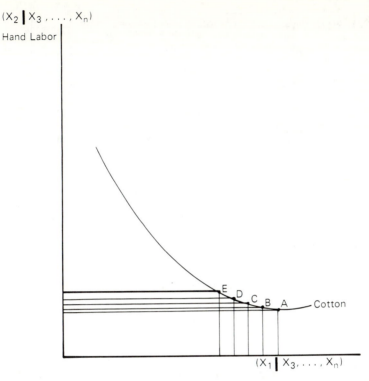

$(X_2 | X_3 , \ldots , X_n)$

Hand Labor

E D C B A — Cotton

$(X_1 | X_3 , \ldots , X_n)$

Figure 16.5 Diminishing marginal rates of factor substitution give isoproduct curves their characteristic shape.

at which one factor may be substituted for another in the production of some particular quantity of Y. Thus, if X_1 is machinery and X_2 is hand labor used in the production of some given quantity of cotton, it takes progressively more and more labor to replace each unit of machinery as we move from A to B to C to D to E along the single isoproduct curve in Figure 16.5. Thus, the diminishing marginal rate of factor substitution between resources causes our isoproduct curves to have precisely the same characteristics as indifference curves for precisely the same reason.

In order to answer the questions concerning the combination of the variable factors that should be selected, we must add some price information to the technical information concerning the substitutability of X_1 and X_2 in the production of Y. The prices for X_1 can be incorporated into an *isocost* line. The isocost line is similar to the budget line used in indifference analysis in that it simply defines the various combinations of X_1 and X_2 that may be purchased with a given cost outlay. But since our objective in the factor-factor analysis is to minimize the cost for producing a given level of product, we are going to use the isocost that minimizes the total expense.

In Figure 16.6, suppose that the price of X_1 is \$4 and that the price of

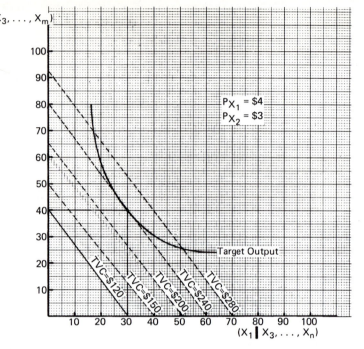

Figure 16.6 Construction of the isocost lines for use in defining the cost–minimizing combination of variable resources.

X_2 is \$3. Let's start with some arbitrary cost outlay, say \$120. We know that we can purchase 30 units of X_1 for this level of cost if all funds are spent on that resource. A similar calculation using the price of X_2 will define the maximum amount of X_2—40 units—that can be purchased. A line connecting these two points will define the combinations of X_1 and X_2 that can be purchased for \$120. But we cannot purchase a combination of X_1 and X_2 that will allow us to achieve our target output. Obviously, we must spend more than \$120 if we are to achieve our production objective.

The slope of the isocost lines is simply the ratio of the prices for the two factors $(P_{X_1}/P_{X_2} = \frac{4}{3}$ in this case), assuming that these factors are purchased under conditions of pure competition. Rather than fixing the isocost at some particular level of cost outlay, we permit the isocost line to "float" parallel to the slope as defined in Figure 16.6. We can do this simply by drawing a series of isocost lines parallel with the first. If we maintain the slope, we are recognizing that we are tied to the market prices for the resources, regardless of the volume purchased. As we continue, we find that the smallest cost outlay that allows the production of the target output is \$240. The cost minimizing combination of resources is 30 units of X_1 and 40 units of X_2.

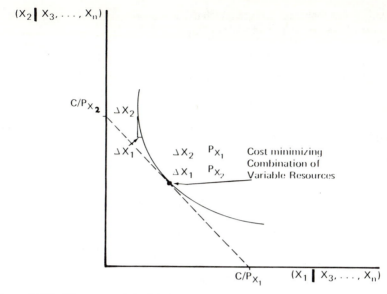

Figure 16.7 The cost-minimizing combination of factors occurs where the marginal rate of factor substitution is equal to the inverse ratio of factor prices.

Now let's move from a specific case to the general case. We have already seen that the slope of the isocost line is defined by the inverse ratio of factor prices. From our elementary school math, we know that the slope of a line may be calculated by the rise over run formula. In Figure 16.7, the rise is measured by C/P_{X_2}, and the run is measured by C/P_{X_1}. Therefore:

$$\text{Slope of the Isocost} = \frac{C/P_{X_2}}{C/P_{X_1}} = \frac{C}{P_{X_2}} \cdot \frac{P_{X_1}}{C} = \frac{P_{X_1}}{P_{X_2}}$$

We have suggested that the cost-minimizing combination of resources occurs where an isocost line is just tangent to the isoproduct curve; that is, where the slope of the isoproduct curve is just equal to the slope of the isocost. The slope of the isoproduct curve may be measured by calculating the change in the level of one resource that is necessary to maintain a given level of output as a result of a one-unit change in the level at which the other resource is used. In other words, the quantity of X_2 necessary to replace one unit of X_1 (i.e., the marginal rate of factor substitution) at any point on the isoproduct curve may be measured by calculating the slope of the isoproduct at that point. Thus in Figure 16.7,

$$\begin{array}{c}\text{Slope of the}\\\text{Isoproduct Curve}\end{array} = \begin{array}{c}\text{Marginal Rate of}\\\text{Factor Substitution}\end{array} = \frac{\Delta X_2}{\Delta X_1}$$

Since we have already suggested that the cost-minimizing combination of variable resources occurs where the slopes of the isocost and isoproduct are equal:

$$\text{Cost Minimizing Combination of Variable Resources} = \frac{\Delta X_2}{\Delta X_1} = \frac{P_{X_1}}{P_{X_2}}$$

or where the marginal rate of factor substitution is equal to the inverse ratio of factor prices.

In other words, if X_1 is priced at \$1 per unit and if X_2 is priced at \$2 per unit, then the minimum cost point for producing some particular level of product (that is, the point on an individual isoproduct curve at which the producer should operate) would occur where one unit of X_2 substitutes for exactly two units of X_1.

At this point, \$1 worth of either of the variable resources will replace exactly \$1 worth of the other and will add exactly the same quantity to the total product. Another way of saying this is that the marginal cost associated with the use of X_1 would be exactly equal to the marginal cost associated with the use of X_2 in the production of the product.

We can define the least-cost combination of resources for producing a given level of product to be the economic optimum for producing that level of output. This least-cost combination of resources occurs at the point where the slopes of the isoproduct curve and the isocost line are equal. Thus, the locus of points of tangency between the various isocosts and isoproducts

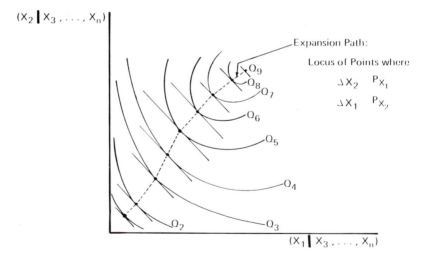

Figure 16.8 The path along which production will be expanded is the locus of points where the marginal rate of factor substitution is equal to the inverse ratio of factor prices.

will show the path along which the production of Y will be expanded (Figure 16.8).

If the product Y were the only product that could possibly be produced, and if the firm had a fixed production budget, then the indifference curve analysis and the isoproduct-isocost analysis would be almost identical. However, since this is rarely the case, rather than being predetermined by some income restriction, the isocost is merely one of a family of isocost lines. This family of isocosts as associated with the family of isoproduct curves defines the expansion path along which a producer will operate. But how are we to decide *where* along that expansion path the producer would operate?

Selecting the Profit-Maximizing Point • When, in the early part of this chapter, we reviewed the factor-product model that is associated with the technical production function that defines the rate at which resources are transformed into products, we found the profit-maximizing position to fall within the range of the second stage of production. This range occurs between the points at which average physical product and total physical product are maximum. Within this range, the point of maximum profit will be where the rate of change in total cost is exactly equal to the rate of change in total revenue; that is, where the marginal cost and marginal revenues are equal.

So far, in our factor-factor analysis, we have been able to define a combination of factors at which the marginal cost of using one of these was exactly equal to the marginal cost of using the other for every possible level of product, given our fixed resource limitation and the prices for the resources. This, of course, defines our expansion path. The problem we now face is that of defining the point along that expansion path where the rate of change in the total cost function is the same as the rate of change in the expansion path. That is, where the value of the marginal product is equal to the marginal cost of using the least-cost combination of X_1 and X_2.

Let's review our factor-factor model in order that we might recall exactly the situation with which we are dealing. Figure 16.9 illustrates the case in which both X_1 and X_2 are essential in the production of Y. (An illustration of this situation might be capital equipment or labor and seed corn used in the production of corn.) If either of these factors is absent from the resource mix, our production surface shows that the level of output is zero. The isoproduct contours along the production surface show the combinations of X_1 and X_2 that can be used in producing any given level of product. The points of tangency between the isocost lines and the isoproduct curves show the least-cost combination of factors for producing those levels of output. The locus of these points of tangency traces out the expansion path along which producers will expand or contract production. The portion of the surface within which profits will be maximized is defined by the

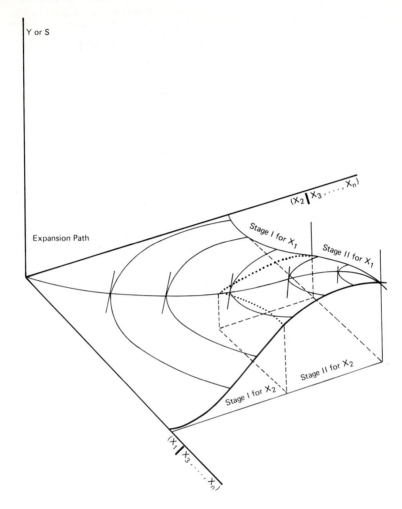

Figure 16.9 Production surface for which both variable resources are prerequisite to production.

portion within which Stage II of production prevails for both variable factors.

The problem we now face is that of defining *where* within the second stage of production we should operate. As we saw in the case of the factor-product model, the rational manager will produce where the change in total revenue associated with increasing or decreasing production by one unit is just equal to the change in total cost associated with that increase or decrease (that is, where marginal revenue and marginal cost are equal). The information that we have used in defining the factor-factor model to this point includes:

1. The technical rate at which the factor X_1 (when combined with a given bundle of fixed factors) may be transformed into the product Y;

2. The technical rate at which the factor X_2 (when combined with a given bundle of fixed factors) may be transformed into the product Y;

3. The varying rates at which the factors X_1 and X_2 may be substituted for each other in the production of Y (as shown by the shapes of the isoproduct curves); and

4. The price ratio at which the factors X_1 and X_2 are purchased, assuming that the individual producer buys under conditions sufficiently competitive that he cannot affect the market prices for the factors (as shown by the slope of the isocost lines).

In order to locate the point along the expansion path at which the value of marginal product and the marginal variable input cost are equal, we need one further piece of information. We cannot talk about value of marginal product until we have first defined the value of the total product. Value of marginal product has been defined as the rate of change in the value of the production surface. To get the value of the production surface, we simply multiply all the values on our production surface by the price at which the product may be sold. If the product is sold under conditions of pure competition (i.e., the individual producer cannot affect the market price for the product), converting our production surface to a value of product surface is simply a matter of multiplying our surface by a constant price. That is, it is simply a matter of scaling the Y axis such that the revenue and production surfaces are identical.

At this point, we need to digress for a moment to consider the meaning of the factor-factor model as related to the factor-product models. We have said that we have included information concerning the individual technical rates of transformation for each of the variable factors into the product Y in constructing our factor-factor model. We have also said that some level of both X_1 and X_2 is required if any product is to be created. Therefore, when we are considering the transformation function for X_2, we must *fix* the usage of X_1 at some given level (Figure 16.10). If we fix X_1 at the level where the production of Y as associated with X_1 is maximum (i.e., at X_{1A} on the diagram), we see the factor-product model for X_2 with X_1 fixed at X_{1A} and all other resources fixed at the levels specified in our factor-factor model. We can calculate the total cost for X_2 by multiplying each level of X_2 by the

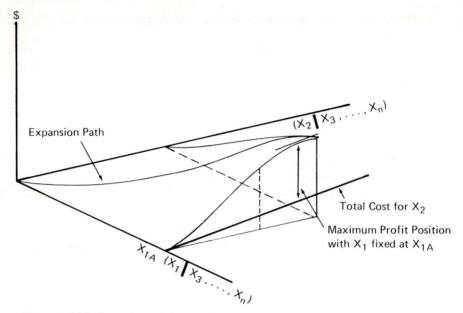

Figure 16.10   Location of the profit-maximizing position on the production surface with one of the variable resources fixed.

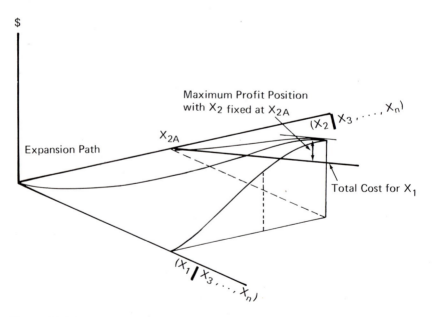

Figure 16.11   Location of the profit-maximizing position on the production surface with the alternative variable fixed.

price paid for X_2, and then locate our profit-maximizing position on the basis of equating marginal revenue with marginal cost.

By the same token, we can fix X_2 at some level and calculate total costs of using X_1 (Figure 16.11). The profit-maximizing point can again be located by equating marginal revenues and marginal costs. The point is, any time we fix one of the variable resources at some level, the price of using that resource no longer comes into consideration when making decisions concerning the maximum profit position. The cost for that resource has already been incurred, and must be paid whether or not the resource is used. The resource that remains variable is now the only factor that will affect our marginal cost curve. Thus, when we fix the level of usage for all resources save one, we are back to a simple factor-product model.

We have seen how the profit-maximizing level of output is defined in the case of the factor-product model in which a single factor of production is varied. It is but a single step now to define the means by which this profit-maximizing position is defined in the case of the factor-factor model. The cost for using *both* variable resources along the expansion path is calculated by multiplying the prices paid for both factors by the levels at which they are combined in achieving the least-cost combination for producing each level of product *along the expansion path.* The rate of change (or slope) in this total cost function is then equated with the rate of change in the level of total revenue along the expansion path (Figure 16.12). That is, the slope of the expansion path along the total revenue surface is measured by the tangent to that surface. When this slope is equal to the slope of total cost at point B in Figure 16.12, the maximum profit position has been defined. At this point, X_{1B} and X_{2B} are the quantities of the factors that are used in producing I_B in total revenue. This point may be defined verbally as being that point at which the marginal cost of X_1 used in the production of Y is equal to the marginal cost of X_2 used in the production of Y is equal to the marginal revenue derived from the sale of Y ($MC_{X_1 Y} = MC_{X_2 Y} = MR_Y$).

It should be pointed out that the factor-factor model is not restricted to analyzing the use of only two factors of production. This model can be expanded to analyze the use of a multiplicity of factors. However, no more than two can be analyzed graphically. To expand the analysis for more than two factors requires the use of some pretty involved mathematical and econometric analysis. However, the theory involved in such an application is precisely the same as we have illustrated in this discussion.

Let's return for the moment to our map of the production surface (or total revenue surface, as the case may be) as shown in Figure 16.13. What are the important things to remember about this factor-factor model? First of all, we learned that the cost-minimizing point could be established for any given level of product Y by equating the slope of the isoproduct curve (which defines the rate at which one factor may be substituted for the other) for that

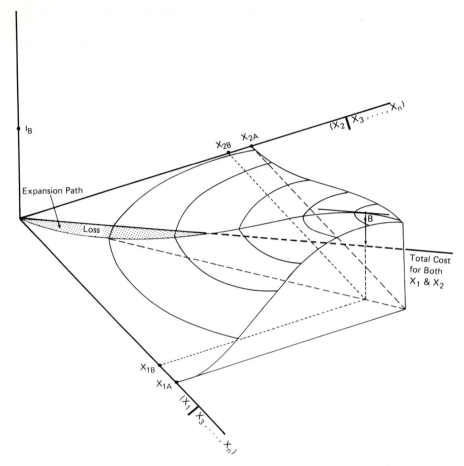

Figure 16.12 Location of the profit-maximizing position along the expansion path on a production surface.

level of product with the inverse of the factor price ratio. This point of equality defines the combination of factors in which the marginal cost of using X_1 is equal to the marginal cost of using X_2. Obviously, the rational manager is going to substitute a cheaper factor for a more expensive factor as long as his total production is unchanged. That is, if X_2 is twice as expensive as X_1, the rational manager will substitute X_1 for X_2 as long as it does not require more than two units of X_1 to replace one unit of X_2. By making this substitution, he can reduce the total cost of producing any particular level of output.

Once the ratio at which minimum cost combinations of the two factors has been defined, the path along which the manager will operate will be

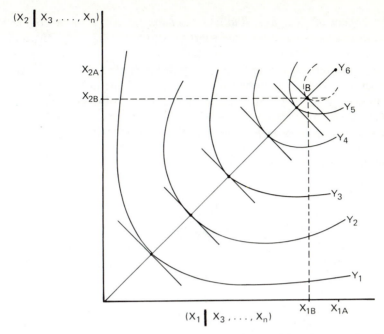

Figure 16.13 Factor-factor model corresponding with the production-revenue surface in Figure 16.12.

defined by the expansion path. As long as the prices for the factors do not change, the expansion path will remain the same. With given prices for the factors, the expansion path defines, for all intents and purposes, a factor-product model in which a fixed ratio of X_1 and X_2 may be treated as a single variable factor. This factor-product model can then be analyzed for purposes of locating the point of maximum profit. (A close examination of Figure 16.12 will show a factor-product model along the expansion path.) If the ratio at which factors are priced should change, a new expansion path would be defined. The least-cost combination of factors would now be a different ratio and the procedure of converting the expansion path to a factor-product model would be repeated to find the profit-maximizing level of production.

   It should be emphasized that the factor-factor model is almost perfectly analogous to our indifference curve analysis. The main difference is that indifference curves measure levels of satisfaction and isoproduct curves measure levels of production. Isoproduct curves exhibit the same characteristics as indifference curves for the same reasons. The isocost line is analogous to the budget line in indifference analysis. However the isocost is not fixed by an income restriction, since we are concerned *not* with finding the maximum level of production, but with finding the cost-minimizing combination of resources for a given level of output.

The Impact of Length of Run and Asset Fixity •   We have confined our discussion to this point to the short-run types of operating decisions that managers face. However, the manager is concerned not only with solving short-run problems within the structure of the market in which his firm must operate; he is also concerned with solving problems over longer periods of time. And while it is true that he must survive in the short run if he is to enjoy any long-run benefits, one of the functions of a manager is to plan for growth and progress in his business over time. He must be concerned with adjusting to the changes that are present here and now, but he must also be prepared to make the more permanent types of adjustments to the conditions that are expected to prevail over longer periods of time.

Since basic farm production occurs under conditions approaching pure competition, for purposes of simplicity let's discuss the length-of-run concepts within the framework of the purely competitive market structure. Because the pure competitor has very little influence in the market, he is often referred to as a price taker. Thus, most of the adjustments made by the manager of the purely competitive business will be concerned with the production or supply side of the question. One of the most convenient means for illustrating the length-of-run concepts is found in the individual firm's supply function as it is generated from the production function and, in the case where there is more than one variable resource, from the production surface.

We know from our analysis of the production function and the factor-product model that the purely competitive firm's short-run supply function is determined by the marginal cost curve faced by the firm. Let's arbitrarily assume that these individual supply functions can be classified into three categories: (1) short run, (2) long run, and (3) intermediate run. This arbitrary classification is obviously to some degree at odds with the facts. The length of run can be defined to be *any* length from the instantaneous or market period in which everything is fixed, to the secular long-term periods in which nothing is fixed.

As you will recall from our earlier discussion of supply and demand, we briefly discussed the long-run and short-run concepts in terms of the *ceteris paribus* conditions that prevailed. That is, in the short run many factors were held constant, and in the long run none of these factors was held constant. In the case of the intermediate run, more of the *ceteris paribus* conditions are permitted to vary than in the case of the short run, but not as many as in the case of the long-run period. Thus, there are an infinite number of lengths of run that might be classified as being intermediate-term types of periods.[2]

---

[2] James S. Plaxico, "Aggregation of Supply Concepts and Firm Supply Functions," *Farm Size and Output Research,* Southern Cooperative Series Bulletin No. 56, pp. 79–80. Stillwater, Okla.: Oklahoma Agricultural Experiment Station, 1958.

In our discussion of the production function, the factor-product, and the factor-factor models, you will recall that we always discussed these models in terms of the fixed and variable factors of production. That is, we defined these models *in terms of the resources that were fixed during the length of the time period with which we were concerned.* The non-farm-produced factors such as fertilizers, feeds, insecticides, fuel, and hourly labor are normally considered to be variable in the short run. The adjustments to situations that managers view as being temporary (or short run) will be made through variations in the levels at which factors such as these are employed. Managers would be unlikely to decide to go out of business or to expand on the basis of conditions that are not expected to persist for any length of time. The responsiveness (or elasticity) of the firm's short-run supply function would depend largely on the relative importance of these inputs that managers think of as being variable in the short run.

The intermediate run is the term used to define conditions the manager may perhaps view as being temporary, but which he will expect to last for several production periods. That is, while it may not be profitable to invest in additional land (or a new plant in the case of an off-farm agricultural business), there are factors of production that, while fixed in the short-run situations, may now be varied. Some of the resources which might become variable as the manager moves to the intermediate-run context include rented land, livestock breeding herds, machinery, salaried labor, and the like.

The truly long-run adjustments that managers may make are those adjustments that are made in response to changes that the manager feels are likely to be permanent in nature. The decision to go out of business is a long-run adjustment. Thus, the changes in the number of firms participating in a business are long-run sorts of adjustments that occur in response to long-run variables such as technological growth.

While the truly long-run types of relationships are of particular interest to persons engaged in agricultural policy types of analyses, the lengths of run that will be of greatest concern to the individual manager will be the short- and intermediate-run type of decisions. The long-run decision most often encountered by the manager of a farm business is the decision whether or not to invest in additional land (or a new plant in the case of a non-farm business) or whether to sell the land he currently owns. The manager will much more frequently face the question of whether or not to take on an investment in the intermediate-term variables such as new tractors, livestock breeding herds, buildings, or additional rented land.

The relationship between short-run and intermediate-term variables gives rise to one of the most puzzling and frustrating problems facing the manager of the farm business. In the first place, the knowledge concerning probable future prices for agricultural products is something less than perfect. About the best the farm manager can do in many cases is to look at recent history and use some sort of average of the prices received over the past several production periods. If he can justify an intermediate-term investment on the basis of such prices, he will often go ahead and invest. Once he has made this investment, he has committed some resources to paying off that investment over the life of the asset. In other words, this becomes a *fixed* factor of production over the period of asset life.

The second difficulty the manager faces in combining short-term and intermediate-term assets is that while he can dispose of an intermediate-term asset, the price at which he disposes of it is nowhere near the price he pays when he acquires the asset. In the case of a tractor, for example, the salvage (or resale) value of the tractor may be reduced by a third the day the manager makes the purchase, even though by no means a third of the potential use of the tractor has been realized.

In our earlier discussion of the factor-factor model, we suggested that a close examination of Figure 16.12 would reveal a factor-product model along the expansion path. The same situation prevails if one of the two variable factors is fixed at some level. For the production surface in Figure 16.14, think of X_1 as being a short-term resource such as fuel or hourly labor and X_2 as an intermediate resource such as machinery. We can readily see that each level of machinery is associated with a particular production function. That is, the available level of machinery places an absolute limit on the output of product Y regardless of how much of the short-term resources of

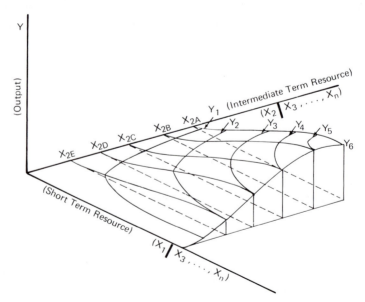

Figure 16.14 Production functions emerge along a production surface as one of the variable resources is fixed at alternative levels.

hourly labor or fuel may be available. Increased availability of machinery (from X_{2A} to X_{2B}, for example) will increase the productivity of any given quantity of the short-term resource.

The factor-factor map of the production surface in Figure 16.14 is shown in Figure 16.15. The horizontal lines labeled X_{2A} through X_{2E} are simply the production functions associated with the alternative levels of the intermediate-term resource as those functions would be perceived if one were looking straight down at the production surface. Obviously, higher levels of output can be achieved with X_{2A} level of intermediate-term resources than can be achieved with X_{2E}.

Almost every productive activity involves the use of some short-term assets (such as feed, seed, fuel, fertilizer, or hourly labor), some intermediate-term assets (such as breeding stock, machinery, building, or salaried labor), and some long-term assets(s) (such as land). As product prices change, the question faced by the manager is how best to combine the factors at his disposal to produce the product in question most efficiently. The long-term factors are totally fixed, and the short-term factors are totally variable. But the intermediate-term factors are pseudo-fixed or pseudo-variable. That is, they are neither fish nor fowl; they can be acquired at one price and salvaged at a lower price. Unless the returns to these intermediate-term factors get so low that the manager would be ahead to salvage them, thus minimizing his losses, these resources are in fact fixed over the short term.

The factor-factor model can be used to analyze the problem we have described. Let's assume that we have one short-term factor, such as hourly

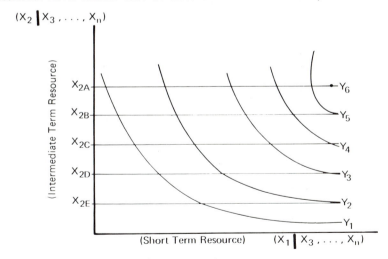

Figure 16.15 A horizontal (or a vertical) line on the factor-factor model is associated with a production function or a factor-product model.

labor or perhaps fuel, and one intermediate-term factor, such as machinery, to use in combination with our fixed factors, such as land, in the production of a given product. Our intermediate-term asset can be acquired at one price and salvaged at a lower price. The acquisition and salvage prices for the short-term asset are the same. Thus, we have one isocost line based on the acquisition price of the intermediate-term asset and the price of our short-term asset (P_{X1}/P_{X2A} in Figure 16.16). We have a second isocost line that is based on the ratio of the salvage price for the intermediate-term asset and price for our short-term asset ($P_{X_1}/P_{X_2 S}$ in Figure 16.16). There are two points on each isoproduct curve that have the same slopes as these two isocost lines. Thus, we have a point on an expansion path in the case of the acquisition price ratio and a point on what might be termed a "contraction" path in the case of the salvage price ratio.

When we expand the scope of our factor-factor model to include more than one level of production for *Y*, we can see the expansion path and the "contraction" path quite clearly as illustrated in Figure 16.17. As product prices increase, the manager will expand output along the expansion path by acquiring more of both factors, if he expects these prices to prevail over

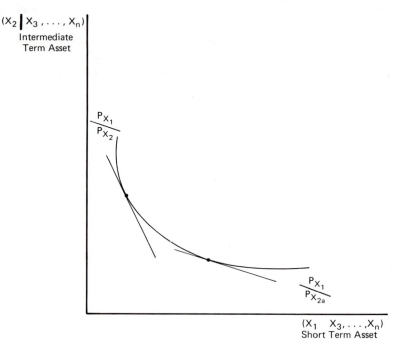

Figure 16.16 Differences in the price at which intermediate-term assets are acquired and salvaged cause different isocosts to be used in decision making.

several production periods. If, after the manager has reached a point such as point *A* (or the level of output Y_3), some change occurs that causes the manager to expect a temporary price decline, he will plan production at the level of Y_2. He does not have the option of reducing his production along the expansion path. The intermediate-term asset of machinery is a fixed resource in the short run, so the manager will make his adjustment to the lower level of production by reducing his usage of the short-term factor (that is, he would reduce his use of resources such as hourly labor, fertilizer, seed, or fuel). In this fashion, he moves back along the production function which is associated with the level of intermediate-term resources he holds to point *B*. When the manager expects prices for the product to improve, he will increase his production back along the line *AB* by increasing his usage of the short-term factor while holding his intermediate-term factor constant.

If prices should get so good that the manager will maximize profits at some level of output above Y_3, and if he expects these prices to be temporary, he will adjust by increasing the usage of X_1 still further along the same path (or the same production function) out toward point *C*. Points *A*, *B*, and *C* all use the same level of X_2 (machinery in our example) and maximize short-run profits by varying the levels at which the short-term

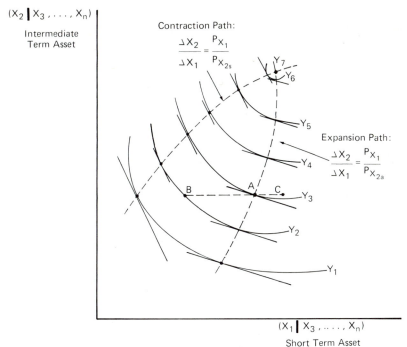

Figure 16.17 Adjustment to a short-term product price change when intermediate-term assets are involved.

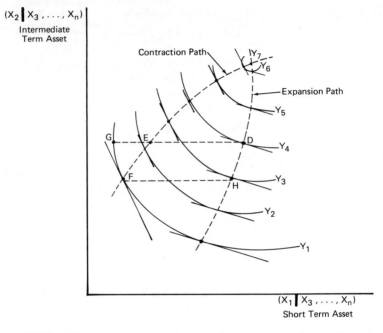

Figure 16.18   Adjustment to an intermediate-term product price change when intermediate-term assets are involved.

factor X_1 (fuel or hourly labor in our example) is combined with fixed levels of intermediate- and long-term factors.

Suppose, however, that the manager has reached a point such as point D in Figure 16.18[3] (output Y_4) when the change in product prices occurs. Let's further suppose that he expects this change to be of a longer-term nature, and that the profit-maximizing level of output would be Y_1 under the new price conditions. The manager would adjust to this situation by reducing the level at which he uses X_1 along the path from point D to point E. If he expected the change to be temporary, he would move on along this path to point G while maintaining his stock of intermediate-term assets. But since he expects the change to be of a more permanent nature, rather than moving all the way to point G, he will salvage some of the intermediate-term assets, X_2, and move down the contraction path to point F on a lower level production

---

[3] College teachers of economics have a nasty habit of asking test questions which involve simply reversing the axes of a diagram such as that in Figure 16.18. That is, the short-term asset will be measured on the vertical axis and the intermediate-term resource will be measured on the horizontal axis. In that case, rather than adjusting horizontally when the intermediate resource is fixed, the adjustment will be made vertically.

function. If at some time in the future product prices should again improve, and if the improvement is expected to prevail for several production periods, the manager will move out to point *H* and on up the expansion path.

What does all of this mean in terms of the supply function for the individual firm? The supply function as related to the expansion path is an intermediate-term supply function since it permits the intermediate factors to vary. This is shown in Figure 16.19 as S_{Ex}. The adjustments made in the short run are shown by the short-run supply function *BAC*. The adjustments that the manager makes as a result of changes that he expects to be more permanent are shown by the "box" labeled *DEFH*. The only parts of this box that are truly long-run sorts of adjustment are the segments *EF* and *HD*. The other adjustments represent the changes that would be made in response to short-run changes in price.

From this analysis, we can draw some conclusions about the impact of the fixity of assets under various length-of-run concepts on the conditions of supply. First, the longer the time period considered, the greater the flexibility the manager has in the adjustment alternatives available, since there are fewer fixed resources to limit his adjustment capability. This means that the elasticity of the supply function at any given price is likely to be greater in the long run than in the short run. Second, as the quantity of intermediate factors (which are fixed in the short run) is changed, the short-run supply function shifts, since a different level of fixed factors means that there is a

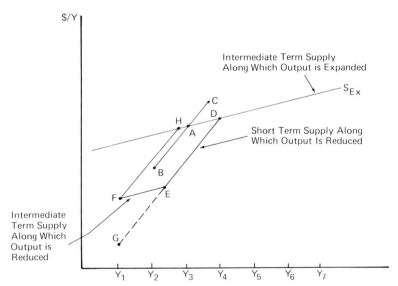

Figure 16.19 Supply functions associated with intermediate-term production assets (derived from the factor-factor model in Figure 16.18).

different short-run production function. The manager can add these inter-mediate factors relatively easily, thus shifting his short-run supply to the right. But the road back is tortuous and painful because he cannot salvage these fixed assets at their full value. Thus, he cannot reduce supply along the same path that it is increased.

A third conclusion is that any point along the intermediate-run supply function will have a short-run supply function that is associated with it. Likewise, any point along a long-run supply function will have both an associated short-run supply function and an infinite number of associated intermediate supply functions. The primary reason for differing lengths of run is the differing periods of time over which production assets are fixed. In general, the fewer the number of fixed assets, the longer the length of run. Another way of saying this is that as more and more of the *ceteris paribus* conditions are permitted to vary, the longer the length-of-run context.

We have conducted our analysis in terms of the supply function. However, the same sort of analysis can be conducted for the demand function. Essentially the same conclusions will be drawn. Each point on the long-run demand function has a short-run demand function and an infinite number of intermediate-run demand functions associated with it. The longer the length of run, the more elastic is demand at any given price and the fewer are the *ceteris paribus* conditions.

The Product-Product Model

We have seen how the factor-factor model is really nothing more than a new application of our old friend the indifference curve analysis. We have further seen how the factor-factor model is nothing more or less than a combination of a family of factor-product models. In our study of the factor-factor model we have considered the situation in which a firm used more than one variable factor of production in the production of a particular product, and we have defined a way in which this situation may be analyzed for purposes of maximizing profits. However, except for the case of certain types of range lands, very few agricultural resources are so specific that they can be used in the production of one and only one good. While we live in a world of agricultural specialization, most agricultural firms still deal in more than one product. For example, most farmers in the Great Plains can produce wheat, all types of livestock, and grain sorghums. Many of them can produce cotton or broom corn, and a few can produce soybeans, sesame, mung beans, safflower, and a variety of other specialty crops. Very few farm supply businesses handle only one product; feeds and fertilizers will often be sold by the same organization. And very few agricultural processing firms deal in only one product: a broiler integrator will many times also deal in turkeys and eggs. Meat packers will normally slaughter hogs, cattle, and sheep. Flour millers will generally process many types of feeds. How, then, is the decision concerning the profit maximizing combination of products to be made? Do we simply select the product with which we like to deal and work with this product to the exclusion of all others? Hardly. If we wish to maximize profits, we must define the alternative types of production that are available to us and then utilize our resources in the production of one or more of these products such that the returns to the owned resources is maximum.

There is a factor-product model and perhaps a factor-factor model associated with each production alternative. How do we go about determining the product mix for which we should strive? For purposes of simplicity, let's assume that we initially have only the factor-product models to consider for each of the two products Y_1 and Y_2—perhaps rutabagas and tomatoes—as shown in Figure 16.20. Let's further assume that the one variable factor with which we are concerned is operating capital, since operating capital can command all the short-term variables. We have certain fixed levels of land, labor, and investment capital with which to combine our operating capital in the production of these two products. We go to the local bank or to the Production Credit Association and say, "Mr. Finance, I've got so much land, so much capital equipment, my own labor, a stout heart, and a sound mind to use as collateral. I can use these resources in producing rutabagas and/or tomatoes.[4] How much money will you lend me for use in producing these two products?"

Mr. Finance asks how much capital you need. You tell him that you need $763,287. After he catches his breath, he asks if you can't get by with $1,500 and the negotiation starts. Finally you agree upon a particular sum of money and Mr. Finance says, "I'll lend you $5,000 for this purpose, but you'd better plan to pay me back the day your crop comes in, hear?"

All right, now you're in business. You have a certain amount of operating capital that you can allocate between producing rutabagas and tomatoes. How do you go about allocating it? You have the two-factor product models of Figure 16.20. Further, you know how much operating capital you have to use. You can put it all into rutabagas or you can put it all into tomatoes, or you can divide it between the two alternatives in any combination that falls on the line connecting the points denoting $5,000 on the operating capital axis of the two production functions. This line connecting the level of available operating capital on the X_1 axis of each of the two factor-product models will define a type of isocost line between the two

---

[4] Rutabagas and tomatoes have been selected simply as proxy products just as operating capital has been selected as a proxy resource simply for convenience. These production functions are *not* empirically derived functions, but are hypothetical functions that are convenient for illustration.

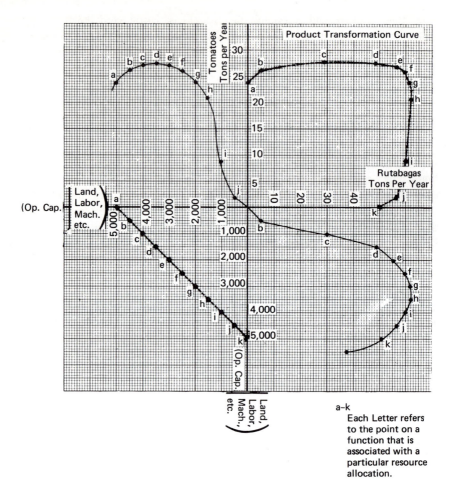

Figure 16.20   A product transformation curve can be constructed from the production functions for two products once the cost outlay is specified.

products. That is, the same cost outlay is allocated differently at each point, but it is the same cost outlay nevertheless.

When we allocate operating capital in the various possible combinations between rutabagas and tomatoes, we find that we are able to define the various quantities of the alternative products that can be produced with our particular level of variable cost. That is, we now have a *product transformation curve* in a product-product model. That is, some rutabagas can in a sense be transformed into tomatoes simply as a result of a reallocation of resources. The product transformation curve defines the combinations of products that may be produced with a given cost outlay. If the amount of operating capital available should be increased or reduced, we would have a new product transformation curve.

In the case of the factor-product model, we pointed out that Stage III was irrational and therefore irrelevant. This shows up again in the case of the product-product model as shown in Figure 16.20. There are ranges within the product-product model where an increase in the production of one product is accompanied by (or complemented by) an increase in the production of the other (those portions between points *a* and *c* and between points *k* and *h* on the product transformation curves). Generally, *complementarity* can occur when the resource is being used into Stage III for one alternative. The removal of some resources from that employment will actually increase the yield. Another situation in which complementarity occurs is the one in which the presence of two crops in the same field (for example, a peanut-grain sorghum rotation in the sandy soils of the Southern Plains) increases the yield of both. (Continuous cropping of peanuts in a field will eventually reduce peanut yields because of the problem of nematodes. A year of grain soghum will get rid of the nematodes, and the grain sorghum yield will be increased as a result of the soil-building quality of peanuts.) In this case, the interaction between the two crops essentially increases the bundle of resources available for use.

A second range in some product-product models is the range of *supplementarity*. This occurs when an increase in the production of one good does not affect the production of the other (between points *c* and *d*, and between points *g* and *h* on the product transformation curve in Figure 16.20). This may occur in the neighborhood of the point of diminishing marginal returns for resources used in the production of one good or the other, or it may occur as a result of an interaction between the products where an intermediate product of one enterprise serves as an input to the other. In the real world, beef cattle grazing on winter wheat pasture or on corn stubble is a good example of supplementarity. Up to a point, the yield of grain is unaffected by grazing. If beef cattle did not utilize the forage produced by winter wheat or corn stubble, that forage would go to waste. Another real world example of product transformation curves exhibiting complementarity, supplementarity, and competitive ranges is the case of beef cattle and deer sharing the same grazing range. A few deer will browse the brush back, allowing more grass to be produced for the cattle and hence increasing beef production from the land resource. Beyond a certain point, further increases in the deer population will not increase or decrease the available grass, but beyond some further point, there is not enough brush to support the deer population, so the deer begin to eat grass, hence competing with cattle for the available forage.

The third range (and the relevant one) in the product-product model is the range within which the products *compete* for resources (between points *d* and *g* on the product transformation curve in Figure 16.20). It is within this range that the profit-maximizing position will be found. Obviously, profits will increase as long as the total production of both products is increased as a result of reallocating resources. Thus, if both products are positively priced, the rational producer will never operate in the range of complementarity. Likewise, if a minor reallocation of resources can substantially increase the production of one good without perceptibly reducing the production of the other (as within the range of supplementarity), the profits will increase from such a reallocation. Only in the range within which products compete for resources can the revenue generated from either alternative be *reduced* by a reallocation of resources. The problem the manager faces is finding the point at which a reduction in the profits from producing one less unit of one product is exactly offset by an increase in the profits from producing another unit of the alternative product.

The complementary, supplementary, and competitive ranges on the product transformation curve can be located very simply regardless of the shape that the curve may take. If the slope of the curve at some point is positive (i.e., if a tangent to a point on the curve slopes upward and to the right) then complementarity prevails at that point. If the slope is negative, the products are competing for resources. If the slope is zero or if it is infinite (i.e., the tangent is perfectly vertical or perfectly horizontal), then there is supplementarity at that point.

Product Transformation Curves Can Take Many Shapes • Figure 16.21 shows what happens to the product transformation curve in the product-product model as the degree of limitation on resource availability changes. The product transformation curves in Figure 16.21 are derived from exactly the same production functions as was the curve in Figure 16.20. Yet there is a world of difference in the appearance of the curves as associated with varying levels of the resource X_1. This shouldn't be surprising, however, when one recognizes the extreme stress faced by the manager of a farm business as his line of credit is curtailed. This typically happens to livestock producers when a severe drop in livestock prices restricts borrowing power. These producers are often forced into short-term management decisions that are not good for the long-term organization and profitability of the business. For example, perhaps a rancher has been following the practice of placing his calves in a custom feedlot, selling 18-month-old steers at 1,100 pounds rather than selling 8-month-old steers at 450 pounds. But the loss of credit prevents his continuing this practice. The need to generate cash flow forces him to sell calves at light weights and low prices.

Different shapes of production functions for the production alternatives can also generate a peculiar-appearing product transformation curve.

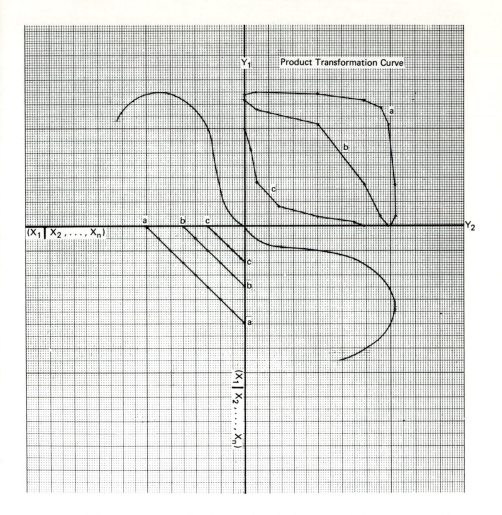

Figure 16.21 A change in the degree of limitation on available resources will change the shape of the product transformation curve.

Figure 16.22 shows a transformation curve for two production functions with which some minimum level of production will occur even in the absence of the short-term variable resource. This is the case, for example, with most crops and fertilizer, or with range livestock production and operating capital spent on winter feeding programs.

The shape that the product transformation curve takes is unimportant. The presence or absence of complementary or supplementary ranges in the product transformation curve is unimportant since it is irrational to produce in these ranges. Regardless of the shape of the product transformation curve,

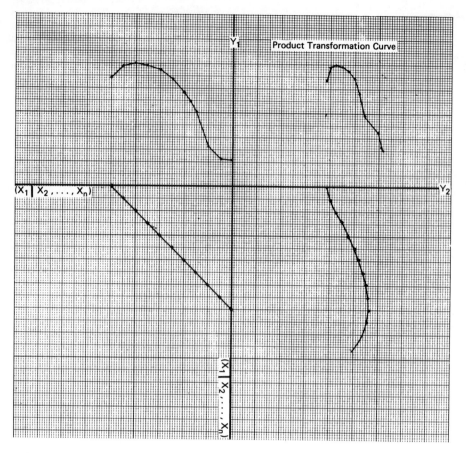

Figure 16.22 Different types of production functions will produce differently-shaped product transformation curves.

the source of the curve is from basic production function information, and the objective is to locate the revenue- (or profit-) maximizing combination of products. For this purpose, the analysis is the same, regardless of these externalities.

Selecting the Profit-Maximizing Point • We have seen where the product transformation curve comes from and we have seen that it can take a multitude of shapes. We have learned that products may exhibit three different types of interaction: complementarity, supplementarity, and competitiveness. But we have not yet gotten around to learning how to accomplish the objective for which this product-product model is designed—that of finding the profit-maximizing product mix with a given cost outlay. Let's redraw our product-

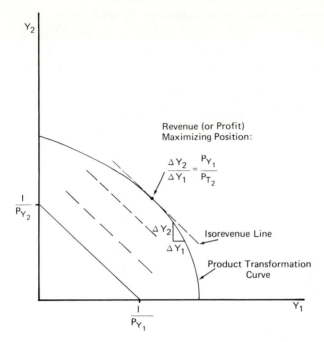

Figure 16.23 Location of the profit-maximizing position with the product-product model: where the marginal rate of product transformation is equal to the inverse ratio of product prices.

product model to include only the relevant range within which products compete for resources, as in Figure 16.23. We immediately recognize the product-product model as being our old friend the production possibilities curve from Chapter 2. The problem we face is finding where on our production possibilities curve we should elect to operate. You will recall that we said our production possibilities curve defined all the possible combinations of Y_1 and Y_2 that could be produced with a given cost outlay. The economic problem we must solve in this case is the problem of producing maximum total revenue (or product) for a given cost outlay. If we maximize revenue, and if costs are not changed, then profits are maximum where total revenue from sales is maximum.

For purposes of simplicity, let's assume that we are still operating in the spirit world of pure competition. The levels at which we produce Y_1 and Y_2 will in no way affect the market price. We can define all the combinations of Y_1 and Y_2 that will provide some target level of revenue by dividing that target level by the price of Y_1 and marking off on the Y_1 axis the quantity of Y_1 that would have to be sold to achieve that revenue (I/P_{Y_1}). The opposite end of our constant income line (or our isorevenue line) can be defined by repeating this procedure using the price of Y_2. The resulting quantity of Y_2 that will yield our target level of revenue is marked off on the Y_2 axis (I/P_{Y_2}). A line connecting these two points will give us an isorevenue line. That is, every combination of Y_1 and Y_2 along this line will yield the same level of revenue. Since we are not concerned with achieving a "target" income, but with maximizing the level of revenue it is possible to achieve with our given cost outlay, we'll let this isorevenue line "float"—maintaining the slope defined by the product-price ratio—to the point that is just tangent to the product transformation curve of our product-product model. At this point the profit-maximizing combination of products for a particular cost outlay is defined. That is, the profit-maximizing combination of products occurs where the marginal rate of product transformation is exactly equal to the inverse ratio of product prices.

The logic of this procedure is that the point at which the slope of the product transformation curve is the same as the slope of the isoincome line is the point at which the value lost by a one-unit reduction in the production of one product is exactly offset by the value gained in the production of the other. For example, if Y_1 is worth \$2 per unit and Y_2 is priced at \$1, the profit-maximizing point would be where a reduction of one unit in the production of Y_1 would be offset by an increase of two units in the production of Y_2. That is:

$$\text{where } \frac{\Delta Y_2}{\Delta Y_1} = \frac{P_{Y_1}}{P_{Y_2}}$$

or where the marginal rate of product substitution is equal to the inverse ratio of the product prices.

Some Special Cases • There are some special types of product-product models that come into effect in the processing and distribution phases of agriculture where conditions other than pure competition may prevail. In the case of products that require exactly the same levels of inputs for exactly the same volume of production, the production possibilities curve is a straight line (Figure 16.24). An example of this is provided by the canning companies that may sell the same canned fruits or vegetables under two different brand names. Gasoline is another product that may be handled in this fashion, and laundry detergent still a third. If these companies were in fact operating under conditions of pure competition, the products would be the same product. But because of the imperfectly competitive market structure, the firm finds it advantageous to sell at one price to one set of consumers under one brand name and to another set under another brand name.

A second special type of product-product relationship that is of particular importance in the agricultural processing businesses is provided by the

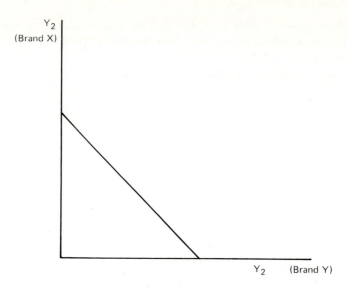

Figure 16.24 The product-product model: a special case in which a single product may be sold under two different brand names.

situation in which one product cannot be produced unless some quantity of another product is produced at the same time (Figure 16.25). For example, wheat flour and wheat bran are jointly produced, as are soybean oil and soybean meal. Other examples are beef and hides, pork and lard, or eggs and chicken manure (sometimes euphemistically called organic fertilizer). The production possibilities curve in the case of joint products is supplemental in nature throughout the entire range of the curve. The only part of it that is

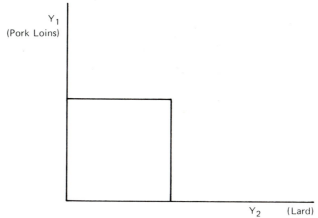

Figure 16.25 The product-product model: a special case in which two products are jointly produced.

really relevant is the point at the corner: that is, these products are produced in this ratio regardless of the price situation facing either one or the other product, and for all intents and purposes are viewed by the producer as being the same product, even though processors and consumers perceive them to be very different.

Selected References

Boulding, Kenneth E., *Economic Analysis,* 3rd ed., Chapters 28, 34, and 35. New York: Harper and Brothers, 1955.

Heady, Earl O., *Economics of Agricultural Production and Resource Use,* Chapters 2, 5, 6, 7. Englewood Cliffs, N.J.: Prentice-Hall, Inc., 1952.

Plaxico, James S., "Aggregation of Supply Concepts and Farm Supply Functions," *Farm Size and Output Research,* Southern Cooperative Series Bulletin No. 56, Stillwater, Okla.: Oklahoma Agricultural Experiment Station, June, 1958.

17

Joint Supply Functions and Derived Demand

In Chapter 14, we discussed how the basic demand functions are the demand at the consumer level; that is, the demand at retail. The basic supply function is the supply at the source of raw materials. Thus, in the case of food, the basic supply occurs at the farm level, while the basic demand is observed in the chain store. The relationships between these market levels are defined by the marketing margins. The farm demand curve for a given product is derived from the demand at retail by way of the demand curves at all the intermediate processing and marketing levels. This derivation may be accomplished by means of simply subtracting the marketing margin for any given quantity of product from the retail price that consumers are willing to pay for that quantity. The retail supply curve is derived from the basic farm supply by adding the cost for marketing (that is, the marketing margin) at each quantity along the farm supply schedule to the price at which farmers are willing to supply that quantity.

In our discussion of production management in Chapter 16, we discovered that rational managerial decisions could be made on the basis of the factor-product, factor-factor, and product-product models. We also recognized that many products that originate on farms and ranches are broken apart during the processing phase and are then used in producing a variety of goods to be sold at the consumer level. Each of these finished consumer items faces a retail demand curve that is often independent to a large degree from the demand of the other jointly-supplied products.

A change in the demand for one jointly-supplied consumer product can have some far-reaching effects on the market prices for the other jointly-supplied products and the quantities of these products available in the market place. Jointly-supplied products are of particular importance in the agricultural processing industries. Changes in the conditions of demand facing one of the finished products will have an impact on the availability of the other products derived from this same raw material. An example of the relationship between joint supply functions and derived demand functions may be found in the case of the products derived from hogs. You get so much ham, so much bacon, so much shoulder, loin, and lard from a hog of a given size. Therefore, the point of intersection for the farm supply of hogs and the farm demand for hogs as derived from all the market demand curves for the pork products will determine the available supplies of all the pork products. Yet the demands for lard and for pork chops tend to be quite independent.

Until 1962, Cuba provided a major outlet for American lard. United States housewives were using vegetable shortenings for cooking purposes, and U.S. lard production greatly exceeded U.S. consumption. In 1962, during the period when the United States and Russia stood with noses touching for a week without seeing eye to eye on the issue of Cuban missiles, an embargo was placed on the export of lard to Cuba. This, in effect, represented a rather sharp reduction in the demand for American lard. Since the demand for pork was unaffected—indeed, we were then importing substantial quantities of canned hams from Denmark and Poland—the primary product of the *meat* derived from hog slaughter was still in demand. The problem that the managers of pork slaughter and processing facilities faced was a problem of analyzing the probable impact of the Cuban embargo on their businesses, and then the problem of planning their operations to offset this influence.

How could we analyze this situation? What would we expect to happen to the demand and price for live hogs? What would happen to the demand and price for pork items? Well, let's define the situation that prevailed prior to the Cuban embargo. The demand for hogs would be determined jointly by the demand for pork and the demand for lard (Figure 17.1). Since lard is much lower in value than are the other portions of the pork carcass, and since approximately 20 percent of the dressed carcass is lard, the demand for a given quantity of live hogs would reflect this relationship along with the marketing margin. The total demand for lard exceeds the domestic demand; that is, the difference in the total and domestic demands may be defined as representing the export demand, which we shall define to be the Cuban demand.

This is the situation prior to the embargo. Along comes the embargo on shipments of lard to Cuba and wipes out that portion of the total demand for lard. What sorts of changes does this create in the rest of Figure 17.1[1]?

The loss of the Cuban lard market caused the domestic demand for lard to become essentially the *total* demand for lard. Therefore, the total demand

---

[1] The relationships in Figure 17.1 are purely for illustration. They do not represent empirically derived estimates of the supply and demand relationships for hogs or pork products.

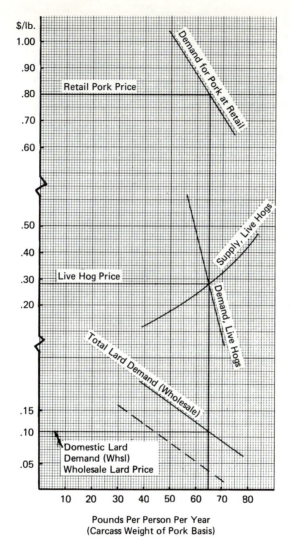

Figure 17.1 Postulated situation in live hog and pork product markets prior to the Cuban export embargo.

for lard shifted sharply downward and to the left when the Cuban embargo was enacted. Since the demand for hogs is partially derived from the demand for lard, and since lard composes about 20 percent of the carcass weight of hogs, about 20 percent of the price change for each quantity of lard would be reflected in the price of that quantity of hogs that produced a given quantity of lard. Thus the demand for live hogs was shifted down and to the left. That

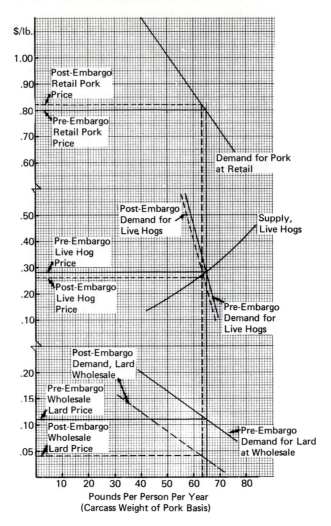

Figure 17.2 Expected change in live hog and pork product markets as a result of the Cuban export embargo.

is, processors were now willing to pay less for each quantity of hogs since the value of about 20 percent of the carcass was worth less (Figure 17.2).[2] This would cause a change in the point of equilibrium where the supply and demand functions for live hogs intersect. The reduced market quantity of

_____

[2] The relationships in Figure 17.2 are purely for illustration. They do not represent empirically derived estimates of the supply and demand relationships for live hogs or pork products.

hogs would be reflected in a reduced quantity of both pork and lard available in the market. Since the demand for pork was largely unaffected by the change in the demand for lard, after all adjustments were made, we would have a simple movement along the demand curve for pork to the higher price associated with the reduced quantity available. A smaller quantity of hogs would be sold for a lower price as a result of the reduced demand for hogs, and the smaller quantity of lard would be sold at a greatly reduced price.

What are the implications of this situation for managers of the various economic units involved in producing, processing, marketing, and consuming hogs and the products derived from these animals? In the end, the adjustment is made largely in the reduced prices for lard and live hogs. Some adjustment is made in the form of a higher price for pork. The consumer of pork pays a higher price for less product. The producer of hogs receives a reduced price and sells fewer hogs. The domestic consumer of lard can buy a great deal more lard at a sharply reduced price. (But who needs it?) The hog processor has reduced receipts since his income from lard is reduced by more than his income from pork is increased. The actual adjustment that eventually evolved from this situation was that much of the lard went into the low-value non-food uses, such as soap making. That is, when prices got to the level where lard was relatively less expensive than alternative sources of fats and oils, the commercial users switched to lard.

Problems such as these are common in the agricultural processing industries. The automotive industry, for example, takes a large number of raw materials and assembles them into a single finished product (hence, the term *assembly line*). Agricultural processors, on the other hand, take a single raw material and "disassemble" it into a large number of finished products. This disassembly nature of agricultural processing brings about all sorts of questions concerning primary products and by-products. Generally, the primary product that is derived from a given raw material is so designated because it represents the largest single portion of the total value that may be derived from *all* the products that are manufactured from that raw material. Thus, since lean meat is greatly in demand, the lean meat is the primary product derived from hogs. Lard, glands, Hush-Puppies (pigskin shoes, not a Southern dietary delight), squeals, and the like are all by-products of pork processing. Land grant colleges are continually working to develop a hog that produces more lean meat and less lard because of the higher value of lean meat. This hasn't always been the case. Prior to World War I, the use and availability of vegetable shortenings were quite limited. Because the hog was the primary source of edible fats and oils, lard was considered to be about as desirable a product as meat. Many of the agricultural textbooks of that era describe as highly desirable types of hogs that today's packer would discount heavily in the market place because of the low dressing percentage.

Changes such as these are by no means restricted to the dim, dark, and distant past. The soybean replaced the hog as the primary producer of edible fats and oils. Soybean production increased rapidly in the 1940s and 1950s and until about 1959–1960, oil was the primary product derived from the soybean. Soybean meal was a by-product used as a source of protein in animal feeds, and as such was considered to be valuable. But the greatest value came from the oil.

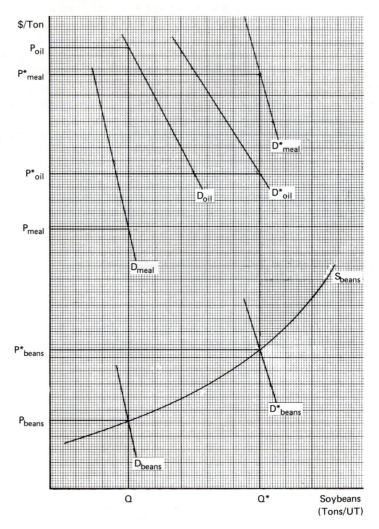

Figure 17.3 When a by-product becomes the primary product produced from an agricultural raw material, dramatic changes in market conditions occur.

By about 1960, the growth in the poultry and livestock industries and the resulting increase in the demand for soybean meal had been so rapid that the meal became the high-valued product. This is shown in Figure 17.3 by some increase in the demand for oil and a very large increase in the demand for meal. The increase in the demand for both basic products derived from soybeans created an increase in the demand for soybeans at the farm level. Farmers moved out along their marginal cost curves to meet this increased demand. But since they could not produce the raw material for soybean meal without also producing soybean oil, the production of both products was expanded at about the same rate. Because the demand for meal had increased more rapidly than had the demand for oil, the price for meal increased while the price for oil declined. As a result, meal became an increasingly important part of the demand for soybeans as derived at the farm level.

The result of this situation has been rapidly expanding demand for soybeans at the farm level, and a tremendous response on the part of farmers in an effort to meet this increasing demand. Through research and technology, we are finding more and more ways to use soybean products, so we would expect the demand for soybeans to continue to increase. For example, many of the so-called synthetic meats (or meat analogs) are based on soybean meal. When the technological processes for this type of production are perfected, we can expect some further increase in the demand for soybeans.

You will undoubtedly have noticed throughout our discussion of the situation facing agricultural products that we derive the farm demand for a farm product from the basic market demand functions for *all* of the goods produced from that raw material. However, we have been very careful *not* to derive the supply functions for the consumer goods from the basic farm supply functions. Why do you suppose we have been so careful to avoid this derivation? The main reason for the avoidance is that since the supply of a by-product depends to an extreme degree on the demand for a primary product, any derivation of a supply function for that by-product would be completely arbitrary. You will recall that we acknowledged in our discussion of derived demand that the derived functions have very little meaning except in the immediate neighborhood of the equilibrium point. Thus, we can simply take the levels of production from the equilibrium point at the farm level and analyze what these levels of production mean in regard to the demand for the products at some higher level in the marketing process. There is no need to derive the supply functions for these products, and furthermore, if such a derivation were made, it would have little if any meaning. This is also the reason it is impossible to define the cost of producing a pound of bacon, a pound of T-bone steak, flour, or any other jointly-supplied good, except in terms of the added costs of processing and marketing. Numerous congressional committees have discovered this reality to their sorrow.

Selected References

Boulding, Kenneth E., *Economic Analysis,* 3rd ed., Chapter 12. New York: Harper and Brothers, 1955.

Heady, Earl O., *Economics of Agricultural Production and Resource Use,* pp. 222–24. Englewood Cliffs, N.J.: Prentice-Hall, Inc., 1952.

Marshall, Alfred, *Principles of Economics,* 8th ed., Book V, Chapter VI. London: Macmillan and Co., Ltd., 1959.

18

Budgeting:
A Management Tool

We have suggested throughout our study of economics that management of any business entity is really a game of alternatives, and that managerial knowledge of economic relationships is useful in defining and evaluating managerial alternatives. It is important that the manager understand how his business affects and is affected by the economic environment within which it exists. The economic theory that we have studied to this point can provide guidance to the manager seeking to solve the problems of his business. For example, the manager who knows that he sells as a pure competitor will not likely make the error of incurring the expense of an advertising campaign. Since his product is homogeneous with that offered by his competitors, he will reap no perceptible price or income benefit from the expenditure. Thus, the competent manager will utilize economic theory as a framework within which to define and solve his problems, and to evaluate the alternative approaches for solving those problems.

It is unlikely that many managers of agricultural businesses will go to the trouble and expense of personally constructing market supply and demand functions, particularly in view of the fact that so few of these managers can really influence these functions. While very few managers will actually chart the cost structure for their businesses, most of them have this information in their accounts and will utilize their business records for purposes of making decisions in much the same fashion as this information would be used if it were actually charted. The method that has been developed to combine economic theory and business records for purposes of defining and evaluating alternative means for achieving business objectives is that of *budgeting*.

Throughout our study of agricultural economics, we have pursued the profit-maximizing objective. We have recognized that we can maximize profits by minimizing costs for a given level of production or by maximizing output (or revenue) for a given cost outlay. We have seen that we will substitute resources for one another as long as a dollar spent on one resource will replace more than a dollar spent on an alternative resource. This was the factor-factor decision. We have also seen that we will increase production of one good as long as a dollar's increase in the value of our production of that good reduces the value of the output of another good by less than a dollar. This was the product-product decision. And finally, we recognized that we wanted to produce every unit of product that added more to revenues than it added to cost and none that added more to cost than it added to revenues. This, of course, was the factor-product decision. The budgeting procedure can be of use in all of these decisions. A *budget* represents a physical and a financial plan for the operation of a business for some future period of time. Hence, budgeting is a tool that can be used in conjunction with our tools of economic theory to aid managers in making decisions that will maximize net returns to their businesses.

The Complete Budget

Two types of budgets are commonly used in business management— complete budgets and partial budgets. The complete budget, used for longer-run decisions, involves a listing of all physical inputs and their cost as well as a listing of all outputs and the expected income. The elements of a complete budget, then, would be *total income* and *total costs*.

By way of illustrating the complete budget, let's suppose that the year is 1976. We know a young man who is in the process of deciding whether or not to become a rancher. His objectives are first to find a line of work in which he can be an independent businessman that works out of doors, and second, a line of work in which he can earn a minimum return of $300 per month or $3,600 per year to his labor and management since this is what he can earn as a cowboy. Obviously, ranching will meet his first requirement (as would a newspaper route), but cattle prices have been reduced by half since the summer of 1973. While prices are currently recovering, we need to conduct some sort of analysis that will tell us whether the income objective can be met. This is where a complete budget—involving not only the variable cost items but also such fixed cost items as interest, insurance, taxes, and depreciation—will be useful.

Imagine that our young friend is the only male grandchild of a 72-year old rancher in northeastern Wyoming. It is important to the grandfather that his ranch continue to be operated under the family name. Since this grandson is the only grandchild who is likely to continue to bear this name, our chauvinistic Grandpa is willing to provide a sweetheart deal for his only male heir. Grandpa cannot sell his ranch and livestock to a member of his family at less than market value without creating all sorts of problems with the collector of inheritance taxes. But there is no law and no tax regulation to prevent his financing the sale of the ranch himself at very advantageous interest rates. He offers to sell his grandson 2,867 acres of land at a price of $60 per acre. There are 150 brood cows that are priced at $365, 6 bulls, at $500 and 24 replacement heifers at $225. All vehicles and machinery are priced at half their new cost for a total equipment investment of $11,835.

The ranch will carry 150 mother cows on a year-round basis (19 acres per cow, including bulls and replacements). The old gentleman is willing to sell the ranch and the livestock on the basis of nothing down. All the grandson has to do is to pay $5,000 annually on the principal of the loan plus 3 percent per annum on the unpaid balance of the principal. The grandfather is further willing to arrange the purchase contract such that upon his death, the grandson has 15 years in which he can operate the ranch under these terms, making the payments to his grandfather's estate. At the end of this

TABLE 18.1

ESTIMATED INVESTMENT NEEDS, 150 BEEF COW
HERD,
Selling Choice Calves in Fall, Northeastern Wyoming

ITEM	NO.	TOTAL ANIMAL UNITS	AVERAGE ANNUAL INVESTMENT	TOTAL INVESTMENT
Land & improvements (in acres)	2,869	—	$60.00	$172,020
Livestock				
Brood cows	150	150	375.00	56,250
Bulls	6	6	500.00	3,000
Replacement heifers	24	10	225.00	5,400
Total		166		
Total Livestock Investment				$64,650
Machinery & Equipment (no. ranches)	1	—	11,835	11,835
Miscellaneous (no. ranches)	—	—	500	500
Total Machinery & Equipment				12,325
Total Investment				$248,295

[1] Includes tractor, truck, pickup trailer, front-end loader, manure spreader, and cattle sprayer, all at half of purchase price.

period, he will have built up enough equity to be able to secure financing from conventional lending agencies, thus providing for settlement of the estate.

The question the embryonic rancher must answer is whether the ranch will be profitable enough to pay 3 percent interest on the fixed investment, pay all other costs of operation, and still return him $3,600 annually for his labor and management. (It should be pointed out that the $5,000 annual payment on the equity in the land will represent a return to the grandson's labor and management since this payment will represent $5,000 increase in his net worth.)

Since an estimate of total costs including both fixed and variable cost items is prerequisite to our total budget, the first calculation we need to make is the total fixed investment (Table 18.1). This calculation will provide us with a basis for calculating our fixed interest charge. We find that the total investment for land, improvements, livestock, and equipment amounts to $248,295. At 3 percent per annum, this represents a fixed interest charge of $7,569.85 the first year. Since he will be paying $5,000 on the principal each year, this interest expense will be reduced by $150 annually.

The variable cost inputs are listed in Table 18.2 and amount to $6,833.50 annually. Fixed cost items such as taxes, interest, insurance, and the like amount to $10,429.32. Total first year annual costs, then, amount to $20,262.82. The annual gross income from the ranching operation must be at least $3,600 above the total annual costs if the business is to enable our young friend to meet his income requirement.

Let's assume that the grandson will be able to maintain a weaned calf crop of 84 percent, selling 41 heifers and 61 steers each fall. Twenty-four heifers are retained for purposes of replacement heifers. If he is selling choice feeder calves at weaning weights of 390–420 pounds, he can probably expect to get an average price per hundredweight of $45 for the steers and $38 for the heifers. He should be able to sell cull cows for about $28 per hundredweight. Thus, his total annual income from sales should amount to about $24,227.20.

Now we can begin to make the final calculations for our complete budget. These can be made from Tables 18.2 and 18.3.

Total annual value of sales (From Table 18.3)	24,227.20
Less annual variable costs (From Table 18.2)	7,833.50
Returns to land, labor, investment capital, and management	17,393.70
Less returns to land, investment capital, depreciation, and insurance (annual fixed costs in Table 18.2)	13,408.42
Returns to labor and management	3,985.28

TABLE 18.2

ESTIMATED ANNUAL PRODUCTION REQUIREMENTS
AND COSTS, 150 BEEF COW HERD,
Selling Choice Calves in Fall, Northeastern Wyoming

ITEM	UNIT	RATE	NO.	TOTAL UNITS	NON-LAND COST PER UNIT	TOTAL COST
Variable Cost Items						
Native hay	Ton	1.08/a.u.	166	180.0	$18.98	$3,416.40
26–30% protein feed	Cwt	2.19/a.u.	166	112.5	7.70	866.25
Salt & minerals	Lb.	32.5 a.u.	166	5,400.0	.025	135.00
Vet and medicine	$	1.54 a.u.	166	255.00	—	255.00
Bull depreciation	$	37.50 each	6	225.00	—	225.00
Hauling & marketing	Cwt	—	6	650.90	1.22	795.00
Interest on op. capital	$/yr.	—	—	5,714.73	.09	603.50
Total annual variable cost						$6,833.50
Fixed Cost Items						
Taxes						
Land	Acre	17.27/a.u.	166	2,867	.61	$1,748.87
Livestock	Head	—	—	180	.92	165.60
General overhead	Ranch	—	—	—	—	596.74
Interest on fixed investment	$/yr.	—	—	248,295	.03	7,488.95
Depreciation on bldg. & equipment	Ranch	—	—			4,045.00
Total annual fixed cost						$13,408.42
Total annual costs						$20,241.92

Labor[1]

[1] Labor requirements amount to 9 hours per cow, or about 1,350 total hours. This amounts to 25–26 hours per week, with no month during the year requiring more than 30 hours per week.

TABLE 18.3

ESTIMATED ANNUAL PRODUCTION AND GROSS SALES, 150 BEEF COW HERD
Selling Choice Calves in Fall, Northeastern Wyoming

ITEM	NUMBER	WEIGHT	PRICE/CWT.	VALUE EACH	TOTAL VALUE
Cull cows	24	950	$28	$266.00	$6,384.00
Cull heifer	1	680	38	248.00	238.00
Heifer calves	41	390	38	148.20	6,076.20
Steer calves	61	420	45	189.00	11,529.00
Total value of sales					$24,227.20

It is apparent that with a labor-management return of $3,985 annually, our young friend can meet his income goal. However, since he is committed to paying $5,000 each year on the principal of his loan, he faces a small problem. The principal payment will take all of his labor-management return plus $1,014.72. Therefore, unless he has a wife that can earn the family living expenses from some job in town, he will have to have a somewhat higher return in order to buy groceries. (Perhaps this explains the popularity of schoolteachers as wives of young farmers and ranchers.) Another alternative might be for him to seek employment off the ranch and attend to ranch work during evenings and weekends, since no more than 30 hours per week is required in any month, and some months require less than 5 hours per week.

If our young rancher can, in fact, arrange for payments on the principal to come from some source off the ranch during the early years, then as he begins to build up equity in the place, he will have the return to his equity for purposes of reinvestment. For example, at the end of six years, he would have $750 return from his equity that he could either apply against the principal of his loan, use for purposes of expansion, or use for family living costs (see Table 18.4). If the value of the land should increase—as agricultural land in the United States has since the Great Depression—his financial position would improve more rapidly than suggested in Table 18.4. But no matter how he slices it, this young man would have to have a burning desire to be in the livestock business to take on even so advantageous a deal as has been offered by his grandfather.

Other complete budgets could be worked out for a steer operation or for some combination of steers and cows in order to examine the decision as to whether some other type of livestock operation might provide a better income. The thing to remember about the complete budget is that it lists *all*

TABLE 18.4

SCHEDULE OF INTEREST AND PRINCIPAL
PAYMENTS, EQUITY BUILDUP AND EQUITY RETURN

YEAR	TOTAL DEBT	INTEREST PAYMENT PAID TO GRANDFATHER	EQUITY PAYMENT AT END OF YEAR	TOTAL OWNED EQUITY AT BEGINNING OF YEAR	RETURN TO OWNER EQUITY @ 3%
1	$248,295	$7,448.85	$5,000	0	0
2	243,295	7,298.85	5,000	5,000	$150
3	238,295	7,148.85	5,000	10,000	300
4	233,295	6,988.85	5,000	15,000	450
5	228,295	6,848.85	5,000	20,000	600
6	223,295	6,698.85	5,000	25,000	750
7	218,295	6,548.85	5,000	30,000	900
8	213,295	6,398.85	5,000	35,000	1,050
9	208,295	6,248.85	5,000	40,000	1,200
10	203,295	6,098.85	5,000	45,000	1,350
11	198,295	5,998.85	5,000	50,000	1,500
12	192,295	5,798.85	5,000	55,000	1,650
.					
.					
.					
20	148,295	4,448.85	5,000	95,000	3,000
.					
.					
.					
30	98,295	2,948.85	5,000	145,000	4,500

Note: Interest rate at 4% per annum is assumed.

expenses and *all* returns in order to give some dependable estimate of the
total income that might be expected from the business.

The Partial Budget

The partial budget only considers the items of receipts and expenses
that are expected to *change* with some change in the organization or operation of the business. It is a logical procedure for comparing a proposed change

in the business with the present method of operation. If, for example, certain items of expense, such as interest on fixed investment, taxes, or insurance, remain the same for the present and proposed method of operation, it is not necessary to list these items of expense to determine which plan is more profitable. Thus, any item of expense or receipts that remains constant for both alternatives may be ignored. It is not possible to estimate expected net income from alternative plans when a partial budget is used. However, expected *gain* or *loss* over the present plan and differences in expected earnings from alternative plans can be derived. (In a sense, the partial budget examines marginal cost and marginal revenues.) The usual problem a business-man faces is to choose the best alternative from those budgeted rather than to determine the net income from each plan. Thus, for most problems a partial budget is entirely adequate if one is careful to include all the receipts and expenses which change.

Partial budgets may be used to analyze a wide variety of business decisions. They can be used to analyze such long-run decisions as: (1) increasing the size of one enterprise in the business (for example, increasing the size of a cow-calf or hog enterprise presently on the farm); (2) adding an enterprise to the existing operation; or (3) comparing machine ownership with custom hiring the machine work. The partial budget can also be used to analyze short-run decisions such as: (1) comparing alternative marketing dates for livestock currently on feed or; (2) making a change in the cropping program for this year because of unusual weather conditions.

The partial budgeting procedure can be either written or unwritten. Many problems are complex enough that the details must be written so that they can be analyzed accurately. However, there are also many situations where the procedure can be used in an informal manner.

The Partial Budget Outline •   A general partial budgeting outline is useful because it indicates the income and expense categories that need to be considered in comparing any present and proposed plan. There are seven parts to the outline.

ADDITIONAL RECEIPTS: This category contains the estimated additional returns resulting from the change under consideration.

REDUCED EXPENSES: This includes a listing of estimated expenses that will no longer be incurred if the change is made.

TOTAL CREDITS: This is additional receipts plus reduced expenses.

REDUCED RECEIPTS: This category lists the returns that would no longer be received under the proposed plan.

ADDITIONAL EXPENSES: This includes a listing of additional expenses that will be incurred if the change is made.

TOTAL DEBITS: This is reduced receipts plus additional expenses.

DIFFERENCE: This is the change in net income. It is equal to total credits minus total debits. It indicates how much more (if positive) or less (if negative) profitable the proposed plan is than the present method of operation.

An example of the use to which the partial budget may be put is illustrated in the case of an intermediate-run change in the organization of a farm business, such as substituting one enterprise for another. Suppose a farmer has 360 acres of bottomland. Of the total acreage, 204 acres are in cultivation, 110 are in native pasture, and 46 acres are woodland and waste area. His usual farm organization, average yields, cash operating expenses, and estimated prices are specified in Table 18.5.

The change that is under consideration is that of transferring 95 acres from oats to alfalfa hay production. The problem that the manager faces is estimating the impact that such a change would have on his total net revenue. The estimated alfalfa yield is 5 tons per acre. It would sell for $45 per ton

TABLE 18.5

CURRENT ORGANIZATION FOR 360-ACRE FARM

	ENTERPRISE				
ITEM	Wheat	Oats	Barley	Rye & Vetch Pasture	Cow-Calf
Usual acreage	38 ac.	95 ac.	63 ac.	8 ac.	25 cows
Average yield	30 bu.	60 bu.	45 bu.	3 AUM[1]	22 500-lb. calves
Estimated returns	$3.50/bu.	$1.60/bu.	$2.00/bu.	—	$4,950 for herd
Cash operating expenses[2]	$72.00/ac.	$76.00/ac.	$74.00/ac.	$33.00/ac.	$2,998 for herd

[1] Animal Unit Month—the grazing required to carry a 1000 lb. cow and her calf for one month.

[2] Cash operating expenses include such items as seed, fertilizer, pesticides, variable costs of machine operation, custom harvest cost, hired labor, and interest on operating capital.

TABLE 18.6

PARTIAL BUDGET OF CHANGES IN COSTS AND
RECEIPTS FOR TRANSFERRING 95 ACRES OF LAND
FROM OATS TO ALFALFA

Additional Receipts	
Alfalfa hay—95 acres @ 5 tons/ac.—475 tons	
sold @ $45	$41,375.00
Reduced expenses	
Cash costs for producing oats—94 acres @ $76	7,220.00
Total credits	$28,595.00
Reduced receipts	
Oats sales—95 acres @ 60 bu./ac.—5,700	
busels @ $1.60	$ 9,120.00
Additional expenses	
Cash costs for producing alfalfa—95 acres @ $128	12,160.00
Total debits	$21,280.00
Difference	$ 7,315.00

and have cash operating expenses of $128 per acre. The farmer would utilize custom cutting and baling. Hence, no new equipment is required by the proposed plan. Any additional labor required is either available on the farm or has been included in the cash costs of operation. The partial budget in Table 18.6 provides means for comparing the present and proposed plans.

In the example above, the manager only had to consider those items of income and expense that changed. The results of Table 18.6 suggest that shifting the 95 acres from oats to alfalfa would increase net returns to the farm by $7,315. A complete budget might have been used to analyze the

TABLE 18.7

ESTIMATED FEED REQUIREMENTS, COSTS, AND
RETURNS FOR FEEDING OUT HOGS

WEIGHT OF HOGS	PRESENT EXPECTED HOG PRICE	TOTAL FEED INPUT	ADDITIONAL FEED INPUT	ADDITIONAL WEIGHT GAINS	PRICE OF FEED
160	$47.00/cwt.	429	—	—	$3.50/cwt.
180	49.00/cwt.	510	81	20	3.50/cwt.
200	45.00/cwt.	594	84	20	3.50/cwt.

same problem. This would have involved listing all the fixed and variable cost items under both types of organizations. The difference in the net returns, however, would have been the same as that obtained with the partial bugeting procedure.

An example of how the partial budget may be used to analyze the impact of a short-run change in the operation of a farm business may be seen in the case where the manager is faced with determining the optimum weight at which to market livestock. Assume Mr. Brown has 100 hogs on feed. The average weight today is 160 pounds. He estimates that the hogs will gain 2 pounds per head per day until they reach an average weight of 200 pounds. Hence, it will take 10 days to add an additional 20 pounds of gain to the hogs and 20 days to add an additional 40 pounds. Mr. Brown expects the hog price to decline over the next month due to seasonal and cyclical effects. The data in Table 18.7 summarizes his price expectation, the feed requirements, and the price of feed. Farmer Brown does not have an alternative use for his labor or feeding facilities. Hence, the only variable cost item is the feed input. He wants to maximize returns to his labor, capital, fixed facilities, management, and risk.

Two partial budgets can be used to analyze this problem. First, Mr. Brown must determine if it will be more profitable to sell at 180 pounds than at the present time (Table 18.8). Second, he must compare the alternative of selling at 200 pounds with the more profitable selling weight determined by the first partial budget (Table 18.9). The results of the partial budget in Table 18.8 indicate that returns to Mr. Brown's fixed resources will be $1,016.50 greater if he sells the hogs at the present time. The results of the second partial budget in Table 18.9 indicate that returns to Mr. Brown's fixed

TABLE 18.8

PARTIAL BUDGET SHOWING COMPARISON OF SELLING AT 180 VERSUS 160 POUNDS

Additional receipts	
18,000 lb. @ $.49/lb.	$8,820.00
Reduced expenses	0.00
Total credits	$8,820.00
Reduced receipts	
16,000 lb. @ $.47/lb.	$7,520.00
Additional expenses	
8,100 lb. feed @ .035/lb.	283.50
Total debits	$7,803.50
Difference	$1,016.50

TABLE 18.9

PARTIAL BUDGET SHOWING COMPARISON OF
SELLING AT 200 VERSUS 180 POUNDS

Additional receipts	
20,000 pounds @ $.45/lb.	$9,000.00
Reduced expenses	0.00
Total credits	$9,000.00
Reduced receipts	
18,000 pounds @ $.49/lb.	$8,820.00
Additional expenses	
8,400 pounds feed @ $.035	294.00
Total debits	$9,114.00
Difference	−$114.00

resources will be $114 *less* if he feeds the hogs to 200 pounds than if he sells them at 180 pounds. Hence, he would plan to feed the hogs for another ten days. If his price expectations in ten days are the same as they are now, he would sell the 100 hogs at that time.

The budgeting examples that we have discussed are illustrating the wide applicability of the partial budget as a management tool. Budgeting cannot replace economic theory. Rather, budgeting serves as a complement to economic theory. In every example, our budgets have presupposed a production function and the use of some economic model. For example, our complete budget required that we define a factor-product model for the cow-calf operation from the beginning, and our first partial budget involved the product-product models. Budgets simply provide a method by which we can systematically apply economic theory. The budgeting technique can, of course, be applied to the problems of non-farm as well as farm firms, and to many of the day-to-day economic decisions that we all must make.

19

The Economics of Land Use and Value

In the early chapters of this book, we analyzed in a very general way the entire process of production. We discovered that a very large part of our stock of national wealth was made up of land and a still larger portion was made up of capital. Further, we decided that capital represented a "storage" of land and labor since it represented the sum total of all the production that had occurred throughout the entire period of human history and had not yet been consumed by mankind. (That is, land and labor are stored in the form of capital.)

By this time, it should have become apparent that the only source of new wealth is Mother Earth. Labor as such can produce nothing without some other resource with which to work. Limited production can and does occur in the absence of human labor: the natural growth of trees, wild game, and fish, for example. Man can live as a parasite of nature simply by harvesting these natural products, provided there aren't too many men. However, if Mother Nature has things all to herself, she's not a particularly efficient housekeeper. Natural productivity can be greatly increased if man provides some managerial direction. This is illustrated by the impact of such activities as scientific farm and forest management. Rather than remaining extractive in nature, the farming industry has become a generative type of industry that improves and builds the basic land resource. Forestry is in the process of becoming such a business. Through this evolutionary process, our planet has been able to support a progressively larger and larger human population.

If we consider population as a part of national wealth (and labor *is* a productive resource) we must remember that population can exist only because of the land. Food, a product of the soil, is required to build and maintain a man. Thus, man comes from and is ultimately returned to the soil.

Land, then, is the basic factor of production. If this is the case, then what is the contribution of land to the production process? If we are talking about land in the philosophical sense that all wealth ultimately comes from the soil, then land contributes *everything* to the process of production. If however, we are talking about the contribution of a *particular* piece of land, then the contribution of land is not nearly so easy to define. The production process requires that two or more resources be combined to produce some product. If only one resource is used, nothing is produced. Unless that resource is combined with some other resource, production is impossible— you merely have that resource. The owner of a single resource, then, must either purchase or otherwise arrange for the use of at least one other resource if he is to make any contribution at all to the process of production.

Since individual ownership of resources has proved to promote the greatest degree of economic efficiency in our society, it has become necessary for us to put prices on these resources. The only way we can set prices for resources is on the basis of the forces of supply and demand, but supply of and demand for resources will be determined by the contribution that these resources make to the production of some particular good or goods. Thus, the problem we face is one of estimating that contribution.

A number of ways have been devised for estimating the contribution of the various resources. When we discussed the concept of derived demand, we examined one method of allocating the value of a product to the various resources used in the production of that good. The procedure we used in our analysis of derived demand was to pay all other resources at the rate set in the market place, and then to attribute all of the value remaining to that resource with which we were concerned. The example we used was the demand for some product at retail as the basic demand function. We then derived the farm demand for that product by paying all resources used in the marketing process the price that was necessary to keep those resources employed in the particular marketing activity. (This price level is defined by the supply curve for such services, i.e., the supply curve defines the quantities of the service that will be forthcoming at the various market prices.) Anything that was left after these resources had been paid was included as a part of the demand at the farm level. As was pointed out at the time we discussed derived demand, this analysis has the greatest meaning in the neighborhood of the equilibrium point.

Economic Rent • The derived demand procedure is particularly appropriate for use in the estimation of land's contribution to production. Land is ordinarily the most fixed of all the resources used. Thus, even though the cost of using land must eventually be paid regardless of the level at which it is used, this payment may occasionally be deferred from one year to the next. The value of that usage can be most effectively estimated through the procedure of paying the short-term and intermediate-term assets the prices that are necessary to retain them in their present employments and then allocating the residual to the value of land usage.

The only unique economic characteristic of land is that it is normally considered to be a *permanent* asset. That is, regardless of the length of time we consider, the land remains after that time period has expired (unless of course one is in the high plains on a windy day). But other than in the time dimension, land exhibits the same economic characteristics as any other resource. Thus, the concept of *economic rent* may be applied to land in the same fashion as to any other resource.

In most cases, the payment to any resource will represent some combination of *economic rent* and *transfer earnings.* In order to define and differentiate between these two ideas, let's examine the situation in which all payment to the resource would be either pure economic rent or pure transfer earnings. By transfer earnings, we mean the amount of payment necessary to keep the resource from "transferring" out of its present employment. By economic rent, we mean that price that a resource is paid *in excess* of the price that is necessary to keep it from transferring to some other use.

In the left side of Figure 19.1, we see that the supply function for the resource is perfectly elastic. This is much the situation faced by the individual housewife when she goes into the supermarket. If she is unwilling to pay the price indicated for a particular good, she simply goes without that product. She has no opportunity for price negotiation. Thus, the price of any product or resource purchased under purely competitive conditions represents a pure transfer income to that product or resource. That is, if any user is unwilling

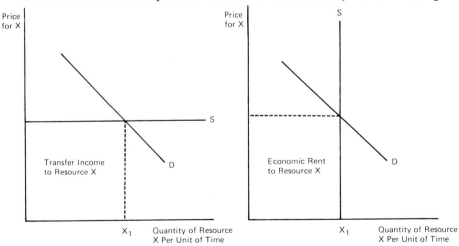

Figure 19.1 Relationship between transfer income to a resource and economic rent to that resource.

to pay the going price, the quantity of the resource that he might have used is transferred to some other user purely on the basis of price. Under these circumstances, the user is such a small portion of the total market that his refusal to pay the going price would affect the market price in no way. In general, the short-term productive assets, such as manufactured feeds, seeds, fertilizers, and petroleum products, will be purchased under conditions approaching the situation illustrated by this example. If supply is perfectly elastic, the resource price is determined exclusively by the supply function.

On the other hand, certain resources are not nearly as versatile as others. Gasoline, for example, can be and is used in almost every type of business. But the needs for land are pretty specific in almost every industry. By far the most land is used for some form of agricultural production and will continue to be used for agricultural production regardless of the market price for land. The supply of land and other resources of this type is almost totally *inelastic;* That is, the supply function tends to be almost perfectly vertical. Under these circumstances, the price for the resource is determined almost exclusively by the position of the *demand* function. No matter what the price

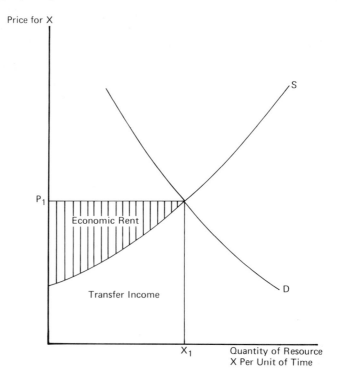

Figure 19.2 Allocation of total revenues generated between transfer income and economic rent.

level might be, the quantity offered for sale is unchanged. No payment is necessary for preventing the resource from shifting to some other form of employment, since there is no alternative use for very much of this resource. Thus, the price of such a resource is exclusively of the economic rent type of income under circumstances in which the supply function is perfectly inelastic.

The examples of perfectly elastic and perfectly inelastic supply functions represent the extremes. The situation we normally use to illustrate the supply functions where the supply curve slopes upward to the right is far more realistic. Under these circumstances, the payment to the resource will include both a transfer income and an economic rent payment (Figure 19.2). The payment to the last increment (i.e., the marginal unit which is sold at the point of equilibrium) of the resource represents a payment that is totally a transfer income *to that unit.* If this price were not paid—that is, if the demand curve were to shift to the left by one unit—this marginal unit would seek some other employment. But the price paid to all the previous units of the resource includes some economic rent since they would stay in their present employment at some lower price.

Since the demand for a resource is derived from the demand for all the products produced by that resource, and since resources will tend to flow into those uses that pay the highest return, the price for any resource will be determined by the income that resource can earn in its highest-paying alternative. We can observe the truth of this statement in areas such as Arkansas, Louisiana, Mississippi, and Alabama. Large acreages of land that were at one time under cultivation in these areas have been planted in tame pasture grasses as a result of relatively increasing cattle prices and relatively declining crop prices. These acreages have been attracted into the production of beef, since beef cattle prices have reached the levels that permit all the short-term costs (hay, protein supplements, vet fees, etc.) and all the intermediate-term costs (cow herd investment, equipment, etc.) to be paid. The earnings in excess of these costs still return more to the permanent asset of land than do the crop enterprise alternatives.

As the returns to land in a particular enterprise such as beef production increase, the demand for land to be used in this enterprise increases. The higher prices that result from the increase in demand attract areas into the business that heretofore were quite content to produce cotton or corn. The prices paid for attracting additional land into the business are by and large in the nature of transfer income to that land. If the income to this land should be reduced, the chances are that it would transfer out of beef production into some other more profitable type of use. However, the land that was already employed in the production of beef has also become more desirable and the prices for the use of such assets have likewise increased. This increase in price represents a windfall gain or an "economic rent" to that land. The owners of such land would not shift their resources into some other employment if the income from beef production were to decline. There are huge acreages of these lands in the seventeen western states. These areas will remain in livestock production under almost any set of circumstances since there are virtually no other alternative uses for these acreages.

An increase in the value of any product or in the technical productive efficiency of any business will ultimately be reflected in the form of increased prices for the use of or the ownership of the most nearly fixed asset used in the process of production. In the case of agricultural production, the most fixed asset is land. In the case of an industry such as electronics or auto-motives, the most fixed asset is often a patent right. Increases in income in these industries will often be capitalized into the patent right that permits the organization to produce the highly lucrative product.

Estimation of Land Value

The world of agriculture is replete with examples of increased production efficiency or increased product prices being bid into the value of land. The introduction of hybrid corn during the 1930s was very quickly bid into the rental rates and purchase prices for land capable of producing corn. Increased cattle prices have brought about enormous increases in the purchase prices and rental rates on pasture land. The acreage allotment and price support program for tobacco during the 1950s increased the price of farms having tobacco allotments by an estimated $4,000 per acre of tobacco allotment.[1] Similar results of the acreage allotment and price support programs were observed in the cases of cotton, wheat and peanuts.

The value of a piece of land is determined by the returns that can be generated by the most profitable enterprise that particular tract of land is capable of supporting. This same product may be produced more efficiently on another piece of land and the greater degree of efficiency will be reflected in a higher price per acre for such land. Any excess of resource price over what would be required to keep any specific resource in its present employment is termed economic rent. Increases in the profitability of an enterprise will cause prices for fixed resources to increase, hence causing the windfall gain of economic rent to occur.

Since World War II, prices for agricultural land (particularly grazing land) have risen sharply. In the 1970s, the investment necessary to provide the forage necessary for each beef cow in the traditional beef areas of the seventeen western states was in the neighborhood of $2,500. Many cattlemen,

---

[1] *Farm Management Manual,* Agricultural Economics Miscellaneous Publication No. 1 (Raleigh, N.C.: North Carolina State College, Department of Agricultural Economics, 1960).

and some economists, feel that this level of investment prohibits expansion of the beef enterprise. We saw in Chapter 18 that entry into the business of ranching is made extremely difficult by the required levels of investment, but the question of whether producers can really afford to pay the current prices for grazing land remains to be answered.

The price for land is determined by the forces of supply and demand for land. The supply of almost any particular sort of land is more or less fixed. Thus, the price of land is going to be determined largely by the demand for land. The demand for land is derived from the demand for the products that land produces. As has already been pointed out, the derived demand function is most relevant in the neighborhood of the point of equilibrium, and the derived demand function represents the residual of what is left after all other resources have been paid at their going rate. Thus, we would make our analysis of the price that ranchers can afford to pay for land on the basis of the return that can be generated to that land in the production of beef cattle.

Since the price of land is derived from the income that that land produces after all the other resources have been paid at their market rates, the first step a manager would take in estimating the price he could afford to pay for a particular piece of land would be to calculate the net income that land would generate to his business.

In Chapter 18 we discussed budgeting as a means of estimating costs and returns for purposes of making managerial decisions. The partial budgeting techniques were used for making short-run decisions such as the scheduling of selling livestock. Intermediate-term decisions, such as those concerning the organization of the particular business, could also be made through the use of a partial budget. The partial budgeting techniques indicated the *change* in the costs and returns that might be expected to result from taking some particular managerial action. We indicated that the *complete* budget was used under circumstances in which it was necessary to estimate the total net income a business would generate, and would be used in making long-run decisions such as the advisability of purchasing land. Therefore, in order to estimate the value of land, we must construct a total budget for purposes of defining the income that land will earn.

For purposes of simplicity, let's return to our embryonic rancher of Chapter 18. But let's assume that he and his grandfather have had a disagreement. Grandpa is an irascible old cuss who still would like to see the land carry his family name. He has offered the same deal we saw in Chapter 18 to a granddaughter's fiance, provided he will go to Hawaii to get married, since the laws of that state permit a husband to take his wife's family name. But while this decision is pending, Grandpa has driven his pickup truck to town. On the way home, the pickup stalls. Grandpa is livid. Out of sheer cussedness, he has an apoplectic seizure and passes to that great squeeze chute in the sky.

In the meantime our young friend has found a rich Montana rancher, Ludwig Von Climax, who has an ugly daughter, Appassionata. As a wedding gift, Ludwig endows Appassionata with the mineral rights to 1,000 acres of land. Three weeks after the wedding, the Big Sky Country Coal Company pays $6 million in hard cold cash for the right to develop a coal bed that has been discovered under this land. So our young friend and his unlovely bride have access to all kinds of capital. He, like his grandfather, has a deep desire to see his ancestral lands continue to be operated under the family name. Since the estate is in the process of being settled, he expresses an interest in purchasing his grandfather's ranch. However, Ludwig counsels his son-in-law that the investment in his ancestral home should be treated as he would treat any other investment. What can he affort to pay for that land after he has made provision for paying all other resources at their market rates?

The Market Demand for Land •   The components that go into making up the demand for land are numerous and in some cases are not subject to objective measurement. Those components include the following:

1. Agricultural productivity;

2. Undeveloped minerals;

3. Speculation (anticipated of appreciation in value);

4. Site or location; and

5. Demand resulting from the desire of a producer to achieve an economic scale of unit (i.e., the value of a quarter section of land added to a section already owned might be greater than the value of the quarter section alone since the machinery and equipment—or in the case of range land, the barns, corrals, and trucks—necessary for the 640-acre operation would be used on the added 160 acres as well. That is, the fixed costs would be spread over a larger volume of production. The operating cost for the total 800-acre unit might be less per acre than for the 160-acre unit alone, thus increasing the value of the *added,* or marginal, 160 acres.)

The demand for land resulting from components 1 and 2 can be measured with some accuracy. The demand associated with possibly increasing market prices of land depends on the expectations of the prospective purchaser. Components 4 and 5 are closely related since location can affect the efficiency of spreading existing equipment over increased acreage. Additional factors that might affect the individual's demand for land include such tangible values as personal satisfaction of owning and operating land.

The components of demand for land that are not readily measurable—such as this young man's desire to own his ancestral home—must be assigned some subjective value when an individual is estimating the total worth of a tract of land. This subjective value is then added to the value calculated for the agricultural productivity and the undeveloped mineral potential. For the time being, let's ignore the subjective questions, and assume that the land we are considering is located in northeastern Wyoming. Let's further assume that the mineral rights to this land are being retained by the estate. Thus, the only factor with which we will be concerned is the agricultural productivity.

The computation of the value of agricultural productivity involves an estimation of the annual returns to land and then capitalization of that return at some specified rate of interest. This estimation is made through the use of the total budget shown in Table 19.1. You will recognize this budget as being based on the same information as the complete budget constructed in Chapter 18. The primary difference is that we had the price of land given in our complete budget in Chapter 18. Now, we need to estimate what we *can afford* to pay for this land. A second difference is that in Chapter 18, since we knew the price of land, we charged off a return to land and calculated the residual return to labor and management. In Table 19.1, we assess a charge for labor and management, calculating our residual return to land.

In addition to the long-term investment of land, we must provide for the intermediate-term assets of machinery, equipment, and livestock. We find that over the life of these intermediate-term assets, there is a total of almost $75,000 in capital tied up in these assets. Further, about $11,400 in operating capital is needed to provide for supplemental winter feeding, taxes, and the like. But some of these funds are tied up for a few days and others for a full year. The most we would need at any given time is $5,700. Since we could place this money in certificates of deposit at 7 percent, we do have an opportunity cost for the use of this money. Thus, the short-term and intermediate-term capital on which the purchaser of this unit will be paying himself (or the bank) interest comes to about $82,000 per year. The interest on this at a rate of 7 percent comes to a little over $5,154. Other cost items are hay, labor (either the operator's labor or someone else's), land tax, and such items as minerals, protein supplement, and vet costs. The total annual cash cost of operation, including interest, comes to about $18,003.

If we figure on a long-term average calf price of $38 for heifers, $45 for steers and cow price of about $28, the total receipts from our operation will be just over $24,000 annually. Labor is charged at $2 per hour, and 4.4 percent of total specified cost is assessed for management. This leaves a return of about $2,722 to land, and risk. This is the annual return that we can expect from 2,867 acres of northeastern Wyoming range. The question we now face is, How much can we pay for an annual return of $2,722 to the fixed items of our land and risk?

TABLE 19.1

ESTIMATED ANNUAL PRODUCTION REQUIREMENTS AND INCOME FOR 150 BEEF COW HERD

NON-REAL ESTATE INVESTMENT NEEDS	NO.	TOTAL ANIMAL UNITS	ESTIMATED VALUE EACH	TOTAL VALUE
Brood cows	150	150	$375	56,250
Bulls	6	6	500	3,000
Replacement heifers	24	10	225	5,400
Machinery & equipment	—	—	—	11,835
Total		166		$76,485

SALES	NO.	WT.	PRICE PER CWT	VALUE PER UNIT	TOTAL RECEIPTS
Cull cows	24	950	$28.00	$266.00	6,384.00
Cull heifer	1	680	38.00	238.00	238.00
Heifer calves	41	390	38.00	148.00	6,076.20
Steer calves	61	420	45.00	189.00	11,529.00
Total receipts					$24,227.20

ANNUAL INPUTS	UNITS	RATE	NO.	TOTAL UNITS	NON-LAND COST/UNIT	TOTAL COST
Land & improvements	Acres	17.27/AU	166	2,867	—	—
Native hay	Tons	1.08/AU	166	180.0	$18.98	$3,416.40
26–30% protein feed	Cwt.	2.19/AU	166	112.5	7.70	866.25
Salt & minerals	Lb.	32.5/AU	166	5,400.0	.025	135.00
Vet. & medicine	Dol.	$1.54/AU	166	255	—	255.00
Bull depreciation	Dol.	37.50/Bull	6	225	1.22	225.00
Hauling & marketing	Cwt.	—	—	650.9		795.00
Interest on operating capital	$/yr.	—	—	5,715	.07	400.05
Interest on non-land investment	$/yr.	—	—	76,485	.07	5,353.95
Depreciation	Ranch	—	—	—	—	4,045.00
Taxes, land & livestock	Ranch	—	—	—	—	1,914.47
General overhead	Ranch	—	—	—	—	596.74
Total specified costs						$18,003.18
Gross returns to land, labor, risk & management labor	Hour	9/cow	150	1,350	2.00	2,700.00
Returns to land, risk & management						3,524.34
Management fee (4.4% of specified cost)						802.43
Return to land & risk						2,721.91

Spring calves born March–April, sold October–November; winter ration, 26–30 percent protein feed, native hay, and range; northeastern Wyoming.

The Capitalization Rate • In estimating the value of a given stream of income, we are immediately faced with the question of *capitalization*. A capitalization rate is simply the inverse of an interest rate. For example, if one were to place $100 in a savings account at an annual rate of 5 percent interest, he would realize an annual income of $5 for that $100 investment. The capitalization question is concerned with calculating the investment necessary to generate the $5 annual income. That is, $5 capitalized at 5 percent would capitalize to $100.

When computing the interest income from an investment, the calculation would be:

$$(\text{Principal}) \ (\text{Interest Rate}) = \text{Income}$$

Capitalization would be accomplished by:

$$\frac{\text{Income}}{\text{Capitalization Rate}} = \text{Principal}$$

Selecting the rate at which the return to range land is to be capitalized depends on the return that might be expected to accrue from funds invested in assets other than land, adjusting for differences in risk, potential value appreciation, etc. For example, if the best alternative investment is government savings bonds, the capitalization rate would be the interest paid by these bonds (about $3\frac{1}{2}$ percent) assuming there is virtually no risk associated with owning land. If blue-chip stocks can be expected to pay an annual 7 percent return, then 7 percent is the appropriate capitalization rate for funds invested in real estate. If land investment is less risky than commodity market speculation, then obviously a lesser return would be required on land investment than on the more hazardous alternatives.

Capitalization of the annual return to land treats the return to land as the interest income from the investment in land. Thus, if the capitalization (or interest) rate selected is 5 percent, we would divide the annual income by .05 to calculate the investment necessary to yield that annual income at an interest rate of 5 percent. The annual income of $2,722, or 95 cents per acre capitalized at 5 percent, would suggest that our young rancher could afford to pay about $19 per acre for his grandfather's ranch, or about $54,000 for land in the entire 150-cow unit. Thus, the value of the agricultural productivity of the grazing land we are considering is about $19 per acre under 5 percent capitalization if long-run average cattle prices are expected to be $45/cwt. for steer calves and $28/cwt. for culled cows. Cattle prices higher than those used in our example, or a capitalization rate of less than 5 percent, would increase the agricultural value of our land.

Expected changes in land prices and the acceptable rate of return on investment are closely related. If land prices are expected to increase at a rate of 10 percent per year, one would be willing to accept a substantially lower annual return on investment than if prices of land were either constant or declining. Thus, that rate of return which would be considered to be acceptable would depend not only on the alternative investment opportunities, but also on the expectations with regard to future land prices.

Let's assume that land prices will likely increase at a rate of about 5 percent per year. (This, by the way, is not a bad assumption. Farmland prices showed an average annual increase of more than 7 percent between 1959 and 1974.[2]) We can now reduce our requirements for returns from 5 percent to perhaps 2 or 3 percent when deciding between land investment and the other investment alternatives. As you will recall, our per-acre return on land was $0.95 per acre. If we divide $0.95 by .03 we get a figure of $31.66 per acre. If we use a capitalization rate of 2 percent, the resulting estimate of value is $47.50 per acre.

We have made no attempt to decide whether or not land is too expensive or whether we could in fact buy land in Wyoming at $32 or $47 per acre. But we have explained why land prices have reached their present levels. The appreciation in value of land has encouraged those who are involved in the business of agricultural production to pay what seems to be extremely inflated prices for land. The fact that many small units have been absorbed by some larger units has also added to the upward pressure on land prices.

Value of Land for Purposes of Expansion ● Now, let's look at the value of this same 2,867 acres of pasture land for an individual who already has a 150-brood cow operation adjoining the land in question. For this purpose we can use the partial budget. We know the costs and returns involved in our current operation (Table 19.1). What we are now looking for is the change that would result from adding the 2,867 acres of grass. Let's assume the same prices as used in Table 19.1.

If we expand to 300 cows, we can easily get along with four additional bulls. Therefore, we can actually expand to 302 cows, giving us a couple of extra calves to market in the fall. Thus, we sell 24 more cows and 104 more calves and one additional cull heifer for a total increase of $10,002.00 in receipts (Table 19.2).

With regard to cost reduction in the increased size of operation, we can cut labor requirements per cow to perhaps 8 hours, thus saving 150 hours of labor and $300 (Table 19.3). Further, our overhead costs are spread over twice as many cattle, giving us a cost reduction of perhaps $200 on our existing unit. Thus, the total of our cost savings and our increased revenue is $10,202.

---

[2] *Agricultural Statistics, 1974,* U.S.D.A., p. 427.

TABLE 19.2

ESTIMATED INCREASE IN GROSS RECEIPTS RESULTING FROM DOUBLING IN SIZE OF AN EXISTING 150 BEEF COW HERD

ITEM	NO.	WEIGHT	PRICE	VALUE EACH	TOTAL VALUE
Cull cows	24	950	$28.00	$266.00	$6,384.00
Cull heifers	1	680	38.00	238.00	238.00
Heifer calves	42	390	38.00	148.20	6,224.40
Steer calves	62	420	45.00	189.00	11,718.00
Total increase in gross receipts					$24,564.40

Note: Spring calves born, March–April, sold October–November, winter ration, 26–30 percent protein feed, native hay, range; northeastern Wyoming.

Our increased costs are of both a capital nature and of an operating nature. The cowherd will be a bit more than doubled. But much of the machinery and equipment can be used on the expanded unit, so machinery and equipment needs will increase by only about half. Since we have been able to utilize our bulls more efficiently, our grass will produce more salable beef. As a result our hauling and marketing costs will increase a bit more than would be the case if we started from scratch. Likewise, using some machinery and equipment on both units causes the added depreciation and interest on non-land investment to be less than would be the case for an independent

TABLE 19.3

ESTIMATED REDUCTION IN COSTS ON EXISTING 150 BEEF COW OPERATION RESULTING FROM DOUBLING THE SIZE OF THE UNIT

ITEM	RATE	NO.	TOTAL UNITS	NON-LAND COST/UNIT	TOTAL COST
Labor (hours)	1/cow	150	150	$2.00	$300.00
Miscellaneous costs	–	–	–	–	200.00
Total reduction in costs for existing unit					$500.00

Note: Spring calves born March–April, sold October–November; winter ration, 26–30 percent protein feed, native hay, and range; northeastern Wyoming.

TABLE 19.4
ESTIMATED INCREASE IN RESOURCE NEEDS AND COSTS RESULTING FROM DOUBLING THE SIZE OF AN EXISTING 150 BEEF COW HERD

INCREASE IN NON-LAND CAPITAL NEEDS

Item	No.	Total Animal Units	Estimated Value Each	Total Value
Brood cows	152	152	$375	$57,000
Bulls	4	4	500	2,000
Replacement heifers	24	10	225	5,400
Machinery & equip.				6,000
Total increase in non-land investment				$70,400

INCREASE IN ANNUAL INPUTS

Item	Unit	Rate	No.	Total Units	Non-Land Cost/Unit	Additional Cost
Land & improvements	Acre	17.27/AU	166	2,867	$ –	$ –
Native hay	Ton	1.08/AU	166	180	18.98	3,416.40
26–30% protein feed	Cwt.	2.19/AU	166	112.5	7.70	866.25
Salt & minerals	Lb.	32.5/AU	166	5,400.0	.025	135.00
Vet. & medicine	Dol.	1.54/AU	166	255.0	–	255.00
Bull depreciation	Dol.	37.50/Bull	6	225	–	225.00
Hauling & mktg.	Cwt.	–		659.0	1.22	803.98
Int. on op. capital	$/yr.	–		5,715.0	.07	400.05
Int. on non-land inv.	$/yr.	–		70,400.0	.07	4,928.00
Depreciation	Ranch	–		–	–	3,045.00
Taxes, land & livestock	Ranch	–		–	–	1,914.47
General overhead	Ranch	–		–	–	0
Labor	Hour	8/cow	152	1,216	2.00	2,432.00
Management fee	(4.4% of specified costs other than labor)					703.53
Total increase in specified costs						$19,124.68

Note: Spring calves born March–April, sold October–November; winter ration, 26–30 percent protein feed, native hay, and range; northeastern Wyoming.

unit. That is, our additional non-land investment is $70,400—about $6,000 less than for the man with no other land or cattle. The depreciation need is $3,045, $1,000 less than for the man with no other land and cattle (Table 19.4).

The main changes in operating costs as compared with Table 19.1 are on bull depreciation, reduced $75; hauling and marketing costs, increased $9; interest on investment capital, reduced about $425; depreciation, reduced $1,000; labor, reduced $268; and management charges, reduced about $99.

There are no reductions in returns to the existing unit to account for, so the total increase in costs is $19,124.68. Consolidating the information in Tables 19.2—19.4 gives us our partial budget (Table 19.5).

The total change in the returns to land, risk, and management is $5,939.72. If we capitalize this at 5 percent, the price that we could afford to pay for this additional land would be:

Value = $5,939.72 ÷ .05

$\qquad$ = 118,794.40, or $41.44 per acre, if long-term cattle prices are expected to average 45 cents/lb. for steer calves and 28 cents/lb. for cows.

As you recall, the value of this land to a man considering going into the business with no other land and no other cattle using a 5 percent capitaliza-

TABLE 19.5

ESTIMATED CHANGE IN INCOME RESULTING FROM
DOUBLING THE SIZE OF AN EXISTING 150 BEEF
COW OPERATION
84% Weaned Calf Crop

ITEM	DOLLAR CHANGE
Increase in returns	$24,564.40
Decrease in costs	500.00
Total credits	$24,064.40
Increase in costs	19,124.68
Decrease in returns	0.00
Total debits	$19,124.68
Difference	$5,939.72

Note: Spring calves born March—April, sold October—November; winter ration, 26—30 percent protein feed, native hay, and range; northeastern Wyoming.

tion rate was only $19 per acre. Thus, the value of this land for purposes of achieving a more efficient unit adds about $22.50 per acre to the price one could afford to pay. This means that the man already in the business can either pay a higher price, or he can pay the same price and survive through periods of lower cattle prices. This illustrates the difficulty that young people face when going into the farming or ranching business. People already in business can simply afford to pay higher prices for resources due to the advantages of improving the efficiency of an existing production unit. This is one reason that the business of agricultural production has come to the point where it is almost invariably hereditary. The capital requirements are so high, and the price one can afford to pay for resources is so dependent on the resources one currently controls that a young man's entry into ranching is determined largely either by birth, by marriage, or by both.

The Influence of Technical Efficiency on Land Value • It must be pointed out that the figures we have used assume that the manager is going to be able to maintain the same level of efficiency in his operation. However, if he can increase his weaned calving percentage from one of 84 percent to one of 95 percent through a program of pregnancy testing, quite a different picture would result. This would mean that he would sell 16 more calves from his original 150 cows and 16 additional calves from his additional 152 cows. It also means that he would be selling 33 head of open cows that were detected during the pregnancy check and replacing them with bred heifers. The partial budget elements in Table 19.5 would be altered as shown in Table 19.6.

  If we capitalize the income from Table 19.6 at 5 percent, the price one could afford to pay for the additional 2,867 acres of grass would be:

Value = $7,902 ÷ .05
  = 158,040 or $55.12 per acre if long-term cattle prices are expected to average 45 cents for steer calves and 28 cents for cull cows.

Thus, the improved technical efficiency from improved management would add $15 per acre to the price we could afford to pay for the land.

Summary and Implications

  Table 19.7 shows the relationship between the producer's operating situation and his production efficiency in determining the price he can afford to pay for land under various capitalization rates. Though the figures in Table 19.7 are for a very specific situation producing beef in northeastern Wyoming, the example does illustrate some general implications.

TABLE 19.6

ESTIMATED CHANGE IN INCOME RESULTING FROM
DOUBLING THE SIZE OF AN EXISTING 150 BEEF
COW PRODUCTION UNIT
95% Weaned Calf Crop

Increased returns	
17 open cows sold @ $28/cwt–(950#) ($.28) (17)	$4,522
24 cull cows sold @ $28/cwt–(950#) ($.28) (24)	6,384
1 cull heifer sold @ $38/cwt/(680#) ($.38) (1)	238
80 steer calves sold @ $45/cwt–(420#) ($.45) (80)	15,120
50 heifer calves sold @ $38/cwt–(390#) ($.38) (50)	7,410
Total	$33,674
Reduced costs	
Labor: 1 hour/cow on existing herd–(150 hr.) ($2/hr.)	$300
Misc. costs	200
Total	500
Total credits	$34,174
Increased costs	
Pregnancy testing @ $1/cow	$150
17 bred heifers @ $375 to replace open cows	6,375
Hauling & mktg. costs on additional tonnage sold:	327
(268.3 cwt @ $1.22)	
Additional management costs	295
Other increased costs from Table 19.4	19,125
Total	$26,272
Reduced returns	0
Total debits	$26,272
Difference	$7,902

Note: Table assumes spring calves born March–April, sold October–November; winter ration of 26–30% protein feed, native hay, and range; northeastern Wyoming.

First of all, an established operator can generally afford to pay a higher price for land than can a beginning operator. This accounts in large part for the fact that the average age of farm operators has grown steadily. That is, the older operator who strives to reduce the per-unit production cost in his business can outbid the young man seeking to enter the business.

Second, those operators who can accept a lower return on investment can afford to pay higher prices for land. Generally, those operators with large equities can get more favorable interest rates than can the operator that is heavily leveraged financially. This also works to the disadvantage of the

TABLE 19.7

RELATIONSHIP BETWEEN CAPITALIZATION RATE,
OPERATING SITUATION, AND DEGREE OF
PRODUCTION EFFICIENCY IN DETERMINING PRICE
A MANAGER CAN AFFORD TO PAY FOR LAND

OPERATING SITUATION	CAPITALIZATION RATE					
	7%	6%	5%	4%	3%	2%
No land; no cattle; 84% weaned calf production; 45¢ steer calves, 38¢ heifer calves, 28¢ cows ($0.95/acre return to land)	$13.57	$15.83	$19.00	$23.75	$31.66	$47.50
Expanding the size of an existing unit; 84% weaned calf production; 45¢ steer calves 38¢ heifer calves, 28¢ cows (2.08/acre return to land)	$29.71	34.67	41.60	52.00	69.33	104.00
Expanding the size of an existing unit; 95% weaned calf production; 45¢ steer calves 38¢ heifers, 28¢ cows (2.76/acre return to land)	$39.43	46.00	55.20	69.00	92.00	138.00

young man seeking to enter the business. It works in favor of the high income individual who can take his living from an outside source and can deduct interest payments from his taxable income. For example, the prospective buyer who is in a 50 percent income tax bracket can pay a market rate of 9 percent interest with much less difficulty than can the buyer who is in a 15 percent tax bracket. The actual post-tax cost of interest to the former is only 4.5 cents per dollar while it is 7.65 cents per dollar to the latter. If the annual increase in land prices is 7 percent, the appreciation in the value of the asset has netted 1.5 percent above interest charges for the high income individual.

The lower income purchaser, however, has to pay .65 percent more interest than he has realized on the appreciation in value. This suggests the truth in the old adage that, Them as has, gets! Since very few young men have, not many get into the business of farm production except through marriage or inheritance.

A third implication is that the better manager who can achieve a greater degree of production efficiency can outbid the less effective manager when seeking to expand. This accounts for the generally increased degree of managerial effectiveness in production agriculture. That is, the entrepreneurial managers who have survived in production agriculture have generally been the most effective among their group. This situation favors the younger manager who is generally better educated and better trained than are those of previous generations. That is, the younger manager who is well trained and who can find a way to get started probably has a very promising future in the business of farming.

Index